D1732826

SOLDIERS OF GOD IN A SECULAR WORLD

SOLDIERS OF GOD IN A SECULAR WORLD

Catholic Theology and Twentieth-Century French Politics

SARAH SHORTALL

HARVARD UNIVERSITY PRESS

Cambridge, Massachusetts

London, England

2021

Library of Congress Cataloging-in-Publication Data

Names: Shortall, Sarah, 1985– author.
Title: Soldiers of God in a secular world : Catholic theology and
    twentieth-century French politics / Sarah Shortall.
Description: Cambridge, Massachusetts : Harvard University Press, 2021. |
    Includes bibliographical references and index.
Identifiers: LCCN 2021011716 | ISBN 9780674980105 (hardcover)
Subjects: LCSH: Catholic Church—Political activity—France—History—
    20th century. | Nouvelle théologie (Catholic theology)—France. | Secularism—
    Political aspects—France—History—20th century. | Church
    and state—France—Catholic Church—History—20th century.
Classification: LCC BX1528 .S56 2021 | DDC 261.70944/0904—dc23
LC record available at https://lccn.loc.gov/2021011716

To my parents and grandmother

CONTENTS

SOLDIERS OF GOD IN A SECULAR WORLD

Introduction

On the morning of June 30, 1880, gendarmes arrived at the Jesuit scholasticate of Laval to dissolve the institution and evict its 155 students and teachers. Splintering into small groups, the Jesuits took shelter in the homes of local laypeople for a few months, before making their way to Saint-Malo, where they set sail for the island of Jersey.[1] For the next sixty years, this small dependency of the British Crown—located just fourteen miles off the coast of Normandy—would host Jesuits from across France while they completed part of their formation to become priests. The reason for the abrupt relocation was the proclamation of the Ferry Decrees, which dissolved the Jesuit order in France. This was the opening salvo in a twenty-five-year campaign by the republican government to dismantle the legal privileges of the Catholic Church in France.[2] Most religious orders soon met the same fate as the Jesuits, including the Dominicans, who moved their Parisian house of studies to Kain, just across the Belgian border, in 1904. By the time the French Republic officially proclaimed the separation of Church and state in 1905, roughly 30,000 religious had been driven into exile.[3]

What few at the time could have predicted, however, was that these two exiled seminaries—the Maison Saint-Louis on Jersey and Le Saulchoir in Belgium—would become the cradles of a revolution in Catholic theology. The French Jesuits and Dominicans who studied at these institutions in exile would go on to develop what became known as the *nouvelle théologie* ("new theology") in the 1930s and 1940s. Born from the ashes of the anticlerical campaign, this movement would play a key role in modernizing the Church and would eventually inspire many of the changes

1

wrought by the Second Vatican Council in the 1960s. But it also transformed French intellectual life more broadly, bringing theologians into a mutually enriching dialogue with secular philosophers. In this way, the separation of Church and state in France inadvertently created the conditions for the revitalization of modern Catholicism. This book tells the story of that renaissance.

The scene at Laval on the morning of June 30 was by no means an isolated event in nineteenth-century Europe. Across the continent, the Church faced a formidable assault on its traditional privileges, as nationalists sought to consolidate their jurisdiction over newly established states while liberals and socialists lambasted Catholicism as an obstacle to economic, political, and intellectual progress. The result of these conflicts was a series of laws that turned areas of public life that had traditionally fallen under the purview of the Church—including marriage, education, health care, Church property, and ecclesiastical appointments—over to the state and either restricted or evicted Catholic religious orders (beginning, usually, with the Jesuits).[4] Meanwhile, the unification of Italy in 1870 left the Holy See without a territorial homeland and the pope a self-proclaimed "prisoner" of the Vatican.[5] The anticlerical campaign in France was only one flashpoint in this broader conflict, albeit one of the bitterest and most polarizing.

And yet, the separation of Church and state did not bring an end to the public role of the Catholic Church in France. Though it marked the end of one kind of Catholic politics, it also marked the beginning of another. One might assume that henceforth it would fall to the laity to spearhead Catholic political engagement and that theology would have little to contribute to this endeavor once Church and state had been separated.[6] But in fact, the events of 1905 forced theologians to reimagine the nature of the Church and its relationship to the political order, as they grappled with the key quandary facing the Catholic Church in the twentieth century: how to maintain a public role for itself once the institutions of public life had been secularized. How could the Church play a robust role in the secular public sphere without compromising its values in the process? By posing this question, I argue, the separation of Church and state had a productive rather than a destructive effect on Catholic theology, inspiring new approaches to the problem of political theology and opening up new avenues for Catholic engagement in public life. The results were transformative not just for the Church, but also for European politics more broadly, as theologians weighed in on debates over fascism and communism, democracy and human rights, colonialism and nuclear war.

In recent years, historians have begun to draw attention to the contributions that Catholics made to the major developments in twentieth-century European politics. They have shown how Catholics contributed to the postwar rebuilding of democratic institutions and the development of an international human rights framework; how they engaged with various parties, trade unions, and philosophies of the left; and the tacit and not-so-tacit support they lent to a slew of right-wing governments from Portugal to Croatia.[7] But what of those Catholics who did not translate their political intervention into the familiar language of party politics or who refused the choice between the dominant political ideologies of their day? Until recently, historians have tended to approach religious actors from the perspective of secular political categories and ideologies, without considering how their subjects might call such categories into question.[8] And yet, what is most striking about Catholic political thought is the extent to which it defied the logic of secular political taxonomies. How does one classify someone like Jacques Maritain, for instance, who made the transition from being a partisan of the far-right Action française (AF) to a leading champion of democracy and human rights? Or Emmanuel Mounier, who graduated from the institutions of the collaborationist Vichy government during the Second World War to become a leading voice of the Catholic left after the war? What makes these figures so difficult to classify is that they often self-consciously conceived their worldview in opposition to the dominant political ideologies of their day. They sought to articulate a religiously grounded alternative to both capitalism and communism, both liberalism and totalitarianism. To understand the protean nature of Catholic politics, it is therefore crucial to grasp the religious commitments that informed it.

In this book, I show how Catholic intellectuals and priests turned to the resources of Catholic theology in order to formulate a public role for Catholicism in a secular age. The key question they confronted was not whether to embrace modernity, but which aspects of the modern settlement were compatible with Catholic teaching. To what extent could Catholics work with secular institutions and ideologies to achieve their ends? Conversely, how could they articulate an explicitly Catholic vision of community and human life without excluding non-Catholics? These were the central problems that theologians faced as they sought to chart a path between accommodation and resistance to the modern world. To solve them, they looked not to the tools of secular political theory, but rather to premodern theological debates about the relationship between the natural and supernatural orders, the nature of the Church, the ends of human life, and the structure of time. This does not mean that theology simply determined their political commitments, however. As we shall see, the same theological model could be deployed to serve a range of different political projects. Instead, theology provided a grid through which these Catholics made sense of the dominant political challenges of their day, but one that they constantly reshaped as well, in light of their experiences and changing historical events. In the process, they fashioned a distinctively Catholic response to the political, social, and intellectual challenges of the twentieth century.

Modernity and Tradition

By examining the rise of the *nouvelle théologie,* this book explores a question that has long fascinated historians: how and when did the Catholic Church make its peace with modernity? At the dawn of the twentieth century, when this book opens, Church leaders were locked in a fierce struggle against "modernism" both within and beyond the Church. This was still the Church of Pius IX, whose famous *Syllabus of Errors* (1864) denounced everything from rationalism and ecumenism to religious freedom and the principle of Church-state separation. And yet, by the time of the Second Vatican Council one hundred years later, the Church had embraced many of these selfsame principles and recognized the need to update its teachings in order to bring them into line with the demands of the modern world. How did this happen? In the past few years, a new generation of European historians has tackled this question anew, showing how the Church came around to such typically modern ideas as religious freedom, human rights, and the distinction between the private sphere of religion and the public sphere of politics.[9] Others have suggested that the Church made its peace with these ideas relatively late or not at all.[10]

Soldiers of God reframes the story of how the Church became modern by asking, not how Catholics came to "accept" or "embrace" typically modern principles, but how they contested and transformed what it meant to be modern. It shows how the "modernization" of Catholicism was, somewhat counterintuitively, anchored in premodern categories and concepts. To bring Catholicism into the twentieth century, theologians returned to the medieval and ancient sources of the Catholic tradition in order to find the resources for an authentically Catholic modernity. They kept one eye trained on their contemporary moment and the other eye focused on the distant past, and this explains why Catholics often fit awkwardly into conventional definitions of modernity. While the figures at the center of this story embraced some aspects of modern thought and politics—the separation of Church and state, for instance—they resisted others, such as the distinction between the private and public spheres, notions of historical progress, the primacy of the nation-state, and the autonomous individual. To be Catholic and modern, in other words, was not to embrace a secular definition of modernity. This suggests that there was rather more continuity between Catholic "modernism" and the traditional antimodernism of the Church than one might expect. But it also indicates that the story of how Catholics became modern should change not only how we understand twentieth-century Catholicism, but also how we define what it means to be modern. After all, Catholics were not the only ones to look back to premodern traditions—invented or otherwise—to anchor a deeply modern worldview, as historians of nationalism and socialism can attest.[11]

Naturally, Catholic theologians and philosophers disagreed on what the Church's engagement with the modern world should look like. This book identifies two broad Catholic responses to the challenge of modernity. Some argued that Catholics should work within the secular institutions of public life, joining forces with non-Catholics to achieve a shared set of practical goals. This position was rooted in neo-Thomist theology, which had come to dominate Catholic thought since the nineteenth-century revival of the work of Thomas Aquinas and his scholastic commentators.[12] Central to the Thomist system was a distinction between the natural and supernatural ends of human life, which allowed it to grant a certain degree of autonomy to temporal affairs—those activities possessing a natural end, which do not directly affect salvation.

In the aftermath of the separation of Church and state in France, this logic underwrote a range of political projects. For those who had not made their peace with the secular Republic, it served to justify a Catholic alliance with the royalist Action française, in spite of the fact that it was led by a nonbeliever.[13] By the late 1930s, however, Thomism took on an entirely new political resonance in the work of Jacques Maritain, himself a former partisan of the AF. In his book *Integral Humanism* (1936), Maritain called on Catholics to give up the dream of restoring the confessional state and work to build a new, "profane Christendom" that would be appropriate to the secular, pluralist reality of modern politics. This did not mean that Catholics no longer had a role to play within the temporal order. But rather than entering it as *"a Christian as such,"* one would now enter it simply *"as a Christian,* engaging only myself, not the Church."[14] By the early 1940s, Maritain had developed these principles into a fully fledged Thomist theory of human rights and democracy, one he sought to implement in his contribution to the debates leading up to the drafting of the Universal Declaration of Human Rights.[15] Meanwhile, others deployed the Thomist distinction between the temporal and spiritual planes to justify an engagement with communism and various forms of working-class activism, as a nascent Catholic left came into its own following the Second World War.[16] Underpinning these very different political commitments was a Thomist framework that allowed for a relatively autonomous realm of human affairs, beyond the direct remit of the Church. It was thus well-suited to a context in which the institutions of public life had been secularized.

Thomism offered one answer to the problem of how to engage with public life in the aftermath of secularization, but it was not the only option. Beginning in the 1920s and 1930s, a group of French Jesuits led by Henri de Lubac began to articulate a powerful critique of the dominant brand of neo-Thomism by turning back to the earliest sources of the Catholic tradition: St. Paul and the Church Fathers. Along with Dominicans such as Marie-Dominique Chenu and Yves Congar, these Jesuits became the architects of a *nouvelle théologie* that would eventually find expression at the Second Vatican Council. They are the protagonists of this book.[17]

This group of French Jesuits came of age in the aftermath of the separation of Church and state, completing part of their religious formation in exile on the island of Jersey. It was here, in the early 1920s, that Henri de Lubac, Gaston Fessard, Robert Hamel, and Yves de Montcheuil developed a close friendship. Formative experiences in the trenches of World War I had convinced these seminarians of the urgent need for new theological tools capable of bridging the gulf between the Church and the modern world. Like Maritain, they recognized that it was no longer possible to revive the medieval alliance of throne and altar, but they were equally suspicious of party politics. Instead, they looked for a way to be *in* the secular public sphere, but not *of* it. They wanted to make Catholicism modern without subjecting it to the corrosive effects of secularization.

But here the Jesuits parted company with their Thomist peers. They could not abide the way neo-Thomism separated the natural from the supernatural order and temporal from spiritual affairs. In fact, Henri de Lubac went so far as to suggest that this theology had inadvertently aided and abetted the secularization of European life. "The relative autonomy it accorded to nature" was "a temptation to independence," he warned, and "the most confirmed secularists found in it, in spite of itself, an ally."[18] Instead, taking his cue from the Church Fathers, de Lubac insisted that it was not possible to imagine an autonomous order of human affairs that was oriented to a purely natural end. Consequently, there could be no question of "closing the Church off from any terrain of human thought or action." If "the supernatural is not separate from nature and the spiritual is everywhere mixed in with the temporal," he concluded, "the Church has . . . authority over everything, without having to step outside of its role."[19] De Lubac and his fellow Jesuits thus looked to the Church rather than the state as the primary framework for collective life.

This might sound like an effort to subordinate the state to the Church. And indeed, the Augustinian tradition on which these Jesuits drew had been associated historically with the theocratic pretensions of the medieval papacy.[20] But de Lubac's circle was by no means calling for the resurrection of this model or the revival of the confessional state. Instead, they wished to return to an even earlier moment in the history of the Church, before it became the official religion of the Roman Empire. They believed that the separation of Church and state, and the secularization of European public life more broadly, presented the Church with an opportunity to recover its original role as a critical force vis-à-vis the powers of this world. Moreover, the "Church" that they had in mind was less the visible institution headquartered in Rome than the Church conceived as the "mystical body of Christ," an entity that would only come into fullness at the end of time. Conceived in this way, they believed, the Church was the only communal body capable of overcoming the limitations of secular ideologies and warring nation-states.

This vision of the Church would inspire all the political activities of these priests, from their critique of the AF in the 1920s to their antitotalitarian activism in the 1930s and 1940s. It found its highest expression during the Second World War, when de Lubac, Chaillet, and Fessard launched the clandestine resistance journal *Témoignage chrétien,* which became the leading voice of the "spiritual resistance" to Nazism in France.[21] After the war was over, it led them to turn their attention to the threat posed by communism and the Catholic left. But in addition to inspiring their anti-totalitarianism, this theological vision also led them to reject the fundamental premises of liberal politics (as they understood it)—including the primacy of the individual, the sovereignty of the state, and the distinction between the private and public spheres. In other words, they were both anti-totalitarian and antiliberal, which makes it very difficult to classify them according to the categories of the modern political spectrum.

French Catholics thus developed two main theological responses to modernity and the secularization of public life—one Thomist and one broadly patristic. And crucially, *both* these approaches cut across secular political distinctions between "right" and "left" or "liberal" and "conservative." As I show, Thomist political theology could be, and was, deployed to serve a range of competing political projects. This was not lost on critics such as de Lubac, who recalled in his memoirs that he had known "a Thomism as patron of the 'Action française,' a Thomism as the inspiration of Christian Democracy, a progressive and even a neo-Marxist Thomism."[22] In fact, Thomism was the red thread that tied the antimodernist Church of the turn of the century to the Church that reinvented itself as the preeminent defender of human rights and democracy in the latter half of the twentieth century. The history of this transformation is in many ways the history of Thomism itself and of the various ways it was reformulated and redeployed in the course of the century, from its neo-scholastic iteration to the very different Thomisms of Maritain and of the Dominican branch of the *nouvelle théologie.*

If Thomism could be, in a sense, "both right and left," the patristic vision of de Lubac's circle was "neither left nor right."[23] For these priests, the political role of the Church was above all a critical one; they looked to theology to articulate a critique of the dominant political ideologies of their day—or what I call a "counter-politics."[24] Theology thus gave them a means to access the political obliquely; it gave them language with which to intervene in political questions even as they claimed to remain at arm's length from politics. This is by no means to suggest that their theology actually *was* above politics, but rather to indicate how this disavowal was itself crucial to theology's political power. This became particularly apparent during the Second World War, when de Lubac's circle was able to circumvent wartime censorship by encoding their resistance message in the language of theology. In this way, they used the resources of ecclesiology, eschatology, and theological anthropology to fashion a response to the dominant political questions that exercised their world.

What the Thomist-patristic typology underscores is the crucial role that theology played in mediating the Catholic response to the modern world. This was not a division between Catholics on the right and those in the center or on the left. Nor was it simply a split between Catholics who embraced modernity and those who refused any such compromise. Instead, we should view these as two different theological modes of engaging with the modern world. Both sought to do so through a return to the premodern sources of the Catholic tradition, and indeed, each accused the other of making too many concessions to modernity. While de Lubac and his friends suggested that Thomist metaphysics had unwittingly reinforced the secular logic of separate spheres, Thomist critics of the *nouvelle théologie* took issue with the way the Jesuits seemed to naturalize the supernatural—a tendency they attributed to the insidious influence of modern philosophy. And they were not entirely wrong. Jesuits such as Gaston Fessard and Jean Daniélou did in fact play a leading role in the Catholic engagement with the Hegelian and existentialist philosophies that dominated France in the 1930s and 1940s, while their brother Pierre Teilhard de Chardin developed a distinctive theory of evolution that wove together the insights of theology and paleontology. It was this effort to engage with modern thought that would eventually, if temporarily, cause this group to be condemned in 1950, when Pius XII issued the encyclical *Humani Generis*.

And yet, it is crucial not to overstate the differences between the Thomist and the patristic models. In the first place, there was considerable diversity within each—especially within what Étienne Gilson called the "great family" of Thomism—and some, especially the Dominicans associated with the *nouvelle théologie,* had affinities with both models.[25] The Jesuits, for their part, were not so much opposed to the work of Thomas Aquinas himself as to the neo-Thomist interpretation of his work. Ultimately, both approaches would place their mark on the Second Vatican Council and go on to set the terms for subsequent debates, influencing everything from liberation theology in Latin America to the worldviews of

Pope Benedict XVI and Pope Francis. At base, both of these theological approaches shared the same goal: to carve out a public role for Catholicism after the separation of Church and state. Emerging from the crucible of the anticlerical campaign in France, both sought to chart a middle path between the old alliance of throne and altar and the privatization of religion demanded by secular politics. In the process, they articulated a way of being and belonging that was modern but far from secular.

Theology and Intellectual History

To be sure, the political positions taken by these theologians and philosophers were not always representative of lay politics, and formed only one component of their much larger contribution to Catholic thought. This book therefore does not aim to provide an exhaustive account of the theological prehistory to Vatican II or of Catholic politics in twentieth-century Europe. Instead, by focusing on how theologians engaged with broader developments in European thought and politics, it seeks to integrate theology into the intellectual history of modern Europe.

The history of theology and modern European intellectual history have traditionally been told as separate stories. While theologians tend to approach theology through the lens of internal debates within the Catholic tradition, historians of modern European thought have, until very recently, devoted little attention to Catholic theology.[26] And yet, theologians made crucial contributions to modern philosophical developments from phenomenology and the philosophy of history to human rights and totalitarianism theory. Doing so brought them into dialogue with a range of interlocutors, from Jean-Paul Sartre and Maurice Merleau-Ponty to Martin Heidegger and Alexandre Kojève as well as Georges Bataille and Raymond Aron, and *both* theology and secular philosophy were reshaped in the process. Specifically, Catholic theologians played a pivotal role in the French reception of Hegel, Heidegger, and the early writings of Marx, as well as the development of Christian existentialism. They also made important contributions to historical scholarship in dialogue with secular historians such as Ernst Kantorowicz and the architects of the Annales School. A major goal of this book, then, is to show that the histories of modern theology and modern European thought are far more intertwined than previously imagined, and in doing so, to begin to integrate theology into the canon of modern European intellectual history.

Working with theology requires a different set of methodological tools of the intellectual historian, and in particular, a new approach to contextualization. Because Catholic philosophers and theologians approached their contemporary moment through the categories of premodern thought, historians must balance two different contexts when making sense of their work. To understand religious ideas, we must attend not only to the particular place and time in which they are articulated, but also to the much longer textual traditions in which they are embedded. In the case of de Lubac, for instance, this means reading his work in the context of both the Church Fathers and the rise of Nazism. The history of theology and religious thought, in other words, requires an approach to contextualization that is both temporally intensive and temporally extensive. Keeping both these contexts in view allows us to see how Catholic intellectuals used premodern theologies to make sense of the dramatic events of the twentieth century, but also how their experiences led them to retool and transform these theologies.

Equally important is the need to attend to the communities and institutions in which religious thought takes shape. This is particularly the case with members of a religious order. In these communities, the distinctive spirituality of the order and the affective bonds forged in the course of religious life are inseparable from intellectual production. The story of the Jesuits at the heart of this book demonstrates the crucial role that friendship in particular can play in the development of ideas.[27] Focusing on these institutional and friendship networks also provides a different perspective on the *nouvelle théologie* than one finds in the existing literature, which tends to group Jesuits such as de Lubac and Daniélou together with Dominicans such as Chenu and Congar.[28] Examining the archives left by these actors and situating them in their institutional and interpersonal context yields a quite different picture, revealing significant fault lines between the Dominican and Jesuit branches of the *nouvelle théologie*.

Religion and Politics in a Secular Age

The story of these priests also has much to tell us about the continuing political power of religion in a secular world. Thirty years ago, many social scientists were convinced that religion was destined to disappear from public life, but in the wake of the rise of the American religious right, anxieties about "political Islam," and most recently, the revival of

Christian nationalism in Eastern Europe, it seems clear that religion is destined to remain a powerful political force.

The perceived resurgence of religion in public life has yielded a growing body of scholarship on secularization and political theology that draws from anthropologists, political theorists, philosophers, sociologists, historians, and scholars of religion. What is most striking about this rapidly expanding field, however, is how rarely the discipline of theology and the work of professional theologians enter into the discussion of political theology.[29] Taking its cue from Carl Schmitt, this literature has tended to focus on the medieval or early modern theological origins of modern political concepts, treating theology as something that existed in the past but whose formal features have now been taken over by the political.[30] The effect is to confine theology's moment of efficacy to a premodern past, foreclosing the possibility that it might continue to play a robust political role in the modern world. *Soldiers of God* offers a corrective to such one-directional accounts. It attends instead to the productive relationship between theology and secularization—the way the secularization of European public life has spurred theological reflection and opened the way for new politico-theological configurations.[31] By demonstrating the ongoing role of theology in a secular political context, this book aims to bring the "theology" back into the literature on political theology.

Doing so is complicated by the fact that many of the priests at the heart of this study did not conceive of themselves as "doing politics," which can make it difficult to grasp the political stakes of their work. In her 2005 study of the women's mosque movement in Egypt, the anthropologist Saba Mahmood lamented the fact that "we have few conceptual resources available for analyzing sociopolitical formations that do not take the nation-state and its juridical apparatuses as their main points of reference."[32] When religious actors, such as the women in Mahmood's study or the theologians in mine, do not frame their goals in the language of party politics, legal rights, or policy-making, they are liable to "fall off the 'political radar'" of most scholars.[33] This is a testament to the continuing power of the secular liberal distinction between the private sphere of religious belief and the public sphere in which political discourse takes place. Liberal political theorists such as John Rawls and Jürgen Habermas insist that religious actors must translate their faith commitments into the universal, neutral, and secular language of public reason in order for their claims to have political purchase.[34] When religious actors do not translate their goals into secular political terms—for instance, by making claims on the state or demanding legal recognition—they tend to become politically illegible.

I argue that we ought to take seriously the political power of religious ideas that refuse this sort of translation, not least because their power often derives from this very refusal. The priests in this story did not take the state as their primary point of reference. Eschewing party politics, they worked through a range of nonstate bodies such as Catholic Action associations, journals, trade unions, pastoral initiatives, and international organizations. But this does not mean that their work did not have political effects or that they simply accepted the modern distinction between the private realm of faith and the public realm of politics. Instead, the very claim to remain above politics itself performed political work for these priests, whether by allowing them to circumvent state censorship, authorizing them to pronounce on questions that might otherwise seem beyond their purview as priests, or clothing their political interventions in the transcendent authority of religious faith. As Gaston Fessard put it during a discussion with several other leading Catholic intellectuals about the Spanish Civil War, "I think it is precisely because I strive to be apolitical that I become supremely political."[35] The difficulty with the logic of separate spheres so central to liberal politics is that it tends to naturalize the distinction between religion and politics. It thus obscures the way in which this distinction is constantly drawn and redrawn, and the ideological work performed in the act of doing so. Just as political authorities can deploy the distinction between religion and politics strategically—as in the recent efforts by the French state to police the public expression of Islam—so, too, can religious actors use this distinction to advance their own ends.[36] Indeed, this is precisely how Catholic priests and theologians were able to carve out a role for themselves in public life after the institutions of Church and state were separated in France.

There is yet another reason why theology can be politically powerful even when it does not purport to engage in politics. While the priests at the heart of this study were deeply suspicious of political parties, ideologies, and state power, their work was nevertheless political in a much wider sense. This was because they firmly believed that Catholicism was an indispensably social faith and that its teachings therefore could not leave the structures of temporal life untouched. The central questions that animated Catholic theology in the twentieth century—questions about the relationship between the individual and the community, the nature and ends of the human person, the direction of history, the dignity

13

of labor, the relationship between Judaism and Christianity—had clear political import, especially in the context of twentieth-century European political developments such as the rise of fascism and communism. The theologians whom I follow were keenly aware of this significance and of the religious and metaphysical assumptions built into even the most secular of political projects. What they recognized, and what gave their thought political purchase, was that all politics presupposes a much wider set of ideas about the relationship between the individual and the community, the source of authority, human nature, and the structure of time. Of course, these are precisely the sorts of questions that theology seeks to answer, which is why it continues to impinge on political life in even the most robustly secular of modern states. But to recognize this, it is necessary to embrace a more expansive view of the political—one that focuses not just on the conventional sites of political action such as the state, the law, and the economy, but also integrates the sorts of anthropological, temporal, and metaphysical questions that are central to theology as well. In this way, the history of the *nouvelle théologie* invites us to rethink what constitutes a political act and where the boundaries of the political lie.

Overview of the Book

At the dawn of the twentieth century, the Catholic Church was locked in a global struggle against the intellectual and institutional foundations of modern life. France found itself at the epicenter of this conflict, and Part 1 demonstrates how the battle between an antimodern Church and an anticlerical Republic inadvertently created the conditions for a major renaissance in Catholic theology. Chapter 1 focuses on the institutional dimension of this story. It traces the roots of the *nouvelle théologie* to the new seminaries-in-exile, which were created to serve the religious orders evicted from France, including the Jesuit scholasticate on Jersey where de Lubac's circle studied in the early 1920s. Chapter 2 examines the interwar revolution in Catholic political theology that was precipitated by the Vatican condemnation of the AF in 1926. The condemnation undercut the dominance of royalism in French Catholic politics, creating a space for the emergence of political and theological alternatives that were no longer bound to the goal of restoring the confessional state. They included the specialized Catholic Action movements that flourished in the interwar period, which drew support from a range of new personalist theologies.

While remaining profoundly critical of liberalism, these theologies shifted the focus of Catholic politics away from the conflict with republicanism to the challenge of totalitarianism, opening up new ways for Catholics to participate in secular public life in the process.

Part 2 turns to the Second World War and shows how the new theological tools developed in the 1930s underwrote the spiritual resistance to Nazism and the collaborationist Vichy regime. Leading the charge was the group of Jesuits who had studied at Jersey in the 1920s: Henri de Lubac, Gaston Fessard, Yves de Montcheuil, and Pierre Chaillet. At first, they confined their resistance to "licit" channels, using theology to circumvent state censorship. But soon they were driven underground, and in 1941, they launched the clandestine journal *Témoignage chrétien* ("Christian witness"). The journal would become the leading voice of the spiritual resistance to fascism, but its editors never ceased to reaffirm that its mission was a purely spiritual one. Chapter 3 argues that in the context of the war, theology became a powerful political weapon precisely because it appeared to be apolitical. Chapter 4 delves deeper into the theological foundations of the spiritual resistance to show how de Lubac's circle deployed the resources of theology to carve out an ideological space that was both antifascist and antiliberal.

The Liberation brought a new spirit of optimism and experimentation to the French Church. Intellectual life in these years was dominated by the "humanism" debates between Marxists and existentialists, and Catholics also threw themselves into the fray. The result was a split within the progressive wing of the French Church between those who were open to a dialogue with the forces of the left and those who preferred to engage with modern philosophies such as existentialism and Hegelianism. At the forefront of the first group were the Dominicans associated with the *nouvelle théologie,* such as Marie-Dominique Chenu and Yves Congar. Chapter 5 shows how they repurposed and transformed Thomist arguments previously deployed by Catholics on the right to support their vision for a new "missionary" Church committed to the working class, anticolonialism, and nuclear disarmament. The Dominicans' Jesuit counterparts took a different path, for they viewed anticommunism as the logical extension of their wartime struggle against fascism. Chapter 6 traces how these Jesuits incorporated the insights of existentialism and Hegelianism to develop a vision of human nature and history that could serve as a counterpoint to both Marxism and liberalism. The postwar period thus saw the division of the *nouvelle théologie* into a Thomist strand that sought to incarnate Catholicism within secular movements, and a patristic strand that resisted such efforts in the name of eschatology.

By the 1950s, both these groups would be condemned by the authorities in Rome. And yet, the opening of the Second Vatican Council in 1962 gave them a chance to redeem themselves. Chapter 7 tells the story of the condemnation and rehabilitation of the *nouvelle théologie,* showing how it helped to shape the revolutionary changes of Vatican II as well as post-conciliar disputes over the relationship between the Church and the modern world. The epilogue widens the lens to explore the legacies of the *nouvelle théologie* for contemporary discussions both within and beyond the Church about the place of religion in public life. Not only did liberation theologians in Latin America and Anglo-American theologians associated with radical orthodoxy turn to these mid-century Frenchmen to reclaim a political role for the Church, but the *nouvelle théologie* also anticipated the efforts of contemporary scholars to understand how and why religion remains such a powerful force today.

PART ONE

SEPARATION

(1880–1939)

CHAPTER ONE

Exile Catholicism

In 1880, the Ferry Decrees unilaterally dissolved the Jesuit order in France. This was the opening act in a bitter campaign to dismantle the power of the Catholic Church, which culminated in the separation of Church and state in 1905. The campaign drove tens of thousands of religious into exile, where they established new houses of formation like the Maison Saint-Louis, a Jesuit scholasticate located just off the French coast on the Channel Island of Jersey.[1] It was here that Henri de Lubac arrived in 1920 to begin his philosophical training, and he later recalled with great fondness his formation in exile: "We were really quite far from the world, away for a time from nearly all the responsibilities of the apostolate; alone among ourselves, as if in a big ship drifting, without a radio, in the middle of the ocean. But what an intense life within that ship, and what a marvelous crossing!"[2] Marie-Dominique Chenu had a similar experience as a student and then teacher at Le Saulchoir, the Dominican house of studies that was established across the border in Belgium after the Dominicans were evicted from France in 1903. "Because it was in exile, and therefore cut off from certain French activities," Chenu explained, Le Saulchoir "lived on its own resources and the emphasis on the contemplative life was therefore stronger there, albeit a life of contemplation nourished by study."[3]

Both men stressed the profound isolation of exile, but their words also reveal that the experience fostered a uniquely intense intellectual environment. This helps to explain one of the great ironies of the French Republic's anticlerical campaign. The two seminaries-in-exile it helped to create—the Maison Saint-Louis and Le Saulchoir—would become the cradles for one of the most important movements of renewal in twentieth-century Catholic theology, known as the *nouvelle théologie*. Emerging in France during the 1930s and 1940s, it would go on to play a vital role at the Second Vatican Council in the 1960s. As a result, many of the most influential theologians at the Council—including de Lubac, Chenu, Yves Congar, Edward Schillebeeckx, and Jean Daniélou—studied at one of these two institutions. This chapter focuses in particular on the Jesuit scholasticate, where de Lubac developed a close friendship with Gaston Fessard, Yves de Montcheuil, Robert Hamel, and René d'Ouince in the 1920s. It is to the friendships and shared experiences of this group that we must look to understand the intellectual origins of the *nouvelle théologie*. Their story testifies to the important but often overlooked role that affective bonds play in the history of ideas. It also shows how the anticlerical campaign in France unwittingly created the conditions for a renaissance in French Catholic thought.

The experience of isolation and exile inspired this group of young Jesuits to elaborate a theological vision capable of overcoming the growing gulf between the Church and French society. This divergence was the product of parallel developments in the French Republic and the Catholic Church around the turn of the twentieth century. While the leaders of the Republic sought to expand the sovereignty of the state over matters traditionally under the purview of the Church, the papacy was in the process of consolidating and centralizing its authority over the Church. These two processes were not necessarily at odds, however. Both relied on the identification and exclusion of internal enemies. For the Republic, this enemy was the religious orders, while the Church focused on the threat posed by Catholic "Modernists." In the process, both Rome and the Republic mobilized the same opposition between Catholicism and modernity to consolidate their sovereignty, jointly producing and reinforcing the very opposition on which they relied for justification.

This paradoxical situation perhaps explains why the neo-scholastic theology that dominated the Church in this period seemed in some ways to mirror the very logic of the secular republicanism it so fervently opposed. Despite their manifestly contrary aims, the neo-scholastic separation between the natural and supernatural orders echoed the logic of separation that was so central to the anticlerical project. These parallels were not lost on de Lubac and his friends. As they completed their formation on Jersey, the experience of physical exile drove home for them the intellectual exile to which neo-scholasticism had confined the Church.

Accusing their superiors of adhering to a "separated theology" that unwittingly colluded with the forces responsible for the separation of Church and state, these young men began to develop a controversial "new theology" devoted to reintegrating the natural and supernatural orders, faith and reason, and the Church and the modern world.

Two Frances at War

The conflict between the Church and the French Republic did not begin in 1880. Ever since the French Revolution and the Civil Constitution of the Clergy, republicanism and anticlericalism had been intertwined, while the Vendée uprising and the writings of Catholic royalists such as Joseph de Maistre and Louis de Bonald solidified the association between Catholicism and counterrevolution.[4] But it was under the Third Republic that the conflict reached its peak. From 1880 to 1905, republican lawmakers mounted a systematic assault on the legal and political power of Catholicism in France, enshrining *laïcité* (secularism) as a defining principle of French republicanism and establishing the legal apparatus that continues to structure the place of religion in the public sphere to this day.[5]

At the center of this anticlerical campaign, as in many other European countries, was the status of the religious orders (*congrégations*). On March 29, 1880, Jules Ferry, then minister of public instruction, fired the opening salvo by issuing two decrees. The first dissolved the Jesuits and the second gave unauthorized religious orders three months to request state authorization or meet the same fate. These measures were integral to Ferry's broader efforts to limit the role of the Church in the French educational system, which included an extensive network of schools run by *congrégations*. The Jesuits in particular administered a prestigious system of colleges that recruited heavily from the upper echelons of French society and served as feeder schools for the nation's top military academies.[6] Republican lawmakers feared that these schools served to inculcate the counterrevolutionary ideology of the Church instead of producing republican citizens, effectively creating two kinds of French youth whose values were incompatible. The school thus became a privileged site in the ideological battle against the Catholic Church.[7] In 1882, the republicans scored a major victory in this struggle when they passed educational reforms that made primary schooling free, secular, and mandatory. Ferry's attack on the religious orders must be understood in the context of this battle over education. As a result of his decrees, the twenty-nine Jesuit colleges in France were closed, moved to other countries, or placed under lay administration.

There was yet another reason for republican suspicion of the religious orders: their status as international bodies that partially escaped the disciplinary purview of the state. Unlike the secular clergy, who fell under the jurisdiction of the French hierarchy, the religious orders reported directly to the Roman Curia, and in many cases their superiors were based in Rome. Republican ministers therefore denounced the orders as an "independent Roman militia," the irruption of a foreign power at the heart of the *patrie*.[8] The Jesuits were particularly vulnerable to such accusations, given the longer history of the conflict between the Gallican Church and Ultramontane Jesuits, who supported the centralization of ecclesiastical authority in Rome.[9] The text introducing the Ferry Decrees drew on this history when it explained the need to dissolve an order "against which the national sentiment has always pronounced itself." But in addition to evicting the Jesuits from "the territory of the Republic," the decrees also refused to authorize any order with a superior residing outside France or that would not submit to the jurisdiction of the local bishop.[10] As a result, the Dominicans, Franciscans, Benedictines, and several other orders were expelled as well and roughly 6,500 religious went into exile.[11]

By the end of the decade, the political situation had changed considerably. Conservatives had made substantial electoral gains and, with the specter of Boulangism threatening the very survival of the Republic, the government toned down its anticlerical rhetoric in an effort to court the Catholic vote. Many exiled religious judged the moment opportune to return to France and discreetly resume their work. Meanwhile, Pope Leo XIII seized on this favorable conjuncture to extend an olive branch to the French government, appealing to French Catholics to make their peace with the institutions of the Republic. In an 1892 encyclical, he reminded Catholics of their duty to obey the established temporal authority whatever its political stripe. And he pointed out that no form of government—including the Republic—was, "in itself, opposed to the principles of sound reason nor to the maxims of Christian doctrine."[12] Leo's call for a *"Ralliement"* breathed new life into the fledgling Christian Democratic movement in France, led by such figures as Marc Sangnier and his Sillon movement.[13] This "first generation" of Christian Democracy in France would prove short-lived, however. Not only were the vast majority of French Catholics too deeply entrenched in their

22

royalism and hostility to the Republic to countenance the pope's appeal, but shortly after he issued it, the nation found itself embroiled in the Dreyfus Affair, which drove the "two Frances" further apart than ever before.[14] The forces of Catholicism, anti-Semitism, and royalism, which backed the army, were now arrayed in a bitter struggle against Captain Alfred Dreyfus's republican defenders.

In the wake of the Affair, the republican government of Pierre Waldeck-Rousseau sought to break the power of the religious orders once and for all. In 1901, it seized the opportunity provided by a broader law on civil associations to insert a specific clause concerning the *congrégations,* forcing them to apply for authorization from the state within three months or face dissolution and the liquidation of their assets.[15] The law also submitted the orders to a regime of state surveillance by requiring them to maintain an exhaustive inventory of their property, which the local prefect could request at any moment. They would also have to submit their statutes to the local bishop, the prefect, and the government for approval. Rather than banning the *congrégations* outright, then, the 1901 law subordinated them to the prerogative of the state, giving it discretionary power to grant or withhold authorization on a case-by-case basis.

The religious orders saw this measure for what it was—a bid to shore up state sovereignty at the expense of the autonomy of the Church. The four Jesuit provincials in France condemned the law as a ploy "to subjugate [the orders] and to prepare the way for the subjugation of the Church itself."[16] As other orders weighed whether to seek state authorization or go into exile, the Jesuits came out strongly in favor of the second option. To seek authorization, they insisted, would be to render the *congrégations* "totally dependent on the government, shackled, paralyzed in their action, and absolutely enslaved." They suggested that the government's effort to submit the religious orders to the jurisdiction of the bishops was part of a broader campaign to domesticate the French Church and "make it into a national, independent church" by separating it from the Holy See.[17] By remaining in exile, they argued, at least they could maintain their autonomy.

But the question of whether to seek authorization rapidly became moot. The following year's elections brought a much more anticlerical government to power under Émile Combes, and all but five requests for authorization were refused. In 1903, the government initiated the process of systematically dismantling the *congrégations,* sometimes having to evict them by force from barricaded residences defended by the local laity. But the Combes administration did not stop there. The following year, it passed legislation that greatly expanded the scope of the Law on Associations and targeted the authorized religious orders as well. Proclaiming that "teaching of any kind and any nature is forbidden in France to the *congrégations*," the law imposed a ten-year timeline for the complete dissolution of all religious orders connected with education.[18] Those who violated this injunction would face possible prison sentences or fines. By this time, relations between the government and the Holy See had soured considerably, not least because Leo XIII had died in 1903 and his successor, Pius X, was far less open to dialogue. In 1904, the French government broke off diplomatic relations with the Holy See, threatening the Concordat that had governed relations between Church and state since the Napoleonic era. It would be officially nullified the following year with the passage of the landmark Law of Separation, which put an end to the subsidization of Church activities and any other privileges that interfered with the state's religious neutrality. The law was the culmination of the efforts of successive republican governments to decouple religious personnel and institutions from the institutions of public life with which they had long been intertwined.

And yet, Church and state were far from cleanly separated in 1905. The regime the law inaugurated was instead built on a number of exceptions. Indeed, the restrictions imposed on religious orders in 1901 were themselves an exception within the broader Law on Associations, which made it easier to form voluntary and civil associations without state authorization. The anticlerical laws were also not applied to the nation's colonies, where missionaries and religious schools played a central role in spreading French values and supplied the imperial project with a cheap labor force.[19] The region of Alsace-Moselle was likewise exempted from the Law of Separation when it returned to French jurisdiction following World War I, and it remains so to this day. Scholars often point to such exceptions as evidence that the French state is by no means religiously "neutral." Indeed, some argue that the various exceptions to the 1905 law are themselves manifestations of the sovereign power of the French state to define the scope of religion and the acceptable forms its public expression can take.[20]

Nevertheless, the radicalization of the anticlerical campaign under the Combes administration also suggests the *limits* of state sovereignty. Instead of submitting the religious orders to state authorization and surveillance, as the 1901 law had done, it made membership in a religious order with perpetual vows incompatible with membership in the body politic. The logic of domestication had given way to the logic of separation, as tens of thousands of religious were driven into exile. Some republican deputies sensed that this move might actually undercut the French state's authority over the orders and called instead for a more lenient approach that would allow the state to "reserve for itself, over these *congrégations*, means of action and control which will escape us completely if they no longer have houses in France."[21] What these deputies grasped was that, far from affirming the Republic's sovereignty, the exile of the religious orders and the Law of Separation served instead to limit its power over the Church.

The Republic's Exiles

Ferry, Waldeck-Rousseau, and Combes certainly could not have foreseen the dramatic effect their laws would have on the development of Catholic theology: in seeking to limit the financial, social, and political power of the Catholic Church, they unwittingly created the conditions for an extraordinary renaissance in French Catholic theology. To understand how the anticlerical legislation paved the way for this renaissance, let us focus in particular on the story of the Jesuits who took refuge on the island of Jersey.

Roughly 30,000 religious went into exile in response to the anticlerical legislation.[22] Preferring destinations that were francophone, Catholic, and close to France, they flocked above all to Belgium, but also to Spain, the Channel Islands, England, Italy, and the canton of Fribourg in Switzerland.[23] The exodus also spurred a marked upswing in missionary vocations, thanks to the colonial exemption from the anticlerical legislation. The exiles' choice of destination was often constrained by the political climate of the host country, and especially by the virulence of local anticlerical sentiment. This problem was particularly acute in Belgium, where an influx of well over 10,000 French religious fueled support for anticlerical parties and put considerable pressure on the Catholic government, leading the Belgian bishops to impose limits on the flow of religious refugees across the border in 1903.[24] In most cases, asylum was sought from and accorded by the local bishop rather than the temporal authorities, which meant that the experience of France's exiled religious orders was often determined by the specific situation in the host diocese.[25]

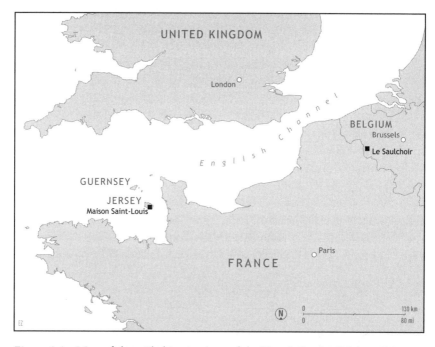

Figure 1.1 Map of the exiled institutions of the French Jesuits (Maison Saint-Louis, St. Hélier, Jersey) and the French Dominicans (Le Saulchoir, Kain, Belgium) discussed in this chapter. *Credit:* Ezra Zeitler.

This was certainly the case with Jersey. In the aftermath of the Ferry Decrees, the Jesuit Provincial of Paris appealed to the local Catholic bishop rather than the government of Jersey—known as the "States"—for permission to move his province's scholasticate to the island.[26] He had already written to the Jesuit Provincial of England, who procured the building that would become the Maison Saint-Louis on behalf of the French Jesuits, since they could not legally acquire property on the island.[27] What most attracted the French Jesuits to Jersey was doubtless its physical and cultural proximity to France. Located just fourteen miles off the coast of Normandy, the island occupied a liminal legal space. As a self-governing Crown Dependency, it did not fall under the jurisdiction of the British government and instead possessed an independent legal system combining elements of Norman customary law, English common law, and French civil law. Residents spoke both French and English, though local politics was largely conducted in French. This linguistic and physical proximity to France, in conjunction with Jersey's legal independence from Britain, made it an ideal destination for France's exiled Jesuits.

Their stay was nevertheless troubled by scuffles with the local government, inspired in part by anti-Catholic sentiment and a suspicion of foreigners. There were several incidents of vandalism and harassment at the Maison Saint-Louis, including one involving a local farmer who attacked a group of students out for an afternoon stroll, striking them in the face with his riding whip.[28] Conspiracy theories about Jesuits abounded in the local media, including a rumor that the Jesuits ate their dead (they had only one recorded death in their first year on the island).[29] One Anglican clergyman even led a legal campaign to expel the Jesuits from the island. In 1880, he introduced a bill in the Jersey States to ban the establishment of any Jesuit institutions on the island. When that failed, he amended the bill to require that all institutions established by foreign religious orders submit to a regime of state inspection.[30] But the bill met with stiff resistance in the States and local newspapers, where it was denounced as a violation of personal liberty and religious freedom. Many islanders perceived the Jesuits as victims of religious persecution at the hands of an irreligious government and argued that they should be left in peace so long as they refrained from proselytizing or meddling in local affairs.[31] Ultimately, the bill was defeated and, as time went on, attitudes toward the Jesuits began to improve. The exiles did their part to show respect for their new home by hosting the lieutenant governor in 1883 and taking part in the queen's jubilee celebrations of 1887 and 1897. In 1901, however, amid fears that the new Law on Associations would inundate the tiny island, the Jersey States passed legislation to prevent any more French religious communities from settling there, which provoked a new wave of vandalism and anti-Jesuit sentiment.[32]

Kicked out of their homeland, at odds with their hosts, and isolated on a tiny island off the coast of Normandy, how could the Jesuit community on Jersey become an incubator for one of the most important movements of renewal in twentieth-century Catholic thought? Several factors help to explain how this unassuming Anglo-Norman island became such an intellectual hotspot. First, the logistics of exile brought together Jesuits from different provinces and countries who would not otherwise have studied together. Each of the order's four French provinces joined with one other to consolidate their houses of formation in exile. The Jersey scholasticate initially served the provinces of Paris and Champagne, but in

1887, the Champagne contingent left for Enghien (Belgium) and was replaced by students from the province of Lyon.[33] This would have important consequences for Henri de Lubac's circle, since it included members of both the provinces of Lyon (de Lubac) and of Paris (Montcheuil and Fessard), who would have pursued their studies at separate institutions had the order remained in France. The exiled religious schools also attracted a much higher proportion of international students, which expanded the intellectual and linguistic horizons of the French students. In addition, Jersey boasted an extremely impressive library, drawn from the collections of the closed Jesuit colleges in France, which nourished the intellectual life of the community.

The isolation imposed by exile also served as a powerful stimulus for intellectual production. In France, the Jesuits had accrued a number of pastoral commitments to the local population they served, such as youth ministries, and these responsibilities took time away from their studies. This was not the case for many of the exiled religious orders, especially in the British Isles and Belgium, where they observed strict limits on their teaching and pastoral activities so as not to arouse local hostility.[34] In Belgium, for instance, the bishops offered asylum to French orders on the express condition that they not open schools or engage in charitable works.[35] As a result, intellectual life took center stage and transformed institutions such as the Maison Saint-Louis and its Dominican counterpart Le Saulchoir into premier centers of Catholic thought. As the recollections by de Lubac and Chenu that opened this chapter attest, the isolation of exile created a remarkably intense intellectual environment. Indeed, when the Provincial of Lyon considered returning the province's theological scholasticate from Hastings to Fourvière in 1926, one of the principal disadvantages he saw to the move was the renewal of pastoral commitments that it would entail, which would distract the students from their studies. He therefore issued a directive establishing strict limits on the time students could devote to such ministries, so as not to damage the intellectual prestige the school had acquired in exile.[36] As one member of the community recalled, "We have never worked so well at the scholasticate as since we have been in England."[37]

The physical isolation of exile was also liberating for another reason: it helped to shield these institutions to a certain degree from the repressive regime of censorship and espionage that was imposed on the major clerical institutions of formation in the aftermath of the Modernist Crisis (discussed in the next section). As Étienne Fouilloux explains, the exiled seminaries and houses of study were "far-removed, materially and psychologically, from the eye of the storm" that "shook great seminaries and Catholic Institutes with its full force during this period."[38] As a result, Chenu recalled, institutions like Le Saulchoir were able "to maintain a space where one could breathe freely, at a time when a police state was being installed" throughout the Church. The Dominicans there even managed to set up a journal that conveyed the school's distinctive historical approach to theology (the *Revue des sciences philosophiques et théologiques*) in 1907—the very same year when the pope condemned historicism as a form of "Modernism."[39]

It is therefore no coincidence that the primary architects of the postwar theological renewal in France had trained at exiled religious schools, and in particular, the Maison Saint-Louis or Le Saulchoir. The republican anticlerical campaign thus turned out to be a kind of *felix culpa*. By driving France's religious orders into exile, it unwittingly created the institutional and intellectual conditions for the extraordinary vibrancy of French Catholicism in the 1930s and 1940s.[40] The founder of Le Saulchoir observed this strange phenomenon as well, noting that the persecutions and evictions of the anticlerical campaign seemed to bring new vitality to the intellectual life of the Dominican order. "The destructions and separations wrought by the hands of men do not destroy the works they touch, but instead perfect them," he concluded. "In the face of the menace that still hangs over our heads even today in Belgium, this is what accounts for the beautiful, pious, and studious serenity of this French Dominican convent of Le Saulchoir."[41]

Modernity on Trial

While the French religious orders languished in physical exile, Catholic theology in this period was also "in a state of emigration or exile from the modern cultural world," as Joseph Komonchak has put it.[42] This self-enforced intellectual exile was the defensive reaction of a Church that felt beset on all sides by the forces of secular modernity. It was not just in France that the traditional privileges of the Church were under attack; throughout Europe, the Church faced assaults on its property, legal privileges, schools, and religious orders from newly established nation-states seeking to shore up their sovereignty and from liberals and socialists who viewed it as an obstacle to progress.[43] While Bismarck waged his *Kulturkampf* in Germany, the Italian Risorgimento left the Holy See without a territorial homeland. It is no coincidence that the doctrine of papal infallibility, which dramatically expanded the spiritual authority of the pope, was pronounced a mere two months before Italian forces captured Rome.[44] Just as European lawmakers sought to consolidate state sovereignty at the expense of ecclesiastical privileges, the forces of Ultramontanism sought to consolidate ecclesiastical authority in Rome.[45] Papal primacy and infallibility were two tools in this arsenal; another was the establishment of neo-scholasticism as the unifying framework for Catholic thought. By the turn of the century, as the "war of the two Frances" reached its peak and the Republic evicted the religious orders, Catholics were consumed by their own civil war over the relationship between the Church and the modern world. These contemporaneous conflicts—the anticlerical campaign and the Modernist Crisis—were in many ways mutually reinforcing; both relied on, but also heightened, the opposition between the Church and the modern world.

In 1864, Pius IX had issued a blanket denunciation of the intellectual and political edifice of the modern world in his infamous *Syllabus of Errors.* But his successor, Leo XIII, took a different approach. He recognized that an effective Catholic response to the challenge of modernity would have to go beyond mere rejection to articulate a positive alternative to modern thought—one that could do battle on the same terrain as its secular counterpart. This he found in the philosophical tradition of Thomas Aquinas and his scholastic commentators. One of Leo's first acts as pope, then, was to enshrine Thomist philosophy as the foundation for all theological inquiry in his encyclical *Aeterni Patris,* which he issued a year before the Ferry Decrees. Just as papal primacy and infallibility centralized ecclesiastical authority in the figure of the pope, this encyclical sought to unify Catholic thought around the figure of Aquinas.

What appealed to Leo XIII was the scholastic tradition's synthetic nature and the primacy it placed on speculative reason. He traced the ills of the modern world to the moment when reason emancipated itself from revelation. When humans sought "to philosophize without any respect for faith," the inevitable result was "that systems of philosophy multiplied beyond measure, and conclusions differing and clashing one with another arose."[46] By restoring reason to its rightful place as the foundation and "steppingstone to the Christian faith," Leo hoped that the revival of Thomism would counteract this corrosive intellectual pluralism. A theology constructed on these "solid foundations" could then assume the "nature, form and genius of a true science" (§6). Additionally, by deploying reason in the service of faith, Leo sought to reappropriate the primary philosophical tool in the arsenal of secular modernity in order "to cut off the head of the boastful Goliath with his own weapon" (§7). While affirming the ultimate superiority and autonomy of faith, the Thomist tradition endowed reason with a central apologetic role in establishing the "preambles of faith," tasked with proving the existence of God and the credibility of revelation prior to any act of faith. By framing Catholic thought in these highly rational and scientific terms, Leo XIII hoped to compete with modern intellectual culture on its own terrain, even as he called for a return to premodern scholasticism.

In this sense, the Thomist revival championed by Leo XIII was not a straightforward rejection of modernity. In an effort to provide a viable alternative to modern thought, neo-scholasticism ultimately echoed many of the rationalist presuppositions most closely associated with it, including its tendency to distinguish between reason and faith, between the natural and supernatural orders. Indeed, the neo-scholastic philosophers at the Catholic University of Louvain were early pioneers in the development of phenomenology—the foundation for much of twentieth-century continental philosophy.[47] But while neo-scholastics were at home in the language of speculative reason, they were far less comfortable with the more subjectivist and historicist aspects of modern philosophy. In contrast to Kantian idealism, neo-scholasticism relied on a realist metaphysics that moved from the sensible created world to an analogous knowledge of God's attributes and conceived of Catholic dogma as a set of objective, intelligible, and immutable truths independent of the individual believer. Toward the end of the nineteenth century, this model faced a serious challenge from Catholic "Modernists" who foregrounded precisely those aspects of religious life and thought neglected by neo-scholasticism.

Though it was by no means a self-conscious and coherent movement, one can identify two main strands of thought associated with Catholic Modernism.[48] The first was an emphasis on the role of history. This included embracing the historical-critical method in biblical exegesis—treating scripture as an object of historical investigation, as Alfred Loisy did in *The Gospel and the Church* (1902).[49] More commonly, it meant acknowledging that the doctrines of the Church develop and evolve over time—as John Henry Newman and the Tübingen school had begun to suggest earlier in the nineteenth century—in contrast to the neo-scholastic emphasis on the immutability of truth and dogma. In addition to foregrounding the role of history, Catholic Modernists also elevated the role of the human subject. They prioritized lived religious experience and non-rational ways of knowing God over the abstract, propositional knowledge afforded by neo-scholasticism. And they approached doctrine as a practical guide to action rather than a rigid credo requiring intellectual assent. This focus on the experiential and practical life of the believing subject was most evident in the work of George Tyrrell and Friedrich von Hügel in Britain and Maurice Blondel, Lucien Laberthonnière, and Édouard Le Roy in France.[50] Although there were significant differences among these figures, they all rejected the abstract rationalism of the neo-scholastic model. Such a critique would resonate deeply with de Lubac's circle and the two central dimensions of Catholic Modernism—the turn to history and the turn to the human subject—later became key themes of the *nouvelle théologie* as well.

When Pius X replaced the more conciliatory Leo XIII in 1903, he mobilized the Church's full disciplinary apparatus to stamp out Modernism. The leading figures associated with the movement had their works placed on the Index of Forbidden Books, and Tyrrell and Loisy were even excommunicated. In 1907, the pope condemned Modernism as "the synthesis of all heresies" in his encyclical *Pascendi Dominici Gregis*.[51] He accused the Modernists of "agnosticism" for denying the role of reason in apologetics and the possibility of an objective, immutable knowledge of revelation. He also charged them with reducing religion to a subjective need for God. Such "immanentism" not only undermined the transcendence of the divine; it also threatened the authority of the magisterium—the teaching authority of the Church—by privileging the subject's direct relationship to God at the expense of the mediating role of the hierarchy and by suggesting that the doctrines of the Church were subject to historical change. This perhaps explains why the Curia took such extreme steps to stamp out the threat of Modernism. Anyone accused of professing these ideas was banned from teaching at a seminary or Catholic university, which led to a ruthless campaign of denunciations and purges. "Councils of Vigilance" and even an international network of spies known as the Sodalitium Pianum were created in order to identify and unmask suspected Modernists, and in 1910, Pius X required all clergy and seminary professors to take an anti-Modernist oath.[52] As a result of these measures, whole fields of study, such as biblical scholarship, fell under a cloud of suspicion that did not lift until the 1940s.

Reinforcing the privileged status of neo-scholasticism became a key aspect of this disciplinary project. Indeed, the first measure that *Pascendi* adopted to combat the spread of Modernism was to reassert the role of scholastic philosophy as the basis for all Catholic thought. At the heart of the Modernist error, the pope insisted, was its repudiation of scholasticism, for "there is no surer sign that a man is on the way to Modernism than when he begins to show his dislike for this system."[53] George Tyrrell therefore quipped that, while *Pascendi* "tries to show the Modernist that he is no Catholic, it mostly succeeds only in showing him that he is no scholastic."[54] If the Thomist revival had begun under Leo XIII as a way to meet the challenge of modernity on its own terms, it had now become a defensive rampart against the threat of Modernism.[55] Thanks in part to the Modernist Crisis, neo-scholasticism became the governing framework for Catholic thought. The manuals and textbooks used to train priests were steeped in this tradition, especially after the 1917 Code of Canon Law made the teachings of Aquinas the basis for Catholic instruction in philosophy and theology, and its dominance would not be seriously challenged until the Second Vatican Council.

Far more than an internal doctrinal quarrel, however, the Modernist Crisis must be situated in the context that produced the anticlerical campaign in France. It is no coincidence that *Pascendi* was issued only two years after the separation of Church and state in France. The pope's hostility was no doubt informed by events in France, not least because some of the most prominent "Modernists," such as Laberthonnière and Blondel, were also active in the fledgling Christian Democratic movement there.[56] Indeed, *Pascendi* explicitly accused the Modernists of supporting the principle of Church-state separation, and therefore of aiding and abetting the Church's enemies. By contrast, in the first decades of the twentieth century, neo-scholasticism became ever more closely aligned with the royalist movement led by Charles Maurras and known as the Action française (AF).

But there is yet another connection between these two contexts, for the campaign against Modernism rather strikingly mirrored the anticlerical campaign in France. Both were premised on the identification and exclusion of internal enemies, and both drew their justification from the presumed opposition between the Church and the modern world. Above all, the Church's antimodernist campaign and the Republic's anticlerical campaign constituted parallel and connected assertions of sovereignty.

Just as the Modernist Crisis dramatically expanded and centralized Rome's control over Catholic thought, the anticlerical campaign extended the sovereign power of the French state over public life. Together, they jointly reinforced the opposition between Catholicism and modernity.

Toward a "New Theology"

When Henri de Lubac, Gaston Fessard, Robert Hamel, and Yves de Montcheuil arrived at Jersey to undertake their philosophical studies in the early 1920s, they entered an institution that was still grappling with the fallout from the Modernist Crisis. But much had also changed. In 1914, the outbreak of World War I interrupted their peaceful life of exile, as priests and seminarians were drafted into military service. The experience of war convinced de Lubac's generation of the urgent need for a Catholic philosophy and theology capable of speaking to the modern mind, a task for which the neo-scholasticism they learned at Jersey seemed manifestly inadequate. In conjunction with parallel efforts in the Dominican order, these young Jesuits would begin to formulate an alternative to neo-scholastic orthodoxy—one that they hoped would rescue Catholicism from its intellectual exile.

Born in the mid- to late-1890s, this generation of priests was in its infancy when the Law on Associations expelled the religious orders from France. The formative experience of their youth was not the anticlerical campaign, but rather the First World War. Because the anticlerical legislation had lifted the clerical exemption on military service, theirs became the first generation of French priests and seminarians to see active duty when war broke out and they were recalled from exile to serve as soldiers, chaplains, or stretcher-bearers in the French army. Over the course of the war, a total of 9,281 members of religious orders were mobilized, including 870 Jesuits and sixty-eight teachers and students from the Maison Saint-Louis.[57] At a political level, the war brought an end to the most intense period of conflict between the Church and the Republic, as the state suspended implementation of the anticlerical legislation and called instead for a "sacred union" between Church and state in the interests of defending the *patrie*.[58]

At a personal level, the war had a profound effect on the "curates with backpacks," as the mobilized priests and seminarians were nicknamed.[59] The leveling and integrating effect of the trenches brought de Lubac, Fessard, and Hamel into contact with a whole class of Frenchmen from whom their own socioeconomic background (the Jesuits recruited heavily from the upper echelons of French society) and the isolation imposed by their vocation had previously segregated them. They were astonished by the level of unbelief they observed among the men they encountered in the trenches, but they also learned that nonbelievers too "were men of courage, of loyalty, of generosity, of intelligence, of integrity," as Fessard later recalled. "That experience opened our eyes," he added, "and when the war ended, there were among us Jesuits those who resolved that we would never again allow ourselves to be cut off from the real world in which we lived. . . . How could we be witnesses to the gospel to the men of our times if we did not know those times and those men?"[60] The experience of the trenches opened the eyes of these young Jesuits to the enormous gulf that had emerged between the Church and the masses, and the need for new apologetic and evangelical tools to bridge it.

But they found few resources to meet this need in their formation at Jersey. Here, Montcheuil complained, students were "carefully locked away in a padded box so as not to be contaminated by the spirit of the times." They were "infused with the philosophy of another age and invited to thank God for possessing the absolute and definitive truth, while their contemporaries, brains sickened and stripped of good sense, lose themselves in chimeras."[61] Instead of providing them with the tools to confront the problem of dechristianization, their teachers seemed to have retreated into the protective cocoon of a premodern philosophy that foreclosed any engagement with the social or intellectual challenges of the modern world. Such an approach could not satisfy the generation formed by the war. Robert Hamel acknowledged the extent to which this experience set them apart from their teachers. "If the war hadn't come, with all the intellectual and social openings it created," he wrote to de Lubac, "would we be any more open-minded, and would we have understood the value of personal initiative and of recourse to the original [texts of the tradition]?"[62] The experience of social engagement and integration that these Jesuits had gained in the military thus brought into sharp relief the material as well as intellectual isolation of their order.

When the demobilized Jesuits arrived at Jersey, they entered an institution dominated by the neo-scholasticism of teachers such as Pedro Descoqs and Gabriel Picard. Like most Jesuits at the time, Picard and Descoqs followed the teachings of the sixteenth-century Jesuit scholastic Francisco Suárez. Descoqs in particular was known to be "savagely Suarezian," which brought him into conflict with both Catholic Modernists and strict Thomists, who prized fidelity to Aquinas himself over the early modern commentators.[63] The curriculum at Jersey therefore excluded works of modern philosophy. Such works were "semi-forbidden fruit," de Lubac recalled, and were "stored in a locked cupboard, which was opened only on holidays."[64] But because clerical formation at the time was based on a series of manuals steeped in neo-scholasticism, students could also emerge from their formation without having read many of the foundational texts of Catholic thought, including the works of Thomas Aquinas himself. This was a source of great consternation among de Lubac's group of friends.[65]

What frustrated them even more was the intellectual narrowness and hostility to innovation that they observed in their teachers. Students at the Jersey scholasticate complained of the "airtight cleavage" between themselves and their teachers, whose attitude was consistently "defensive and guarded, as if faced with an enemy coming to attack them and against which they must defend themselves."[66] They were particularly scathing about Descoqs, "whose combative teaching was a perpetual invitation to react" and whose penchant for impossibly recondite philosophical questions was a frequent source of amusement.[67] De Lubac and his friends also poked fun at their rector, Gabriel Picard (depicted on the top left of Figure 1.2), for his rigid sense of orthodoxy.[68] This irreverent attitude is reflected in the cartoons the students drew of their teachers at Jersey. It is particularly evident in the two-panel series depicting Father Bonnet (on the right of Figure 1.2). The top drawing shows him with a furrowed brow, muttering "it seems vexing . . . ," while in the panel below it he appears to breathe a sigh of relief, concluding, "our position . . . is secure. . . ." Here we can see the students mocking their teachers for their fear of new ideas that might challenge their established orthodoxies. In this way, the teachers at Jersey furnished de Lubac's circle with a negative intellectual model against which to define themselves.

In response to the insufficiencies of the curriculum at Jersey, de Lubac, Fessard, Montcheuil, and Hamel, along with Alfred de Soras, Charles Nicolet, and René d'Ouince, developed their own parallel curriculum. They formed an independent study circle, which met on a weekly basis to read and discuss works not included in the official curriculum.[69] Readings included the foundational texts of medieval and ancient thought—such as Augustine, Plotinus, Aquinas, Bonaventure—as well as the classics of modern philosophy, including Descartes, Malebranche, Kant,

Figure 1.2 Cartoons drawn by the Jesuit students at Jersey during Fessard and de Lubac's time there. The top left cartoon depicts Gabriel Picard, and the caption in the pair of images on the right roughly translates: "It seems vexing . . ." (top) and "our position . . . is secure . . ." (bottom). *Credit:* Fonds Gaston Fessard, 62/5, reproductions © Compagnie de Jésus—Archives Jésuites.

Leibniz, Pascal, and Spinoza. They also read more recent work by French philosophers such as Maine de Biran, Henri Bergson, and Alexandre Koyré. But what had perhaps the greatest impact on this young group of Jesuits were the contemporary Catholic philosophers they read together, including Maurice Blondel, Joseph Maréchal, Pierre Rousselot, and a little later, Pierre Teilhard de Chardin. They were introduced to many of these works by Auguste Valensin—a close friend and disciple of Blondel who had recently been removed from his teaching post at Jersey. It was through Valensin that many of these texts, which were considered too controversial to be stocked in the library, made their way to the island. The very fact that these students were permitted to pursue their independent study is noteworthy, however, and it suggests that Picard and Descoqs may not have been quite as rigid and uncompromising as their students believed.[70]

It was through their collective engagement with this "para-curriculum"—which blossomed into a more formal study circle calling itself "la Pensée" later on, during their theological studies—that de Lubac and his friends began to develop many of the ideas that would launch them to the forefront of Catholic intellectual life in the 1930s and 1940s. Above all, the activities of the group testify to the central role that friendships can play in intellectual development, especially in the absence of a supportive intellectual or institutional environment. What Fouilloux writes of Yves de Montcheuil—that he "built his personality on the margins, on friendships, on readings and an intense work of collaborative elaboration"—was just as true of the other members of the group.[71] Their collaborative readings and discussions brought into focus the lacunae of their teachers' neo-scholastic paradigm and provided them with the affective and intellectual resources to begin to articulate an alternative vision.

It was at Jersey, for instance, that de Lubac first began to cultivate a lifelong commitment to the role of mystery in human affairs. This was above all a reaction against the overweening rationalism he associated with neo-scholasticism, and it would form a key premise of the *"esquisse,"* or "sketch," for a theory of knowledge that he cowrote with Fessard during their last year at Jersey. While distancing itself from the intuitionism of Bergson, the *esquisse* also stressed the limits of reason, insisting that "there is, within all the particular problems that philosophy studies, a mystery" that is "insoluble in purely rational terms."[72] This approach elicited predictable consternation from Picard and Descoqs, but de Lubac and Fessard never lost their sense of "the mystery on which all of philosophy, like all of life, depends . . . the incomprehensible thing without which everything else would be incomprehensible."[73] This vision would inspire Fessard's most important intellectual achievement at Jersey, his thesis on Maine de Biran, which would have an impact on the development of Christian existentialism after Fessard finally managed to publish it in 1938.[74] But more than any of his friends, it was de Lubac who returned again and again to the theme of mystery. Nourished above all by his reading of the Church Fathers, he would make it a central preoccupation of his life's work.

Like the Modernists before them, de Lubac and his friends also sought to foreground the role of the human subject in both epistemology and metaphysics. They found crucial resources for this endeavor in Blondel's work, but also in that of Pierre Rousselot and Joseph Maréchal, who sought to bring Thomism into dialogue with modern philosophy, and especially with Kant. Their work, which would go on to influence the "transcendental Thomism" of Karl Rahner and Bernard Lonergan, was proof that Thomism was by no means monolithic or exclusively antimodernist in these years. But in an order dominated by Suarezianism, this was a controversial position, and in 1920, Jesuits were forbidden from teaching Rousselot in their seminaries.[75] What attracted de Lubac and his friends to Maréchal and Rousselot was that, in stark contrast to neoscholastic epistemology, they stressed the role of the human subject in the act of knowing.[76] Montcheuil credited Maréchal in particular with rescuing the human subject from the passivity to which neo-scholastic realism had reduced it, by showing that the world "is intelligible and becomes an object of knowledge only by what the thinking subject adds to it."[77] For these young Jesuits, it was crucial to restore the role of the subject, not just in epistemology, but also in metaphysics. Following Blondel, de Lubac insisted that "metaphysics must be the science of the subject," rather than a science of the object, as it had become under neo-scholasticism.[78] This meant recognizing that there is an intimate relationship between the human subject and the divine, or as Montcheuil put it, that God "is not heteronomous to us; he is sufficiently transcendent to be immanent to us."[79]

It was in these years that de Lubac also became fascinated with the relationship between the natural and supernatural orders, which would become the central concern of his career. A second *esquisse* that he cowrote with Fessard in 1924 posed the key question: "If the supernatural is gratuitous, which is to say that it exceeds the possibilities of human nature, how can it be obligatory, which is to say necessarily sought out by man as his only possible end?"[80] He began to realize that resolving this question would require a departure from the neo-scholastic account of the relationship between the natural and supernatural ends of human life—a critique that would reach its full expression in his most famous and controversial work, *Surnaturel* (1946). These early reflections on the relationship between the natural and the supernatural were inspired in part by de Lubac's exposure to the early work of Teilhard de Chardin. Teilhard had been among the first group of Jesuits to arrive on Jersey when the Ferry Decrees evicted the students at the Laval scholasticate. He went on to train as a professional geologist, and by the 1920s, he had begun to develop some controversial ideas about evolution and original sin. His superiors quickly forbade him from publishing on these topics, but his works nevertheless circulated in manuscript form and had a potent influence on de Lubac's circle from the mid-1920s on.[81]

But it was above all the work of Maurice Blondel that offered de Lubac and his friends the tools to reconnect the natural and supernatural orders, and no figure played a more important role in the intellectual development of this little group. Blondel was deeply dissatisfied with what he called the "extrinsicism" of neo-scholastic thought—the sharp distinctions it drew between the natural and supernatural, especially in the realm of apologetics. In landmark works such as *Action* (1893) and *The Letter on Apologetics* (1896), he developed an alternate apologetics grounded in the dynamism of human action. He called this approach the "method of immanence" because it took the human subject as its point of departure and sought to identify, within the immanence of human action, evidence of something that transcends it. Blondel reasoned that each particular object willed by the human being (the "willed will") presupposes a much deeper will for something beyond that object (the "willing will"), which is the driving force behind all human action. Within each immanent act of the human will, and making each one possible, is a deeper will for the supernatural "one thing necessary" that lies utterly beyond our powers of achievement.[82] By beginning from the immanent realm of human action, Blondel concluded, it was possible to establish the necessary human exigency for the supernatural. And this was absolutely critical if Catholic philosophers wished to engage with modern philosophy. They had to begin from an immanent starting point because this was "the very condition of philosophizing" in the modern world.[83]

This model had an enormous impact on the Pensée circle. "I cannot fail to tell you the personal gratitude I owe you," Montcheuil wrote to Blondel in 1931. "Your books, and especially *Action*, have been not merely an object of speculative study for me."[84] Montcheuil would go on to cowrite a book on Blondel with Auguste Valensin in the 1930s, and his friends shared his enthusiasm.[85] In Blondel's work, Hamel enthused, "the synthesis of modern thought and Catholic thought is truly accomplished, although this does not mean that it cannot be further perfected."[86]

Perhaps the best evidence of this debt was de Lubac's inaugural lecture following his appointment to the Theology Faculty at the Catholic University of Lyon in 1929. In it, the newly ordained priest echoed Blondel's critique of neo-scholastic "extrinsicism." By starting from a sharp distinction between reason and faith, the natural and supernatural orders, de Lubac argued that neo-scholastic apologetics was forced "to establish a totally extrinsic connection between the two, just as one builds a makeshift bridge to connect two separate banks."[87] But the effect of this extrinsic apologetics was actually to heighten the separation between the natural and supernatural orders, he explained. In seeking to protect the transcendence and autonomy of the supernatural realm of faith, neoscholastic theology had transformed dogma "into a kind of 'superstructure,' believing that, if dogma is to remain 'supernatural,' it must be 'superficial' and that, by cutting it off from all human roots, it is making dogma all the more divine."[88] As de Lubac went on to explain in his first book, this approach only served to heighten the abyss between the Church and the modern world, and thus unconsciously played into the hands of the anticlerical forces:

> Such a dualism, just when it imagined that it was most successfully opposing the negations of naturalism, was most strongly influenced by it, and the transcendence in which it hoped to protect the supernatural with such jealous care was, in fact, an exile. The most resolute secularists found in it, in spite of itself, an ally.[89]

In this way, de Lubac concluded, neo-scholasticism had become an unwitting accomplice in the secularization of French society. Its "separated theology" simply mirrored, and therefore intensified, the separation of Church and state enacted by the French Republic.

De Lubac was thus conscious of the way in which Catholic antimodernism and secular republicanism tended to mirror and reinforce one another. For him and his friends, the most important task for Catholic thought was to overcome the opposition between Catholicism and modernity that animated both neo-scholasticism and secular republicanism.

Rather than retreating into a protective ghetto, they argued, Catholicism needed to incarnate itself more fully in modern intellectual life, in order to steer it in a Catholic direction. As Robert Hamel explained:

> If there has been this break between Catholic thought and modern thought, it is because, for several centuries now, the Church is no longer at the forefront of intellectual movement. Instead of locating ourselves at the heart of those centers from which new ideas shine forth, in order to force them, so to speak, to refract themselves through our prism before shining out onto the world, we are indolent spectators playing some old man's game in solitude. And when others come to warn us that the century is leaving us behind in order to run off to the idols, the anathemas we launch back at them are the subject of mockery for our enemies and of pain for our friends.[90]

But so long as neo-scholasticism dominated Catholic philosophy, these young Jesuits despaired of being able to heal this breach. "How can we hope to resurrect Catholic thought," de Lubac wrote to Fessard, "when there are those who are determined to deepen the ditch between what one calls 'scholastic philosophy' and what one calls 'modern thought,' a determination coupled with an absolute bias against understanding the latter?"[91] This was all the more frustrating because many of the neo-scholastic doctrines that these churchmen sought to protect were in fact relatively recent inventions in the history of theology. "The so-called 'traditional doctrine' that an army of fossilized professors brandishes with constant threats is not, for the most part, any more traditional than it is satisfying to the spirit," de Lubac complained to Montcheuil.[92] He would go on to develop this line of critique in works like *Corpus Mysticum* and *Surnaturel,* which revealed the extent to which the early modern scholastic commentators had departed from the Church Fathers and Thomas Aquinas himself. The Penseurs were thus acutely aware of the way in which neo-scholasticism, for all its antimodernism, unwittingly mirrored and reproduced aspects of the very modernism it despised.

As we shall see in chapter 2, there was also an important political dimension to this group's critique of neo-scholasticism. In 1909–1910, as the Modernist Crisis raged, Blondel had written a series of articles criticizing the affinities that he perceived between neo-scholastic philosophy and the politics of the Action française. His opponent in that exchange was none other than Pedro Descoqs, one of the AF's staunch defenders.

Given the Penseurs' relationship to both Blondel and Descoqs, it is perhaps not surprising that this exchange molded their own political engagement as they became increasingly drawn into such questions in the 1930s. The political and theological vision of de Lubac and his friends would, of course, evolve considerably between their formation at Jersey and the heyday of the *nouvelle théologie*. Through the 1920s and 1930s, they would increasingly turn their attention from Blondel to the Church Fathers, from Modernism to *ressourcement*, and from a subject-centered metaphysics to the historical and social dimensions of the faith. And yet, the themes and concerns they began to explore at Jersey would remain at the heart of their theological vision.

But it was the friendships they developed at Jersey that would have perhaps the most lasting impact on their work. Built on the solid foundation of shared intellectual and spiritual commitments, and especially on a shared contempt for the worldview of their teachers, these friendships played a pivotal role in the intellectual development of this group of Jesuits and, by extension, in the genesis of the *nouvelle théologie* more broadly. Their letters reveal a strong sense of shared mission to renovate Catholic thought. Writing to de Lubac in 1923, Hamel resolved that since the Church had not managed to provide the kind of philosophy and theology that modern people were searching for, "we will strive together to satisfy their desires, and in order to do that, let us remain united and love each other."[93] "Every time, your letters bring me a renewed confidence," de Lubac replied. "We must hope that we will eventually be able to accomplish some real work together. Then we will sketch out grandiose plans, and what's more, with the help of a few others like Fr. Fessard, we will realize them."[94]

Such friendships were particularly important given the institutional context that these Jesuits inhabited. Faced with tremendous pressure to conform to the dominant neo-scholastic paradigm and the powerful disciplinary apparatus that was deployed to enforce it, their friendships gave them a safe space in which to test out new or unorthodox ideas without the threat of ecclesiastical sanction. In their correspondence and conversations, they could be far more honest than in their published works, which were subject to ecclesiastical censorship. In the process, they gained useful feedback and critical interlocutors with whom to discuss the foundational texts of the tradition as well as contemporary philosophy. Given their sense of embattlement within the Church and their order, such friendships also provided these Jesuits with the emotional

Figure 1.3   Photograph of Henri de Lubac, Robert Hamel, and Gaston Fessard taken in 1927. *Credit:* Fonds Henri de Lubac, 52, reproduction © Compagnie de Jésus—Archives Jésuites.

support they needed to resist the pressures of conformity and pursue their own distinctive vision.[95] The connection between the affective and intellectual dimensions of these relationships is evident throughout their letters. Writing to Montcheuil from Lyon, de Lubac expressed his joy to "have a whole band of friends here now, which makes the atmosphere of the house pleasant to breathe, and gives one a taste for work."[96] "It is so good to feel in full communion of thought and desire with friends like you!" he wrote again; "to achieve this to such a degree is a rare thing, since it requires a truly complete harmony of thought."[97] Hamel's letters convey a similar sentiment. "I am still under the spell of our long conversations from our vacation, when all three of us [de Lubac, Fessard, and Hamel] found ourselves so alike," he wrote to de Lubac in 1926. "It would be better to say that we are friends, and that the little group Rev. Picard so feared will not have the pernicious effect he dreaded."[98] The project of theological renewal that these young Jesuits were beginning to develop at Jersey was thus inseparable from their close affective ties, sentiments reinforced by their physical as well as intellectual isolation. For these young men banished from their home-land, alienated from the neo-scholastic orthodoxy of their Church, cut off from their families, and bound by the vows of celibacy, such affective bonds took on immense significance.

The story of the Pensée circle thus illustrates the crucial role that friendships can play in supporting intellectual innovation.[99] Intellectual historians often overlook such relationships, and the role of affect more generally, when accounting for the genesis of an intellectual project. Yet the story of de Lubac's circle reveals how important they can be, not only in explaining a particular individual's intellectual development, but also in illuminating how innovation occurs within highly centralized, conservative, and hierarchical institutions like the Church. Throughout his career, de Lubac would frequently pay tribute to the role these friendships had played in his own intellectual trajectory. "I increasingly understand," he wrote to Fessard in 1935, "that our Jersey adventure is more extraordinary than, in our innocence, we had realized . . . one must admit that we did not 'educate' ourselves in the same way as all these other good and docile theologians."[100]

Le Saulchoir

The experience of de Lubac's circle, though idiosyncratic, was not entirely unique. At the same time that they were developing their para-curriculum and yearning to bring Catholic thought into contact with the modern world, another French Catholic seminary-in-exile was developing a similar program (though the archival record is thinner in this case). This was the Dominican studium of Le Saulchoir, which was established just across the Belgian border in 1903 (see Figure 1.4). Just as de Lubac's circle abandoned the pedagogy of the neo-scholastic manuals to focus on their own para-curriculum, Le Saulchoir also broke with the manual tradition and developed a distinctive program of study. Like his Jesuit contemporaries, Marie-Dominique Chenu was appalled by the "pitiful" state of theological instruction at the time.[101] The first rector of the exiled Le Saulchoir, Ambroise Gardeil, had been determined to do things differently. Chenu credited him with establishing a climate of learning that fostered creativity and a spirit of independent inquiry. At its core was a commitment to studying the original sources of the Catholic tradition and placing them in their historical context.[102] The situation at Le Saulchoir thus differed in important respects from the one at Jersey. Whereas de Lubac and his

Figure 1.4 Postcard image of Le Saulchoir during its exile in Kain, Belgium.
Credit: Archives de la Province dominicaine de France.

friends found themselves intellectually at odds with their teachers and thrown back on their own resources, the students and teachers at Le Saulchoir were instead united in their intellectual approach.

What the two groups did share was a common antipathy toward the regnant neo-scholastic orthodoxy. But while the Jesuits turned to contemporary philosophers like Blondel, the community at Le Saulchoir turned for inspiration to their fellow Dominican Thomas Aquinas. When the German invasion of Belgium forced the Dominicans to evacuate Le Saulchoir during World War I, Chenu went to Rome to study at the Angelicum, the Dominican pontifical institute. There he entered a world dominated by the aftermath of the Modernist Crisis. He was particularly appalled by the way in which Thomism had been weaponized in the course of that conflict, which he considered a deep betrayal of the spirit of Aquinas. For Chenu, fidelity to St. Thomas did not mean adhering to a set of "theses" defined as orthodox by the magisterium, but rather to imitate the spirit and example of the Angelic Doctor in one's own work. As with de Lubac's circle, the limits of the prevailing neo-scholastic the-

ology were driven home to Chenu by his own teachers, including Réginald Garrigou-Lagrange, a staunch neo-scholastic who would later become one of the fiercest critics of the *nouvelle théologie*. Although he had
great respect for Garrigou-Lagrange's erudition, Chenu was alienated by
his teacher's tendency to reduce theology to a "sacred metaphysics" anchored in deductive reasoning, which, according to Chenu, made him "a
complete stranger to history."[103] The young Dominican attributed this
problem to the influence of the early modern commentators, and he made
it his mission to return to the historical Thomas behind the accretions of
a "baroque" scholasticism.

When he returned to Le Saulchoir in 1920 as professor of the History
of Dogma, Chenu and five or six other faculty members began a program
of study—not unlike de Lubac and his friends' para-curriculum—devoted
to understanding the broader historical context that had given birth to
Aquinas. Through these readings, Chenu got his first taste for historical
scholarship, and he would go on to become a leading historian of the
twelfth and thirteenth centuries, as well as an early proponent of the
Annales School, which foregrounded the social and economic aspects
of cultural history.[104] The study group he helped launch quickly developed into a more formal program of study known as the Institut historique d'études thomistes, and it was soon followed by other initiatives,
such as the formation of the Société Thomiste.[105] Le Saulchoir thus became the center for a new kind of Thomism—one anchored in a deep
historical sensibility. It reached its highest expression under Chenu's
stewardship as regent of studies, and his student Yves Congar credited
Chenu with awakening an entire generation of Dominican priests.[106]

In 1937, Chenu wrote a little book explaining the history of the school
and its distinctive approach, titled *Une école de théologie: Le Saulchoir*.
In the book, he drew a direct parallel between the thirteenth-century historical context in which Thomas Aquinas had lived and the context in
which Le Saulchoir was founded. Just as the Church of St. Thomas's day
was confronted with a social crisis, as well as an intellectual crisis provoked by the rediscovery of Aristotle, Le Saulchoir came into being at a
moment when Christianity was under siege at both a political level (from
republican anticlericalism) and an intellectual level (from the forces of
Modernism). Aquinas had known how to confront the challenges of his
day effectively, by integrating the useful aspects of Aristotelianism into
Christian thought rather than simply rejecting it altogether as a threat to

the faith. But Chenu lamented that the Church had not always followed his example. Instead of going out into the world and engaging with new ideas, it had become a "closed fortress." As a result,

> Christianity has been, from the perspective of intellectual life, at the margins, in *exile* from the real thought of men. It seems that St. Thomas has been too weighty a heritage for us to bear. We have safely buried it away in order to be sure not to lose it; we have surrounded it with learned ramparts like a fortress . . . and we have continued to respond to the same old problems, which are no longer being posed, in order to comfort ourselves for not understanding the problems that are being posed.[107]

The language of exile is perhaps not incidental, given that Chenu wrote these lines while Le Saulchoir was still in Belgium. For Chenu, the mission of the school was to follow St. Thomas's example and do for modern thought what he had done for Aristotle. This mission required an engagement with contemporary ideas, but it also meant returning to the primary sources of the Catholic tradition and reading them in their historical context.[108] Only by steeping themselves in these foundational texts, he insisted, could Catholics engage effectively with modern thought and make theology more responsive to the challenges of modern life. Here, Chenu articulated the logic of *ressourcement,* which would become the defining feature of the *nouvelle théologie* and would distinguish it from both Catholic Modernism and neo-scholastic antimodernism. At its core was the notion that fidelity to the tradition implies a constant effort of renewal; that the Church must constantly move out into the world rather than retreating into the secure fortress of its own orthodoxy. In the 1930s, these intellectual commitments would take a more practical form when Le Saulchoir became an important center for new apostolic initiatives oriented to the working class. As with de Lubac's circle, there was an important political dimension to these rarefied theological debates, which forms the subject of the next chapter.

Homecoming

It is striking that, from their separate institutions, the Dominicans at Le Saulchoir and de Lubac's circle at Jersey arrived at a very similar diagnosis of the political and theological challenges of their day. Both dispensed with the manual tradition that dominated seminary education at the time in favor of a return to the original sources of the Catholic tradition. Both were sharply critical of neo-scholastic orthodoxy and the intellectual ghetto into which the Church had retreated as a result of the Modernist Crisis. That both groups separately arrived at the same position is perhaps no coincidence, however. What they shared was a common experience of exile, an experience that brought into focus the extent to which their Church, too, was in a state of exile from the modern world. It convinced them of the urgent need to develop new theological tools to reverse this process, not least because they observed that both neo-scholasticism and the anticlerical ideology of the Republic tended to reinforce it. Both clung to the language of separation as a means to protect the integrity and autonomy of their respective spheres. As de Lubac pointed out, "There was a sort of unconscious conspiracy between the movement which led to secularism and a certain theology, and while the supernatural found itself *exiled* and proscribed, there were those who believed that this placed the supernatural beyond the reach of nature, in the realm where it must reign."[109] The language of exile here is noteworthy. Coming on the heels of the enforced social integration of the First World War, it was the experience of exile that brought into focus for de Lubac and his friends the precise relationship between neo-scholastic dualism and *laïcité*.

But exile also had unexpected benefits. The fact that so many of the leading architects of the Second Vatican Council trained or taught at either Le Saulchoir or the Maison Saint-Louis is a testament to the extraordinary intellectual fecundity of the exile experience. The institutional changes it brought about—the merging of separate Jesuit houses of formation, the absence of distractions, and the distance it afforded from the excesses of the Modernist Crisis—converged to produce the unique conditions for theological renewal. From the unlikely context of an isolated Channel Island or a Belgian village, caught between an anticlerical Republic and an antimodernist Church, a powerful movement to bridge the abyss between Church and world would emerge. These young priests perceived in their experience of exile an allegory for the broader exile of the Church in the modern world. The 1930s would see the beginning of a homecoming.

CHAPTER TWO

From Royalism to the Mystical Body of Christ

After completing his philosophical formation at Jersey, Henri de Lubac moved to England to begin his theological studies at the exiled Jesuit scholasticate of Ore Place. But he was disappointed by the intellectual and political climate he found there. In a letter to his friend Robert Hamel, he complained about the "thrall of the Action française" at Ore Place, where support for Charles Maurras's royalist and nationalist movement had become "a real madness, or at least, an obsession."[1] De Lubac and Hamel were used to this problem. In the wake of the anticlerical campaign, the Action française (AF) had come to dominate clerical politics in France.[2] This was certainly the case at Jersey, where de Lubac and Hamel were taught by the prominent Maurrassian Pedro Descoqs. And just as they had pushed back against Descoqs's neo-scholastic philosophy, they also rejected his politics. The problem with Maurras, Hamel complained, was that he "has not understood Catholicism and has seen in it only a social order without God, without a soul, without love." Hamel here diagnosed the central problem confronting Catholic supporters of the AF—the fact that Maurras himself was a nonbeliever. In the very same breath, the Jesuit anticipated the collapse of this alliance and the emergence of an alternative Catholic politics anchored in the dignity of the person. "The fascist and royalist movement has no chance of success," he insisted, because it "puts society above, not the individual, but the *person,* and cares much more about France than about the French."[3]

Hamel's prediction was borne out in December 1926, when Pius XI condemned the AF and placed several of Maurras's works on the Index of Forbidden Books. This event sent shockwaves through the French Church. In some ways, it was even more consequential for Catholic political thought than the events of 1905 or the onset of the Great Depression. It broke the deeply rooted bond between Catholicism and royalism, reorienting Catholic politics away from the goal of reversing the separation of Church and state. Instead, Pius promoted an alternative form of Catholic engagement in temporal affairs—one that sought to inject Catholic values into public life while remaining above the fray of party politics. Known as "Catholic Action," this movement endowed the laity with a central role in reversing the secularization of European life. The laity would henceforth be the "yeast in the dough" of the temporal order, leavening it with Catholic values and compensating for the dwindling temporal power of the clergy. Catholic Action took a particular form in France, where it targeted specific sectors of the population such as the working class, pitting Catholic Action militants against communists in a battle for the hearts and minds of workers. By the 1930s, the focus of Catholic politics in France had shifted from the threat posed by republicanism to the threat posed by communism, and to a lesser extent, Nazism. And yet, the legacy of the Action française crisis continued to shape how Catholics responded to the political challenges of the 1930s and 1940s.

This chapter tells the story of this profound transformation in French Catholicism, which opened the way for new forms of Catholic engagement in public life and new theological models to go along with them. The condemnation of the AF dealt a severe blow to both the royalist movement and the neo-scholastic theology associated with it. Into this vacuum stepped a host of younger theologians, including de Lubac and his friends, who rejected the possibility of a return to the confessional state. They concentrated on developing a theology appropriate to the new realities of the secular political order—one that would enable Catholics to be *in* the secular public sphere but not *of* it. If these Catholics had made their peace with the separation of Church and state, however, this did not mean that they simply embraced liberal democracy. Instead, they sought to establish a distinctly Catholic alternative to the dominant secular ideologies of the day: liberalism, communism, and Nazism. Known as "personalism," this movement presented Catholicism as the only social force capable of transcending the excesses of liberal individualism and totalitarian collectivism, and it furnished the Catholic Action movement with a theological justification.

Historians have struggled to define the politics of personalism, often describing personalists as "non-conformists" whose politics were "neither right nor left."[4] This chapter seeks to account for this political ambivalence by focusing on the theologies that informed personalism, and in particular, on the Thomist personalism of Jacques Maritain and the ecclesial personalism of the Jesuits and Dominicans associated with the *nouvelle théologie*. A layman and a convert, Maritain was, by the 1930s, well on the way to establishing himself as one of the most important Catholic philosophers of the twentieth century. His Thomist account of the dignity of the person became a crucial source for the development of totalitarianism theory—the notion that Nazism and Soviet communism were structurally similar, despite the ideological differences between them—as well as the postwar turn to human rights and Christian Democracy.[5] How was it possible, then, that Maritain had been a partisan of the AF until 1926? To answer this question, I argue, we must look to the theological vision that inspired Maritain's work, which accounts for the continuity between these two apparently contradictory political positions.

But there was another form of French Catholic personalism—one that has received much less attention from historians—and it was even more difficult to classify politically. This was the "ecclesial personalism" developed by the *nouveaux théologiens*. Like Maritain, these priests sought to articulate a personalist response to both liberalism and totalitarianism, but they took a very different kind of person as their point of reference. Returning to St. Paul and the Church Fathers, they figured the Church itself as a person—the "mystical body of Christ"—and as the primary framework for collective life. Proponents of this vision argued that a robust Catholic response to totalitarian ideologies could not limit itself to defending personal freedom and the autonomy of civil society, as Maritain did. Instead, it had to offer a competing model of collective unity—one that would empower rather than crush the human person. The totalitarian state, many French priests came to believe in the 1930s, could only be effectively challenged by a "totalitarian Church."

If historians have tended to overlook this strand of Catholic anti-totalitarianism, it may be because it was elaborated within the field of ecclesiology, a domain presumed to be apolitical by definition. Instead, I argue that the mystical-body ecclesiology constituted a "counter-politics"— a form of critique that allowed theologians to intervene in political questions while rejecting the terms of secular politics.[6] Recovering the political stakes of this ostensibly apolitical theological discourse thus provides a fuller understanding of how Catholics engaged with public life in a secular context. But it also sheds new light on the roots of anti-totalitarianism more broadly, demonstrating that the critique of totalitarianism need not emerge from a basically liberal defense of individual rights and civil society.

"Maurras Has Been Condemned; Will Thomas Be Next?"

Among Catholic priests who had lived through the trauma of Church-state separation, support for the Action française ran deep.[7] Born in the polarized climate of the Dreyfus Affair, at the height of the battle between the Church and the Third Republic, the AF appealed to many Catholics with its royalist, nationalist, and anti-Semitic message. Maurras himself recognized the Church as a useful ally in his struggle against the forces of republicanism. A year after the separation of Church and state, he wrote a paean to "the Roman Church, Church of Order," asking Catholics to choose between the AF and the Christian Democratic Sillon movement.[8] That choice would effectively be made for them when, in 1910, Maurras's well-placed clerical supporters secured the condemnation of Sillon from Rome. Henceforth, in the memorable words of Yves Simon—a longtime friend of Maritain and future theorist of Christian Democracy—the AF exercised "an almost complete dictatorship over Catholic intellectual circles. Whoever came out as a democrat in these circles was doomed to be the object of an ironical and scornful pity; he was looked down upon as a person behind the times, a survivor of another age."[9]

This dominance was particularly pronounced among the exiled religious orders, where support for the AF became entwined with the Thomist revival. There were a number of reasons for this politico-theological affinity. First among these was Maurras's neoclassicism, which dovetailed with the Aristotelianism of neo-scholastic philosophy. This may explain why neo-scholastic philosophers and theologians—including de Lubac and Hamel's teacher Descoqs, as well as Dominicans such as Réginald Garrigou-Lagrange, Humbert Clérissac, and Thomas Pègues—were among the leading clerical defenders of the AF.[10] These priests were drawn to Maurras's nationalist narrative, which painted France as the heir and defender of the great classical civilizations of Rome and Athens against the onslaught of modern (and implicitly Protestant) philosophies imported from Germany. Maurras was well aware of the affinity between his own worldview and neo-scholasticism. In a 1924 article, he praised the "doctrines of St. Thomas" over and against "the pale substitutes of Kantianism and Hegelianism." "There exists an inhuman Germanism," he complained; "we will never overcome it unless we once again return to civilizing our Europe through the teaching of Aristotle and St. Thomas."[11]

The Modernist Crisis solidified the alliance between neo-scholasticism and the AF, not least because several leading Catholic Modernists also supported Social Catholicism and Christian Democracy. As Maritain later recalled, the attraction that the AF exerted on priests such as his confessor, Humbert Clérissac, had everything to do with "the dangers that, in those days, 'modernism' posed to the dogmatic formulae of the faith." The fact that the AF "denounced without fail the influence of a Bergson, the anti-intellectualism of a Blondel, of a Laberthonnière—all this endeared it even more."[12] This politico-theological conflict reached its highest expression in a public polemic between Blondel and Descoqs in 1909–1914.[13] In that exchange and in later works, Blondel argued for the deep theological affinity between neo-scholastic "extrinsicism" and the politics of the AF. Because neo-scholastics held that nothing in the natural order prepared the way for grace, it became something "purely extrinsic . . . a heavy yoke contrary to the claims of nature and of reason: supreme and incomparable lesson of passivity."[14] According to Blondel, this authoritarian understanding of grace was the theological corollary to the hierarchical model of authority that the AF advocated in the political arena. The common denominator between neo-scholasticism and the politics of the AF, in other words, was their shared emphasis on the passivity of the human subject. And this was also borne out in the realm of ecclesiology, where most theologians continued to embrace the early modern vision of the Church as a "perfect society"—a hierarchical and juridical institution analogous to the state. Each was sovereign in its own sphere, and each should be structured according to the principles of hierarchy, order, and top-down authority. Spiritual and political authoritarianism, in other words, went hand in hand.

To be sure, Catholic priests (especially those exiled under the anticlerical legislation) had strong reasons to support the AF's anti-republican agenda quite apart from these sorts of theological affinities. But there was one major problem to contend with: Maurras himself was not a believer. Indeed, as a disciple of the positivist philosophy of Auguste Comte, he was in some ways closer to the secular worldview of the republicans. He held that the social order exhibited the same lawlike regularity as the natural order, but he happened to believe that the laws of "political physics" mandated a hierarchical society governed by a king and supported by the Church. What attracted Maurras to the Catholic Church, then, was not its religious or ethical teachings, but rather its institutional form. Like the young Carl Schmitt, he was full of admiration for the hierarchical, centralized Church, whose "religious essence, for its external admirers, corresponds to the most general notion of order."[15] Whatever metaphysical differences they might have with him, Maurras invited Catholics to bracket these and put "politics first [la politique d'abord]," rallying around their shared goal of overturning the Republic.

How did Catholic philosophers and theologians who supported the AF make sense of Maurras's unbelief? Here again, neo-scholastic philosophy provided useful resources. What permitted many of them to circumvent this awkward detail was the Thomist principle that the natural order exhibits a rational structure that is intelligible to human reason without the aid of revelation. This meant that nonbelievers like Maurras and Catholics could discern the same set of truths about the social order that were prescribed by natural law, even if they disagreed on the origin of that law. Pedro Descoqs made precisely this point in his 1911 defense of Maurras. Because it would be a theological error to claim "that reason cannot attain certain truths of the natural order without the notion of God and the aid of revelation," Descoqs argued that the "considerable differences" between Maurras and Catholics in matters of "dogmatic and moral speculation" did not imply an "irreducible opposition in matters that affect the domain of political practice."[16] Just as St. Thomas had selectively appropriated the rational truths of Aristotle's pagan philosophy in the service of a higher Christian synthesis, Catholics could successfully appropriate the "partial truths" discovered by Maurras in the service of a truly Catholic politics.[17]

But the pope ultimately rejected this logic. In a series of pronouncements from fall 1926 into early 1927, he condemned the Action française for its anti-Christian doctrines and for subordinating religion to politics. He denounced the philosophy of Maurras and his allies as a form of "paganism" and "naturalism" attributable to the "modern and secular" education they had received in the public schools of the Third Republic.[18] But this was not enough to convince some of the movement's diehard clerical supporters to break with the AF. Recalcitrant Maurrassians such as Marie-Albert Janvier and Thomas Pègues instead turned to their neo-scholastic arsenal in order to challenge the pope's authority to forbid Catholics from supporting a political movement. Citing the encyclical Immortale Dei (1885), which left Catholics free to determine their own political allegiances, Pègues argued that the condemnation in no way restricted the right of French Catholics "to adhere fully to the movement of political doctrine and action that is the A.F."[19] The approach taken by these refractory Maurrassians was thus to decouple the spiritual and political principles of the AF, claiming that the condemnation applied only to the former. The pope had no authority to condemn the political principles of the AF, they argued, since the temporal order "entirely escapes papal infallibility."[20] Pius XI was quick to point out the hypocrisy of these integrists, who had been the first to champion the authority of the pope in their bitter battles against Catholic Modernism and the Sillon. In January 1927, the Holy Office forbade Catholics from reading the AF's newspaper, and in September, the prominent Maurrassian Louis Billot resigned from the Cardinalate.

Maurice Blondel, who had lived under a cloud of suspicion since the Modernist Crisis, suddenly found himself vindicated. He and his disciples eagerly defended the condemnation and chastised the refractory priests for suggesting that the political goals of the AF could be disentangled from the anti-Christian philosophy of Maurras. He also rejected the claim advanced by Descoqs and Maritain that this philosophy contained "partial truths" that could be integrated into the higher synthesis of Thomism. "It is not the Scholastic theses which enlighten and complete the Maurrassian doctrines, but rather the reverse," Blondel insisted; "it is St. Thomas who collapses into Aristotle, Aristotle into Comte."[21] One could not simply bracket the problematic aspects of Maurras's worldview and selectively appropriate those elements that were consonant with Catholic teaching. This refusal to disentangle the political goals of the AF from its philosophical presuppositions or to countenance a strategic collaboration with an atheist ideology would later form the basis for Catholic anti-totalitarianism in the 1930s and 1940s.

The Theory of Indirect Power

Blondel's reaction to the condemnation of the Action française surprised no one. But the other leading defender of the sanctions was a much more unlikely figure. In 1926, Jacques Maritain was a young professor of philosophy at the Institut Catholique and the undisputed star of the "Catholic revival" that spurred a wave of conversions among French intellectuals in the late nineteenth and early twentieth centuries.[22] Jacques and his Russian-Jewish wife, Raïssa, converted in 1906, just one year after Church and state were separated. Through their spiritual director, the Dominican Humbert Clérissac, they were introduced to a world in which neo-scholastic thought went hand in hand with support for the AF. Although the Maritains would later downplay this youthful dalliance with the far right, Jacques was one of the leading intellectual forces behind the pro-AF *Revue Universelle,* which he described as "a platform for the ideas of the Action française in the political order" and "a platform for Christian thought, and in particular Thomist thought, in the philosophical order."[23] As editor of the journal's philosophy section, Maritain strove to establish Thomism as the official philosophy of the AF, on the grounds that the two shared the same enemy: "false liberal dogmas."[24] Moreover, like Descoqs, Maritain initially defended the "partial truths" of Maurrasianism and tried to forestall a full Vatican condemnation.[25] It took Maritain a full year to reconcile himself to the condemnation, break off his ties with Maurras, and suspend his involvement with the *Revue.* This decision seems to have been motivated in no small part by a sense of obedience. "Alas," he sighed, in a letter to his friend Charles Journet. "What can we do now? We can't be seen to be contradicting the Pope."[26]

But Maritain's very public affiliation with the AF also made him an ideal candidate to lead the defense of the condemnation. In a private audience in September 1927, the pope therefore charged Maritain with the task of explaining its doctrinal basis to French Catholics. The philosopher would oversee the publication of three collaborative works on the subject with contributions from high-profile Thomist theologians.[27] Although Maritain—a layperson with no formal training in theology—was an unorthodox choice, Pius XI recognized that his fame and past ties to the AF made him an invaluable ally in the campaign against it. But rather than focusing on the anti-Christian elements of the Maurrassian worldview, Maritain set himself the more modest goal of defending the pope's right to condemn the Action française.

The most common objection raised by Catholic defenders of the AF was that, in condemning a political movement, the pope had ventured beyond the limits of his jurisdiction. Maritain responded by citing a principle developed by the scholastic jurists Robert Bellarmine and Francisco Suárez—the notion that the pope possessed an "indirect" power over temporal matters when "the good of souls" was at stake.[28] Maritain here reaffirmed the scholastic teaching that the temporal and spiritual authorities were autonomous and sovereign in their own spheres but that the former was ultimately subordinate to the latter. Maritain's close friend and disciple, the Swiss theologian Charles Journet, further expanded on the Thomist basis for this theory, anchoring it in the Aristotelian distinction between substance and accident. The domain of indirect power, Journet argued, covers all things that are "by their nature temporal" but become "*spiritual by accident . . .* when the spiritual good of souls is at stake."[29] Crucially, however, Journet maintained that indirect power was "a power of *jurisdiction* and not of mere *persuasion*."[30] This meant that the Church was truly sovereign when it pronounced upon such questions. In condemning the AF, the pontiff was simply exercising his indirect authority over political matters in the name of saving French souls.

It is rather remarkable, however, how closely this approach hewed to the model Descoqs had offered in *defense* of the AF. As a good Suarezian, Descoqs was very much a proponent of the theory of indirect power. In *À travers l'oeuvre de Charles Maurras,* he had anticipated Maritain and Journet by stressing that the spiritual and temporal power each retains "autonomy in its own sphere." But he also qualified the autonomy of the temporal authority over matters that impinged on the salvation of souls. On these matters, he insisted, "the legislation and political statutes of a country will be subject to the judgment of the religious authority."[31] For Descoqs, the political theology of indirect power was compatible with support for the AF because, although Maurras sought to order society according to natural law and without reference to supernatural principles, he nevertheless upheld the Church's traditional jurisdiction over spiritual affairs and "mixed matters" such as marriage and education.

The theory of indirect power, then, could be employed to both underwrite and repudiate a commitment to the AF. This is a testament to the political ambivalence of certain theological positions. But it also helps to illuminate the peculiar trajectory of Maritain who, in the 1940s, would repurpose the same Thomist worldview that had once drawn him into the orbit of the AF to advocate for democracy and human rights. This politico-theological mutability was particularly pronounced in the case of Thomism because of its emphasis on natural law and the autonomy of the temporal order. Such a theology could be used to justify a pragmatic collaboration between Catholics and secular or even atheist political ideologies of various stripes. As we shall see, in the wake of the Second World War, some Catholics would even use it to justify working with communists—a position that some labeled an "AF of the far left."[32]

That both supporters and critics of the AF shared a common political theology was not lost on Henri de Lubac. While he wholeheartedly supported the condemnation of the AF, he nevertheless rejected the indirect-power thesis that Journet and Maritain relied on to defend the pope's intervention. For de Lubac, the problem lay with the jurisdictional model of Church-state relations on which the theory of indirect power relied, and which had formed the basis for Catholic political thought since the early modern period. "Why should the authority of the Church in temporal matters," he asked, "be represented as a 'jurisdiction over the temporal?'"[33] The effect of conceiving of the temporal and spiritual orders as "jurisdictions" was to place them on the same level, reducing the Church to a visible institution on the same order as the nation-state. Far from expanding Church authority, de Lubac insisted, such an approach only served to undermine it by downgrading the Church "to the rank of the powers of this world." "Treating the civil authority as a pure instrument of the spiritual authority," he concluded, "degrades the Church just as much as it humiliates the State."[34]

Instead, the Jesuit insisted upon the *qualitative* distinction between the Church's spiritual authority and the form of authority possessed by states, such that there could be no real contradiction or conflict between the two. Rather than seeking to carve out a legitimate jurisdiction for the Church within the temporal order, in the manner of Journet or Maritain, de Lubac argued that the Church could only achieve a truly universal authority if it ceased to think and act like a state:

> The authority of the Church is entirely spiritual. . . . This is not, to tell the truth, a restriction. It is not a question of closing the Church off from any terrain of human thought or action; there is none, as profane as it might seem, in which, one way or another, faith and morals are not implicated. Christianity is universal, it has happily been said, not only in the sense that all men have Jesus Christ as their Savior, but also in the sense that *all of man* has its Savior in Jesus Christ. . . . The Church is thus also Catholic in this latter sense that nothing which is human can remain foreign to it.[35]

This brief passage contains, in embryo, an entire revolution in Catholic political theology. In contrast to the neo-scholastic theology of grace, which clearly distinguished the natural from the supernatural, de Lubac stressed the internal dynamism of human nature, in which the supernatural was already at work, infusing and raising up the natural order from within. "It is from the inside that grace takes up nature," he argued, and "that the Church influences the State. Messenger of Christ, the Church has not come to place the State under her tutelage; on the contrary, she ennobles it, inspiring it to become a Christian state, and thereby, to become more human."[36] Because the natural and supernatural were bound together, it was impossible to carve up human life into separate and exclusive jurisdictions. "Given that the supernatural is not separate from nature and the spiritual is everywhere mixed in with the temporal," de Lubac concluded, "the Church has . . . authority over everything, without having to step outside of its role."[37] By dispensing with a jurisdictional model of Church authority, then, de Lubac made it possible to expand the authority of the Church to encompass all areas of human life.

De Lubac's ideal of an incarnated Church working within the temporal order to leaven it with spiritual values would become the animating principle for the specialized Catholic Action movements that gained traction in the wake of the condemnation of the Action française. As de Lubac and many others realized, the era of the Church's entanglement with the French state—of its jurisdiction over certain areas such as education—was now definitively at an end. In no uncertain terms, de Lubac told Catholics to "renounce the dream of a return, pure and simple, to the institutions of the past" and the model of Church-state relations they presupposed.[38] Indeed, he suggested that the separation of Church and state might even prove to be a blessing in disguise if the Church emerged with "a purified notion of spiritual authority."[39] The dream of the confessional state was now dead, and it fell to a new generation of Catholic theologians and philosophers to replace it.

"The Yeast in the Dough": Catholic Action and the Specter of Communism

The condemnation of the Action française was a key turning point in the history of Catholic politics in twentieth-century France. As a result, many Catholics abandoned the goal of reversing the separation of Church and state and sought out alternative ways to incarnate their values in the secular public sphere. In light of the Vatican condemnation of the "politics first" approach championed by Maurras, many French Catholics eschewed the domain of party politics in favor of new Catholic social movements that sprang up during this period. In doing so, they began to reconceive the relationship between Catholicism and public life in ways that were not exhausted by the institutional relationship between Church and state. Moreover, as the 1920s turned into the 1930s, their attention increasingly shifted from the traditional bugbear of republicanism to the threat posed by new mass ideologies such as communism and, to a lesser extent, Nazism.

The best example of this transformation was the rapid expansion of social movements led by the laity and known collectively as Catholic Action. This initiative certainly predated 1926; it was one of the signature projects of Pius XI's papacy and even informed his decision to condemn the AF. He made this explicit in the condemnation itself, warning that the AF threatened "the apostolate of the true 'Catholic action' to which all of the faithful, youth above all, have been called to collaborate actively for the extension and affirmation of the reign of Christ in individuals, in families, in society."[40] The key agents of Catholic Action were the laity—and specifically, lay youth—albeit with significant clerical oversight. This was an important innovation because the apostolate of the Church had long been considered the exclusive purview of the clergy, and it reflected one of most important trends in twentieth-century European Catholicism more broadly: the progressive laicization of Catholic politics.[41]

The second defining feature of Catholic Action was that it stood "over and above all problems of purely material and political concern."[42] Catholic Action militants were invested with a spiritual rather than a political mission. They were to be the "yeast in the dough" of the temporal order, leavening it with Catholic values in order to rechristianize Europe. In part, this was a response to the restrictions on Catholic politics imposed by Italy's fascist regime.[43] And yet, the precise line between promoting "Christian values" and outright political activism was never entirely clear. The pope deliberately hedged on this question by distinguishing between "*piccola politica*"—the conventional realm of party politics—and the "*grande politica*" that Catholic Action would address. "Though not engaging in party politics," Pius announced, "Catholic Action is preparing the terrain for the making of good politics, of *grande politica,* is preparing the terrain to shape the political conscience of citizens in a Christian and Catholic manner."[44] In this way, Pius sought to maintain an avenue for some form of Catholic politics in Mussolini's Italy, inaugurating a new approach to Catholic engagement in temporal affairs that would spread throughout the Catholic world.

Though it was a Vatican-led initiative, the structure and aims of Catholic Action varied substantially by national context. In Italy, it was a fairly centralized operation under the close control of the clergy. But in France it drew on a much longer tradition of Social Catholicism dating back to the nineteenth century, which had birthed such organizations as the Association catholique de la jeunesse française (ACJF), the Action populaire, and the Semaines sociales.[45] Starting in the mid-1920s, Catholic Action took on a new form when the French adopted the "specialized" model of Catholic Action pioneered by Joseph Cardijn in Belgium.[46] This approach divided Catholic Action along professional lines, in order to target particular social milieus more effectively. It gave rise to a veritable alphabet soup of new organizations in the late 1920s: the Jeunesse ouvrière chrétienne (JOC), Jeunesse agricole catholique (JAC), and Jeunesse étudiante chrétienne (JEC). Each of these groups in turn operated a distinct branch for women—the JOCF, JACF, and JECF—and a group for married workers soon developed as well (the Ligue ouvrière chrétienne [LOC]).

Founded less than a year after the Vatican condemnation of the AF, the JOC was the first of these specialized Catholic Action organizations to emerge in France.[47] Its primary goal was to offset the recruitment efforts of the Communist Party (Parti communiste français [PCF]) and rechristianize the working class. The idea was to reach workers where they worked. "Before we can convert Christians in the workshops, we must make the workshop Christian," one JOC slogan proclaimed.[48] Setting itself up as a counterpoint to the Jeunesse communiste, the JOC specifically targeted young male workers—those around the age of thirteen who had just left primary school to enter the workforce—and preached a cooperative approach to industrial relations. Rather than encouraging them to strike for better wages, the JOC sought to cushion the boys' transition into the workforce. It provided practical services such as job training and placement programs, educational opportunities, a savings bank, and even leisure activities. But it also preached a strong moral message of chastity, propriety, temperance, and hard work. Above all, these "jocistes" were to remain outside the arena of conventional politics and were expressly forbidden from affiliating with a political party. By 1929, this approach proved so successful that the Jeunesse communiste now considered the JOC its "most dangerous adversary."[49]

Jocistes were taught the organization's distinctive "see, judge, act" technique to evaluate their surroundings and respond in a manner that would promote Christian values. Through this pedagogy, Catholic Action sought to form "new men," just as the communists did. In contrast to the revolutionary masculinity of the Jeunesse communiste, however, JOC chaplains instilled a vision of Catholic masculinity rooted in chastity and virtue, through which *jocistes* would become men "who are stronger than others, who are afraid of nothing, who triumph over difficulty."[50] The female branches of Catholic Action organizations sought to formulate a complementary vision of femininity, although this proved rather more challenging. The idea that young women could be active members of the workforce and lay apostles was difficult for many clerics to accept.[51] Nevertheless, these organizations reflected a broader shift in Catholic gender norms—one likewise evident in the personalist philosophies discussed in the next section.[52] Both Henri de Lubac and Yves de Montcheuil served as chaplains to the JECF, and through it, Montcheuil met women like Germaine Ribière who would go on to play key roles in the clandestine networks of the "spiritual resistance" during the war.

As the 1920s gave way to the 1930s, the political situation in and beyond France evolved considerably and the apolitical stance of Catholic Action came under severe strain. The onset of the Great Depression placed the social question front and center, and as the liberal democracies of Europe and America struggled to resolve the economic crisis, many turned to more extreme political ideologies. One symptom of the waning fortunes of liberalism was the rise to power of the Nazi Party in Germany and the growth of right-wing authoritarianism from Portugal to Croatia. But the Catholic Church remained much more concerned with the threat of communism, especially after the election of the Popular Front in Spain and the outbreak of the Spanish Civil War. While many Catholics (including Vatican officials) perceived this conflict as nothing less than a "crusade" against godless communism, a minority led by Jacques Maritain, among others, vigorously rejected the logic of crusade and refused to take sides in the conflict.[53]

These debates became much more immediate for French Catholics when France elected its own Popular Front government in May 1936. As in Spain, the victory was a product of the Comintern's new strategy to battle fascism in Europe by forming electoral coalitions with other parties on the left, which prompted the PCF to make overtures to left-leaning Catholics. In the weeks leading up to the 1936 election, PCF leader Maurice Thorez gave a radio address in which he extended an "outstretched hand" to Catholics who shared the party's commitment to social justice.[54]

This was not simply a last-ditch effort to secure votes. Thorez and other party members continued their appeals in the pages of *L'Humanité* throughout 1936 and 1937, calling on Catholics and communists to set aside their theoretical differences and work together to improve the lot of the working poor.[55] Some Catholics, such as Robert Honnert, accepted this call to practical cooperation. Despite the "very deep, if not irreducible, latent opposition" between Catholicism and communism, Honnert nevertheless affirmed that "one and the other agree in desiring all that the old world refuses us: security for all workers."[56] Arguments such as these rather strikingly echoed the logic that Catholic defenders of the AF had used ten years earlier. The Communist Party's "outstretched hand" thus became another test case for the possibility of Catholic collaboration with atheist political ideologies.

The "outstretched hand" elicited a wide variety of Catholic responses ranging from utter refusal to full-fledged Catholic-communist syncretism.[57] One of the most philosophically rigorous responses came from the pen of Gaston Fessard, Henri de Lubac's close friend from Jersey, who rejected the possibility of pragmatic collaboration with the PCF. Just as Blondel had refused to decouple the politics of the AF from the atheist philosophy that informed it, Fessard asserted that any such partnership would be vitiated by the utter "incompatibility of the attitudes prescribed to the Catholic by the Gospel and the Spirit of Love, on the one hand, and to the communist by Marxism and the materialism of class warfare, on the other."[58] No compromise was possible because one could not selectively appropriate certain elements of the communist worldview without taking on board all the rest. In "the smallest fact, the totality of the system is implicated," Fessard insisted.[59] Moreover, even if Catholics and communists could agree upon shared values such as "equality" and "justice," one could never be sure that these words meant the same thing to communists because they refused any objective standard of truth. "For the communist," Fessard warned, "words take on the meaning that best serves the interests of the party, without any regard for truth."[60] The same was true of "Hitlerian morality, which is entirely subject to the interests of the race."[61] Absent a shared standard of truth, the Jesuit concluded, there was little hope for a good-faith dialogue between Catholics and representatives of these ideologies.

But Fessard did not entirely foreclose the possibility of Catholic-communist dialogue. Instead, he developed an immanent critique of Marxist materialism, turning Marx against Lenin in order to recover a variant of Marxism capable of entering into meaningful conversation with Catholicism. In doing so, Fessard revealed his own deep engagement with nineteenth-century German philosophy. Indeed, his book contained one of the earliest systematic analyses in French of Marx's *1844 Manuscripts*, which had only just been discovered and were translated into French in 1937.[62] While Marxist intellectuals such as Henri Lefebvre and Norbert Guterman found in Marx's early works the resources for a Marxist humanism that complemented the PCF's popular front policy, what is perhaps less well-known is that the "young Marx" also elicited a robust engagement on the part of Catholic intellectuals. For some, the more idealist, philosophical Marx of the *1844 Manuscripts* opened up the possibility of a rapprochement between Marxism and Catholicism; for others, the text provided fodder for a critique of the Communist Party and the Soviet Union by allowing them to turn Marx against the Marxists.[63]

Fessard was situated in the latter camp. A central protagonist in the French Hegelian revival of the 1930s, Fessard privileged the more Hegelian Marx of the *1844 Manuscripts*, who had not yet embraced the strict materialism of his mature thought. In the works of the young Marx, Fessard found a philosophy that was in some sense open to transcendence. It was Lenin, he argued, who had foreclosed these possibilities by reorienting Marxism toward a more robust atheism and "reduc[ing] historical materialism to a vulgar materialism."[64] But Fessard still hoped that communists might reclaim their lost heritage and embrace a philosophy of history that did not necessarily imply atheism. "Renouncing the negation of God," he argued, "would give the communist the chance to speak the same language as the Catholic and . . . the way would be open for dialogue."[65] Until this day came, however, any collaboration with communism would poison the religious faith of those who entered into it. The "outstretched hand" would become a "closed fist."[66] Instead, Fessard endorsed Catholic Action as the only model that allowed Catholics to engage in meaningful action on behalf of social justice without compromising their values.[67]

The same year Fessard published *La main tendue,* the Vatican issued its own response to the "outstretched hand" in the form of an encyclical, "On Atheistic Communism" (*Divini Redemptoris*). "Communism is intrinsically wrong," the pope warned, "and no one who would save Christian civilization may collaborate with it in any undertaking whatsoever."[68] The pope then reaffirmed his commitment to Catholic Action as "the means best calculated to save these, Our beloved children, from the snares of Communism."[69] Just over ten years after the condemnation of the AF, Pius XI had once again intervened to forbid Catholics from entering into a political alliance with a party whose ideology was explicitly atheist. Five days earlier, he had issued a companion encyclical against National Socialism, warning Christians against the idolatry implicit in Nazi ideology. "None but superficial minds," he cautioned, "could stumble into concepts of a national God, of a national religion; or attempt to lock within the frontiers of a single people, within the narrow limits of a single race, God, the Creator of the universe."[70] Scholars have made much of the differences in tone, language, and circulation between these two encyclicals, which together endowed the anticommunist encyclical with much greater force.[71] Nevertheless, the two documents laid the groundwork for a growing Catholic anti-totalitarian discourse. When de Lubac, Fessard, and Montcheuil launched themselves into the underground networks of occupied France, these encyclicals would provide much-needed ammunition for their work of spiritual resistance.

Catholic Personalism and the Challenge of Totalitarianism

The late 1920s and 1930s were a tremendously fecund period for Catholic thought in France. A flurry of new Catholic periodicals came into existence in these years—*La Vie intellectuelle, Esprit, Temps present, Sept,* and *L'Aube,* to name but a few—and Catholics forged new connections with secular philosophers as they contributed to the development of French Hegelianism and existentialism.[72] At a social and political level, the key concern for Catholic intellectuals was to elaborate a theory of Catholic engagement that would avoid the dangers condemned by Pius XI, first in 1926 and then in 1937. How could Catholicism play an active role in public life without engaging in compromising alliances with secular parties and ideologies? Put another way, how could Catholics work within the terrestrial City without being corrupted by it? These questions exercised most of the leading Catholic intellectuals of the day, and their various responses are often grouped under the amorphous label of "personalism."

Personalism was the dominant paradigm for Catholic thought in the 1930s, but it was by no means a unified movement. What the various strands of Catholic personalism had in common was a vision of the human person as a transcendent, social being and the basis for a third way between liberal individualism and totalitarian collectivism. But the political implications of such a model were far from clear, not least because most personalists explicitly conceived their vision in opposition to the dominant political ideologies of the day. This has not prevented historians from attempting to yoke them to a political project, however. Those who focus on Maritain's personalism tend to view him either as a conservative who never fully overcame the illiberalism that had drawn him to the AF or as the man who helped to liberalize the Church and inspired it to embrace human rights and democracy.[73] Those who focus on the more communitarian personalism of Emmanuel Mounier or the Ordre nouveau circle tend to view these figures as either crypto-fascists or as leftists.[74] What gets lost in the effort to shoehorn these Catholics into secular political categories is the deep political ambivalence of their work—the way it drew from both sides of the political spectrum, or indeed, from neither. This comes into view only when one attends to the theological commitments that informed personalism and account for its political plasticity.

The most well-known of these models was the Thomist personalism of Jacques Maritain. While his approach is already well documented, historians remain perplexed by its relationship to Maritain's earlier antimodernism and support for the AF. I argue that the key lies in Maritain's Thomism, which remained constant across his political evolution. But in what follows, I focus primarily on a different kind of Catholic personalism—one that has received far less attention from historians. This was the ecclesial personalism developed by the Jesuit and Dominican theologians of the *nouvelle théologie,* who drew on the early sources of the Christian tradition as well as the cosmic personalism of Pierre Teilhard de Chardin. Like Maritain, these priests sought to develop a personalist alternative to both liberalism and totalitarianism. But unlike Maritain, the person at the heart of their vision was a collective rather than an individual one: the Church, conceived as the mystical body of Christ. Although they explicitly formulated their vision of the mystical body in opposition to political projects, this does not mean that it was apolitical. For the *nouveaux théologiens* believed that the totalitarian state could only be resisted by a "totalitarian" Church—one that ennobled rather than trampled the human person.

Jacques Maritain and Thomist Personalism

Published roughly ten years after his break with Maurras, *Integral Humanism* (1936) signaled a dramatic evolution in Maritain's political thought. The book exhorted Catholics to abandon once and for all the dream of reviving the medieval alliance of throne and altar. That era was unequivocally at an end, Maritain insisted, and Catholics needed a new approach to temporal affairs that was suitable to the changed historical circumstances in which they now found themselves. Instead of longing for the restoration of medieval Christendom, Maritain invited Catholics to build a "new Christendom" that would "correspond to the historical climate of the period into which we are entering."[75] He thereby departed from the "thesis-hypothesis" model affirmed by Leo XIII, which established the confessional state as the ideal type for Church-state relations and treated any other form as less than ideal. Maritain instead argued for the equal legitimacy of the "old" and "new" Christendoms as the Christian regimes best suited to their respective historical circumstances. To make this argument, he deployed the principle of analogy, which was central to Thomist metaphysics, to argue for an updated model of Church-state relations. The best way to preserve the principles of medieval Christendom, he reasoned, was to apply them analogically to the modern context and develop a model that would serve as "a new concrete *analogue*" to medieval Christendom.[76]

Whereas medieval Christendom rested on a sacral conception of the temporal order, Maritain went on to explain that the "same principles (but applied analogically)" to the modern world "would entail a *secular Christian* and not a sacral Christian conception of the temporal order."[77] In other words, the new Christendom should allow for the autonomy of the temporal order and the "*holy freedom* of the creature" who inhabited it.[78] But Maritain was at pains to distinguish this defense of personal freedom from the abstract individualism of liberal theory. Here, he invoked the classic personalist distinction between the "person" and the "individual."[79] Whereas liberalism envisioned the individual as abstract and interchangeable—its essence unchanged by its relationship to other people or to God—the concept of the "person" instead recognized that humans are both spiritual and social beings embedded in multiple overlapping communities (family, nation, Church, etc.). Maritain argued that the political model most appropriate to the new Christendom was one that enabled these aspects of the human person to thrive by allowing for a robust civil society that was independent of the state. Invoking the Thomist principle of "subsidiarity," he therefore argued for a decentralized, pluralist polity.[80] "Civil society is made up not only of individuals, but of particular societies formed by them," he explained, "and a pluralist polity allows these particular societies the greatest autonomy possible."[81] Maritain thus called for a political model that would avoid the excesses of both liberalism and totalitarian collectivism, and one can already see how this commitment to civil society, personal freedom, and pluralism would lead him toward a fuller embrace of democracy and human rights in the 1940s.

Given Maritain's "Christian secular" conception of temporal life, what were the avenues for Catholic intervention within it? By affirming the autonomy of the temporal order from spiritual affairs, Maritain left it to individual Christians to bring spiritual values to bear on temporal life. He nevertheless did reserve for the Church the right to pronounce on certain questions that affected the temporal order because they inhabited a third plane "of the *spiritual* as *joining the temporal.*"[82] Maritain thus reiterated the position he had defended in *Primauté du spirituel,* while moving away from the jurisdictional language he had relied on in that work. But the Thomist distinction between temporal and spiritual affairs remained the operating principle. This was equally evident in the distinction Maritain drew between the forms of Christian action that were appropriate to each sphere. "On the plane of the spiritual," he explained, "I appear before [people] *as a Christian as such,* and to that extent I engage Christ's Church." But when intervening in temporal affairs, "I must act instead *as a Christian,* engaging only myself, not the Church."[83] It fell to the laity to incarnate Catholic values in the temporal order, in other words, while the Church and Catholic Action had to confine themselves to spiritual affairs and the "third plane" of mixed matters.

Maritain thus continued to adhere to a characteristically neo-scholastic approach to the relationship between spiritual and temporal affairs. As a good Thomist, he stressed the autonomy of a natural order governed by the principles of natural law and oriented to a natural end. This allowed him to argue that believers could cooperate with nonbelievers on "a *common practical task*" in the temporal order without sharing "a *common doctrinal minimum,*" which was precisely the argument that Catholic defenders of Charles Maurras had made ten years earlier.[84] Despite his political evolution, Maritain thus remained bound to the same theological model that had informed his support for the AF. But he now repurposed it in the service of political pluralism, a robust civil society, and the dignity of the person. Indeed, Maritain's first forays into personalism date not from the 1930s, but from the period of his involvement with the AF, and he first articulated the distinction between the individual and the person in *Three Reformers* (1925), his antimodernist screed against Luther, Descartes, and Rousseau.[85] In other words, we should not overstate the break between the early right-wing, antimodernist Maritain and the later champion of democracy and human rights. The common denominator between them was a commitment to Thomism. And these sorts of theological continuities may go some way toward explaining how the Catholic Church more broadly made the transition from a refusal to a qualified embrace of democracy and human rights in the mid-twentieth century.

Pierre Teilhard de Chardin and Cosmic Personalism

For many intellectuals steeped in the tradition of Social Catholicism, Maritain's personalism seemed to linger too long on the dignity of the individual person, at the expense of emphasizing the bonds of community. This was certainly Maurice Blondel's view. Despite its distinction between the "individual" and the "person," Blondel argued that personalism risked reinforcing the very individualism it was meant to combat, by elevating the person into an absolute end in itself.[86] Many Catholic intellectuals therefore devoted themselves to developing a personalism that placed greater emphasis on the constitutive bonds between person and community. Mounier led the way, forging an eclectic personalism that drew on the phenomenology of Max Scheler and a Catholic reading of Henri Bergson.[87] Meanwhile, Alexandre Marc and the Ordre Nouveau group articulated a corporatist vision that was vigorously antiliberal and indebted to Proudhonian socialism.[88] But neither of these movements was explicitly or exclusively Catholic, and they drew on a range of both secular and religious sources. At a theological level, then, the most significant alternative to Maritain's Thomist personalism was the mystical-body theology articulated by the *nouveaux théologiens*.

A crucial but often overlooked source for this ecclesiology was the idiosyncratic work of the Jesuit paleontologist Pierre Teilhard de Chardin. As we have seen, Teilhard had a profound influence on de Lubac's circle during their formation. By 1925, however, Teilhard's controversial views on the subject of evolution and original sin had aroused the suspicion of his superiors. He was forbidden from publishing on anything but scientific questions and would spend the next twenty years in China, where he worked on the dig that unearthed the fossil remains of *Homo erectus pekinensis*, popularly known as Peking Man. It was during this period that Teilhard developed the substance of his distinctive cosmic personalism in works such as *Le phénomène humain*. But because these works were not published until after Teilhard's death in 1955, historians have underestimated his impact on intellectual life in the first half of the century. And yet, Teilhard's writings did circulate in a kind of *samizdat* form among French Catholic intellectuals in the interwar period and began to attract a cult following, making him a key inspiration for Catholic personalism.[89]

Whereas Maritain's personalism centered on the individual human being, the central person in Teilhard's account was not the individual human creature, but the universe itself. The Jesuit was a professional paleontologist and, as such, he embraced the science of evolution. But, rather like Henri Bergson, he sought to develop an all-encompassing theory of evolution that would apply to material as well as spiritual phenomena, thus overcoming the artificial separation between matter and spirit. According to Teilhard, all phenomena—from the smallest subatomic particle up to the cosmos itself—tend to organize into ever more complex entities with ever greater levels of interiority and consciousness. When this process reached a key threshold, it allowed first for the emergence of life from inorganic matter (the biosphere), and then for the emergence of consciousness with the advent of human life (the noosphere). This same process was now driving human life to converge at both a biological and a psychic level, yielding new forms of collective consciousness.

And yet, Teilhard insisted that this process of human convergence, or "totalization," was not a threat the freedom and personality of the individual. Indeed, he claimed that the rise of collective consciousness actually served to enhance the incommunicable uniqueness of the individual person because the driving force behind it was also a person. For Teilhard believed that Christ was the telos, or Omega Point, of evolution itself. He defined evolution as the progressive "personalization" of the universe—the process by which the universe progressively takes on the features of the "Cosmic Christ." This is what draws human life to converge, and consequently, the unity it achieves tends to enhance rather than destroy the personality of those whom it joins together. Indeed, Teilhard insisted, humans become more fully conscious of themselves as persons through their integration into this broader consciousness, with each person "becoming all the more itself, and therefore more distinct from the others, the more it approaches the Omega." The result is "not only the conservation, but the exaltation of the elements through their convergence!"[90] Through the divine personalization of the universe, individuals become at once fully persons and fully united with other persons.

To illustrate this principle that "union differentiates," Teilhard invoked the model of conjugal love, which does not abolish the personality of each spouse but instead tends "to differentiate the two beings it brings together." Such an argument was based on the logic of heterosexual complementarity—the paradigmatic form of a union based in difference. And for Teilhard, it was proof of "the necessary synthesis of the masculine and feminine principles in the edification of the human person."[91] This model of conjugal love based on complementarity dovetailed with the gender ideology associated with the specialized Catholic Action movements and represented something of a departure from the more vertical, patriarchal vision of the family that had long dominated Catholic teaching on the family.[92] Like other personalists, such as Gaston Fessard, Teilhard instead figured the complementarity of the sexes as the germ and model for the love that secures social bonds and, eventually, union with Christ. It goes without saying, however, that this was a deeply unequal vision of gender relations and relied on an essentialist and instrumental vision of femininity.[93]

Conjugal love was particularly central to Teilhard's vision because he believed love was the driving force behind evolution itself and served to distinguish true union from the false unity imposed by totalitarian regimes. Human persons could not give themselves to some impersonal higher force, he argued, but only to a universe that "takes on a face and a heart," becoming a personal being and thus an object of human love. While the collectivism of fascist and communist regimes might appear to be manifestations of the growing trend toward cosmic unity, Teilhard warned that they should not be confused with the truly personalist societies that would prepare the way for the full unity of the cosmic Christ, which would enhance rather than suppress the human person. Because of the "impersonal, material character of the Red 'Omega,'" Teilhard argued, "communism ends up, to all intents and purposes, suppressing the person" and "making man into a termite."[94] The surest sign that such a society was not authentically personalist was that relations between the individual persons within it were governed by coercion rather than love. The union they enacted was externally imposed, rather than arising from the internal bond between persons who "enter into contact through the foundations of themselves, each interiorized to the other."[95] But Teilhard had little patience for liberal democracy either. The privilege it placed on individual liberty, with "each monad jealously falling back on itself," seemed to him like the opposite of evolutionary progress. "The age of tepid pluralisms is definitively past," he concluded.[96] The Jesuit thus shared Maritain's antipathy toward both liberalism and totalitarianism, albeit for very different philosophical reasons.

Given the rather unorthodox nature of Teilhard's views, one might well wonder why his work held such powerful appeal for a generation of Catholics. The answer, I believe, lies in its wholesale rejection of the characteristic features of neo-scholasticism: dependence on medieval or early modern categories, a sharp distinction between the natural and supernatural orders, and a penchant for ahistorical speculative reason. Like many secular philosophers at the time, Catholics in the 1930s were searching for an alternative to the abstract, ahistorical philosophies of the day—whether it be neo-scholasticism or Neo-Kantianism—in favor of a turn to history and the concrete.[97] This explains why so many Catholics were drawn to Hegelianism and existentialism in these years, as we shall see in Chapter 6, and it also explains the appeal of Teilhard's evolutionary worldview, with its emphasis on the interpenetration of matter and spirit, the natural and the supernatural, and the human and the divine. Of course, these features also made Teilhard's work deeply controversial, as critics accused him of straying into pantheism and Pelagianism (denying the doctrine of original sin). Though many of his closest intellectual allies were critical of the pantheist—or, more properly, panentheist—tendencies in his work, the sheer dynamism and novelty of his approach made a profound impact on a rising generation of Catholic theologians.[98]

Ecclesial Personalism: The Mystical Body of Christ

Teilhard's influence was particularly palpable in the case of the mystical-body theology that dominated Catholic ecclesiology in the 1930s and 1940s. It was based on the idea that the Church is the "mystical body of Christ"—a model with roots in St. Paul and the Church Fathers, but which had fallen out of favor with the rise of scholasticism. In the 1920s and 1930s, Catholic theologians began to revive this model by returning to the patristic sources of the tradition and the work of the nineteenth-century Tübingen theologian Johann Adam Möhler. Among the leading proponents of the mystical-body theology were the French Jesuits and Dominicans associated with the *nouvelle théologie*—people such as de Lubac, Fessard, Montcheuil, Chaillet, Congar, and Chenu. De Lubac offered his interpretation of this ecclesiology in his first book, *Catholicisme: Les aspects sociaux du dogme,* which was published in 1938. The book was the first fruit of de Lubac's lifelong project of *ressourcement*—an effort to return to the sources of the Catholic tradition, and especially to the Church Fathers. But de Lubac likewise drew on Teilhard de Chardin to elaborate his vision of an ecclesial body that enhances rather than destroys the personality of those whom it joins together. In this way, de Lubac used the resources of the Church Fathers to translate Teilhard's cosmic personalism into an ecclesial personalism.

De Lubac's efforts to revive the mystical-body theology were above all a reaction against the juridical and hierarchical ecclesiology associated with neo-scholasticism. In contrast to the visible and institutional Church, the vision of the Church as the mystical body of Christ foregrounded the organic, communal, and invisible aspects of the Church. The Church is not just an earthly institution, de Lubac insisted; it is also an eschatological body that will only come into fullness at the end of time. It is "both the way and the goal" of salvation, both a particular church and the universal human community that will be incorporated in Christ.[99] For de Lubac, this was a productive tension that militated against the tendency to reduce the Church to its visible, institutional form. "The Church which is the Body of Christ is not merely that strongly hierarchical and disciplined society," he insisted, "and the Catholic is not only subject to a power but is a member of a body as well. The purpose of his legal dependence on the former is that he may participate vitally in the latter."[100] De Lubac thus figured the visible Church as the imperfect but indispensable vehicle for the mystical body, but because the two were not simply identical, he recognized that it was possible to belong to one but not the other.[101] In this way, the idea of the mystical body allowed for a more open, ecumenical ecclesiology that did not restrict salvation to members of the institutional Church—a principle that Yves Congar would develop more fully in his pathbreaking ecumenical work in the 1930s.[102]

This ecclesiology was central to de Lubac's broader goal of demonstrating that, in its dogma, scripture, ecclesiology, sacraments, and soteriology, "Catholicism is essentially social."[103] He believed that Catholics had progressively lost sight of this fact, in part because they had abandoned the patristic understanding of the Church and the sacraments. The Church Fathers had understood that the purpose of the Eucharist was to incorporate the faithful with each other in the unity of Christ's body. Such a vision necessarily entailed a social model of salvation, according to which, "the salvation of the individual could only be obtained within the salvation of the community."[104] This argument was echoed by fellow Jesuit Henri Rondet in an address to the Catholic Action militants of the JECF. Citing de Lubac, Rondet credited the doctrine of the "mystical body" with "rescuing us from the murderous individualism of the nineteenth century, according to which each person struggled to achieve his own salvation in isolation."[105] If Catholics had lost sight of the social dimension of their faith, de Lubac blamed this in no small part on the dominance of neo-scholasticism, which "begins by separating, 'defining,' isolating objects in order to then artificially reconnect them."[106] Not only did this approach lead to an impoverished understanding of history; de Lubac suggested that it also reinforced the prevailing individualism of the age. He even speculated that "perhaps the error of Marxism and Leninism would not have arisen and been propagated with such terrifying effects if the place that belongs to community in the natural as well as in the supernatural order had always been given to it."[107]

Instead, de Lubac looked to the mystical body as the best weapon against totalitarianism because it provided an alternative vision of community—one that did not sacrifice the value of the individual person. Whereas collectivist societies tended to crush the person, "by integrating himself into the great spiritual Body [the mystical body of Christ] . . . man does not lose or dissolve himself. On the contrary, he finds himself, he liberates himself."[108] After all, "we are fully persons only within the Person of the Son."[109] Here the Jesuit revealed his profound debt to Teilhard de Chardin. To support this argument, he cited Teilhard's account of the way in which "union differentiates" in the biological development of complex organisms but added theological weight to this claim by invoking the doctrine of the Trinity. Just as God is composed of three persons whose unity preserves their distinction, he argued, "true union does not tend to dissolve into one another the beings that it joins together, but rather to bring them to completion by means of one another." Instead of "distinguishing in order to unite," then, as Maritain sought to do, de Lubac insisted that one must "unite in order to distinguish."[110] Like Teilhard's cosmic personalism, de Lubac's ecclesiology thus refused the sharp distinction between the natural and supernatural that was so central to neo-scholasticism. But he insisted that doing so provided a more effective answer to the secular ideologies of the day. By revealing that the supernatural end of human life was the only authentic grounds for social action, such an approach militated against the tendency of these ideologies to reduce the human person to "a mere instrument."[111] Only the mystical body of Christ could overcome the inevitable contradictions between the individual and society that arose when humans tried to build the Kingdom of God on earth.

But translating Teilhard's cosmic Christ into the language of the mystical body also led to a dangerous slippage between the Church and the human race as a whole. This was evident when de Lubac explained the basis for the mystical-body theology in the doctrine of the Incarnation. By incorporating himself into humanity, the Jesuit explained, Christ "incorporated it in himself. In assuming a human nature, it is human nature *itself* that he united to himself, that he enclosed in himself, and it is the latter, in its entirety, that in some sense serves as his body."[112] Here, the mystical body seemed to encompass, not just the more limited community of the Church, but the whole of humanity. This was not lost on critics, such as his former teacher Pedro Descoqs. Commenting on a number of personalist texts, Descoqs complained about precisely this tendency to equate the Church with humanity *tout court,* and rightly identified Teilhard as the source of the problem. "From the idea of the 'mystical Body,'" Descoqs lamented, "they would immediately transport us to that of the 'cosmic Christ,'" a slippage he blamed on the personalists' "refusal to distinguish the two orders of the natural and the supernatural."[113] And indeed, Descoqs was not entirely wrong. The difficulties of an ecclesiology that effectively identified the Christian and the human would become more apparent during the war, when de Lubac's circle used it to defend the rights of Jews.

This danger was particularly evident in Fessard's contribution to interwar personalism, *Pax Nostra* (1936). Ostensibly an effort to mediate between the pacifist and nationalist responses to German rearmament, the book was in fact a much broader exploration of personalism and the theology of history that revealed Fessard's deep engagement with Hegelianism and existentialism. Fusing St. Paul and Hegel, Fessard argued that both the individual person and history as a whole are governed by a "Jew-Gentile dialectic" that raises human beings from particular communities up to the universal unity of the mystical body of Christ. Just as Christ had overcome the opposition between Jew and Gentile in his own person, according to Paul's Letter to the Ephesians, each person must repeat the same process. Each Christian had to overcome the opposition between their inner Jew and Gentile so as to become a Christian "person" in whom the particular and the universal coincide—a unique "me" who is also "an irreplaceable part of an organic whole: the mystical Body of which Christ is the Head and we are the members."[114] And Fessard applied the same logic to collective persons such as the family, nation, and the community of nations, which he labeled "moral persons," to show how these communities could reconcile the demands of internal solidarity with their duty to the larger communities in which they were embedded.

The difficulty with this logic was that it seemed to equate the process of becoming a person with the process of becoming a Christian, a problem that becomes clear when one examines Fessard's account of how the Jew-Gentile dialectic functioned after the Incarnation.[115] Henceforth, he claimed, the mission of the Jewish people was fundamentally "negative" (in the Hegelian sense), for it was destined to remain radically opposed to Christianity. However, following Paul's Letter to the Romans, Fessard argued that this negation was also the precondition for the second and final reconciliation of the Parousia (the Second Coming of Christ).[116] Fessard's account attracted criticism from the Jewish intellectual Jules Isaac, who felt that the Jesuit's language of negation reinforced the long-standing Catholic tradition of anti-Judaism.[117] This was certainly not Fessard's intention, and he was at pains to insist that the Jew and Gentile in his account did not designate ethnic groups; they were figures for universal tendencies that existed within all societies and individuals. Christians should therefore understand the dialectic between the "converted Gentile" and the "unbelieving Jew" as "an opposition that is immanent to myself" and part of the process of "becoming-Christian" through which all humans must pass.[118] But the fact that Fessard framed his analysis in these loaded terms reveals precisely the risks involved in conflating the mystical body of Christ with humanity *tout court*.

The Mystical Body and Catholic Action

By the late 1930s, the "mystical body of Christ" had come to dominate discussions of ecclesiology in France and beyond.[119] It provided an alternative to the ecclesiastical model that had once been championed by partisans of the AF and quickly became something like the official theology of Catholic Action.[120] The Dominican theologian Yves Congar recalled the "veritable 'craze' for the doctrine of the mystical body of Christ" that "emerged parallel to the rise of Catholic Action and was partly due to it."[121] Like de Lubac, Congar had turned to the mystical body as a reaction against the excessive focus on the visible and juridical elements of the Church in Catholic ecclesiology since the Reformation. And he also shared de Lubac's desire to reassert the public and social role of the Church against the rising tide of secularization that had confined the Church to the private sphere—a process in which he felt the Church itself had been partly complicit.[122] In keeping with the lay apostolate of Catholic Action, Congar looked to the mystical-body theology to "give the lay members their organic place within the Church."[123] This effort to endow the laity with their rightful role in the mission of the Church would become one of the defining goals of Congar's career, culminating in his magisterial work, *Jalons pour une théologie du laïcat,* in 1953.[124]

Figure 2.1 Yves Congar at Le Saulchoir (Kain, Belgium) in 1937.
Credit: Archives de la Province dominicaine de France.

Few people expressed the central connection between Catholic Action and the mystical-body theology more forcefully than Congar's former teacher Marie-Dominique Chenu. Chenu had hosted retreats for the JOC at Le Saulchoir throughout the 1930s, and in a 1937 article dedicated to "the chaplains of the JOC," he identified the doctrine of the Incarnation as the key link between such initiatives and the mystical-body theology.[125] The Incarnation "did not happen once and for all in a corner of Judea," Chenu explained, but instead *continues* and "accomplishes itself in the 'mystical body' of Christ."[126] Catholic Action was this "Incarnation continued" in the context of modern capitalist society. It was "the yeast thrown back into the dough," the leavening agent that penetrated a particular sector—worker, student, peasant, and so on—in order to incorporate it into the mystical body of Christ.[127] In sum, Chenu concluded, "the doctrine of the mystical body of Christ is the richest food for the JOC and its peers."[128]

Like de Lubac, Chenu interpreted the mystical-body theology as proof that nothing within the human person escaped the transfiguring power of the supernatural. No region of human life was beyond its purview:

> If God incarnates himself in order to divinize man, he must take *everything* in man, from the top to the bottom of his nature. . . . It is all of man, according to his resources and with all of his works, that is assumed by grace. Divine life does not infuse itself in our life through an elimination of its human content or a reduction of its native structure, but through a *totalitarian* [*totalitaire*] elevation to the supernatural plane.[129]

This use of the term "totalitarian" was, of course, highly significant, and Chenu deployed it to underscore that no arena of human action was immune to the penetrating light of grace. It followed that there was also no social milieu so unchristian as to resist the transformative power of Catholic Action—including the factory. It was only by going into the factory that the factory could be brought to Christ, Chenu insisted. Thanks to the actions of the JOC, the working-class milieu was no longer "*as such* refractory to the presence of Christ," and labor had been transformed into a vehicle of evangelization.[130] For Chenu, this was proof of the superiority of Catholic Action to the traditional means of Catholic engagement in temporal affairs, party politics. Parties or political movements, such as the AF or the Communist Party, merely served an "external" function, whereas Catholic Action was "a slice of the internal life of

Christendom, growing the mystical Body."[131] In other words, Catholic Action was a stage in the historical Incarnation that would progressively incorporate all that is human into Christ.

While Chenu's language here recalls Maritain's vision of a "new Christendom," the fact that the Dominican's approach seems in some ways closer to that of de Lubac is indicative of the growing internal diversity within the Thomist tradition by the 1930s.[132] The condemnation of the AF had shaken the dominance of neo-scholasticism and revealed fractures in what Étienne Gilson called "the great family" of Thomism.[133] In the process, it opened up new avenues for the embattled minority of "historical Thomists," such as Chenu and Congar. By returning directly to Aquinas, these theologians recovered many of the Augustinian and Platonic inflections in his work that the "baroque theology" of the neoscholastics had downplayed in favor of the Aristotelian elements. The Dominicans' impulse to return to the "authentic" Thomas dovetailed with the Jesuits' efforts to revive the ecclesiology of St. Paul and the Church Fathers as part of a broader project of *ressourcement,* which would become the hallmark of the *nouvelle théologie.*[134] Their shared historical, mystical, and social sensibility, as well as their commitment to overcoming the separation between the natural and supernatural orders, distinguished both groups from Maritain.[135] But there also remained important differences between the Dominicans and the Jesuits, most notably over the status of Thomas Aquinas, and these differences would increasingly come to the fore after the war.

The Counter-Totalitarian Church

In the context of the late 1930s, Chenu's use of the term "totalitarian" was no accident. In fact, a growing number of theologians began to deploy this language in order to contrast the "good" totalitarianism of the Church, which empowered rather than stifled the human person, with the dangerous totalitarianism of the communist or fascist state. Yves de Montcheuil, for instance, made such an argument in his contribution to a volume celebrating the hundredth anniversary of the Tübingen school, which was edited by Pierre Chaillet and Yves Congar and published in both German and French in 1939. Given the context, there could be little doubt as to the target of Montcheuil's remarks:

> Christianity is, to employ a contemporary expression, totalitarian, but not in the manner of ideologues that impose identical solutions

upon everyone and therefore suppress personal freedom and autonomy. It binds its faithful, who thenceforth no longer belong to themselves and must no longer think, will, or do anything but by it and for it. But because it exercises its control from within, far from limiting their personal activity, it kindles this activity. It increases and cultivates human liberties . . . [136]

Montcheuil thus presented Christianity as a counter-totalitarianism that liberates rather than oppresses the human person.

Henri Rondet had been making a similar argument since 1934. In an essay provocatively titled "L'Église totalitaire," Rondet essentially blamed the rise of Nazism on Protestant ecclesiology.[137] He argued that the "invisible church" of Protestantism, because it lacked the "visible" element central to Catholic ecclesiology, looked instead to the state to provide this visible form. Here, Rondet may well have been thinking of the German Christian movement, which sought to align the German Evangelical Church with National Socialism. Catholic ecclesiology avoided this trap, Rondet reasoned, because the visible structures of the supranational Church prevented it from ever being identified with a single nation. The Catholic form of totalitarianism instead allowed for distinctions within the unity of its body, just as the limbs of the body of Christ possessed distinct functions. The "Totalitarian Church," Rondet explained, is a "unity that does not require the disappearance, but instead the maintenance of differences of race, culture, colour . . . in order to make their value understood, to give them their relative place in the harmony of the whole."[138] The Church is authentically totalitarian, in other words, because it alone can reconcile the individual ends of each person with the ends of all persons. Just as the ends of a body and those of its limbs cannot be at odds, "in the Church, mystical body of Christ, the Frenchman will be a better Frenchman to the extent that he is a better Catholic."[139] Here, once again, the influence of Teilhard's vision of a union that differentiates was powerfully in evidence. And it led Rondet to assert that a "totalitarian State in which the human person attains its full development does exist, and it is the Church."[140]

Such appeals to the "totalitarian Church" provide the clearest expression of the political stakes of ecclesial personalism. Against both totalitarianism and liberal individualism, the doctrine of the "mystical body of Christ" erected its own counter-totalitarian mystique—one based on love rather than coercion and empowering rather than stifling the human person. For proponents of this model, the challenge of the totalitarian state could only be met by a rival totalitarianism; the "mystiques" of communism and fascism could only be met by a rival mysticism; the "total politics" of Carl Schmitt could only be met by a "total ecclesiology."[141] "Faced with the racist and communist mystiques," the founder of the Belgian JOC explained, we must "erect the Christian mystique—the true one" and "build up a truly Christian society, in which everyone will live for everyone, like the members of a single body, the mystical Body of Christ."[142] This was very different from the Thomist personalism advanced by Maritain, with its clear-cut distinctions between the spiritual and temporal planes. The totalizing language that the Jesuits and Dominicans used to describe the mystical body suggests that they saw the Church not as an institution alongside the state, but rather as the primary framework for collective life. For them, Catholic Action was not simply a way to infuse Catholic values into civil society through the agency of individual Catholic laypeople, as it was for Maritain; it was a vehicle for the progressive edification of Christ's mystical body. And they therefore rejected totalitarianism, not just because it infringed on the rights and dignity of the individual person, but also because it violated the unity and sanctity of Christ's person.

The mystical-body theology thus demonstrates that resistance to totalitarianism need not emerge from a defense of individual rights, pluralism, and civil society. If Maritain's distinction between acting "as a Christian" and acting "as a Christian as such" was foreign to people like Teilhard and de Lubac, this was not least because it seemed to map all too readily onto the classic liberal distinction between the public and private spheres. What appealed to these theologians about the mystical-body ecclesiology was precisely that it refused such distinctions between the natural and supernatural, spiritual and temporal, or public and private. In the aftermath of Church-state separation, it offered these priests a means to resist the privatization of religion and reclaim a robust public role for the Church, but without yoking it to a particular political project as Catholic partisans of the Action française did. Specifically designed to be inassimilable to a political ideology, ecclesial personalism thus reveals the difficulty with using political categories derived from a secular context to make sense of theological concepts. Instead, the mystical-body ecclesiology should be viewed as a "counter-politics," one that resisted the terms of secular politics, including the primacy of the state, the logic of the right-left political spectrum, and the distinction between the private and public spheres.

And yet, the mystical-body theology did not prove to be quite as resistant to political appropriation as these priests hoped. The coming of the war and the German occupation would show just how easy it was for some Catholics to make the jump from the organic holism of the mystical body to the nationalist and racist politics of Vichy and the Third Reich. Indeed, some German theologians such as Karl Adam had already made this leap.[143] The danger of this sort of political appropriation of the mystical-body theology became much more apparent to the *nouveaux théologiens* during the war, when many French Catholics—including many who had gotten their start in Catholic Action—were drawn in by the Vichy regime's promise of a National Revolution. De Lubac and his friends would be forced to reckon with these problems in their wartime resistance writing, ultimately leading them to revise their ecclesiology and distance themselves in some respects from the language of the mystical body.

Toward Vichy

French theologians and philosophers seeking to articulate the nature and scope of Catholic engagement in public life faced a particular set of challenges in the 1930s. The separation of Church and state and the condemnation of the Action française led them to rethink the traditional approach to Church-state relations they had inherited from the great early modern jurists. No longer could Church and state be conceived as analogous "perfect societies" with distinct jurisdictions and ends, negotiating their respective spheres as two states might negotiate a shared border. The rise of the lay apostolate and specialized Catholic Action movements inspired theologians to imagine the relations between the temporal and spiritual orders in ways not exhausted by the interaction between Church and state. Maritain's "new Christendom" and the mystical-body theology constituted two such efforts to elaborate a personalist model that could successfully compete with both liberal individualism and the growing threat posed by communism and fascism. Despite their differences, both approaches avoided directly politicizing the faith, even as they sought to carve out a space for Catholic engagement in the secular public sphere.

But the new approaches to Catholic politics that emerged in the 1920s and 1930s would soon face their greatest test. Three events in 1939 took the wind out of the sails of the politico-theological renaissance that had been inaugurated by the condemnation of the AF. In February of that year, Pope Pius XI died and was succeeded by his secretary of state, Eugenio Pacelli. It soon became clear that Pius XII had a different temperament and vision for the Church's role in European politics.[144] As if to signal this change in outlook, one of the pope's first acts was to lift his predecessor's condemnation of the AF. Then, in September, Hitler invaded Poland and suddenly Europe was at war. The new pope's decision to lift the condemnation of the AF would have significant consequences for French politics after France surrendered to the Germans in 1940. Pétain's National Revolution took significant support from Catholic partisans of the AF, some of whom took up high-profile positions in the new regime. Catholics who had only grudgingly submitted to the 1926 condemnation now felt themselves vindicated, and when the Vichy government began to roll back much of the anticlerical legislation enacted under the Third Republic, it was easy for many to forget the difficult lessons of the 1920s and 1930s. The separation of Church and state no longer seemed as irreparable; the dream of restoration no longer seemed like a romantic yearning for a bygone era.

But it was not just dyed-in-the-wool royalists who lined up behind Pétain in 1940. By drawing on the anti-individualist language of personalism and the rhetoric of "spiritual revolution," Pétain managed to recruit from the ranks of Catholic Action as well. Vichy and the Occupation thus brought to the surface sharp political differences that the rather vague language of 1930s Catholic personalism had managed to conceal. Once again, the debate over collaboration would center on the question of whether Catholics could cooperate with an anti-Christian ideology. And once again, these political debates would be carried out obliquely, with the tools of ecclesiology, Eucharistic theology, and biblical studies. Indeed, these theological domains proved to be particularly fruitful channels for communicating political dissent in the context of state censorship and political persecution. As a result, it was precisely the proponents of the counter-political ecclesiology of the mystical body—above all, de Lubac, Chaillet, Fessard and Montcheuil—who would emerge as the leaders of the spiritual resistance to fascism. The war gave them the opportunity to put their ecclesial personalism into action, revealing both its political possibilities and its limitations as they struggled to adjust their theology to the messy terrain of history.

PART TWO

RESISTANCE

(1940–1944)

Fighting Nazism with the "Weapons of the Spirit"

When war broke out in 1939, priests were once again called up to serve in the military, as they had during the First World War. Henri de Lubac's service in that conflict left him with a piece of shrapnel lodged in his head, which rendered him unfit to serve, but his two close friends, Gaston Fessard and Yves de Montcheuil, were mobilized. Their military service was rather short-lived, though, because in June 1940, the French forces surrendered to the German army. Shortly after Marshal Pétain announced the armistice—which divided the country between an Occupied Zone in the north and a "Free" Zone that would soon be administered by a new French State headquartered at Vichy—Montcheuil wrote to de Lubac from his garrison. He had few illusions about "the honorable façade of an old and impotent Pétain" and predicted that the new regime would try to appropriate the Church's "vocabulary of sacrifice, effort, and discipline" for its own, rather less lofty aims. He hoped, nevertheless, that the Catholic hierarchy would manage to see through this gesture:

> I hope that our spiritual leaders will not allow themselves to be compromised and that authorized voices will know to speak clearly and firmly. We will perhaps have occasion to know what it means to take a risk in order to ensure the freedom of the word of God. This will be the moment to prove that everything we said before the war was more than the sterile chatter of people living in security.[1]

These words proved chillingly prophetic. In August 1944, Montcheuil was executed by the Gestapo while serving as a chaplain to the young resistance fighters, the *maquisards,* who were battling to liberate the country from the German forces. It was not by chance that Montcheuil found himself in their ranks. While the Catholic hierarchy embraced Pétain and his National Revolution as a heaven-sent redemption from the secular ills of the Third Republic, Montcheuil, de Lubac, Fessard, and fellow Jesuit Pierre Chaillet led an embattled Catholic resistance against Nazism and the collaborationist government of Marshal Pétain.

At first they confined their protests to the licit channels of official publications that were subject to state censorship. But as they faced increasingly restrictive censorship on two fronts—from the French State and their religious superiors—they chose to move underground and publish anonymously. Thus was born the clandestine journal *Témoignage chrétien* ("Christian witness"), which the Church hierarchy denounced as the work of "theologians without a mandate" because it was published without ecclesiastical *imprimatur*. As its authors never ceased to affirm, the publication's aims were spiritual rather than political. It sought to educate the French people about the crimes committed throughout Europe in the name of National Socialism and the duty incumbent on all Christians to resist it, even when the victims of the Nazi "New Order" were not Christians. As its name suggests, *Témoignage chrétien* was an ecumenical as well as a transnational enterprise. The editors compiled testimony from popes and from Catholic bishops across Europe, but also from Protestant leaders, in order to counteract official propaganda and demonstrate that Nazism and Christianity were fundamentally irreconcilable.

In many ways, this project represented the logical continuation of the political positions that de Lubac's circle had taken during the 1920s and 1930s. Emboldened by the Vatican's decision in 1939 to lift its condemnation of the Action française (AF), Catholic Maurrassians were among the most enthusiastic partisans of the National Revolution. Consequently, the charges that de Lubac and his brothers leveled against Vichy's Catholic supporters echoed arguments they had made against the AF in the 1920s about the danger of collaborating with an unchristian regime simply because it shared the Church's penchant for order and hierarchy.

Yet Vichy did not just recruit from the ranks of the traditional French right; it also rallied a sizable segment of the interwar Catholic Action movements that de Lubac's circle had helped to guide, revealing once again how Catholic politics tended to elude clear-cut distinctions between right and left. The war therefore forced these Jesuits to reconsider the movement's theological foundations, including the mystical-body ecclesiology they had helped to elaborate. They were particularly troubled by the way in which some veterans of Catholic Action now invoked its mission to incarnate Catholic values in the temporal order as a means to justify the politics of "presence"—the notion that Catholics should work within the structures of the National Revolution in order to orient it in a Catholic direction. In response to such claims, de Lubac's circle continued to stress the importance of Catholic engagement in temporal affairs, but they also sought to balance the discourse of incarnation, which was so central to Catholic Action, with a healthy dose of eschatology. And yet, their turn to eschatology did not imply a retreat from politics, even though they ceaselessly maintained that their resistance work was strictly a spiritual and not a political act.

The story of *Témoignage chrétien* thus demonstrates that even the most otherworldly and ostensibly apolitical discourses can have powerful political effects. Indeed, the very claim to remain above politics performed crucial political work for these theologians in the context of the war. In this sense, their resistance activities should be viewed not as apolitical but as *counter-political*. To combat Nazi and Vichy ideology, they deployed the "weapons of the spirit"—the resources of theology, and specifically, of ecclesiology, biblical studies, and Eucharistic theology. But precisely because they conceived their resistance in theological terms, it is difficult to make sense of the activities of these priests by means of categories derived from a secular political framework. One might assume that those who resisted fascism—and who were not communists—did so out of a commitment to liberal democracy. But these theologians rejected all three of these options, and in fact they blamed the rise of Nazism and communism squarely on the excesses of liberalism. Instead, they sought to articulate a theology of resistance that was at once antifascist and antiliberal.

This chapter introduces the history of the spiritual resistance and situates it in the context of the National Revolution. Just as Vichy officials mobilized support for this project by presenting it as a moral rather than a political one, priests such as de Lubac, Fessard, and Montcheuil framed their resistance to Vichy and Nazi ideology in strictly spiritual terms. As in the case of Vichy, the claim to remain above politics was politically expedient for these priests, especially in the context of wartime censorship. Chapter 4 then goes on to delve more deeply into the intellectual foundations of the spiritual resistance, examining how theology not only shaped the resistance activities of de Lubac and his brothers, but was itself reshaped in the process. In an effort to forge an alternative to both totalitarianism and liberal democracy, these priests transformed the fields of biblical studies, ecclesiology, and Catholic teaching on Judaism in ways that were to have a profound impact on postwar Catholicism.

The National Revolution

On June 25, 1940, Marshal Pétain took to the airwaves to communicate the terms of France's surrender to the Germans, offering an explanation for France's humiliating defeat as well as a program for the physical and spiritual regeneration of the nation. More than just a question of military unpreparedness, the hero of Verdun blamed the defeat on the moral "laxities" of the Third Republic, which had promoted a "spirit of pleasure" at the expense of the "spirit of sacrifice." To counteract the effects of this moral failure, Pétain enjoined his listeners to embark on the difficult work of "intellectual and moral revival," thanks to which "a new order [was] beginning."[2]

Known as the National Revolution, this order was not simply a German import or mere caretaker regime, but rather a distinct ideological project with its own French roots.[3] It was also a deeply divided enterprise founded on an alliance between Catholics and anticlericals, Maurrassian nationalists and pro-German collaborationists, proponents of state planning and decentralizing corporatists. What this motley crew shared was a distaste for the "decadence" of the Third Republic, however they defined it. For many Catholics, it was the Republic's commitment to laïcité that had sealed its fate, while those on the left blamed the corrosive effects of capitalism and those on the right bemoaned the triumph of liberal individualism. All could agree, however, that the Third Republic was to blame for France's humiliating defeat. Indeed, many perceived the débâcle of 1940 as nothing less than divine punishment for the sins of the Republic. Seen from this perspective, Pétain was the providential man sent to lead the nation in its penance, or as the bishop of Marseille put it: "God is at work through you, M. le maréchal, to save France."[4] Against the "spirit of pleasure" that had led France astray, Pétain trumpeted the virtues of sacrifice and hard work. Against the republican emphasis on individual rights, he privileged the duties that derive from membership in a community. Against the "false idea of the natural equality of men," he promised "a social and hierarchical regime."[5] And against the republican slogan of "liberty, equality, fraternity," he offered his own trinity: "work, family, fatherland."

Far from a coherent political program, the National Revolution was thus a rather vague project of moral and physical regeneration. But this was precisely what allowed it to appeal to such a wide audience. At its heart was a biopolitical effort to mobilize the bodies of French men and women in the service of a healthy body politic. This commitment manifested itself in a variety of signature policies, including the regime's natalist measures and vigorous promotion of the cult of motherhood, initiatives extolling physical activity among the youth, and, most infamously, laws directed against those who were deemed a threat to the national body—foreigners and Jews.[6] Such an emphasis on the physical regeneration of the nation was inextricable from its spiritual and moral resurrection, as Vichy politicians blended a Catholic discourse of sacrifice and redemption with the social-scientific language of health and hygiene.[7] But precisely because the National Revolution was presented as a moral and physical project, it was able to marshal support from across the ideological spectrum. Pétain styled himself a father figure who transcended political parties, even addressing his speeches to "my children."[8] As historian Francine Muel-Dreyfus explains, the power of the National Revolution stemmed from its capacity to win "forms of adherence to the regime that were not necessarily political but that had political effects."[9] From a Catholic penitential discourse of redemptive suffering to essentialist visions of the "eternal feminine" and medical fantasies of a purified social body, Vichy was able to mobilize a range of ostensibly apolitical commitments to secure its legitimacy. Whether grounded in the imprescriptible authority of Providence or of nature, these discourses had very real political effects.

This goes some way toward explaining Catholic support for Vichy. For the regime recruited not just from the ranks of the traditional Catholic right, but also Catholics who saw themselves as "neither right nor left," such as "non-conformists" and Catholic Action militants. Historians have offered various explanations for why these Catholics were drawn to the institutions of the National Revolution. In the case of the "non-conformists," John Hellman and Zeev Sternhell point to their spiritualist and communitarian commitments, as well as their hostility to the liberal institutions of the Third Republic.[10] Others, such as Muel-Dreyfus, stress the role that gender ideology played in securing support from across the political spectrum. The regime was able to appeal to such a wide range of constituencies, she argues, because it anchored itself in gender and family norms that were considered natural and therefore beyond the political. From this perspective, support for the regime was a "political consequence of the collective identification with a cause presented as apolitical."[11] Such accounts help us to understand how the French State was able to mobilize support from beyond the traditional bastions of the Catholic right. They also convincingly demonstrate the political power of putatively apolitical discourses such as religious or gender norms, which are all the more powerful precisely because they anchor themselves in the unshakable authority of nature or the divine.

But accounts such as these cannot adequately explain those Catholics who rejected Vichy and its collaborationist enterprise. Many of the regime's fiercest critics, including the authors of *Témoignage chrétien*, sounded in many ways just like its Catholic supporters. These critics shared Vichy's communitarian ethos as well as its gender norms, and they were just as critical of liberalism as their Pétainist counterparts. To understand why these antiliberal Catholics stood at the forefront of the resistance to fascism, we must attend to their specifically religious and theological motives. Doing so makes it possible to recapture the multivalent political possibilities embedded within apolitical discourses—the way they functioned, not just to reinforce the power of the new French State, but also as vehicles to critique or resist it. For, much like Pétain, the regime's Catholic critics secured support for the spiritual resistance by presenting it as a project that transcended the petty divisions of the political order.

The "Politics of Presence"

Such Catholic voices of protest were few and far between, however, especially in the heady early days of the National Revolution. The new regime—with its promise of moral and spiritual regeneration, its neomedieval corporatism, and the pride of place it accorded to the family and traditional gender roles—found a kindred spirit in the Church. But the affinities between the regime and the Catholic Church were not purely rhetorical or ideological. By rolling back the most excessive elements of the anticlerical legislation enacted under the Third Republic, the Vichy government achieved a degree of Church-state harmony not seen since the 1870s.[12] In September 1940, the French State allowed religious orders to resume their teaching activities and reversed elements of the 1901 Law on Associations, although the Church had hoped for more sweeping revisions. It had more success in the realm of education. Thanks to the efforts of the Catholic philosopher Jacques Chevalier, the primary school syllabus was modified to include instruction on "duties to God," and under Chevalier's ministry, religious instruction was even introduced into state schools as an optional subject.[13] But the measure met with stiff resistance from the teachers' union—as well as anticlerical forces within the regime—and Chevalier's successor quickly replaced it with scheduled free time for voluntary religious instruction. By way of recompense, the Church was granted limited state subsidies for its network of parochial schools.

Such measures reinforced Pétain's reputation as a "providential man" sent to redeem France. The marshal inspired a tremendously powerful cult of personality within the Church, owing to his image as a suprapolitical father figure and hero of World War I, in which so many clergy had served.[14] Church services frequently culminated in prayers for "our beloved leader" and his "work of national salvation," and the Marshal's portrait adorned the walls of religious houses and schools "at the head of the beds, between the images of the Sacred Heart and of the Holy Virgin."[15] Catholic support for the *maréchal* persisted even after most had become disillusioned with the regime's failures, which were blamed on the "unscrupulous politicians" who surrounded Pétain—especially his anticlerical deputies, Pierre Laval and François Darlan.[16] Many Catholics could therefore agree with Archbishop Pierre-Marie Gerlier of Lyon when he infamously declared that "Pétain is France; and France, today, is Pétain!"[17]

What is most striking about Catholic allegiance to the regime is the way it transcended the political divisions of the interwar period. Predictably, Vichy drew some of its strongest support from Catholic partisans of the Action française (AF), many of whom were delighted to see France's longest experiment in republican government come to an end, and looked to Vichy to restore the Church's lost privileges. The Dominican theologian Réginald Garrigou-Lagrange is a case in point. Like so many neoscholastic theologians of his day, Garrigou-Lagrange had been a staunch supporter of the AF and he was equally enthusiastic about the National Revolution. In 1941, he wrote to his erstwhile disciple Jacques Maritain, extolling the virtues of the new regime. "I am entirely with the Marshal," he enthused. "I see him as the Father of the *patrie,* blessed with a good sense verging on genius, and as a truly providential man."[18] Maritain's own politics had, of course, evolved considerably by then, and he quickly became one of the regime's sharpest critics. From the perspective of Garrigou-Lagrange, such an evolution could only be explained by "deviations" in Maritain's Thomist philosophy.[19] Other Thomists of a Maurrassian persuasion likewise drew a connection between their philosophical commitments and the principles of the National Revolution—especially its cult of authority, hierarchy, and order rooted in the unchanging dictates of natural law. Indeed, as we shall see in the next chapter, the Vichy regime itself deployed Thomist principles to justify its anti-Semitic legislation. Father Gillet—Master General of the Dominican Order and a key player in the negotiations that led to the Vatican lifting its ban on the AF—was widely suspected of having supplied the French state with the Thomist ammunition that it trotted out to justify these laws.[20]

It is no surprise that such archenemies of the Republic would rally behind the National Revolution. But why did so many of the traditional critics of the AF, including left-leaning Catholics and leaders of the Catholic Action movements, do the same? The positions of Gustave Desbuquois, Paul Doncoeur, and Emmanuel Mounier offer some clues to the regime's appeal for Catholics who were not associated with the AF. It was the rhetoric of spiritual renewal that spoke most forcefully to these figures, for they hoped that the National Revolution might inaugurate Charles Péguy's dream of a moral and mystical revolution. The celebrated poet was claimed with equal fervor by both proponents and opponents of Vichy, no doubt because his own politics were so idiosyncratic—a heady mixture of philosemitism, socialism, nationalism, and antimodernism.[21] In 1942, Doncoeur penned a paean to the dead poet that portrayed him as the heir to Joan of Arc and appropriated both figures in the service of the National Revolution, whose "essential goal" was "to restore in our people the meaning and respect for the sacred," thus opening the way for a Christian revolution.[22] Mounier likewise shared the Péguyan, communitarian sensibilities of the new regime, as well as its contempt for the "established disorder" of the Third Republic.[23] Like many Catholics with broadly anti-capitalist politics, he perceived potential affinities between the regime's corporatism and the tradition of Social Catholicism.[24] Most of these figures would ultimately break with the regime or be forced out, but their initial support is a testament to the extent to which Catholic attitudes toward Vichy transcended the logic of right and left.

The position these figures adopted vis-à-vis the new regime came to be known as the "politics of presence."[25] Those who adopted it did not necessarily share all the priorities of the National Revolution and some were in fact quite critical of the new regime, but they believed that Catholics should work within the new order to channel it in the right direction. Few expressed this position more clearly than Mounier, who initially played an important role in Vichy youth projects such as the Uriage school for functionaries and the cultural organization Jeune France.[26] Invoking the logic of presence, Mounier argued that Catholics ought to "profit from the verbal similarities between our values and the publicly proclaimed values in order to introduce . . . the content we desire."[27] This was also the approach adopted by Gustave Desbuquois, director of the Jesuit-led social movement Action populaire. Desbuquois explicitly counseled Catholics to "enter into the new regime," on the grounds that "the spiritual and the supernatural cannot refuse to penetrate this or any political form."[28] Such an approach dovetailed with the incarnational spirituality of Catholic Action, which called on the laity to incarnate Catholic values in the temporal order. For Desbuquois, this meant that the National Revolution and Catholic Action should be conceived as "two complementary sectors" operating in tandem to cure the moral and spiritual ills of the fallen nation. "Catholic Action must effectively act in conjunction with the National Revolution," he argued, "like a radioactive body on a specified tumor."[29] Desbuquois thus justified the politics of presence by framing it as a form of moral and spiritual engagement, and therefore, as consistent with Catholic Action's claim to remain above politics. And he could do so precisely because the National Revolution was framed as something that transcended party politics.

But not all Catholic Action leaders drew the same connection between the movement's incarnational discourse and the aims of the National Revolution. Perhaps because the injunction to "incarnate" Catholic values in the temporal order was so vague and indeterminate, Catholic Action had managed to recruit widely in the interwar period. By 1942, its organizations' ranks had swelled to at least 380,000 members, but the war brought substantial political, tactical, and theological cracks to the surface.[30] These differences manifested themselves in the various ways in which Catholic Action organizations responded to the National Revolution. The Jeunesse agricole catholique and the Scouts were most favorable to the new regime, attracted as they were by its "return to the land" social policy, its emphasis on discipline, and the high-profile positions given to Scout leaders within the regime's youth movements. At the other end of the spectrum, the spiritual resistance recruited heavily from the Jeunesse éudiante chrétienne and, in fact, the women's branch (JECF) played a particularly important role in the resistance network of the French Jesuits, several of whom had served as chaplains to the organization before the war. The Jeunesse ouvrière chrétienne and the broader Association catholique de la jeunesse française were more divided, and all were wary of the possibility that the regime might abolish independent Catholic Action organizations in favor of a unified youth movement under state auspices. Most of these groups would turn against the regime when it imposed the Service du travail obligatoire (STO) in February 1943, drafting all men aged twenty through twenty-three to work in German factories. But until then, Catholic Action remained divided over how to interpret the duty to incarnate Christianity in the temporal order, and thus over the appropriate attitude to adopt with regard to Vichy.[31]

The French episcopacy was not so divided—at least not publicly. When the Assembly of Cardinals and Archbishops (ACA) met for the first time after the defeat, it initially adopted a cautious line, seeking to remain above the political fray while reminding Catholics of St. Paul's injunction to obey the established temporal authority. But by July 1941, the ACA had moved from cautious reserve to a more forthright endorsement of the regime:

> We wish that, without subservience [inféodation], a sincere and complete loyalty be practiced toward the established authority. We venerate the head of State and . . . encourage our faithful to take their place at his side in the work of recovery that he has undertaken in the three domains of the family, work, and the fatherland, with the aim of achieving a strong, united, coherent France.[32]

The duty to obey the governing authority was one of the key theological justifications to be deployed in the service of the new regime. This Pauline injunction had previously been used to very different political effect when Pope Leo XIII invoked it in 1892 to convince French Catholics to rally behind the Republic, but now the wartime French hierarchy used it to secure obedience to Pétain's authoritarian regime instead. Not all bishops were equally enthusiastic about the new regime, of course, but despite scuffles with Vichy over areas such as youth policy and the STO, the episcopacy did not substantially revise its 1941 position and remained stubbornly Pétainist until the bitter end.[33]

The bishops' steadfast obedience was something that the regime's Catholic critics found difficult to forgive. When Bishop Pierre-Marie Théas of Montauban later asked Gaston Fessard to write a report for the pope on how the bishops had acquitted themselves during the war, the Jesuit made no secret of his disappointment with the lack of leadership exhibited by the shepherds of the French flock. He lamented that caveats such as "'without subservience' seemed entirely forgotten. 'Complete loyalty to the established authority' became 'obedience without reservation'" and "the Catholic conscience was delivered defenseless to every order that emanated from Vichy." Even as the hierarchy claimed to confine its directives to purely religious questions, Fessard argued that they "amounted to the French Church siding with Vichy." It was left to isolated theologians like himself to remind Catholics of the difference between "a legitimate and illegitimate regime—in short, true and false authority."[34]

Reading between the Lines

Along with his friends Montcheuil and de Lubac, Fessard soon emerged as one of the leading voices of a fledgling spiritual resistance that had begun to develop in Lyon. With Paris under German occupation, Catholic Action organizers, intellectuals, demobilized clergy, and the editorial boards of Catholic journals streamed into the city, in what amounted to a gathering of the leading lights of the Catholic intelligentsia. The Jesuit journal *Études*, like every other periodical, was dissolved after the defeat. In order to continue publishing, its editors acquiesced to the censorship regime imposed by the French State and renamed the journal *Cité nouvelle*—a title that reflected the politics of presence favored by its editor-in-chief, Gustave Desbuquois. Nevertheless, the journal also drew contributions from some of the regime's fiercest critics, including de Lubac, Montcheuil, Fessard, and Jules Lebreton. In 1940, these priests still hoped that they could offset the Pétainism of the editorial team and outmaneuver the Vichy censor in order to make their anti-Nazi message heard. Theology proved a particularly useful vehicle for such an endeavor because it was less likely to arouse the censor's suspicions. In other words, theology became a key political tool in the context of the war precisely because it seemed to be apolitical. But in order to glimpse what the censor missed, it is necessary to read between the lines of these texts to recover the political messages encoded within them. This is all the more important because such works were subject to a *double* regime of censorship—at once governmental and ecclesiastical. By late 1941, de Lubac and his friends found themselves increasingly squeezed on both sides of this censorship regime and they were forced to move underground.

Gaston Fessard had been warning Catholics against the twin dangers of Nazi and communist totalitarianism since the mid-1930s—most notably in *Pax Nostra* (1936) and *Épreuve de force* (1939). He presented the two ideologies as the logical outgrowths of liberalism, which had decoupled state from society, and *homo politicus* from *homo economicus*.[35] After the French defeat, however, Fessard could no longer profess his anti-totalitarianism openly and was forced to couch it in more abstract, eschatological language in order to outwit the censor. One of the earliest examples of this strategy was a sermon Fessard gave on the third Sunday of Advent in 1940, at the church of Saint-Louis in Vichy. The sermon is particularly interesting because a censored version of it was later published in *Cité nouvelle*. A comparison between the two texts reveals why theology became such a useful weapon in the context of censorship.

In his sermon, Fessard initially appeared to adopt the rhetoric of the National Revolution, blaming France's defeat on the decadence of the Third Republic. But he was quick to clarify that the democratic ideology of the Republic was not the source of the problem; it was only a symptom of the broader decadence brought on by the secularization of public life since the Middle Ages. The current crisis was not specific to France, but stemmed instead from the rationalist ideology at the heart of modern Western civilization, which "accustomed peoples to search for the meaning of their history in the limits of the here and now."[36] By evacuating the supernatural, Fessard argued, rationalism had paved the way for the rise of Nazism and communism: "From the rationalist ideology common to the West, two new mystiques were born: that of the Race and the People [Nazism]; that of Labor and the Classless Society [communism]."[37] But the censored version of the text suppressed the second half of this statement and replaced it with a much vaguer reference to "two new mystiques, both daughters of the rationalist ideology reigning in the West."[38] Later in the sermon, Fessard once again compared the cult of "the Race" to that of "Labor," but the first of these references was suppressed in the published version.[39] The Vichy censor evidently sought to transform Fessard's anti-totalitarian discourse into an anticommunist one, as the following passage makes clear (the censored sections are shown with a line through them):

> [Hope] will put us on guard against appeals which seek to drag us ~~either~~ into the venture of the communist apocalypse, ~~or in the service of a triumphant Will to power.~~ With her help, we will discern behind the mask of Class, ~~as well as behind that of Race,~~ our eternal enemy . . . [40]

In addition, the published version omitted a passage in which Fessard blamed the war on the alliance between the "two mystiques"—no doubt an allusion to the Molotov-Ribbentrop Pact—as well as his references to Pius XI's twin 1937 encyclicals against communism and Nazism.[41]

Because Fessard was unable to denounce Nazism by name or even in this implicit manner, he turned instead to the language of eschatology to communicate his message in print. He warned his fellow Frenchmen that neither the "two mystiques" nor the liberal rationalism that had given birth to them could supply the ultimate answer to the mystery of human history.[42] Only the history of salvation could resolve the contradictions of human history and bring about "the universal reconciliation of man with God and of men amongst themselves, whatever be their tribe, their language, their nation."[43] Here, Fessard invoked St. Paul's vision of the mystical body of Christ as an oblique critique of the racist policies of Vichy and the Third Reich. Such policies represented an attack on the unity of Christ's body, in which "there will be neither Jew nor Greek, neither man nor woman, neither master nor slave."[44] From Fessard's perspective, the eschatological vision of the mystical body offered an alternative to "the narrow and petty future embraced by human politics," one that militated against the "insidious appeals of the watchmen of despair, of selfishness, and of a base servility."[45] Here, Fessard managed to get in a swipe at Vichy defeatism, although the censor suppressed more overt references to the crimes of the occupier and the servility of collaborators. Nevertheless, these passages show how Fessard was able to mobilize theology to articulate a clear, if coded, indictment of the regime.

In this way, Fessard deployed the eschatological vision of the mystical body of Christ as a weapon against the Third Reich and the French State, while also offering a corrective to the rhetoric of incarnation and "presence" invoked by the regime's Catholic supporters. But by turning from incarnation to eschatology, Fessard was certainly not advocating *attentisme* or a retreat from political engagement. Because salvation history was not like the linear time of human history and was instead omnipresent within each moment of human time, Fessard insisted that bearing witness to one's eschatological destiny in no way implied withdrawing from the contemporary historical crisis. In fact, salvation history provided the best interpretative grid for making sense of the current moment, by teaching Christians to reject any order that violated the unity of the mystical body and to orient their own profane history toward its coming. "How, then," he asked, "could the lessons we must draw from this Christian anticipation of salvation not have a bearing on the political and social spheres through which our personal destiny must accomplish itself?"[46] Far from implying a retreat from political affairs, he insisted that the demands of eschatology placed an even heavier burden on Christians to work toward the advent of a reconciled humanity, for the mystical body of Christ "depends upon you *now* in order to become more and more real, *hic et nunc.*"[47] Rather than retreating from political affairs, Fessard was accessing them by other means.

Fessard's analysis quickly found an echo in the work of his closest friend, Henri de Lubac, who articulated a similar account of the causes of the defeat in a lecture he gave in October 1941 at Uriage, the school created to train future Vichy cadres. While some historians have suggested that de Lubac's presence at the school lent moral weight to the National Revolution, the content of the Jesuit's remarks makes clear that they were written with precisely the opposite goal in mind.[48] In fact, like Fessard, de Lubac turned to theology to articulate a critique of Nazism and Vichy ideology—one that he could nevertheless get past the Vichy censor, as he managed to do when the speech appeared in print a few months later.

Like Fessard, de Lubac initially appeared to endorse the Vichy narrative that blamed the French defeat on a bankrupt liberalism. Yet, also like Fessard, de Lubac insisted that "we are not simply dealing with a crisis of liberalism or of democracy," but with a much more fundamental crisis of European civilization rooted in secularization.[49] Recalling the social Catholicism that he had advocated in his first book, de Lubac blamed this crisis on the progressive privatization and individualization of Christianity since the Renaissance. The effect of evacuating Christianity from public life was to open the door to rationalism in intellectual life and liberalism in the political order. But these secular ideologies could not offer a viable replacement for Christianity, de Lubac declared. Instead, they inspired an "*absolute* hunger and thirst, because they are an impotent hunger and thirst *for the Absolute.*"[50] As a result, Europeans were left at the mercy of the "two totalitarianisms," against which a privatized Christianity and an impotent rationalism were equally powerless.[51] Conceiving of Nazism and communism as replacement religions that were "at once the antipode and the caricature" of Christianity, de Lubac's analysis strongly echoed the philosopher Eric Voegelin's claim that totalitarian ideologies constituted "political religions" and anticipated Raymond Aron's postwar work in the same vein.[52] The Jesuit's critique of liberalism and rationalism must be read, then, not as an endorsement of the National Revolution, but as a much broader theory of secularization that was also a theory of the origins of totalitarianism.

This was evident from the solution de Lubac proposed to the crisis in which France found itself. If the crisis facing France was a fundamentally spiritual one, he argued, it necessarily required a remedy of the same nature. Here de Lubac returned to the personalist ecclesiology he had begun to develop in the interwar period, distinguishing his own communitarian vision from that of both the National Revolution and the Third Reich. Although he granted that the family and the nation were natural outgrowths of the human need for community, de Lubac warned that they were ultimately only provisional and suffered from the same problems that beset all purely terrestrial societies. Above all, they could not resolve the intractable tension between individual freedom and communal solidarity. Instead, they tended to privilege one at the expense of the other, thus degenerating into either totalitarian collectivism or liberal individualism. "Either the person is crushed by a system that makes of men a society of termites," de Lubac explained, "or on the contrary, the human community and the national communities of which it is composed are dislocated by an anarchic liberalism."[53] Only the Church, he insisted, could reconcile these competing imperatives, precisely because it was not of this world:

> So that the person finds his complete fulfillment, so that he arrives at full interiority, at the full possession of himself, he must be enfolded into a vaster and deeper community, a community of a different nature—no longer simply terrestrial, as the family and the nation still are, but a community whose essence is eternal, as the person himself is. Such is the Church, this Church which the Apostle Paul called the "Body of Christ" and which we still commonly call the "mystical Body of Christ."[54]

De Lubac here recapitulated his interwar counter-politics, presenting the Church as the only human community capable of overcoming the limitations of secular political projects. But in the context of wartime France, this ecclesiology also served a more specific role as a weapon against the siren song of the National Revolution.

De Lubac drove home this political message in the conclusion to his talk, putting the students on guard against a purely instrumental use of Christian rhetoric by those in power. "It is not enough to pronounce the name of 'God' to truly believe in him," he warned. "Behind this word, a pagan idol may still be hiding."[55] This was no doubt a dig at the Vichy regime's lip service to Catholic values, but in case his auditors had any doubts about his target, de Lubac reminded them that all "national revolutions" have as their necessary condition a "human revolution" that includes "respect for the person."[56] More pointedly, he told them to "be especially wary of a certain form of anti-Semitism which is nothing other than an anti-Christianity and which, by that very fact, leads . . . to our own destruction by ripping out our soul."[57] From these lines it should be clear that, although de Lubac invoked the rhetoric of personalism in vogue at Uriage, he did so precisely in order to channel it into a critique of Nazism, anti-Semitism, and the excesses of the National Revolution. If the mystical body alone could reconcile the freedom of the human person with the unity of the human race, he maintained, Catholics were obligated by their participation in this body to reject here and now any political order that violated these principles.

While de Lubac and Fessard were dueling with the Vichy censor to communicate their message of resistance, their friend Montcheuil was engaged in a similar combat against the much more restrictive censorship regime of the Occupied Zone. In *Construire,* the Parisian sister-journal to *Cité nouvelle,* Montcheuil amplified de Lubac's warning against the French State's instrumental use of Catholic rhetoric. Without mentioning Vichy or the National Revolution by name, Montcheuil criticized the educational reforms enacted by the new regime, which had added instruction on the "duties to God" to the primary school curriculum, as a companion to familial and patriotic duty. Montcheuil was fiercely critical of the way in which the new French State deployed the "idea of God" as a means to secure the obedience of its subjects. "An education founded upon such an idea may produce submissive citizens," he warned, "but it will not form moral beings." Such a utilitarian promotion of the faith only served "to make the State and its functions into an absolute end and allow it to subordinate everything to itself, even spiritual realities."[58] Montcheuil thus sought to disabuse those Catholics who perceived the educational reforms as a boon for the Church by showing that they amounted to a purely instrumental use of religion—one designed to secure obedience to Vichy.

But Montcheuil was not simply concerned about the end to which religious instruction was yoked. He also condemned the way in which it was carried out, which allowed him to embed an even more forceful critique of the French State in his essay. The Jesuit rejected the Vichy education minister's justification for the educational reforms—the notion that the idea of God can be demonstrated on purely rational grounds. Proving the *fact* of God's existence, the Jesuit pointed out, is not equivalent to demonstrating its rightfulness.[59] Montcheuil then used this distinction to authorize a much broader claim about the right to resist an illegitimate regime, thus offering a corrective to the French bishops' insistence on the duty to obey the established authority: "The refusal to submit before the *fact* of a domination that is not at the same time a *right* is a requirement of every spiritual being, a requirement that we Christians need not doubt because we recognize that it has been instilled in us by God himself."[60] Montcheuil's critique of a moral education founded on the primacy of obedience to God thus served as a pretext for a much more extensive assault on the authoritarian tendencies of the French State and an endorsement of the Christian duty to resist tyranny. But because he embedded this message within an ostensibly apolitical essay about moral philosophy, he was able to get it past the German censor.

One might wonder what effect these sorts of coded critiques actually had on public opinion, but there were few other available avenues for political critique, short of crossing the boundary into illegality and going underground. By late 1941, however, even these limited avenues for licit resistance had been closed off. In August of that year, progressive Christian publications such as *Esprit* and *Temps nouveau* were shuttered. By December, Victor Dillard had to inform de Lubac that the Vichy censor had rejected his latest article in its entirety, and even pastoral letters from the bishops and Radio Vatican broadcasts were severely restricted.[61] Yet in themselves, these restrictions might not have forced the Jesuits underground had they not been matched by parallel restrictions from their religious superiors. An exchange between de Lubac and his Jesuit superiors in mid-1941 provides a fascinating insight into their attitude to the new French State, which closely mirrored that of the French bishops. It shows how both the regime's critics and its defenders justified their respective positions in strictly religious terms while accusing the other side of playing politics.

In a long letter to his superiors dated April 25, 1941, de Lubac lamented that Church leaders in France had not done enough to warn Catholics of the threat that Nazism posed to Christianity and the way Vichy ideology played into the Nazis' hands.[62] He worried that the hierarchy had been duped by the euphoria of the National Revolution and that it risked betraying its mission because it was more concerned with protecting its own institutional privileges than denouncing the anti-Christian ideology of the occupier:

> Shouldn't we also be reminded more often that laws can be contrary to Christianity even if they do not attack the institutions or men of the Church? Just as the official honors the latter may receive do not necessarily coincide with a Christian revival, so it is not just when our own personnel begins to suffer that Christian morality and the faith itself are in peril. Every time that charity and justice are harmed . . . the Church is thereby harmed.[63]

By way of example, de Lubac pointed to the anti-Semitism that was so central to both Vichy and Nazi ideology and argued that it constituted an attack on the doctrine and scripture of Christianity itself. De Lubac therefore exhorted his superiors to speak out against the spiritual dangers of Nazism and promote a "deepened and more integrally lived Christianity," instead of one that prioritized institutional self-preservation.[64]

De Lubac's appeal did not have the desired effect. In lieu of a direct response, Assistant General Norbert de Boynes issued a circular letter to all French Jesuits instructing them to stay out of politics. In a statement clearly directed against de Lubac's circle, de Boynes complained that the activities of a few bad apples threatened to derail the sensitive, ongoing negotiations between the Church and the French State over the status of the religious orders and the Catholic youth movements. He commanded Jesuits to choose "respect for authority and obedience" over "a critical and rebellious spirit," and to set an example through their submission to the laws of both Church and state.[65] This he justified on the grounds that their vocation as priests and religious necessarily precluded political engagement, arguing that "the priest who devotes himself to politics compromises not only his apostolate, but also his ascension toward divine union."[66] And yet, in the very same breath, de Boynes affirmed that Vichy was the only "legitimate government" of France and lauded the virtues of the *maréchal,* who "promotes the return to a Christian culture." Indeed, he went so far as to suggest that Jesuits had a religious duty to submit to the French State and persuade all Catholics to do the same:

> What must our attitude be, as members of the Society [of Jesus]? We must first of all accept the established government and obey it in everything that is not contrary to the law of God. . . . We must even use our influence where we can to lead souls, if necessary, to practice the obedience that all, especially Catholics, owe to the head of State. . . . For the same supernatural reasons, we must in no way promote dissidence.[67]

In taking this position, de Boynes claimed that he was merely "recalling the duties required of all Catholics" by their faith. He thus invoked the apolitical vocation of the priesthood to authorize support for a political regime.

De Lubac pointed out this contradiction in a second letter written in response to de Boynes's circular. He agreed wholeheartedly with the assistant general's statement that "it is not our place to get involved in politics."[68] But he insisted that the concerns he had expressed to his superiors were not political in nature, for he viewed Nazism as a specifically *religious* threat. Turning de Boynes's words back against him, de Lubac accused his superiors of applying the duty to remain above politics selectively. "If, contrary to the affirmations of principle contained in the Rev. Fr. Assistant's letter, a *wholly religious* action were . . . to be declared a political and subversive action," he wrote, "it is impossible for me, in conscience, to consent to what would be today, in my eyes, a very grave sin of omission." In such a context, he concluded, "I do not think it would be enough for me . . . to act solely in accordance with my immediate Superior."[69] This was a bold affirmation of the primacy of conscience over the duty to obey—one that no doubt informed de Lubac's decision to enter the ranks of the clandestine resistance a few months later. In this letter, de Lubac signaled his intention to disobey the orders of his superiors, on the grounds that these directives were politically rather than religiously motivated, while justifying his own disobedience as a religious rather than a political act. What is so remarkable about this exchange is the way in which *both* the regime's clerical supporters and its critics justified their position in strictly doctrinal terms, while each accused the other side of venturing onto political terrain. This is a striking illustration of the political work performed by the very claim to remain above politics.

"A Front of Spiritual Resistance": *Témoignage Chrétien*

By late 1941, de Lubac and his friends were facing increasingly restrictive censorship from both the French State and their religious superiors. As a result, they chose to move their resistance underground by launching the clandestine journal *Témoignage chrétien* in November 1941. Under the cover of anonymity, they could evade both state and ecclesiastical censorship and articulate a much more forthright condemnation of Nazism. Nevertheless, their licit resistance activities should not be interpreted as a failure, nor did they cease in 1941. The pressure of censorship enabled these Jesuits to clarify the relationship between their theological vision and the political challenges of the moment. It forced them to distinguish their own understanding of the causes of defeat and the duty to incarnate Catholic values in the temporal order from the politics of presence that dominated Catholic circles after the French defeat. As a result, the licit wartime writings of these priests reveal a clear shift from the priority of incarnation to that of eschatology—a reorientation that would shape their postwar theological work in crucial ways. But in 1941, they were casting about for a way to get around the state and ecclesiastical censors. Their friend Pierre Chaillet furnished them with the opportunity they were seeking.

Chaillet was a fellow Jesuit from the Province of Lyon who had studied at the Jersey scholasticate only a year or two after Fessard, de Lubac, and Montcheuil. He had spent the 1930s traveling between Lyon, Rome, Germany, and Austria, and his stint in Central Europe convinced him early on of the formidable threat posed by Nazism. In 1939, he wrote a book on the *Anschluss,* denouncing it as a step in the "gigantic enterprise of dechristianization undertaken by National Socialism."[70] After the French defeat, the work was quickly placed on the "Otto List" of books forbidden by the occupying power, along with Fessard's *Épreuve de force.* Like Fessard, Montcheuil, and de Lubac, Chaillet's hostility to Nazism was closely connected to his vision of the Church. He was a leading expert on the ecclesiology of Johann Adam Möhler and the nineteenth-century Tübingen school. Writing in the age of Hegelian idealism and German Romanticism, the Tübingen theologians drew on the Church Fathers to elaborate a vision of the Church as an organic body that evolves over time. A shared appreciation for Möhler's ecclesiology and its ecumenical possibilities brought Chaillet into close collaboration with Yves Congar during the 1930s, when the two worked on a new translation of

Möhler's *Die Einheit in der Kirche*. Writing to the Dominican in 1936, Chaillet expressed his full solidarity with Congar's efforts to "bring theology back into contact with the living realities of the great collective consciousness of the Church as the body of Christ," and both priests conceived the translation as part of a broader effort to "replace the Counter-Reformation juridical ecclesiology with an ecclesiology of the Mystical Body."[71]

As in the case of his Jesuit brothers, Chaillet believed that this ecclesiology provided the key to formulating a Christian response to the political challenges of the day. Just like de Lubac, he presented the mystical body as an alternative to both liberal individualism and totalitarian collectivism, for in this body "the personality develops itself all the more as it seems to absorb itself in the whole."[72] In a 1938 article, Chaillet clarified the political implications of this ecclesiology in ways that illuminate the logic behind his subsequent resistance efforts and the project of *Témoignage chrétien*. Faced with the threat of totalitarianism, Chaillet argued, following Möhler, that the Church should model itself on the early Christians under the Roman Empire. In the face of pagan persecution, the early Christians had testified to the eternal vocation of the Church by heroically affirming its independence from the state, while also refusing to retreat into a private faith without social repercussions. It was the "intimate connection" between the interior and exterior aspects of the faith, according to Chaillet, that endowed the Church with this public mission to "bear witness without fear and without reproach."[73] And he was convinced that this model of engagement without enslavement should likewise guide the Church's response to totalitarianism. Chaillet insisted that the Church cannot be "enlisted or simply aligned" with political ideologies, particularly when they "display the totalitarian pretensions of a mystique." Instead, it was paradoxically by remaining detached from politics proper and bearing witness to its eternal mission that the Church could engage most effectively in temporal affairs. Even though this might "seem on the purely temporal plane like an escapist doctrine," he maintained, "it is in fact a doctrine of radical dissatisfaction and overcoming."[74] Like Fessard and de Lubac, then, Chaillet transformed the eschatological vocation of the Church into a kind of critical counter-politics designed to do battle with totalitarian ideologies.

This shared counter-political theology would provide the theoretical basis for the spiritual resistance these Jesuits helped to lead. After being mobilized in 1939 and dispatched to Hungary on a secret mission, it took Chaillet six months to get back to France after the defeat, traveling via Turkey and Syria. When he arrived in Lyon toward the end of December 1940, he was severely disappointed to observe that the intoxicating spirit of the National Revolution had penetrated even the most progressive Catholic milieus, such as Mounier's *Esprit* circle. "I called in vain upon our friends to put an end to a politics of presence in the gears of the National Revolution," he later recalled, but "the illusions of presence were not ready to yield to the exigencies of refusal . . . the detestation of Hitlerism was unable to counterbalance the bourgeois and Christian confidence of the myth of the Marshal."[75] He did, however, find likeminded allies among his fellow Jesuits living at the Fourvière seminary.

Since his return to Lyon, Chaillet had been looking for ways to warn the public about the spiritual dangers of collaboration, including authoring short essays on this subject for Henri Frenay's resistance newspapers. In fall 1941, just as the state was shuttering a number of Catholic publications, Frenay met with Chaillet and they decided to split the political and spiritual wings of the clandestine press. *Combat* would become the mouthpiece for the first, while Frenay offered Chaillet funds, a printer, and an all-important supply of paper to set up its spiritual counterpart.[76] Louis Cruvillier, a former Catholic Action militant who had distributed the defunct *Temps nouveau,* furnished the necessary distribution network, which was staffed largely by Catholic Action militants.[77] The name that Chaillet chose for his clandestine newspaper reflected his Möhlerian vision of an ecumenical commitment to bearing witness to Christian values: *Témoignage chrétien.* At the very moment when the pressures of both state and ecclesiastical censorship had become too burdensome for de Lubac and his friends, this project gave them the opportunity to circumvent both censorship regimes by publishing anonymously and clandestinely. De Lubac would share the editorial functions with Chaillet and author numerous contributions of his own, while it fell to Fessard to pen the very first issue.

Composed in July 1941, "France, Take Care Not to Lose Your Soul" is widely regarded as the text that launched the spiritual resistance. It appeared in November as the inaugural issue of the *Cahiers du Témoignage chrétien,* with a print run of 5,000 copies—a figure that climbed to 30,000 when the editors reprinted the essay a year later.[78] Unburdened of the weight of censorship, Fessard could voice a much more pointed critique of Nazism, even as he rehearsed many of the themes he and his friends had explored in their licit resistance writings. As in those earlier works, Fessard presented Nazism as a religious phenomenon first and foremost. "Before being a political regime," he explained, "National Socialism is a *Weltanschauung,* a worldview as totalitarian and intolerant as a religion because it is founded on a mystique." Consequently, "no conciliation, no distribution into zones of influence is possible between Christianity and Nazism: one of the two must disappear."[79] Quoting extensively from Nazi ideologues such as Adolf Hitler and Alfred Rosenberg, Fessard sought to demonstrate the "inherently *anti-Christian character*" of this neopagan mystique founded on the idols of blood and race.[80] Such a mystique was fundamentally at odds with Christian teaching on the dignity of the person and the unity of the human race. Indeed, Fessard suggested that Nazism represented an even greater threat than communism because at least communism proclaimed its hostility to religion openly, whereas Nazism sought to co-opt Christianity from within. Here Fessard pointed to the example of the German Christian movement, which sought to Aryanize Christianity and strip it of its "Jewish imports."[81] Even though Nazi leaders paid lip service to Christianity, Fessard warned that this language merely served as a Trojan horse, implicating Christians in an "idolatrous cult" that divinized the *Volk* and vitiated Christianity from within.

In addition to demonstrating the radical incompatibility between Nazism and Christianity, Fessard sought to disabuse French Catholics of the notion that support for the Vichy regime did not imply collaboration with the Germans. He pointed out that in every country the Germans occupied, their strategy had been to seduce local Christians with the illusion of a "shared goal, whose dubious nature conceals itself under honest words and appearances."[82] In the French case, this shared project was the National Revolution—the promise of a religious revival at the expense of republican *laïcité*. Although this might seem like a worthy project, Fessard warned that the superficially religious rhetoric of the Vichy regime in fact enlisted Christians in an unwitting collaboration with the pagan ideology of the occupier. "To the extent that the Catholic is duped by this equivocation and embarks on this path," Fessard cautioned, "he is compromised and 'begins to lose his soul.'"[83] The effect was to co-opt French Christians into carrying out the Nazis' anti-Christian agenda, while those who protested were censored or intimidated into silence. Fessard thus sought to dispel the widespread illusion that Vichy remained substantially independent from the occupying power and its ideology. And in case this message remained at all unclear, he spelled it out in capital letters: "COLLABORATION WITH THE GOVERN-MENT OF THE MARSHAL = COLLABORATION WITH THE NEW ORDER = COLLABORATION WITH THE TRIUMPH OF NAZI PRINCIPLES."[84]

As this text suggests, what differentiated *Témoignage chrétien* from other resistance newspapers was that it claimed a strictly spiritual mission. The very first issue opened with a disclaimer: "The Frenchmen who present you these *Cahiers* do not engage in politics."[85] Instead, they sought to fight Nazism with "the weapons of the spirit" and show Christians that "on this level of the spirit, the duty is to oppose and to organize resistance to Nazism."[86] Central to this spiritual mission was a pedagogical objective. The goal was to "inform consciences" about the fundamental incompatibility between Nazi ideology and the teachings of the Church by "reporting censored facts" as well as "doctrinal directives emanating from the leaders of the Church."[87] To this end, large portions of each issue were given over to quotations from both Nazi ideologues (one issue was titled "The Racists in Their Own Words") and the Church hierarchy. In keeping with its editors' transnational and ecumenical vision, *Témoignage chrétien* included testimony not only from Catholic bishops and theologians across Europe, but also from Protestants such as Karl Barth, Roland de Pury, and Marc Boegner, the spiritual head of the French Protestant community. The journal also reported what the official press could not—the systematic persecutions being carried out in the territories of the Third Reich, including, in 1943, an account of the extermination of Jews then underway in Poland. "There can be no possible doubt," the authors insisted, "concerning Hitler's plan to completely exterminate the Jews of the European continent."[88] In this way, the journal aimed to offer an antidote to "a press that has been enslaved or bought," by providing "the facts, naked, concise, and confirmed."[89] By framing the mission of *Témoignage chrétien* in these terms, Chaillet and his team thus carved out a new public role for themselves as priests in a context in which Church and state had been separated. They envisioned themselves as something like the spiritual directors of the nation, who sought to form the consciences of French men and women by providing them with the necessary tools to make an informed Christian judgment.

But presenting their mission in spiritual and pedagogical terms also performed a certain amount of political work for these priests. In the first place, it allowed them to engage in politics without appearing to do so and to pronounce on questions that might otherwise seem beyond their purview as priests. But it also helped to justify their decision to depart publicly from the directives of their superiors. Because the Jesuit authors of *Témoignage chrétien* published anonymously and clandestinely, they did so without acquiring the mandatory *nihil obstat* and *imprimatur* from their superiors. They were therefore careful to insist that their work in no way implicated or spoke for the Church and merely reflected the commands of their own conscience. And yet, they *also* relied on the pronouncements of the hierarchy—whether French, Roman, or otherwise—to authorize their claims:

> If we do not have the ability to speak in the name of our Churches, we can, however, recall the authentic witness of the Churches of which we are members . . . because our personal Witness as Christians is the faithful echo of the judgment of our hierarchical superiors.[90]

In this passage, the author at once claims to speak from personal witness while also invoking the authority of the hierarchy to support his position. Indeed, one could argue that appealing to the authority of likeminded bishops served, in this instance, to authorize the demands of personal conscience and to defend the priests' divergence from the position of the French hierarchy.

This was certainly how it was interpreted by the bishops themselves. They rightly perceived that *Témoignage chrétien* drew on the pronouncements of Church leaders outside France—including testimony from the German, Dutch, Polish, Greek, Croatian, Norwegian, and Belgian churches—precisely because such statements authorized its position and undermined that of the French episcopacy. The Assembly of Cardinals and Archbishops was therefore quick to denounce *Témoignage chrétien* as the work of "theologians without a mandate," of "guerrillas [*franc-tireurs*] more or less in revolt against the authority of the Church."[91] De Lubac responded to this attack in the September 1943 issue by turning once again to the resources of the mystical body ecclesiology. Such a vision of the Church, he argued, implied a transnational solidarity that exceeded the exclusive authority of any single national hierarchy:

> The Church is one; there are no closed compartments within it; an active and living solidarity unites each Church with all of the Churches, each Christian with all of his brothers in Christianity. In the universalism of its charity, its solicitude knows no selfish

withdrawal into the frontiers of the nation. "We are all one body in Christ," says St. Paul.[92]

Montcheuil echoed this sentiment in his own resistance writings. "There is not a German Church and a French Church," he insisted; "there is the Catholic Church, which is one because it is the body of Christ in the world. To interfere with the Church in any one of its parts is to interfere with it as a whole."[93] Statements such as these affirmed the transnational solidarity of the Catholic Church against an equally transnational enemy. But they were also politically efficacious for these priests, allowing them to invoke the voices of Catholic prelates and intellectuals outside France who were critical of fascism against the authority of the Pétainist French bishops. By framing the Church as the transnational, ecumenical body of Christ, they privileged the solidarity that binds all Christians over their duty to their immediate superiors.

While *Témoignage chrétien* articulated the theory behind the spiritual resistance, Amitié chrétienne put these ideals into practice.[94] It was an interconfessional initiative under the patronage of Cardinal Gerlier and Pastor Marc Boegner, in which Catholics, Protestants, and Jews worked together to provide material assistance to people fleeing Nazi persecution. Chaillet played a leading role in this organization, which quickly evolved, as the anti-Semitic campaign intensified, into a clandestine rescue operation secretly funded by leading Jewish organizations.[95] The operation included a "laboratory" for manufacturing false papers that produced over 30,000 identity cards and 50,000 ration cards in three years.[96] In addition to furnishing refugees and deportees with false documents and financial support, Amitié chrétienne developed an extensive network to smuggle people across the border into Switzerland or hide them in Catholic convents and schools. Chaillet's key ally in this endeavor was a young woman, Germaine Ribière, who became a close disciple of Montcheuil during his prewar stint as chaplain to the JECF, when she served on its national steering committee. In his postwar report to his superiors, Chaillet praised Ribière as the "unflagging agent" of the rescue effort, who was called on to carry out the most dangerous operations on behalf of the clandestine spiritual resistance, thus earning the nickname "Joan of Arc."[97] Her story is a testament to the critical but often overlooked role that women played in the spiritual resistance.[98] During the infamous roundups of Jews in summer 1942, Ribière and Amitié chrétienne helped to spirit away over a hundred Jewish children bound for the German death camps. When the police intendant returned for the children two days later, Chaillet and his colleagues refused to hand them over and they were secretly dispersed to local families.[99] As a result of this episode, Chaillet was placed under house arrest at a psychiatric hospital in Privas. But he was nevertheless able to steal away to work on the November issue of *Témoignage chrétien,* which published the first major protests of the French bishops and Protestant leaders against the roundups.

In November 1942, the Germans invaded the Unoccupied Zone, dramatically intensifying the danger of these clandestine activities. Chaillet immediately went underground, but he was captured in a Gestapo raid on the Amitié chrétienne headquarters in January 1943. Fortunately, his captors did not recognize him and he was released the same day. The next day, Ribière managed to warn away those who arrived to pick up their false papers by disguising herself as the building's cleaning lady.[100] That same month, the Gestapo seized the forthcoming issue of *Témoignage chrétien* as it lay on the presses, although it would be reprinted and distributed that summer. The journal had already lost its primary distributor a year earlier when Cruvillier was arrested with forty-seven other members of the *Combat-Témoignage chrétien* network, although he managed to flee to Switzerland, where he served as an international go-between for the French resistance. By the end of 1943, de Lubac was forced to leave Fourvière and go into hiding. Fessard only narrowly eluded the Gestapo the following year, with the help of his friend René d'Ouince, who was imprisoned in Fessard's stead.[101]

Despite these setbacks, the print runs of *Témoignage chrétien* continued to grow, from 5,000 to 60,000 copies per issue, and after the German invasion of the southern zone, the journal established a second printing operation in Paris in April 1943. It was around this time that the *Courriers du Témoignage chrétien* were launched as a companion to the *Cahiers,* roughly tripling their circulation.[102] Under the leadership of André Mandouze—a layman and veteran of the fledgling left-Catholic journal *Sept*—the *Courriers* aimed to bring the message of the spiritual resistance to a wider readership. Not only did they have a larger print run, they were shorter, less abstract, and more attentive to the practical demands of spiritual resistance in a rapidly evolving political climate. The addition of the *Courriers* brought the message of *Témoignage chrétien* to a new audience, but it also set the stage for a bitter battle over the journal's postwar editorial line. By the end of the war, roughly 1,235,000 copies of the *Courriers* and 550,000 copies of the *Cahiers* had been printed.[103]

A Self-Effacing Politics

What should we make of the claim that the spiritual resistance to Nazism was an essentially apolitical project? Again and again, the Jesuits who led it reaffirmed that their resistance writings "are of a purely religious and theological nature" and "do not give any political orders."[104] And yet, the very claim to remain above politics was itself a political act, and a particularly powerful one in the context of the war. This was true at the most practical level, because it enabled these Jesuits to circumvent wartime censorship by encoding their critique of Nazism and the policies of Vichy in the apparently apolitical language of theology. But presenting their spiritual resistance in apolitical terms also enabled these priests to carve out a legitimate space for clerical intervention in public affairs. In the process, they articulated a rejoinder to those bishops and religious superiors who claimed that obedience to Vichy was a spiritual duty incumbent on all Catholics. By framing Nazism as a religious rather than a political threat, one that could only be fought with the "weapons of the spirit," these Jesuits instead presented resistance as the primary spiritual duty required of French Catholics.

This argument was the logical extension of these Jesuits' prewar vision of a Church that was in the world but not of it, engaged in the life of the City but refusing to collaborate with secular political ideologies. But their wartime writing also marked something of a departure, as they sought to downplay the language of incarnation in favor of the language of eschatology. In doing so, these Jesuits were no doubt reacting against the way Catholic supporters of Vichy mobilized the discourse of incarnation, which had been so central to interwar Catholic Action, in the service of the politics of presence. In response, they stressed the difference between a true incarnation of Christian principles and the institutional privileges accorded to the Church under Vichy. "There are Christians today who would like to save the *material* first," de Lubac warned. "But what is all that worth in the eyes of God if it is not the incarnation of the spirit of His Son? It is a long way, alas, from 'Crucifixes everywhere' on the walls of schools and courtrooms to 'Christ everywhere' in the hearts of real Christians."[105] These words were clearly directed against those, such as Doncoeur and Desbuquois, who looked to the state to reintroduce Christianity into the hearts and minds of the French people. In their haste to incarnate Christianity in the temporal order, de Lubac argued, these priests mistook the external trappings of piety for an authentic revival and undermined the very faith they sought to protect. Instead, the only way to make Christianity "present" in the here and now was precisely to look beyond the present. As Montcheuil put it, "the infinite viewpoint of the Kingdom of God" is not "a path to evasion, but rather a new dimension given to life and to duty."[106]

This turn to eschatology on the part of de Lubac, Fessard, and Montcheuil should not, therefore, be read as a disavowal of the commitment to Catholic engagement in public life that de Lubac and his friends had made during the first enthusiasms of Catholic Action. For it was precisely this commitment to eschatology that inspired them to enter the spiritual resistance to Nazism. Eschatology gave them a language with which to resist the totalizing pretensions of the political under Nazi ideology without having to rely on the notion of a private sphere in which religion would be protected from state overreach. Only one community could lay claim to totality, for these theologians, and that was the mystical body of Christ. Such a totalizing vision of the Church necessarily refused strong distinctions between the public and private spheres, and indeed, these priests blamed the rise of totalitarianism precisely on the privatization of religion in modern Europe. Christianity affected "all of life, social life as much as individual life," de Lubac insisted, and consequently, the battle in which these theologians found themselves engaged during the war "is purely about religion. But it is also about total religion."[107] While de Lubac and the other architects of the spiritual resistance drew a strong distinction between religion and politics, then, they actually used this distinction to expand rather than limit the public role of religion. In short, they used it to colonize the realm of the political.

To recognize what these priests were doing, however, it is necessary to dispense with a presumptively secular definition of the political, which takes the distinction between the spheres of religion and politics as a given. Rather than naturalizing this distinction, it is crucial to attend instead to the political work performed in the act of drawing it and the way it can be used to advance religious as well as secular projects. Doing so allows us to understand how appeals to ostensibly apolitical discourses served to underwrite the politics of *both* collaboration and resistance in wartime France, and to grasp the power of theological discourses that tend to be dismissed as politically inconsequential. Such discourses rarely fit neatly into secular political categories. De Lubac's memoirs confirm this, insisting that "it was not any tendency toward the right or the left which determined the action of men like Chaillet, Fessard, or Montcheuil."[108] As the following chapter will show, the architects of the spiritual resistance instead used theology to fashion a vision that was both antifascist and antiliberal.

CHAPTER FOUR

The Theoretical Foundations of the Spiritual Resistance

If *Témoignage chrétien* was the logical extension of the theological work that de Lubac and his friends had been doing since the 1920s and 1930s, the war also forced them to confront the inadequacies of some of the positions they had taken before the war. Montcheuil, for instance, expressed his concern that the personalist critique of liberalism and individualism risked driving some Catholics into the arms of fascism. "We cannot forget," he warned, "that totalitarianism as well as personalism is anti-individualist. Consequently, the critique of individualism ought not to be made in such a way that, seized with dizziness or panic, we would throw ourselves into totalitarianism as the only means to escape the misfortunes born of individualism." And yet, Montcheuil remained no less convinced that the critique of individualism was justified.[1] While he and his friends sought to revise those aspects of their theology that had lent themselves to political misappropriation, the experience of the war did not inspire them to embrace liberal values. Instead, they continued to stake out a position that was both anti-Nazi and antiliberal. They elaborated a critique of anti-Semitism without embracing religious pluralism; they defended the right of legitimate resistance without appealing to the principle of popular sovereignty; and they articulated a discourse of human rights that did not derive from the preeminent dignity of the individual. By delving deeper into the theological foundations of the spiritual resistance, this chapter shows how de Lubac's circle turned to theology to carve out an ideological space that was neither fascist nor liberal.

This chapter thus leaves behind the narrative focus of the previous chapter to move into a more analytic register. We have seen how theological commitments partly determined the political choices that Catholics made under the Occupation; this chapter instead explores how the events of the war reshaped Catholic theology itself. The resistance activities undertaken by de Lubac and his allies were consistent with their prewar theological commitments to Catholic personalism, anti-totalitarianism, and the mystical-body ecclesiology, but the war also forced them to clarify and refine these positions. The result was a number of innovations in ecclesiology, anthropology, and Catholic teaching on Judaism that would have a significant influence on postwar Catholicism and, eventually, the Second Vatican Council. The story of how they arrived at these positions reminds us that theology is not a rarefied activity undertaken far from the chaos of the City; it is shaped by the messy, unpredictable terrain of historical life. This contingent process of negotiation is what this chapter seeks to recover.

Totalitarianism and Political Religion

One might expect that the experience of the war and the Pétainist sympathies of the French hierarchy might have inspired de Lubac and his friends to reconsider their previous hostility toward liberalism. But as we have seen, these theologians did not perceive liberal democracy as the natural enemy of totalitarian ideologies and instead maintained that liberalism had created the very conditions for their rise. "One of the reasons for the success of totalitarianism," Montcheuil insisted, "was the kind of fragmentation and isolation into which an excessive liberalism and individualism had thrown humanity." Together, they had "deprived man of his need for communion and led him to seek out a distorted satisfaction for it in totalitarian movements."[2] Despite Montcheuil's concern that the critique of individualism might play into the hands of the fascists, he therefore insisted that Nazism could not be fought with the resources of liberal ideology. What was needed was an alternative form of community that could provide a bulwark against the excessive power of the state and satisfy the natural human yearning for community. He believed that the Church was uniquely qualified to serve this function, because it alone could offer an alternative system of value—one that avoided the excesses of liberal individualism without reducing the person to a cog in the collectivist machine.[3]

During the war, Montcheuil and his fellow Jesuits developed this theory of totalitarianism in greater detail, expanding in particular on the religious dimension of totalitarian ideology. De Lubac offered the most systematic account in a speech to Jeunesse ouvrière chrétienne (JOC) activists in spring 1942, which circulated clandestinely and would form the basis for his book *The Drama of Atheist Humanism*.[4] While he granted that Nazism and communism were fundamentally at odds, de Lubac insisted that they were nevertheless alike in the challenge they posed to Christianity. "At the base of their two constructions is a critique of religion," he argued, which "precedes all of the economic, social, and political critiques established by each."[5] And yet, de Lubac insisted, communism and Nazism do not so much negate religion as continue it by other means. What makes both these ideologies "complete, 'totalitarian' systems" is that "they present themselves as a complete conception of the world and of existence, and as a complete form of salvation. As such, they are therefore real 'religions,' albeit 'replacement religions.'"[6] De Lubac here made a crucial, early contribution to the discourse on "political religions" that is more often associated with the work of Eric Voegelin and Raymond Aron.

But de Lubac did not believe that Nazism and communism were equally dangerous to Christianity. Wary of the appeal that Nazi anticommunism held for some Catholics, he took pains to show that the frank atheism of communism was, in fact, less dangerous than Nazi neopaganism. Because National Socialism sought to co-opt Christianity from within rather than attacking it head-on, as communism did, he warned that Nazism risked lulling Christians into "a secret complicity."[7] The Jesuit here pinpointed what was peculiar (and in his view, peculiarly dangerous) about Nazi ideology—that it was at once anti-Christian and crypto-Christian. Historians have long debated whether Nazism constituted a "political religion" that sought to replace Christianity with its own neopagan cult of the *Volk,* or a "religious politics" that preserved and co-opted Christianity by "Aryanizing" it.[8] In fact, both of these elements coexisted somewhat uneasily within the ideological family of National Socialism, and for de Lubac, they were simply two complementary weapons in the service of the Reich's broader campaign against Christianity. The first, exemplified by the German Faith Movement, sought to take the place of Christianity, "replacing its God with a pagan God, its morality with a pagan morality, its sacraments with pagan sacraments."[9] The second instead brought about "the internal corruption of

Christianity through the invention of a 'Nordic Christianity.'"[10] Here, de Lubac took on the German Christians. By stripping Christianity of its Jewish inheritance, he argued that they had "emptied it of everything that constitutes its essence."[11] From de Lubac's perspective, the effects of neopaganism and the German Christian movement were therefore essentially the same: to destroy Christianity.

If anti-Christianity was the common denominator holding together the disparate factions within National Socialism, then Christianity was also the best weapon against it. By framing Nazism and communism as political religions, de Lubac asserted that the subversion of traditional religion, rather than the suppression of individual liberty or democratic governance, was the defining feature of totalitarianism. He thus replaced the opposition between liberalism and totalitarianism that informed so much of twentieth-century secular politics with an opposition between true religion and ersatz political religions. As we have seen, this claim served to justify the project of "spiritual resistance" in which de Lubac and his friends were engaged. For if Nazism was fundamentally a religious scourge, then it necessarily had to be fought with the "weapons of the spirit."

Sovereignty, Obedience, and Legitimate Resistance

The spiritual resistance was not just engaged in a battle against Nazism, however; it also had to contend with Vichy. Consequently, its intellectual leaders did not limit themselves to condemning totalitarianism, but sought to develop a broader critique of state sovereignty—one that placed clear limits on the Christian duty to obey the established temporal authority taught by St. Paul. In doing so, they took aim at the central principle invoked by the French bishops to secure Catholic obedience to Pétain and defended the Christian's right to resist an unjust or illegitimate regime. Charles Journet, for instance, recalled the teachings of Thomas Aquinas on the duty to resist a tyrant, while de Lubac reminded Christians that the duty to obey the established authority never trumped one's primary duty to God. French Catholics therefore possessed a "limited but *real right to judge, and sometime to resist.*"[12] Mgr. Bruno de Solages, rector of the Institut Catholique de Toulouse, echoed this sentiment, telling his students that "the sovereignty of the State is not absolute" and must be subordinated to the dictates of conscience.[13]

Starting in 1943, such arguments took on even greater urgency. In February of that year, the French State imposed the Service du travail obligatoire (STO), which drafted men between the ages of twenty and twenty-three to support the German war effort by working in German factories. This was a crucial turning point in Catholic support for Vichy. Cardinal Achille Liénart advised compliance but acknowledged that Catholics were not obligated in conscience to comply.[14] De Lubac went further, asserting that all Christians were bound by their faith and patriotic duty to *refuse* the draft and to help other draftees to escape.[15] At the same time, that year also saw a dramatic expansion of the Allied bombing campaign and attacks by the internal armed resistance, as many young men chose the *maquis* over deportation to Germany.[16] But as late as May 1944, months before the Liberation, the French bishops denounced the activities of the *maquisards* as "acts of terrorism."[17] *Témoignage chrétien* replied by devoting its next issue to defending the legitimacy of armed resistance. In it, Montcheuil appealed to Catholic just war theory, arguing that the war against Germany had not ended with the armistice and had not ceased to be a just war, since it was directed against Nazi aggression.[18] But he insisted that the use of force must be proportionate and could never justify reprisals or excessive violence.

The Occupation thus prompted Catholics to explore the question of what constitutes a legitimate political authority and the circumstances under which it might be justifiably overthrown. One of the most detailed and idiosyncratic meditations on this subject came from the pen of Gaston Fessard. Known as the "Slave-Prince Treatise," it was written at the behest of Cardinal Emmanuel Suhard in fall 1942 and circulated widely in the form of a six-page summary.[19] Fessard had actually first begun to explore these questions in the context of the Spanish Civil War, when the political valence of insurrection was rather different.[20] In his 1942 treatise, Fessard developed the Hegelian principles he had used to make sense of that conflict and brought them to bear on the problem of the legitimacy of the Vichy government.

Following Leo XIII, Fessard looked to the common good as the basic criterion of legitimacy in the temporal order and posited that it included three hierarchically ordered components: material survival, justice and law, and the higher values or vocation of a particular community. The defeat and armistice, Fessard argued, had split apart these elements of France's common good, forcing the country to choose between material survival and its higher ideals. The result was something akin to Hegel's master-slave dialectic, which had become a key concept for the French Hegelian revival since Alexandre Kojève made it the centerpiece of his celebrated lectures on the *Phenomenology of Spirit* in the 1930s—lectures that Fessard had attended religiously. According to this reading of Hegel, the origins of social life lie in a battle to the death between two consciousnesses seeking recognition. One combatant chooses survival and, in doing so, submits to the other's mastery and becomes his slave. This was what had happened, Fessard argued, when France chose survival over the values that had led it to war and surrendered to the Germans. The political regime that emerged from the armistice therefore could not lay claim to "the genuine legitimacy of a government of right" because it remained at least partially enslaved to the victor of the war.[21] Pétain was nothing but a "Slave-Prince," Fessard concluded, and "a half-free Head of State is owed only a half-obedience."[22] To the extent that Pétain secured the survival of the nation or worked to restore the other elements of the common good, he deserved obedience. But to the extent that he denied the higher values of the national or international common good (for instance, by serving the anti-Christian ideals of his German master), he could, and should, be resisted.

Fessard recognized that putting this "half-obedience" into practice was not as straightforward as it might seem, however, given that the German occupation had sundered the lower and higher elements of France's common good and set them against one another. Because the slave-prince had chosen slavery in order to secure the material survival of the country, he could not *also* defend its higher ideals, and it therefore fell to his people to fulfill this higher element of the common good. "The more the slave-prince is reduced to going down the path of 'collaboration,'" Fessard concluded, "the more his people must anchor themselves in an obstinate resistance."[23] The Jesuit thus affirmed that French citizens had a duty to "move, in all *security of conscience,* from resignation to a passive and active *resistance.*"[24] And yet, Fessard also stressed that this was an *exceptional* duty occasioned by the circumstances of the Occupation. Normally, it was the role of the head of state to mediate the common good for the members of the national body.

Fessard thus offered a Hegelian counter-reading of St. Paul that placed limits on the duty to obey the "established authority" and even endowed Catholics with a duty to resist when this authority was neither sovereign nor legitimate. But in making this claim, Fessard was certainly not endorsing the democratic principle of popular sovereignty. Like most Catholic philosophers at the time—even those, like Maritain, who had openly embraced democracy—Fessard remained highly suspicious of this principle.[25] Instead, he derived the right to resist from a higher duty to the common good, and not from the principle that political authority flows from the people. Once again, Catholic opposition to Vichy did not imply a corresponding embrace of liberal principles.

A Virile Christianity?

On matters of gender, the discourse of the spiritual resistance was similarly fraught with ambiguity, as it sought to resist both the masculinist language of fascism and the perceived feminization of religion. As with so many regimes of the far right, the French State made the family a key plank in its program of national regeneration. For Pétain, the causes of France's defeat at the hands of the Germans were simple: "too few children, too few weapons, too few allies."[26] Too many women had succumbed to the seduction of interwar liberalism, abdicating their childrearing responsibilities to work outside the home. To counteract this, Vichy offered financial incentives to stay-at-home mothers and large families, while severely restricting access to employment for married women. It even made abortion a capital offence.[27] Alongside such legal measures, the regime promoted a cult of motherhood rooted in Catholic ideals of feminine self-sacrifice and maternal devotion. According to Francine Muel-Dreyfus, this close affinity with the gender ideology of Vichy made the French Church as a whole complicit in shoring up the regime. The differences between Catholic Pétainists and those engaged in the spiritual resistance mattered little because "the crusade to return women to the home and to keep them there was unanimously accepted by the clergy," which "placed the Church in its entirety within the sphere of influence of the National Revolution."[28] Yet a closer examination of the gendered rhetoric of the spiritual resistance suggests a more complicated story.

To be sure, the martial rhetoric of the spiritual resistance was just as masculinist as its secular counterpart, betraying a profound anxiety about the possibility that Christianity had become "feminized." In part, this was a reaction to the humiliation of defeat. But it also drew on a much larger set of concerns about the perceived "feminization" of religion since the late eighteenth century.[29] These fears provoked much hand-wringing in even the most progressive Catholic circles. Catholic journals published roundtables on the question, "Has Christianity de-virilized man?," and calls for a "shock Christianity" capable of producing "virile souls" rose up from both the partisans of Vichy and the ranks of the resistance.[30] For the latter, the vision of a heroic, forceful Christianity offered an antidote to the Nazi critique of Christian meekness, as well as to the virtues of submission and obedience preached by Vichy.

And yet, such rhetoric risked reinforcing aspects of the very ideology that these Catholics sought to combat. After all, the German Christian movement also sought to restore the virility of Christianity, but believed that doing so meant stripping Christianity of the "feminine" qualities it had purportedly inherited from Judaism. De Lubac was acutely aware that resistance appeals to a "heroic Christianity" might unwittingly play into this discourse. He rebuked Catholics who complained that Christianity had become "effeminate," warning that critiques of "feminized" Christianity could all too easily "turn into critiques of Christianity itself" and ultimately reinforce the Nazi critique of Christianity as a "slave-morality."[31] Yves de Montcheuil agreed, reminding Catholics that, in their effort to undermine the critique of Christianity as "a school of weakness," they must not present it "as a purely human heroism."[32]

To counteract this danger, de Lubac and Montcheuil reappropriated the language of virility but tied it to precisely those "effeminate" qualities disavowed by the Nazis. Christian heroism "does not consist in speaking constantly of heroism and babbling about the virtues of strength," de Lubac chided. Instead, it rests on "kindness and goodness, gentleness toward the weak, pity—yes, pity—toward those who suffer . . . this is what Christian heroism will save."[33] Just as de Lubac invoked "the strength of charity," Montcheuil argued that "true love is not a weak man's feeling"; it is instead the very source of Christianity's power.[34] Comparing the saint to the hero, Montcheuil insisted that the saint is no less strong for knowing that his strength comes from a higher power. The saint "has all the virility and maturity of a man" despite being "a child before God," because "to lack humility, is to lack strength."[35] Such a "heroic Christianity" was evidently very far from the "virile Christianity" promoted by the German Christians. Instead, de Lubac and Montcheuil combined appeals to the masculine rhetoric of "spiritual combat" and the need to stand courageously against the enemies of Christianity, with appeals to the ostensibly "feminine" virtues of love, humility, and sacrifice execrated by the Nazis. Indeed, they framed these virtues as the very source of Christianity's strength. They thus inverted the gendered tropes of Nazi anti-Semitism by reappropriating its rhetoric of virility in the service of those values it deemed feminine, weak, and "Judaized."

We should therefore not be surprised to note, along with the prominent role that women such as Germaine Ribière and Marie-Rose Gineste played in the spiritual resistance, that fully one-third of the national committee of *Témoignage chrétien* militants and an even greater proportion of the Amitié chretiénne staff were women.[36] Though the movement's clerical leaders were very far from embracing the values of liberal feminism, it does not follow that their work simply reinforced repressive gender norms or that the women who participated in the movement in such great numbers were mere victims of ideology. As Saba Mahmood and Brenna Moore have shown, understanding the complex gender politics of religious worldviews requires moving beyond a model of agency which presumes that women are either victims of oppression or empowered agents, but not both.[37] The Catholic women and men of the spiritual resistance instead refused *both* the gender politics of fascism and the individualist premises of liberal feminism. For them, human agency was premised on submission to a higher power; freedom and obedience were necessarily intertwined.

The Mystery of Israel

No aspect of the spiritual resistance manifested this double refusal of both fascist and liberal ideology more acutely than the Catholic critique of anti-Semitism. Like most of the planks of the spiritual resistance, this critique did not emerge fully formed in the 1940s. Instead, it grew out of prewar theological efforts to chip away at the Church's traditional anti-Judaism—what Jules Isaac called "the teaching of contempt"—which held that the Jews were responsible for the death of Christ and cursed to suffer through the ages.[38] The war added new urgency to this effort because of the way religious anti-Judaism tended to reinforce the racist anti-Semitism of the far right.[39] This was certainly the case with Vichy, which presented itself as the inheritor of medieval Christian anti-Judaism, even as its laws defined Jews in racial terms. And Catholic theologians were not immune to this logic either. Georg Bichlmair and Joseph Eberle, for instance, conflated racist anti-Semitism with religious anti-Judaism, arguing that Jews continued to bear the stain of their forefathers' rejection of Christ like an original sin written into their genetic code—one that baptism was powerless to wash away.[40]

As John Connelly has shown, anti-Judaism was so deeply embedded in Catholic theology that even the most robust critics of anti-Semitism in the 1930s and 1940s remained in many ways bound by its assumptions.[41] The French Catholics who led the spiritual resistance, including the authors of *Témoignage chrétien,* were no exception. They were among the most progressive voices of their day on Catholic-Jewish relations and they helped lead the spiritual resistance against Vichy and Nazi anti-Semitism, often at great personal risk. But they did not do so out of a commitment to liberal values such as religious freedom and pluralism. For these theologians, anti-Semitism was a scandal because it constituted an attack on Christianity itself. Christianity was the fulfillment of the covenant that God had made with the Jews, and consequently, any attack on them was an attack on Christianity. In making this argument, these theologians sought to resist and correct some aspects of traditional anti-Judaism. But they had not yet fully shaken off its heritage. Their critique of anti-Semitism continued to rely on a basically supersessionist understanding of the relationship between Judaism and Christianity, according to which Christianity completed and superseded the Jewish covenant. Such a model did not ascribe an independent value to the Jewish tradition, considered apart from its relationship to Christianity. Instead, what grounded this critique of anti-Semitism was the prospect of the eventual conversion of the Jews. As with the other aspects of the spiritual resistance, then, this was at once an antifascist and an illiberal project—one that rejected anti-Semitism without embracing religious difference.

These tensions were in many ways the legacy of a distinctively French Catholic tradition of philosemitism, an early but equivocal effort to revise Catholic teaching on Judaism that was first developed by Charles Péguy and Léon Bloy around the time of the Dreyfus Affair. Bloy firmly rejected the virulent anti-Semitism that pervaded Catholic circles in these years and was one of the first Catholics to argue that the Jewish people continued to enjoy divine favor despite having rejected Christ. Rather than interpreting Jewish suffering throughout history as a punishment, he viewed it as a "sign of the permanence of the Holy Spirit upon these men who have been so scorned."[42] But in making this argument, Bloy also reinforced many of the most damaging tropes of anti-Judaism, including the notion that Jews were fated to suffer until the end of time.[43] Bloy's work would go on to exert a powerful influence on Jacques Maritain and his Jewish wife, Raïssa, whose shared conversion to Catholicism he oversaw. In 1937, with Jews across Europe facing increasingly violent assaults on their lives, property, and rights, Maritain issued his own con-demnation of anti-Semitism as a violation of the dignity of the human person.[44] But alongside strikingly liberal appeals to pluralism and religious freedom, Maritain also rehearsed many of the illiberal tenets of anti-Judaism he had inherited from his godfather, Bloy.[45] Turning to the role of the "mystery of Israel" in the history of salvation, Maritain argued that the Jews had chosen the world over Christ and that their "punishment is to be held captive by their choice"; to be "prisoners and victims of this world" without ever fully belonging to it.[46] Like Bloy, however, Maritain believed that this fate endowed the Jewish people with a positive role in advancing the history of salvation. Both he and Bloy thus exemplified the central tension between idealization and abjection at the heart of prewar Catholic philosemitism.

Leading up to the war, then, the French Catholic engagement with Ju-daism was marked by a powerful ambivalence. Especially compared to their counterparts in Germany and Poland, French Catholics were among the most progressive voices in Europe on this question.[47] But the tension between idealization and abjection within French philosemitism shows how deeply rooted was "the teaching of contempt." Only when the war brought the systematic persecution of the Jews to French soil would some French Catholics begin to reevaluate this teaching.

In October 1940, without any encouragement from the Germans, the French State issued the first of two Jewish Statutes. The law excluded Jews from public service employment and other "professions that influence people," and a second law the following June went even further in re-stricting their access to the professions and higher education.[48] At the same time as it issued the first law, the Vichy government endowed pre-fects with the power to intern "foreign" Jews, and by the end of the year roughly 60,000 people were interned in French camps. In addition, the French State began revoking the citizenship of some 15,000 naturalized French citizens, including 6,000 Jews.[49] In March 1941, Pétain created the General Commissariat on Jewish Questions and appointed the prom-inent Catholic Maurrassian, Xavier Vallat, to administer it.[50] The "Final Solution" reached France the following year. In July 1942, the occupying authority rounded up 13,000 Jews at the Vélodrome d'Hiver in Paris and deported them to the death camps of Central Europe. Vichy followed suit by handing over 10,000 Jews from its own territory, leading several bishops to break their long silence and issue public protestations in Au-gust 1942.[51] Despite this complicity in the worst crimes of the Third

Reich, however, Vichy anti-Semitism was far from simply a German import.[52] The Jewish policy of the French State drew on an indigenous mélange of Maurrassian anti-Semitism, Catholic anti-Judaism, and a more generalized xenophobia that privileged "French" over "foreign" Jews.

In their justification for the anti-Semitic legislation, Vichy lawmakers drew extensively on Catholic anti-Judaism and even sought to articulate their own theological rationale for the laws. In August 1941, two months after the second Jewish Statute, Pétain instructed his ambassador to the Vatican, Léon Bérard, to take the temperature of the Church hierarchy. A month later, Bérard reported back that "nothing ever told to me at the Vatican suggests, on the part of the Holy See, any criticism or disapprobation of the legislative acts and rules in question."[53] The ambassador did acknowledge the "irreducible" incompatibility between scientific racism and Church teaching on the unity of the human race, as Pius XI had affirmed in his 1937 encyclical *Mit brennender Sorge*. But Bérard sought to differentiate French anti-Semitism from the more extreme racism of the Third Reich, arguing that Church teaching was compatible with the first but not the second.

To add further theological weight to this claim, Bérard argued that a precedent for the Jewish Statutes could be found in the work of Thomas Aquinas himself:

> While proscribing all politics of oppression toward the Jews, St. Thomas nevertheless recommends taking suitable steps to limit their action in society and restrict their influence. It would be dishonorable to allow them, within a Christian state, to govern and therefore to submit Catholics to their authority. From this it follows that it is legitimate to deny them access to public service, and it is equally legitimate to admit them to universities and liberal professions only in a fixed proportion.[54]

Bérard here invoked the anti-Jewish practices of the medieval Church to legitimize the racist measures of a modern secular state. Moreover, to guard against the possibility of any future objections from the Church, the ambassador hedged his bets by deploying another weapon from the Thomist arsenal—the thesis-hypothesis distinction. Ironically, Leo XIII had used this distinction to justify a pragmatic acceptance of the democratic principle of religious freedom. But the Vichy ambassador deployed it to very different ends. Although the anti-Semitic laws might not correspond to the Catholic ideal on this question (the thesis), he argued that the Church would consent to them as a less than ideal "practical arrangement" (the hypothesis).[55] In this way, Vichy officials elaborated a Thomist political theology that lent sacred authority to the regime's racism. They were aided in this endeavor by Thomist partisans of the Action française, possibly including the Dominican Master General, Martin Stanislas Gillet, whom the Vatican nuncio suspected of supplying Bérard with the Thomist bona fides for his report.[56] In his memoir, de Lubac recalled that during the war he had encountered many such Maurrassians at his university library, where they mined the Thomist sources for "a little bouquet of texts capable, they thought, of bolstering Pétain and encouraging Vallat in their saving work."[57]

De Lubac himself was appalled by the way Vichy officials covered themselves in the mantle of medieval Catholicism to justify their anti-Semitic agenda. But rather than condemning the practices of the medieval Church, he sought to differentiate medieval anti-Judaism from modern anti-Semitism. The latter "could only germinate in a dechristianized milieu," de Lubac insisted, because racism was foreign to the medieval worldview.[58] While he recognized that medieval Jews were subject to civil restrictions and persecution at the hands of Christians, he claimed that neither of these things "have anything to do with the recent phenomenon of doctrinaire anti-Semitism," which "can never be anything but a more or less veiled form of anti-Christianity."[59] Charles Journet made a similar point in a text reproduced in the issue of *Témoignage chrétien* devoted to anti-Semitism. Journet denied that medieval anti-Judaism was racist since it extended the same civil status to Christian converts. But he also firmly rejected the possibility that this model could be resurrected in the twentieth century, as the Vichy regime sought to do. The medieval system of ghettos only made sense in the context of a sacral order that presupposed the temporal authority of the Church and tied citizenship to religious belonging. Such anti-Jewish measures, Journet insisted, could have no place in a secular regime like the French State.[60] Both Journet and de Lubac thus relied on a narrative of historical rupture that divorced medieval Catholic anti-Judaism from modern anti-Semitism. In doing so, they avoided attacking the Church's history of anti-Judaism head-on.

Nevertheless, the war did prompt greater theological reflection on the relationship between Judaism and Christianity.[61] Leading the charge against the anti-Semitic policies of Vichy and the occupying authorities were a group of biblical and patristics scholars based in Lyon, whose work drew attention to the Jewish sources of the Gospel and its relationship to the Hebrew Bible. In spite of the cloud of suspicion that had lingered over Catholic biblical scholarship since the Modernist Crisis at the turn of the century, a number of these theologians had begun to venture onto this controversial terrain once again in the 1920s and 1930s. They included Jules Monchanin and de Lubac's mentor, Victor Fontoynont, whose fascination with the Greek Fathers led him to delve further into the relationship between the Greek and Jewish sources of the Gospel. Under their influence, de Lubac developed a keen appreciation for the way the Hebrew scriptures anticipated and prefigured the Gospel. This was a key claim of his *Catholicism* (1938), which affirmed that the two Testaments "formed one body, and to rend this body by rejecting the Jewish books was no less a sacrilege than to rend the body of the Church by schism."[62] De Lubac's appointment at the Catholic University of Lyon in 1929 likewise brought him into contact with Abbé Joseph Chaine, who held the chair in Old Testament studies there, and with the Sulpician theologian Louis Richard. In 1940, they were joined by Joseph Bonsirven, a Jesuit who had fled the German invasion of Belgium and taken refuge at the scholasticate of Fourvière, where de Lubac and Fontoynont both lived. Bonsirven was perhaps the leading Catholic expert on Second Temple Judaism and the Jewish sources of the Christian tradition, which earned him the suspicion of his superiors.[63] Since 1927, he had also authored a regular column on contemporary Judaism in *Études*.

This group of theologians would author the first institutional Catholic protest (under the aegis of the Lyon Faculty of Theology) against the Vichy anti-Semitic laws. It was the brainchild of Joseph Chaine who, in the wake of the second Jewish Statute in June 1941 and the continuing silence of the French bishops, suggested to his colleagues at the university that they issue their own public protest. The ensuing declaration, which he coauthored with de Lubac, Bonsirven, and Richard, condemned the law as an exercise in collective scapegoating that bore all the markers of German influence. While they did not dispute the notion that there was a "Jewish question" to resolve, the authors dismissed the idea that Jews were in any way to blame for the country's misfortunes and condemned the anti-Semitic legislation as an affront to human dignity, Christian morality, and the French legal tradition. Above all, the theologians appealed to the special solidarity that bound Jews and Christians together as heirs to a common religious heritage:

> The Church cannot forget that the Israelites are the descendants of the people who were the object of *the divine election of which She is the culmination,* of the people from whom Christ, our Savior, the Virgin Mary and the apostles sprang; that they have in common with us the books of the Old Testament . . . [that], like them, we are sons of Abraham, the father of the believers, and that the blessing promised to his descendants is still upon them, *to call them to recognize in Jesus the Christ who was promised to them.*[64]

But this statement also revealed the limits of the Catholic critique of anti-Semitism. As the last line makes clear, such a critique remained bound to the logic of supersessionism, albeit a softened version that conceived of Christianity as completing but not abrogating the Jewish covenant. According to this logic, Christians bore a particular responsibility to protect their Jewish brothers and sisters from the depredations of anti-Semitism, not because of the independent value of the Jewish tradition, but because it had prepared the way for the coming of Christianity.

The "Chaine Declaration" would have been the first public protest by the French clergy against Vichy anti-Semitism, but the priests' colleagues and superiors feared that it might provoke the authorities to close the university and, in any case, would never get past the censor.[65] As a result, the document circulated clandestinely but never became the official cry of Catholic conscience its authors intended it to be. Undeterred, the four theologians found another means to publicize their position. Through the intercession of Charles Journet in 1942, they managed to publish a more expansive meditation on the theology behind the Chaine Declaration in Switzerland, whence it was smuggled into France. Bearing the title *Israel and the Christian Faith,* the volume expanded on the special relationship between Christianity and Judaism.

De Lubac's contribution was an essay the Vichy censor had blocked him from publishing in 1941. In it, the Jesuit expanded on his argument for the close bond between the Christian and Jewish traditions, which meant that anti-Semitism "can only be a more or less veiled form of anti-Christianity."[66] To do this, he appropriated the Nazis' own logic but turned it to very different ends. What the various ideological factions within National Socialism shared, de Lubac argued, was a Nietzschean contempt for the elements of the Christian tradition that they attributed to its Jewish roots. Some within the German Christian movement even sought to purge the Old Testament from the Christian canon in order to

"Aryanize" it.[67] But what would remain of the Christian faith, de Lubac asked, if these elements were torn from it? One could not attack the Jewish sources of the Christian tradition without destroying Christianity itself. The Jesuit thus embraced the Nazi claim that Christianity was "Judaized" through and through, but he reversed its normative valence. "These adversaries are often right," he asserted, "when they see in many points of [Christian] doctrine a contribution owed to Israel." This was the source of the very solidarity that Christians owed to Jews in the contemporary crisis, for "the defense of Christ would be incomplete if it did not extend to those who prepared his coming, and to the whole order of things which He himself proclaimed He had come not to abolish but to accomplish."[68]

Here, once again, we glimpse the limits of the wartime Catholic critique of anti-Semitism. On the one hand, de Lubac and his colleagues insisted that the coming of Christianity had not abrogated the Jewish covenant, which "places, between Israel and us Christians, a first bond of solidarity."[69] This marked an important departure from traditional anti-Judaism. But they also insisted on the need for the eventual conversion of the Jews, because Christ died "not only for his people, but to reunite all of the dispersed children of God in a single body."[70] Consequently, the authors argued that the only possible solution to the so-called Jewish question was the eventual incorporation of the Jewish people into the mystical body of Christ. Such sentiments are, of course, very far from a liberal, pluralist embrace of religious difference as a good in itself, and they are a testament to the deep roots of Christian anti-Judaism, which meant that even the most forceful Catholic critics of anti-Semitism in the 1940s found it difficult to fully break with the logic of supersessionism and conversion.

But the fact that de Lubac tended to project the prospect of Jewish conversion into an eschatological future was already an indication of the way in which Catholic theology was beginning to change, thanks in part to a renewed engagement with Paul's Letter to the Romans. This change was evident in a commentary on Romans 11 published by de Lubac's mentor, Victor Fontoynont, in 1941. Fontoynont firmly rejected the notion that God had repudiated the Jewish people, even though he shared de Lubac and his colleagues' conviction that divine favor remained contingent on the "final conversion of Israel." But Fontoynont made clear that this development was to be understood in eschatological terms, as something that would happen only at the end of time, thereby shifting the focus away from efforts to convert Jews in the present. Articulating a view later endorsed by the Second Vatican Council, Fontoynont argued that the Jews' refusal to recognize Christ had not invalidated their covenant with God because "the gifts of God are irrevocable."[71] In fact, this very refusal was what had allowed the Gentiles to enter into the divine covenant. If the "apostasy" of the Jews "was fecund for the salvation of the world," he reasoned, "how much more will it be so, the day that they return to us with the 'plenitude' of Christianity?"[72] The Jewish people thus possessed a privileged role in the history of salvation—one that should inspire respect rather than contempt:

> Israel's place awaits it, and it is superior to our own. It possesses rights that we do not have, and our own rights come to us from it. Paul uses the image of the transplant, reversing it to adapt it to his subject, because here it is the trunk that gives its superiority to the branches that are grafted onto it. This trunk of the cultivated olive tree is the Israel of the promise, the Israel of the Patriarchs. The Jews are its natural branches. We, stock of the wild tree, we have taken their place on the trunk of the olive tree. One day they will take this place back, the first place. We must not forget it and treat them as if they were damned.[73]

Writing in the wake of Vichy's anti-Semitic legislation, Fontoynont was explicit about the contemporary relevance of Paul's teaching. It was a reminder to Christians to treat their Jewish neighbors with respect, for as St. Bernard had warned, "if you mistreat them, you risk wounding the Lord in the apple of his eye."[74]

Fontoynont's exegesis is indicative of the kind of soul-searching that the war inspired among Catholic theologians. It was likewise evident in a brief text by Louis Richard that circulated clandestinely in 1942, in which the Sulpician theologian rejected the notion that the Jews were solely responsible for the death of Christ.[75] Such texts echoed work being done by a few German-speaking theologians and partially anticipated the much more sweeping revision of Catholic teaching on Judaism at Vatican II.[76] But such sentiments were still rare in the 1940s, and it was not until the 1960s that they would become the official teaching of the Church.

Human Rights and Christian Rights

Though the theologians associated with the spiritual resistance mounted a vigorous campaign against Vichy and Nazi anti-Semitism, it should be clear by now that they did not do so out of a commitment to liberal values such as religious freedom, pluralism, and human rights. This does not mean that they did not invoke human rights in their critique of anti-Semitism; they certainly did. But they understood these rights in ways that were at odds with a liberal account of human rights. In fact, the war witnessed the first flowering of a distinctively Catholic human rights theory—one that, as Samuel Moyn and Marco Duranti have shown, would have a significant impact on postwar human rights projects like the Universal Declaration of Human Rights and the European Convention on Human Rights.[77] French Catholics played a formative role in the development of this Catholic rights theory. Two of its earliest elaborations were published in 1942—one by Jacques Maritain from exile in the United States and one by *Témoignage chrétien*. Both presented the Church as the preeminent defender of a universal human dignity imperiled by the racist and totalitarian ideology of the Nazis, while also distancing themselves from the liberal rights tradition inherited from the eighteenth century. This has led historians such as Moyn and Duranti to label Christian human rights a fundamentally conservative, right-wing project.[78] Yet categories such as "right" and "left" or "liberal" and "conservative" fail to adequately capture the human rights vision developed by French Catholics during the war. Conceived as a moral and spiritual project first and foremost, it eluded the logic of secular political taxonomies.[79]

Maritain articulated his theory of human rights in an essay titled *The Rights of Man and Natural Law,* which he soon followed with an essay on the Christian foundations of democracy. Together, these two works signaled that the philosopher's political evolution from Maurrassian to defender of democracy and human rights was complete. But Maritain did not simply accept the rights model inherited from the French Revolution and Enlightenment philosophy. The problem with this model, he argued, was that it was based on the subjective will of the individual. It therefore lacked an objective metaphysical foundation, a sense of the correlative duties that go along with individual rights, and an account of social rights such as the rights of workers. In his contribution to a 1947 UNESCO report on the philosophical grounds for human rights, Maritain therefore insisted on the need to complement "the declarations of the eighteenth century by a statement of the rights of man, not only as a human and a civic personality, but also as a social personality."[80] This was reflected in his 1942 essay, which balanced the traditional liberal emphasis on civil and political rights with an attention to "the social rights of the working person," including the right to a fair wage, unemployment benefits, and the right to unionize.[81]

In order to counteract the subjectivism of liberal rights theory, Maritain developed an alternative account of human rights that was grounded in the Thomist natural law tradition. He argued that such rights necessarily follow from the natural law that God has inscribed on every human heart, which is intelligible to all human beings by virtue of their humanity. Natural law decrees that humans are ordered to certain ends by virtue of their very nature as human beings. Consequently, Maritain reasoned, they must have a right to the things that are necessary to fulfill the ends prescribed by their nature, including life, liberty, work, and the freedom to worship. Natural law was central to Maritain's account because it allowed him to circumvent the limitations he perceived in liberal rights theory—that it lacked an objective foundation beyond human will. "It is because we are enmeshed in the universal order, in the laws and regulations of the cosmos," he explained, "that we possess rights before other men."[82]

By grounding human rights in natural law, of which God was ultimately the author, Maritain avoided the risk of relativism. But because natural law was also, in theory, intelligible to humans without the aid of revelation, non-Christians could apprehend it and appreciate its binding force as well. This was crucial because, as Maritain had argued in *Integral Humanism,* Christianity could no longer serve as the foundation for political life in a modern world characterized by a plurality of religious commitments. Maritain believed that human rights could provide the shared moral framework for a pluralist society instead, precisely because they were accessible to all human beings by virtue of the natural law inscribed on the human heart. And this meant that Christians and non-Christians could agree on which rights should be protected and work together to implement them, even if they disagreed quite radically on the source and justification for these rights. This was the logic that would underwrite Maritain's involvement in nonconfessional projects such as the UNESCO report on the philosophical bases for human rights, which was prepared in the lead-up to the Universal Declaration on Human Rights in 1948.[83]

At the same time that Maritain was formulating his rights model, Pierre Chaillet and Henri de Lubac were developing their own, quite different account of human rights in the pages of *Témoignage chrétien*—one that presented an even more formidable challenge to liberal rights theory.

This challenge was implicit in the very title they chose for the fifth issue of the publication: "The Rights of Man and Christian," which was a clear reference to the 1789 "Declaration of the Rights of Man and Citizen." In striking contrast to Maritain's pluralist approach rooted in natural law, the authors of *Témoignage chrétien* identified human rights with Christian rights. As Chaillet later explained, "In the clandestine struggle of countries subjected to the oppression of the Hitlerian order, we knew that the rights of man and Christian, indissolubly bound together, were jointly exposed to the same oppression, the same denial" and therefore had to be "united together in the same defense and the same protest."[84] De Lubac went even further, arguing that the very distinction between man and Christian was "no doubt arbitrary":

> The Christian is man re-created, re-established in Christ, and nothing that is human can be foreign to him. Everything that affects man, everything that wounds his honor, his dignity, his reason, his sense of justice, affects and wounds the Christian at the same time. One can even say it affects the Christian first of all, because Christianity is not a layer of varnish applied to the surface of man; it is the heart of his heart and the soul of his soul, such that it would be easier for him to give up being a man than to give up being a Christian.[85]

This was a remarkable assertion of the identity between man and Christian, but what is most striking is that it was actually being deployed in this instance to defend the rights of Jews.

Strange as it may seem, this argument followed from the mystical-body ecclesiology that had become such a central resource in the spiritual resistance to fascism. If the Declaration of the Rights of Man and Citizen yoked human rights to citizenship in the nation-state, the authors of *Témoignage chrétien* instead derived these rights from membership in Christ's mystical body. But from their perspective, the mystical body included not just the existing membership of the Church, but future members of Christ's body as well. This meant that all human beings were *potential* Christians and should be treated as such. The notion that the rights of the human person derive from a collective and ecclesial source was in evidence throughout *Témoignage chrétien*. "The Church cannot be unconcerned with the fate of man wherever his inviolable rights are unjustly harmed," the authors proclaimed, because "when one member suffers, the whole body suffers with him."[86] Such a vision was of course very far from the liberal account, which grounded human rights in the nature and dignity of the individual. Yet the Jesuits' approach should also be distinguished from the much more illiberal rights model articulated by some Eastern European Catholics at the time, which limited these rights to practicing Christians.[87] In identifying Christian rights with human rights, de Lubac and Chaillet were not suggesting that *only* Christians have rights. Instead, they maintained that all human beings are endowed with dignity because all are called to be members of the body of Christ. And this call is written into the very structure of human nature itself, as de Lubac would explain in greater detail in his controversial *Surnaturel* (1946). The architects of *Témoignage chrétien* did not react to the fascist assault on human dignity by embracing the tradition of the rights of man, then, but rather by articulating their own distinctively Christian human rights model.

Biopolitics and the Body of Christ

As the story of this fledgling Catholic rights discourse indicates, the theologians behind *Témoignage chrétien* continued to turn to the vision of the Church as the mystical body of Christ to underwrite their resistance to Vichy and Nazi ideology. They looked to it to anchor their account of human rights and the unity of the human race against the depredations of anti-Semitism. As de Lubac had argued in *Catholicism,* "the unity of the mystical Body of Christ . . . presupposes a prior natural unity, the unity of the human race."[88] In addition, the transnational solidarity of the mystical body provided a bulwark against the overweening power of totalitarian states. For all these reasons, the Jesuits found in the mystical-body ecclesiology a powerful resource for their work of spiritual resistance. Yet not all Catholic theologians drew the same political lesson from this ecclesiology. The war therefore forced de Lubac's circle to confront the limits of the mystical-body theology and refine their vision of the Church. This experience did not, however, induce them to retreat from the collectivist premises of their prewar ecclesiology. Instead, they sought to forestall any political misappropriation of Catholic ecclesiology by anchoring it more firmly in the central mystery of the Eucharist. This Eucharistic ecclesiology would eventually be taken up by the Second Vatican Council in the 1960s. But in the context in which de Lubac first articulated it, in the midst of war, it also served as a theological answer to fascist biopolitics. For de Lubac and his friends, it seems, the body of Christ was the best weapon against the divinization of the ethnonational body.

Political theology functioned differently in different contexts, and it was in Germany that the pitfalls of the mystical-body ecclesiology were most apparent. Here, it was susceptible to a particularly virulent political appropriation as it dovetailed with the Reich's vitalist discourse of blood, race, and *Volk*.[89] Some German theologians, particularly those steeped in the interwar liturgical movement, found it difficult to disentangle the communal aspirations of the Church from those of the Reich. A case in point is the Tübingen theologian Karl Adam, who was an early proponent of the mystical-body ecclesiology. In *The Spirit of Catholicism* (1924), Adam had stressed the unity and universality of the mystical body of Christ but also recognized that "the Body of Christ, if it be a true body, must have members and organs," and is therefore "of its nature differentiated."[90] He would take this principle much further in a 1933 essay on "German Nationality and Catholic Christianity," in which he welcomed Hitler as the savior of the national body. Although Adam did not deny the catholicity of the Church, he argued that one necessarily enters it through the particularity of an ethnonational community—one he identified with "blood purity." The Church is "the true mother of all national-racial identity," he argued, and it thrives when it "carefully observes the blood-given determinations of a race or people." Church and *Volk* were thus "organically linked" for Adam, who insisted that "they belong together as the natural and supernatural orders."[91] The corporeal metaphors of *völkisch* ideology and the mystical-body theology fused in his thinking, and by figuring the body of Christ organologically, Adam sought to square the tension between Catholic universalism and ethnonational particularity. He was not alone in drawing such a connection between the mystical-body theology and the racial politics of the Third Reich, although as Robert Krieg has shown, this ecclesiology could also be deployed *against* Nazi ideology, as it was by Romano Guardini and Engelbert Krebs.[92]

Such thinking was a cause for concern among the theologians associated with the *nouvelle théologie*. Louis Bouyer, for example, worried that the mystical-body ecclesiology lent itself all too readily to a secular political appropriation. Just as the interwar Catholic Action movement had interpreted this theology as a call to incarnate Catholic values in the temporal order, Bouyer suggested that the same logic had led Catholics to embrace the "politics of presence" and the need to work within the structures of the National Revolution. The danger with this language of incarnation was that it opened the way for secular bodies like the state to appropriate the sacral authority of the mystical body for their own ends. "Given all this," Bouyer demanded, "why would the State, the totalitarian State . . . not lay claim to the supreme benefits of this universal divinization of the purely human?"[93] We should not be surprised, he concluded, that "during the first wave of totalitarianism, so many non-mediocre young Christians, even so many directors of Catholic Action, were able to pass so easily from Christ to the new idols."[94] For Bouyer, the solution was to reaffirm the visible structures of the Church hierarchy, which he thought the mystical-body theology had undermined. The pope took a similar approach in his 1943 encyclical *Mystici Corporis Christi,* which embraced the mystical-body ecclesiology while anchoring it firmly in the principle of ecclesiastical hierarchy.[95]

Henri de Lubac took a different approach. While he too acknowledged the political dangers of the mystical-body theology, his solution was to ground it more firmly in the mystery of the Eucharist in order to offset the possibility that it might be deployed in the service of a secular political project. De Lubac laid out his Eucharistic ecclesiology in *Corpus Mysticum* (1944), which was based on lectures he had given just before the war. He began by pointing out that neither St. Paul nor the Church Fathers had ever used the term "mystical body." Instead, they referred to the Church simply as the "body of Christ" and stressed the inextricable relationship between the ecclesial body of Christ (the Church) and the sacramental body of Christ (the Eucharist). Far from just an individual communion with the divine, the Fathers understood the sacrament as a communal act, through which the faithful are incorporated with each other in and through their incorporation in Christ. "Quite literally," they believed, "the Eucharist *makes* the Church. . . . Through its hidden power, the members of the body achieve unity among themselves by becoming more fully members of Christ."[96] When the term "mystical body" was initially used in the ninth century, de Lubac explained, it actually designated the *Eucharist* rather than the Church. But over the course of the next few centuries, this term was progressively transferred from the Eucharist to the Church, as theologians sought to emphasize the "real presence" of Christ in the Eucharist to counteract the Berengarian heresy, and the two bodies were disarticulated. By the twelfth century, the Eucharist became known as the "real" body of Christ, in contrast to the "mystical body," which now designated the Church.

From de Lubac's perspective, this transformation had at least two negative effects. First, it tended to individualize Eucharistic piety and dilute ecclesial solidarity by disarticulating the celebration of the Eucharist from the edification of the ecclesial community. Second, conceiving of the Church as a "mystical body" also made possible an analogy between the Church and secular political bodies that left the Church vulnerable to the forces of secularization. To show this, de Lubac pointed to the fourteenth-century papal bull *Unam Sanctam,* which mobilized the concept of the mystical body in a bid to expand the pope's authority over temporal affairs. While it was meant to expand the Church's power, de Lubac argued that this move instead had the effect of reducing the Church to a juridical body akin to the state. As a result, the "mystical body would now be conceived . . . in terms of an analogy with human societies."[97] The effect of this slippage from mystical body to juridical body was that the emerging European nation-states would henceforth appropriate the term "mystical body" to hallow their own institutions, as the historian Ernst Kantorowicz would demonstrate in greater detail in *The King's Two Bodies,* a book heavily indebted to de Lubac.[98] In this way, *Unam Sanctam* opened the door to a secular political appropriation of the mystical-body concept and the Church became an unwitting agent in the secularization of European life.

Writing at the height of the war, de Lubac was keenly aware that the political dangers of the mystical-body theology were not limited to the medieval past. He made this clear in the conclusion to *Corpus Mysticum.* In light of "the tragic needs of our time," he warned, it was all the more important to anchor the Church firmly in the mystery of the Eucharist. Otherwise, "the very strength of the communal aspirations which can be felt everywhere throughout the Church today, and which are driving the liturgical movement in particular, cannot be without peril. Here or there, they could degenerate into a naturalist impulse."[99] Like Bouyer, de Lubac was concerned that Catholics would identify the communal aspirations so central to the mystical-body theology with the goals of collectivist political projects or earthly communities such as the nation. He had already made this point in a 1942 volume edited by the Catholic corporatist and Vichy functionary François Perroux, sensing perhaps that Catholic Pétainists were especially vulnerable to this risk.[100] But it was not just Catholics that de Lubac was worried about. Because he viewed Nazism and communism as "political religions" modeled on Christianity, he was also wary of the way such ideologies could appropriate theological concepts for their own ends. Indeed, in his resistance writings he argued that "the idea of the Reich itself is conceived after the fashion of the idea of the mystical Body in Christianity."[101] *Corpus Mysticum* in a sense expanded on this critique by situating Nazi political theology in a longer genealogy of secular political appropriations of the mystical body that extended all the way back to the fourteenth century.

De Lubac's efforts to revive the Eucharistic ecclesiology of the Church Fathers should therefore be viewed as an extension of his wartime resistance work. His sacramental vision of the Church might well seem like a retreat from politics, but for de Lubac, this was precisely the point. It disrupted the logic of political theology—the mobilization of theological concepts for secular political ends. Such a logic presupposed an analogy between theology and the political, but by reviving the Eucharistic ecclesiology of the Church Fathers, the Jesuit reminded Catholics that the Church was a body with no secular analogue. It was not *a* mystical body, but rather *the* body of Christ continuously enacted in and through the Eucharist, which distinguished it from any other collective body. Eucharistic ecclesiology thus furnished de Lubac with a means to salvage the communal focus of the mystical-body theology while (he hoped) making it less susceptible to political misappropriation. "Everywhere, men are searching for a communal doctrine, a communal spirituality," he explained in 1942. "By preaching with insistence the meaning and purpose of the Eucharistic mystery, we are combatting in a direct and effective manner one of the principal errors of the present day."[102]

If Catholics had lost sight of the true significance of the Eucharist, de Lubac believed, it was because they had an impoverished understanding of "presence." The Church Fathers had understood the presence of Christ in the Eucharist in eschatological terms. The role of the sacrament was to recall the sacrifice of Christ on the cross as well as to anticipate his coming at the end of time, and to make both these times present in the here and now. But the Jesuit lamented that this dynamic vision had progressively given way to a much more static and spatial understanding of presence thanks to the emphasis on sacramental realism since the eleventh century. Yves de Montcheuil shared this suspicion of the spatial logic that was implicit in the concept of "real presence," which applied categories derived from the world of natural bodies to a body that was not of this world.[103] Both Jesuits drew a connection between this faulty theological understanding of "presence" and the "politics of presence" embraced by Vichy's Catholic supporters, who believed that physical presence within the structures of the National Revolution was equivalent to making Christianity "present" in the temporal order. In fact, they insisted, the only way to achieve this goal was by "bearing witness" (*té-moignage*) to our common destiny in a body that is not of this world but is sacramentally present in the Eucharist. As Fessard explained in a wartime sermon, the Eucharist "makes us contemporary to this salvation history, and, by making us relive it, teaches us at the same time to play in the very midst of our own profane history the role that will permit us to orient it to its destiny, to the Presence of God."[104] Fessard and his fellow Jesuits thus looked to the Eucharist to ground a competing politics of presence. In place of a spatial model derived from the secular world of natural bodies and nation-states, they articulated a temporal model shot through with eschatological time—one that they hoped would permit them to be present to their political moment without compromising the transcendence of their faith.

Rather than retreating from the political, these theologians thus looked to the Eucharist as the basis for a counter-politics capable of resisting the overweening power of the state. At the heart of both Vichy and Nazi ideology was a biopolitical fantasy to create a "pure" national body through natalist policies, experiments in eugenics, and racial purity laws. To counteract the biopolitical deployment of human life under fascism, theologians such as de Lubac, Fessard, and Montcheuil looked to the body of Christ to anchor a competing order of bodies. Such a battle could not be fought with the resources of liberal ideology, they argued, because totalitarianism was itself a historical outgrowth of liberalism, which had forced the Church out of the public sphere and left individuals naked before the state. Anticipating more recent reflections on biopolitics by Giorgio Agamben and William Cavanaugh, these theologians thus perceived a hidden kinship between liberalism and totalitarianism.[105] Against the individualism of the former and the biopolitical violence of the latter, they anchored their resistance in the alternative community formed by the Eucharist. As Cavanaugh explains, in his contemporary rendition of this theology, the only way to resist "the fragmenting discipline" of the state is to incorporate people into a "counter-body"—the body of Christ formed by the celebration of the Eucharist.[106] And yet, as with the model of human rights advanced by de Lubac's circle, it is difficult to see where non-Christians fit into such a vision. Even as theologians like de Lubac sought to correct the limitations of the mystical-body theology, they continued to cling to an ecclesiology that effectively conflated human and Christian, the body of Christ and the human race.

Toward the Liberation

Central to the resistance theology articulated by Montcheuil, de Lubac, Chaillet, and Fessard, then, was a double refusal of both liberalism and totalitarianism. Instead, they turned to the resources of their theological tradition—ecclesiology, scripture, and Eucharistic theology—to respond to Vichy and Nazi ideology. But would the counter-political vision that they had forged under the Occupation remain effective once these conditions were lifted? This was the key question these theologians faced by 1944, when the tide of the war had definitively turned and they began to consider what should come after the Liberation.

At this point, the first visible fractures began to emerge within the united front of the spiritual resistance, and they did so at the heart of *Témoignage chrétien* itself. In spring 1943, the journal's Jesuit creators had launched the *Courriers du Témoignage chrétien,* a shorter and more accessible companion to the *Cahiers,* which was overseen by a largely lay editorial staff led by André Mandouze. Given his leftist commitments, there were some fears that the new publication might compromise the apolitical stance of the movement. But as long as Nazism remained the most immediate threat, Mandouze's priorities and those of the Jesuit editors of the *Cahiers* were very much aligned. As we have seen, these Jesuits did not apply the logic of totalitarianism symmetrically during the war, largely because they did not wish to supply ammunition to collaborationists who used anticommunism to rally Catholics to their cause. In one of the last texts he published before he was executed, which appeared in the November 1943 *Courrier,* Montcheuil welcomed the fact that Christians and communists were united in the struggle to liberate the nation from the Nazi yoke. Despite the irreducible opposition between Catholicism and communism at the level of doctrine, Montcheuil acknowledged "all that is just, human, and expansive in the aspirations to which communism seeks to respond."[107] Praising its concern for social justice, he presented communism "less as something to destroy than as something to save from itself."[108] Such statements harmonized with Mandouze's desire to orient the *Courriers* to a working-class audience and show that "the Church is not an ally of a certain bourgeois class."[109]

By 1944, though, with the Liberation close at hand, Nazism no longer seemed like the greatest threat facing France and the editorial team at *Témoignage chrétien* lost the common enemy that had held together these disparate voices. Even before Allied troops landed at Normandy, de Lubac, Chaillet, Montcheuil, and Germaine Ribière expressed concerns that Mandouze was dragging the *Courriers* onto political terrain that lay beyond its purview as an organ of the spiritual resistance. If the lay and clerical members of the team had agreed on the wartime mission to resist Nazism with the "weapons of the spirit," they could not agree on how to extend this mission into the postwar period. Its Jesuit founders conceived the task of *Témoignage chrétien* primarily as a negative and critical one, in keeping with their belief that the role of priests was to denounce political ideologies that violated the principles of Catholic faith without advocating for a positive political program. But their lay counterparts at the *Courriers* were of a different mind. They believed that the logical next step for the antifascist journal was to play a leading role in the emerging Catholic left.[110] The philosopher Jean Lacroix, who joined the team in 1944, explained the journal's postwar predicament thus:

> The occupation was a time when bearing witness [*témoignage*] and politics were identical . . . to resist meant, above all, to bear witness. For four years, we lived in what might be called an infra-political stage, since all politics presupposes a minimum of sovereignty. It was therefore a question, not of pursuing a particular politics, but of recovering the very conditions of possibility for politics. . . . As strong as [*Témoignage Chrétien*'s] position was during the occupation, it was correspondingly difficult after the Liberation.[111]

In other words, it was precisely the limits on political action under the Occupation that made the counter-political approach of the Jesuits so powerful during the war. The question was whether it would remain relevant after these limits had been lifted.

At issue was a difference of opinion over the appropriate scope of Catholic political engagement, but also a disagreement about which political force constituted the gravest threat to Christian values now that Nazism had been defeated. Fessard immediately turned his sights on the Communist Party, which was then enjoying an enormous boost in popularity thanks to its role in the resistance. Rebranding itself as the "Party of the 75,000 martyrs" (a reference to the many communists shot by the Gestapo), the Parti communiste français (PCF) had even made inroads among Catholics. In the spring of 1945, Fessard reminded his readers that French communists had been quick to sacrifice the interests of the *patrie* to those of the Party when they fell into line behind the Nazi-Soviet pact in 1939. If, by "a happy coincidence," the interests of Party and *patrie* had coincided since 1941, he warned that this loyalty might well be short-lived and that the Party's policies could one day lead France "back into a slave-prince state," this time under orders from Moscow.[112] Fessard expanded on these reflections in *France, Take Care Not to Lose Your Freedom,* the anticommunist follow-up to his essay, "France, Take Care Not to Lose Your Soul," which had launched the spiritual resistance to Nazism. When Fessard offered the manuscript to *Témoignage chrétien,* it provoked a bitter quarrel within the editorial team that would eventually lead Chaillet to abandon the publication he had founded. Mandouze and the lay editors at *Témoignage chrétien* would henceforth take the journal in a very different direction, enlisting it in the service of the postwar experiments of the Catholic left. The Jesuits who had led the struggle against Nazism did not simply abandon the public sphere with the end of the war, though, for the Liberation brought them new political and theological battles to fight. With Nazism defeated, they turned their sights on communism and launched themselves into the great postwar struggle among Marxists, Catholics, and existentialists for the mantle of humanism.

PART THREE

RENEWAL

(1945–1965)

CHAPTER FIVE

The Postwar Catholic Engagement with the Left

On Christmas Day 1943, Henri de Lubac put the finishing touches on one of his most popular books. Written at the height of the German occupation, *The Drama of Atheist Humanism* recapitulated the totalitarianism theory that the Jesuit had developed in his resistance writings. As if to acknowledge the characteristically French roots of Vichy ideology, de Lubac joined his critique of Nazism and communism to a critique of the positivist tradition that was central to the far-right ideology of Charles Maurras. The book was thus an attack on what the Jesuit perceived to be the three most dangerous political ideologies of his day: Nazism, communism, and the Action française (AF). But because he was writing under the strict censorship of the occupation, de Lubac was obliged to encode his political critique as a religious and philosophical one. To do this, he adopted a genealogical approach, tracing the political ideologies that he opposed back to their philosophical roots in the work of, respectively, Friedrich Nietzsche, Ludwig Feuerbach, and Auguste Comte. By charting a path from these pioneers of atheist humanism to the authoritarian ideologies of his own day, the Jesuit sought to demonstrate how the philosophical effort to emancipate man from God in the nineteenth century had paved the way for new extremes of violence and inhumanity in the twentieth. "It is not true . . . that man cannot organize the world without God," he concluded, but "without God, he can ultimately only organize it against man. Exclusive humanism is an inhuman humanism."[1]

Although de Lubac had written these lines with the German occupation in mind, his emphasis on the humanism question allowed the book to transcend the immediate context of the war, for the Liberation inaugurated a veritable cultural obsession with humanism.[2] "Nowadays, everybody is a humanist," quipped the writer Pierre Naville in 1945, and he was not far from the truth.[3] The end of the war brought an urgent need to unite the various ideological families of postwar France in the service of national reconstruction, and the language of humanism proved sufficiently capacious to perform this task. It provided the ideological cement for a coalition between the newly created Christian Democratic party (Mouvement républicain populaire), the Socialists (SFIO), and the Communist Party (PCF)—a coalition known as *tripartisme,* which governed the country from 1945 to 1947. Each of these constituencies rushed to stake their claim to the mantle of humanism. Communist intellectuals such as Henri Lefebvre and Roger Garaudy looked to Marx's early writings on alienation to elaborate a Marxist humanism.[4] Not to be outdone, Catholics asserted their own claim to the humanist tradition, led by an emerging Catholic left and Christian Democrats eager to exorcise the specter of wartime collaboration and reinvent the Church as the guardian of democracy and human rights.

But the language of humanism was not just a unifying framework. It quickly became a stick with which to beat one's ideological opponents, especially after the Cold War ramped up and *tripartisme* fell apart. This was clear from the dominant intellectual debates of the period, which pitted Marxists, Catholics, and existentialists against one another, each claiming to be the authentic inheritor of the humanist tradition. Thus, when Jean-Paul Sartre announced in October 1945 that existentialism was a humanism, he was responding to Catholic and Marxist critics who claimed just the opposite.[5] And while Catholics like de Lubac argued that atheist humanism was a contradiction in terms, the communist Pierre Hervé quipped that the very idea of Catholic humanism was "as contradictory as atheist Catholicism."[6] This was not, however, a battle in which Marxists, Catholics, and existentialists confronted each other as unified blocs. In fact, the shared vocabulary of humanism concealed rifts within each of these camps, divisions that come into focus when we approach the intellectual debates of this period, not just through the categories of secular politics and philosophy, as historians have tended to do, but also through the lens of theology.

No one expressed these divisions more clearly than de Lubac's disciple and fellow Jesuit, Jean Daniélou. Appointed to the Chair of the History of Christian Origins at the Institut Catholique de Paris in 1943, Daniélou also had close ties to secular philosophical milieus thanks to his studies at the Sorbonne. In a 1945 essay for *Études,* he mapped out the primary coordinates of postwar French thought. Though he identified Marxism, existentialism, and Catholicism as the three main intellectual "families," Daniélou also argued that each of these groups was internally divided between a "materialist" and a "spiritualist" pole. In other words, he posited that the primary fault line in French thought was a metaphysical one, pitting Marxist humanists against "vulgar materialists" and atheist existentialists against their religious counterparts. In the Church, the quarrel was between "two great currents" of thought pulled apart by the conflicting demands of incarnation and eschatology.[7] The first of these currents, which Daniélou labeled "humanist socialism," included both "the Christian democratic family" and the variety of figures that the following chapter will group together under the (admittedly imperfect) umbrella of the Catholic left.[8] As we shall see, one of the great innovations to come out of these circles was a distinctive form of Catholic materialism—a theological account of the spiritual dignity of the material world and of labor in particular. Against this materialist current in postwar Catholic thought, Daniélou identified a competing strand of "Christian existentialism." In this group, he included not just Catholics like himself, de Lubac, Fessard, and Gabriel Marcel, but also Orthodox and Protestant thinkers. What they shared was a debt to Kierkegaard—the father of Christian existentialism—and the "eschatological expectation . . . that all men will be gathered together in the unity of Christ."[9]

By interpreting French thought through a theological framework, Daniélou's taxonomy gives us a different perspective on intellectual life in postwar France. Far from a story of three blocs—Catholics, Marxists, and existentialists—battling for intellectual dominance, his account testifies to the considerable traffic between the three, as well as the internal divisions within each. In the case of Catholic thought, his essay reveals an emerging split within what might broadly be construed as the progressive wing of the French Church. Despite the dominance of Christian Democracy in the historiography of postwar European Catholicism, this split had little to do with the Mouvement républicain populaire (MRP), and in fact, both the groups I will discuss were suspicious of Christian Democratic parties.[10] Instead, these Catholic theologians and philosophers were divided between those who were open to some form of engagement with the left and those who were more interested in a dialogue with existentialist philosophy. The first group sought to work with communists in the service of shared practical goals such as international peace, anticolonialism, and organized labor. The second refused any such collaboration but saw no harm in engaging with the dominant philosophies of the day. Both were committed to "bearing witness" to Catholicism in the public sphere and engaging with the modern world, but they had very different visions of how to accomplish this goal. The first argued for the need to "incarnate" Catholic values in the temporal order, while the second invoked the countervailing demands of "eschatology" and the need to retain a critical distance from secular politics. The first is the subject of Chapter 5, while the second will be explored in greater detail in Chapter 6.

As Daniélou surmised, this split was as much theological as political. Though one might assume that the postwar experiments of the Catholic left emerged organically from the ranks of the resistance, the reality was much more complicated.[11] In fact, there were more than a few continuities between the prewar right and the postwar left, as progressive Catholics repurposed the same Thomist arguments that Catholic royalists had once used to justify their support for the AF. The political differences between the Catholic right and the Catholic left thus belied a more fundamental theological continuity, something that was not lost on de Lubac:

> I have known a traditionalist Thomism à la Bonald, a Thomism as patron of "the Action française," a Thomism as the inspiration of Christian Democracy, a progressivist and even a neo-Marxist Thomism. . . . This is what still makes it difficult for me to loudly proclaim myself a Thomist.[12]

By contrast, Jesuits like de Lubac and Fessard redeployed the theological resources they had used in their battle against fascism—the eschatological language of St. Paul and the Church Fathers—to resist any sort of compromise between Catholics and communists. Far from simply a battle between right and left, then, this was a theological conflict between Thomism and patristics, between the logic of incarnation and the logic of eschatology, revealing once again how Catholic politics tended to defy the logic of the secular political spectrum. And for the first time, it drove a wedge into the heart of the *nouvelle théologie,* as Jesuits such as de Lubac and Fessard and Dominicans such as Marie-Dominique Chenu and Yves Congar found themselves on opposite sides of the debate over the Catholic left.

This divergence reflected the different wartime experiences of the two groups, which magnified existing theological differences between them. While the Jesuits were leading the spiritual resistance to Nazism in the pages of *Témoignage chrétien,* the Dominicans had spent the war forging a new kind of missionary Church. At the forefront of this movement was Marie-Dominique Chenu. In 1942, Chenu was dealt a severe blow when the Holy Office placed his book *Une école de théologie: Le Saulchoir* on the Index of Forbidden Books for, among other things, advocating a historical approach to the study of theology.[13] Far from retreating into silence, however, the Dominican threw himself into developing new apostolic tools for engaging the working class. Though Chenu had been a vocal supporter of the Jeunesse ouvrière chrétienne (JOC) before the war, he became convinced by the 1940s that the methods of Catholic Action were ultimately inadequate. Rather than developing separate confessional organizations to cater to workers, he argued that Catholics needed work within the existing structures of worker solidarity, even if these were secular or actively hostile to Christianity. This was the approach taken by the worker-priests, whom Chenu did so much to inspire, and it also led him to embrace such projects as the peace movement, anticolonialism, and the labor movement, even when these were led by communists.

Just as the Jesuits' wartime experiences transformed their theology, so did Chenu's engagement with the Catholic left. In both cases, theology provided a grid through which these priests made sense of their experiences, but was also transformed in the process. Whereas the Jesuits increasingly stressed the demands of eschatology, Chenu instead placed the accent ever more firmly on the value of incarnation and the things of this world. Turning to the resources of Thomas Aquinas, he developed a theology of labor that endowed material forces with new religious significance, and in doing so, he transformed Thomism itself. In an effort to overcome the neo-scholastic distinction between the natural and supernatural orders while maintaining the traditional Thomist emphasis on the autonomy of earthly affairs, Chenu arrived at the remarkable conclusion that the secularization of social, economic, and political affairs was itself the sign of God's grace. Ultimately, it was this commitment to Thomism that distinguished Chenu and his fellow Dominicans from their Jesuit counterparts and helps to explain the postwar divergence at the heart of the *nouvelle théologie.*

"France, Take Care Not to Lose Your Freedom!"

Before turning to Chenu, however, it is worth picking up the postwar story of *Témoignage chrétien,* since nothing set the terms for the debate over the Catholic left like the crisis at the journal over the publication of Gaston Fessard's *France, Take Care Not to Lose Your Freedom* in 1946. Five years earlier, Fessard had helped to launch *Témoignage chrétien* and the spiritual resistance to Nazism with "France, Take Care Not to Lose Your Soul," and in the opening lines to its sequel, he explained the connection between the two texts. "In July 1941," he wrote, "we denounced the danger with which Nazism, under the cover of Vichy, threatened the French soul. . . . Now, eighteen months after the Liberation, we must signal a new peril which, under the cover of the Resistance, threatens France: *Communism*."[14] The formal similarities in the title and structure of the two texts were deliberate. Fessard wished to show the "inherent likeness, beyond any surface opposition" between communism and Nazism, which meant that communism "currently threatens our country every bit as much as Nazism did in 1941."[15] For Fessard, the Catholic critique of communism was simply the logical corollary to the Catholic critique of Nazism.

But not everyone who had fought in the ranks of the spiritual resistance perceived the necessary relationship between anticommunism and antifascism. If "France, Take Care Not to Lose Your Soul" had launched the spiritual resistance to Nazism, its sequel marked the end of that project and transformed *Témoignage chrétien* into something very different than its Jesuit founders had intended. No longer united by the shared goal of defeating fascism, the editors were split over whether the journal's antifascist stance should translate into a postwar rapprochement with left, given the bonds that Catholics and communists had forged in the ranks of the resistance, or whether the logical extension of the resistance to Nazism should be anticommunism. The debate tended to pit the Jesuits who had founded the *Cahiers du Témoignage chrétien*—Pierre Chaillet, de Lubac, and Fessard—against the laypeople who had come on board in 1943 to launch the *Courriers du Témoignage chrétien*. But it was not until late 1945, when Fessard brought the manuscript for *France, Take Care Not to Lose Your Freedom* to the journal's editorial board, that these differences reached a point of no return.

Fessard was entirely explicit about the connection between the two iterations of *France, prends garde*. The structure of the anticommunist tract closely replicated that of his celebrated resistance pamphlet, although it was roughly ten times longer. The first half of the text, which was devoted to theoretical questions, constituted an elaborate rejoinder to Marxist humanism, the logic of *tripartisme,* and those who trumpeted the resistance credentials of the French Communist Party (PCF). Fessard did not simply approach these questions from the perspective of Catholic theology, but instead deployed the logic of the dialectic to elaborate a "truly immanent" critique of Marxism.[16] Specifically, he adopted a dialectical method based on Hegel's *Logic,* according to which every concept taken to its extreme invariably passes into its opposite. This allowed him to show how the Communist Party's openness to working with Christians invariably degenerated into anti-Christianity, its patriotism into treason, and its humanism into inhumanity.

A closer examination of Fessard's rejoinder to Marxist humanism illustrates how this method functioned in practice. The Jesuit was responding first and foremost to communist intellectuals who turned to Marx's early writings on alienation in order to present communism as the authentic heir to the humanist tradition. Fessard also turned to these early writings, just as he had in the 1930s, but he did so in order to show how the contradictions within the Marxist philosophy of history vitiated its humanist pretensions. He zeroed in, in particular, on the tension between the quasi-religious and "scientific" aspects of Marxism. In the *1844 Manuscripts,* Marx had described the end of history as the "resolution of the conflict between man and nature and between man and man."[17] Fessard pointed out that this "mystique" of the end of history, upon which Marxist humanists sought to build a communist morality, was palpably at odds with the claim that Marxism constituted a rational system grounded in "the continuous progress of science and technology."[18] And indeed, the postwar history of the PCF was plagued by tensions between proponents of Marxist humanism and those who favored a stricter materialism.[19] For Fessard, this conflict grew out of a tension within the Marxist theory of history itself, between faith in indefinite progress and the notion of the end of history. "Communism," he argued, "can be either the true end of man's conflicts with man and with nature, or a continuous progress toward their resolution, but it cannot be both at the same time."[20] Unable to secure the link between historical progress and the reconciliation that would come at the end of history, communists simply projected this end into an ever-receding future, while using it to justify all manner of violence, deceit, and inhumanity in the present. "By launching man in pursuit of a constantly receding limit," Fessard concluded, "Marxist humanism thereby proves itself incapable of truly liberating him."[21]

This inability to square the logic of historical progress with the end of history followed implacably, the Jesuit argued, from the atheism of

Marxist theory. It lacked what Christianity possessed in the form of the Incarnation and the sacraments—a nexus between historical time and the end of history. Here Fessard rehearsed the account of Nazism and communism as pseudo-religions that he had developed in his resistance writings. If communism "takes on the appearance of a religion" resembling Christianity, he reasoned, it is because Christianity alone can resolve the tensions within Marxist theory.[22] But so long as communists clung to their atheism, they would never be able to achieve the reconciliation between man and nature that Marx had promised. For without the mediating power of Christ, man and nature could only be reconciled by absorbing the first within the second. From Fessard's perspective, this was evident in the way Marxist rationalism approached the human being as a scientific object like any other. By treating "human history as a fragment of natural history," Marxism tended "to reduce man to the level of an animal or a thing."[23] In other words, the logical outcome of Marxist humanism was dehumanization. Once Christ had been rejected as the only means to divinize the human race, "man must choose for himself another means within 'nature' to realize his project of a Humanity-God. We already know where this has led those who chose the master Race. The result must be the same for those who prefer the messianic Class."[24]

In addition to showing how Marxist humanism invariably negates itself, Fessard devoted much of the book to undermining the PCF's much-vaunted patriotic credentials. Having appointed itself the official party of the "patriotic resistance," PCF support was at an all-time high when Fessard wrote *France, prends garde*. The Jesuit was therefore keen to remind his compatriots that the communists had only entered the resistance after Hitler invaded the Soviet Union and abrogated the Nazi-Soviet pact. For the Jesuit, this was proof that French communists placed loyalty to the Soviet Union—the country in which socialism was incarnated—above loyalty to their own countrymen. During the war, Fessard had argued that Pétain was a "slave-prince" whose government could not command full legitimacy because it remained beholden to the occupying power. In 1946, he applied this same logic to the PCF. "Between its members and the regime in Moscow," he insisted, "there exists a relationship of dependence at least as close as the one that linked the government of Vichy to the regime in Berlin."[25] In both cases, the rhetoric of patriotism hid a reality that was anything but patriotic.

Coming as it did at the height of the postwar Catholic opening to the left, this argument scandalized many of Fessard's erstwhile companions from the spiritual resistance. When Chaillet decided to publish the book through the newly established Éditions du Témoignage chrétien in October 1945, he met with stiff resistance from the younger members of the editorial staff who had taken charge of the journal following the Liberation. Led by André Mandouze, they objected that Fessard's polemic was "in complete contradiction" with the journal's commitment to bridging the divide between the Church and the working class.[26] The disagreement quickly escalated into a conflict between those, like Fessard, who refused to compromise on the incompatibility between Church doctrine and communist ideology, and those who felt that the particular historical moment and the interests of evangelizing the working class required a more charitable attitude, particularly given how many communists had fought valiantly in the ranks of the resistance. As Mandouze explained, this split tended to fall along generational and status lines, pitting the Jesuits who had founded *Témoignage chrétien* against "a certain number of laypeople who, though no doubt less competent on the terrain of doctrine, are, because of our estate, in greater contact with temporal realities."[27] They worried that Fessard's anticommunist tract would play into the hands of the journal's political enemies and reinforce the longstanding association between the Church and the right. Fessard, on the other hand, warned that the Church now risked making the same mistake "with communism that we are reproached for having made in the case of fascism."[28]

As with previous political conflicts within the Church, each side accused the other of mixing religion and politics. While Mandouze faulted Fessard for placing himself "on terrain that is no longer Christian, but political," Fessard insisted that it was Mandouze and his allies who had conflated religion and politics by placing *Témoignage chrétien* on the side of the working class.[29] Just as the Jesuits had always maintained that their resistance to Nazism was driven by religious rather than political motives, Fessard characterized his own position as a "Christian and spiritual anti-communism with political effects." But he also recognized that "no Christian witness [*témoignage chrétien*] can avoid this politics . . . precisely because the act of bearing witness takes place within a history."[30] As he himself acknowledged, theology still had political effects even when it did not explicitly address political questions, and both sides used this fact to discredit the other.

Ultimately, neither side really won the argument. Fessard's book was temporarily shelved in response to the objections of his critics, but the conflict convinced Mandouze that the journal no longer reflected his own desire for "a constructive coexistence with the communists."[31] In November 1945, he stepped down from his position as editor-in-chief of *Témoignage chrétien* and took up a teaching post in Algiers, where he went on to become a vocal advocate for Algerian independence.[32] With Mandouze no longer holding up publication, the Éditions du Témoignage Chrétien released *France, prends garde* in May 1946. It elicited an immediate backlash from those within the organization who objected to the way Fessard had appropriated their wartime struggle by dedicating his book to "the memory of the executed and the deported who died in Germany, and to all the militants of the clandestine teams of *Témoignage chrétien.*" In a collective letter to Fessard and Chaillet, these dissenters expressed their respect for Fessard's contribution to the antifascist struggle but declared, "with great sadness that we must now part company. Since *France, Take Care Not to Lose Your Freedom,* there no longer exists within the team at *T.C.* the unity that we had found during the Resistance."[33] And yet, Fessard did not win out either. Under lay leadership, the journal he had helped to launch would go on to become one of the leading voices of the Catholic left, joining the ranks of *Esprit, Économie et humanisme, Vie intellectuelle,* and, later on, *La Quinzaine.*[34]

The publication of *France, prends garde* thus brought to the surface an emerging tension between progressive Catholics who were open to some form of engagement with the left and those who refused any such collaboration. Far more than just a conflict between right and left, this dispute revived the old prewar debate about whether Catholics could work with nonbelievers to achieve shared political goals. On one side stood those like Mandouze and Emmanuel Mounier, who, in his review of *France, prends garde,* insisted that the atheism of the Communist Party should not prevent Christians from "adopting the majority of its political and economic positions and establishing practical alliances with it."[35] In arguing for the legitimacy of Catholic collaboration with an atheist political party, these Catholics reiterated precisely the argument that Catholic supporters of the AF had made twenty years earlier. And just as Fessard and de Lubac had objected to this argument when it was made by the right in the 1920s, so they rejected it when it was deployed by the left in the 1940s. Though de Lubac had significant reservations about the tone and timing of Fessard's polemic and did not share his friend's view that communism was just as dangerous as Nazism, de Lubac was entirely convinced that Catholics could not engage in a purely practical collaboration with communists.[36] If some had fallen into this trap, he blamed it on the misguided belief that Marxism constituted a kind if science whose political and economic findings could be adopted without taking on board its atheism. "Marxism is a complete doctrine," de Lubac replied. "Its 'temporal' program is wholly permeated by its spiritual negations."[37] This emphasis on the unity of theory and practice, metaphysics and politics, was the logical extension of the argument these Jesuits had been making for twenty years against the possibility of Catholic collaboration with secular political ideologies on the right. Only now it put them at odds with an emerging Catholic left, which included many of their erstwhile comrades from the resistance as well as the Dominican branch of the *nouvelle théologie*.

A Missionary Church: The Challenge of the Worker-Priests

As with Mandouze and the veterans of the spiritual resistance, the Dominicans' opening to the left did not emerge from the conventional arena of political parties and trade unions, or any particular sympathy for Marxism. Instead, it grew out of a religious initiative. Born at the height of the war, the internal missionary movement brought many priests into personal contact with communists for the first time and eventually led to forms of practical and intellectual cooperation. While Jesuits like de Lubac, Fessard, and Chaillet were organizing the spiritual resistance to Nazism in the pages of *Témoignage chrétien,* then, Dominicans such as Lebret, Loew, Chenu, Congar, and Féret were busy developing their own projects to reimplant Christianity within the working class. These apostolic initiatives emerged organically out of the interwar Catholic Action movements such as the Jeunesse ouvrière chrétienne (JOC). As we have seen, the Dominicans of Le Saulchoir had hosted retreats for the chaplains of the JOC in the 1930s, and the interwar engagement with Catholic Action had helped to inspire a new theological emphasis on the role of the laity and the need to incarnate Catholic values in secular milieus—to be "the yeast in the dough" of the social order. Whereas the experience of the war had led Jesuits like de Lubac and Fessard to temper this language of incarnation with an emphasis on eschatology, the Dominicans' very different wartime experience only redoubled their commitment to the theology of incarnation as the foundation for their working-class apostolate.

But these postwar projects were not simply an extension of the interwar Catholic Action movements. By the late 1930s, many JOC militants found themselves increasingly dissatisfied with the Catholic Action model, and these concerns found expression in a groundbreaking pamphlet published in 1943 by two JOC chaplains, Henri Godin and Yvan Daniel. *France, pays de mission?* was a dramatic wake-up call about the growing dechristianization, not just of the urban working class, but also of the rural populations that had long formed the backbone of French Catholicism. While French Catholics were focused on evangelizing the far-flung peoples of Africa and Asia, they had failed to notice that their own countrymen had begun to desert the Church en masse. "There are entire regions of human activity," the authors warned, especially "within the proletariat of our great cities, where *Christ is not being preached and where he cannot be preached.*"[38] Catholic Action had done little to reverse this process, hamstrung as it was by the focus on the parish as the primary unit of Christian life. What was needed, the authors argued, was a new kind of missionary activity led by priests rather than laypeople and focused on Christianizing the social milieu rather than the individual. These missionaries would form a "base community" firmly rooted in the working-class milieu and operating alongside the parish.[39]

The publication of *France, pays de mission?* caused a major stir. Shaken by its findings, Cardinal Suhard, the archbishop of Paris, quickly authorized Godin and Daniel to organize teams (*équipes*) of priests to go out and implement their new missionary model. By 1952, there were 280 such priests active in twenty-seven dioceses.[40] These *équipes* required the formation of a new kind of priest, and Suhard therefore oversaw the creation of two new seminaries that would train priests for the demands of the domestic missionary field. The most significant of these was the Mission de France, established under the direction of Louis Augros in 1942 near Lisieux. It was joined in 1943 by the Mission de Paris, which was created specifically to cater to the working class of Paris and its environs. These institutions sought to implement Godin and Daniel's blueprint, pioneering a new pedagogy in which "Marx was studied alongside St. Thomas and St. Paul."[41] The goal was to train a new kind of priest—one who would prioritize evangelization above all else, including the dispensation of the sacraments. This sacerdotal model, Godin and Daniel argued, proceeded directly from the logic of the incarnation and amounted to a "renewal of the gesture of Christ, who was incarnated and came into this world in order to save us."[42] Their approach thus stood in sharp contrast to the Eucharistic ecclesiology that emerged from the resistance writings of de Lubac and his fellow Jesuits, with its emphasis on the centrality of the sacraments and the horizon of eschatology.

Few conveyed the theological significance of the new missionary endeavor more passionately than Marie-Dominique Chenu. He had provided the *nihil obstat* for the publication of *France, pays de mission?* and participated in the founding session of the Mission de Paris.[43] Chenu and fellow Dominicans Yves Congar and Henri-Marie Féret quickly became key consultants at the Mission de France.[44] For Chenu, the missionary movement represented a clear departure from the interwar lay apostolate, abandoning its logic of conquest and conversion in favor of a commitment to dialogue and *témoignage* (bearing witness). Whereas Catholic Action militants had established specifically Catholic organizations to target and take charge of the working class, the new missionary *équipes* understood their role primarily as one of *presence,* of "being with" the workers and sharing in their struggles and aspirations. Rather than approaching the factory or the docks as "a foreign land run by nonbelievers who needed to be steered into Christian institutions," the missionaries approached them as sites of an *"indigenous Christianity"* that had to be nurtured with its own internal resources, much as foreign missionaries sought to foster indigenous Churches in Africa and Asia.[45] This meant acknowledging the presence of grace in even the most secular and anticlerical milieus.

At stake in this model was not just a new method of evangelization, but a very different understanding of the relationship between nature and grace, Church and world. Following Aquinas, Chenu insisted that grace does not come to destroy nature, but rather to perfect it. In much the same way, he argued, the missionaries had to work within the natural communities formed by human beings, including communities of class. They had to cultivate the forms of solidarity and social life that were indigenous to these communities, in which grace was already at work, rather than importing pastoral models developed for a bourgeois context. Such a vision of missionary work had crucial implications, Chenu believed, for the nature of the Church and its relationship to the world more broadly. It meant conceiving of this relationship in terms of dialogue rather than conquest and recognizing that "the world itself is the site of evangelical presence."[46] "The task of the missionary is not to figure out how the

Church, as it is now, will be the shape of the world," he explained; "it is to discover how the world, as it is now, will be the material for the Church."[47] This understanding of the relationship between Church and world would eventually find expression in the Second Vatican Council's Pastoral Constitution on the Church and the Modern World (*Gaudium et Spes*).

In addition to reimagining the relationship between Church and world, the postwar missionary movement also demanded a new approach to the priestly vocation—something that lay-led Catholic Action had not required. This became clear when the missionary movement gave birth to a much more radical form of working-class apostolate. At the Mission de Paris, some began to feel that true solidarity with the working class required priests not just to live among the proletariat, but also to share in the conditions of their labor. Thus was born the controversial "worker-priest" movement.[48] It owed much to the context of the war, when a few priests and seminarians had joined the ranks of the Frenchmen drafted to work in German factories under the Service du travail obligatoire. Emboldened by this experience and the example of priests like the Dominican Jacques Loew, who became a dockworker in Marseille in order to observe the conditions of the working class, some priests began to argue that they were called by the very logic of the Incarnation to be "a worker among the workers, just as Christ was a man among men."[49] But as these priests became increasingly engaged in the life and labor of the working class, they were also drawn into union activism, which was dominated by the communist-led Confédération générale du travail (CGT). Some even became local union representatives and played a role in organizing the strikes of 1947 and 1950. This form of engagement would ultimately seal the fate of the worker-priests. Not only did it strike the bishops as a betrayal of the Catholic trade union (the CFTC); Church leaders also worried that such activism distracted the worker-priests from their priestly duties and exposed them to the seductions of communism.[50] In 1954, the French bishops ordered the priests out of the factories.

Dominicans such as Chenu, Congar, Pierre Boisselot (editor-in-chief of the publishing house Cerf), and Féret were staunch defenders of the worker-priests. "Everyone knew that I was the 'theologian' of the worker-priest apostolate," Chenu later recalled, and he viewed the movement as nothing less than "the greatest religious event since the French Revolution."[51] What attracted him to the worker-priest experiment was the new sacerdotal vision it promised. In a controversial article, Chenu argued that the challenge posed by the worker-priests was above all theological, rather than political. Against a traditional model of the priesthood, one defined by prayer, the dispensation of sacraments, and the activities of the parish, the worker-priests pointed the way to a "total theology of the priesthood."[52] They understood that their liturgical and sacramental functions "presupposed, as their foundation and vital principle," an even more basic mission: *to bear witness to the faith.*[53] The first duty of the priest was to bring the word of God to all people—and indeed, many worker-priests did not even administer the sacraments because they did not wish to differentiate themselves from their fellow workers.[54] Faced with the challenge of dechristianization, they understood that it was first necessary to make the Church present where it was currently absent. "How can we baptize a civilization if we are not present to it?" Chenu demanded. "Presence" was "the very condition for words, including the Word of God" and had to precede any effort to evangelize or incorporate people into the life of the sacraments.[55]

Yves Congar made a similar point in his own defense of the worker-priests, which appeared in the pages of *Témoignage chrétien*. Like Chenu, he stressed the inadequacies of existing pastoral models such as Catholic Action. The great theologian of the laity admitted that it was not enough to rely on laypeople to bridge the divide between the Church and the working class; the clergy, too, had to engage with workers, and this meant not just "talking to" them, but "being with" them.[56] The worker-priests thus filled a spiritual need that by definition the parish system could not meet.[57] It was only natural, Congar reasoned, that once priests entered the factories, they would be drawn into the workers' struggle for human liberation and dignity. But like Chenu, he insisted that the engagement of the worker-priests should not be understood as a political phenomenon. It was "a thing of the Church," something that concerned the basic requirements of the faith. The worker-priests had grasped that workers' demands "translate in a concrete manner the requirements of human dignity, which is an exigency of the faith" and "conditions the very possibility to access the Gospel."[58]

While Church leaders complained that the worker-priests had become politicized, Dominicans like Chenu and Congar insisted that theirs was a theological revolution first and foremost. Not only did it imply a new vision of the clerical vocation—one better suited to the demands of the modern industrialized world—but it also fit into a broader theological revaluation of earthly affairs. As Chenu later explained, the "earthly hopes" of the working class are a "refraction of the hope of Christ," and "the witness of the worker-priests was to provide a Christic dimension to earthly hopes."[59] For Chenu and so many of the priests who entered the Mission de France or became worker-priests, it was this set of theological and pastoral concerns, and not any sympathy for communist ideology, that drove their engagement. Like the Jesuits who had launched the spiritual resistance to Nazism, the Dominicans regarded their engagement as a form of *témoignage*. But what the two groups understood by this term differed dramatically and revealed quite different visions of the Church and the role of the priesthood. Whereas the Jesuits sought to anchor the Church in the celebration of the Eucharist, the Dominicans downplayed the role of the sacraments. Whereas the Jesuits adopted the language of eschatology to critique fascism, the Dominicans embraced the logic of incarnation—the need to make Catholicism "present" in even the most secular corners of French society.

And yet, this was precisely the language that Catholics had used during the war to justify working within the institutions of Vichy. Albeit in a very different political context, the story of the worker-priests raised a similar set of questions about the line between "presence" and collaboration. Most of these priests were far from sympathetic to communism when they entered the factories, but in the solidarity of the factory floor and the struggle to improve the lives of workers, they began to form personal bonds with communists. One worker-priest reported that the local communist union delegate had been the first to welcome him, despite the hostility of his fellow dockworkers, while others were surprised to discover that some of the communists they met seemed to embody the spirit of the Gospel more fully than many practicing Catholics.[60] What began as grudging respect, cautious friendship, or a shared mutual aid project soon blossomed into more formal modes of cooperation in the ranks of the trade unions or the peace movement. Some priests began to argue that they could not truly incarnate themselves in the life of the proletariat without also engaging in the class struggle.[61] In the polarized context of the Cold War, the working-class apostolate thus became a vehicle for political radicalization, especially after the Church forced the priests to choose sides. When the Vatican ordered them out of the factories in 1954, seventy-three (of roughly one hundred) worker-priests responded by issuing a public manifesto. "We cannot see," they wrote, "how priests can be forbidden, in the name of the Gospel, to share the conditions of millions of oppressed humanity or to be on their side in their struggles."[62]

This pattern repeated itself in other Catholic social movements. The Mouvement populaire des familles (MPF), for example, with its focus on the family as the fundamental unit of social life, was able to thrive under Vichy. By the end of the war, the organization boasted 158,000 members.[63] What began as a relatively traditional charitable operation—an effort to secure basic material needs for working-class families hit hard by wartime scarcity—underwent a marked radicalization after the Liberation. The MPF soon aligned itself with the CGT and began to drop the religious references from its publications. As in the case of the worker-priests, the goal of being "present" to the working class increasingly translated into active engagement in the class struggle.

But the case of the MPF is significant for yet another reason, for it reveals that the impetus for the postwar Catholic left did not simply emerge from the ranks of the spiritual resistance, but also drew from the institutions and personnel of Vichy France. The MPF was one example of this trend, but so was the economic think tank Économie et humanisme, which was founded at the height of the National Revolution by the Dominican Louis-Joseph Lebret and a group that included the economist François Perroux, a key architect of Vichy economic policy.[64] Like so many Catholics, this group was initially drawn to the rhetoric of the National Revolution because it seemed to provide an opportunity to implement their corporatist model of an economic "third way" between capitalism and communism.[65] But after the war, Économie et humanisme became associated with the burgeoning Catholic left, advocating for an economic system that would foster the full development of the human person as both a material and spiritual being. In the 1950s, Lebret went on to establish a leading think tank for Third World development policy.[66] The model of "integral development" that it pioneered would eventually find expression in Paul VI's encyclical *Populorum Progressio*.[67]

That both Économie et humanisme and the MPF could make the transition from Vichy to the postwar Catholic left so readily is a testament to the remarkable ideological ambiguity of Catholic economic thought. Corporatism in particular possessed affinities with both right- and left-wing economic principles, which explains how figures like Perroux could find common cause with both the National Revolution and the Catholic left. But the story of these groups also highlights the broader continuities between Vichy and postwar France.[68] In some cases, there were direct institutional or ideological connections between Vichy and the postwar Catholic left. In other cases, however, the links were purely semantic, as left-wing Catholics with no sympathy for Vichy redeployed the logic of "presence" in the service of radically different political ends. This is by no means to suggest any kind of moral equivalence between the two positions, but simply to show how the same theology could be mobilized in the service of both the right and the left. This became all the more apparent as the practical experiments of the war and early postwar years yielded more robust theological reflections on the possibility of Catholic-communist collaboration.

The "Progressive Christians" and the Dilemma of Catholic-Communist Collaboration

As the story of the worker-priests shows, the postwar Catholic engagement with communism arose out of the practical bonds that Catholics forged with communists through a series of common endeavors. For some, like Mandouze, the crucible for this engagement was the shared experience of the Resistance; for others, it was the working-class apostolate and the relationships formed in the ranks of the trade unions. As these experiments brought Catholics into contact with communists, they soon gave rise to a more detailed theological reflection on the legitimacy of Catholic-communist collaboration.

This question became much more vexed with the onset of the Cold War in 1947. That year, the Soviet Union established the Cominform under Andrei Zhdanov to bring Europe's communist parties more fully into line with Soviet policy, and the following year, the United States launched the Marshall Plan. These events substantially reconfigured the French political landscape. France's political constituencies found themselves having to line up behind one or the other great power, and the alliance between the Catholics, socialists, and communists quickly broke apart. In May 1947, the communists were kicked out of the Ramadier government, while the founding of the Gaullist Rassemblement du peuple français (RPF) gave French Catholics on the right an alternative to the MRP. Far from bringing an end to Catholic engagement with the left, however, the death of *tripartisme* and the beginning of the Cold War instead polarized the debate between the mainstream of the French Church and an increasingly radical minority committed to working with the Communist Party.

The Union des chrétiens progressistes (UCP) became the face of this increasingly embattled minority, drawing together the more radical elements within the postwar Catholic left.[69] The group rose to notoriety in 1947 with the publication of its manifesto, "Christians Take a Position"— the most unambiguous call yet for Catholic-communist collaboration. André Mandouze, fresh from his break with *Témoignage chrétien*, helped provide the intellectual inspiration for the movement. He communicated his position in a 1948 article titled "Grasping the Outstretched Hand," a reference to the PCF's overtures to Catholics in the 1930s. In it, Mandouze argued for a purely pragmatic alliance between Catholics and communists on political matters.[70] To justify this, he leaned heavily on the distinction between the spiritual and temporal orders, defending the Catholic's freedom to make his or her own political choices and not "take orders from the representative of God where Caesar's domain is concerned."[71] Such practical cooperation was essential, he insisted, because, "if one can be progressive without necessarily subscribing to Marxist doctrine, one cannot engage in progressive politics without the help of the communists."[72] Nevertheless, he made clear that the "progressive Christians" were Christians first and foremost, with "progressive" functioning as the modifier rather than the noun.

This position found a sympathetic echo from other left-leaning Catholics. Although Mounier differed from the "progressive Christians" on the question of whether Catholics should actually join the PCF, he maintained that "the fact of being Christian" should not preclude "lucid collaboration with the communists" and pointed to the resistance as a case in point.[73] He also insisted that Marxism contained "certain truths capable of being detached from those which we do not accept."[74] The Dominican Maurice Montuclard took a similar position in his own contribution to the volume that included Mandouze's essay on the "outstretched hand." Montuclard was the founder of Jeunesse de L'Église, a progressive Catholic group in which the famous Marxist theorist Louis Althusser got his start.[75] Montuclard agreed with Mandouze that conflating Christianity and politics tended to distort both. It was crucial for the Catholic to hold these two realities apart, because "the consciousness of this distinction permits him, on the one hand, to rediscover political reality and, on the other hand, puts him on the path to a rediscovery of the Church."[76] Only by rigorously distinguishing faith and politics could the Catholic do justice to the demands of both.

This position was, of course, anathema to Gaston Fessard. In January 1949, the Jesuit launched a blistering attack on the "progressive Christians" in the pages of *Études*. The article targeted not only his nemesis Mandouze, but also Mounier and Montuclard. Fessard was particularly exercised by Mandouze's claim that the Vatican could not pronounce on temporal affairs because its authority was "exclusively spiritual."[77] What becomes of Catholic social teaching, Fessard demanded, when one accepts Mandouze's rigid distinction between Catholic doctrine and "economico-political action"?[78] Who decides where the boundary between the two lies and when it has been transgressed? For the "progressive Christians," Fessard argued, it is ultimately the Marxist dialectic that decides. Far from maintaining a distinction between the theological and the political, then, Mandouze had elevated the Marxist dialectic into a *theological* tool. In this way, he resembled those Catholic followers of Charles Maurras who believed that their leader's atheism "would in no way rub off on the consciences of the faithful," and that they could embrace his *"politique d'abord"* while remaining above reproach at the level of faith.[79] "The 'progressivism' of our Christians [would] thus take us twenty years backwards," Fessard concluded, for it amounts to an "AF of the extreme left."[80]

In response, Fessard offered his own theological vision of the dynamic relationship between theory and practice, between spiritual and temporal affairs. He reminded readers that the spiritual authority of the Church extended not just to questions of individual faith, but also to social questions, precisely because salvation was not an individual affair. Here, Fessard invoked the eschatological vision of the mystical body of Christ that had been so central to his wartime resistance writings. The Church defines man as a social being, Fessard explained, because "all men [are] destined to form a single body, that of the New Man, at the end of history. That is what underwrites the jurisdiction of the Church over all of the temporal order and obliges it to have a *social doctrine*."[81] For Fessard, Catholic social teaching flowed necessarily from the social nature of salvation and endowed the Church with a power that was "properly, but not exclusively, spiritual."[82] Even though it could not prescribe a positive political program, the Church could and should fulfill an important critical function vis-à-vis political ideologies, by determining whether they advanced or hindered progress toward the end of history. This critical function was something Mandouze had sacrificed when he abandoned the social teaching of the Church in favor of the Marxist dialectic: "As soon as social man was no longer viewed as dependent on the Church, the Body of Christ was bound to become, in Mandouze's eyes, a spiritual reality with an exclusively spiritual magisterium. In this way, the Church found itself totally disincarnated."[83] In seeking to disentangle Catholic doctrine from the arena of social action ostensibly governed by the Marxist dialectic, Fessard concluded, the "progressive Christians" had only reinforced the privatization of Catholicism.

Fessard's attack elicited a number of vigorous rejoinders, the most sophisticated of which came from the Dominican editors of the Catholic journal *La Vie intellectuelle*. Without endorsing the position of the "progressive Christians," Fathers Jean-Augustin Maydieu and Alain-Zacharie Serrand sought to dispel what they perceived to be the theological errors underwriting Fessard's critique.[84] As we have seen, Fessard derived the temporal authority of the Church from its eschatological role as the institution which "makes present *hic et nunc* the End of history."[85] But for Maydieu and Serrand, this argument conflated two quite distinct eschatological realities: the body of Christ that will come at the end of time, and the Church that exists within time and prepares the way for this eschatological coming. Thomists, by contrast, scrupulously distinguished the end of history from the means to this end, in order to preserve the distinction between the natural and the supernatural orders. Such a distinction allowed the Church to "maintain a sense of its limits" and recognize that "certain temporal determinations" of an economic or political nature fell beyond its purview.[86] But Fessard had violated this Thomist principle by "mixing theological considerations with economico-political preferences."[87] This they blamed on Fessard's fascination with Hegel, who had replaced the transcendent God with a world-spirit immanent to human history.[88] Fessard's tendency to confuse theology with politics and the natural with the supernatural was, for these Thomists, evidence that he had been corrupted by Hegel's pantheism.

By reiterating the classic Thomist distinction between the natural and supernatural ends of the human person, Maydieu and Serrand sought to carve out an autonomous space for Christian activity in the temporal order. In doing so, they rejected Fessard's vision of the Church as a purely critical force in public life. It was not enough, they argued, for Catholics to be mere "opponents and protesters" who denounced ideologies that endangered human salvation.[89] Such an approach might have been necessary under the German occupation, but the coming of the Liberation meant that Catholics now had to work toward a "positive project."[90] And in order to do this, they would need to look to ideological resources beyond the Christian tradition. After all, neither Fessard's meditations on the end of history nor Catholic social teaching could "supply the Christian citizen with the norms for determining whether to affiliate with the MRP rather than the RPF."[91] Instead, Catholics needed to anchor their political engagement in a theory derived from "the temporal ends and ways of knowing natural to man."[92] Although Maydieu and Serrand did not specify which theory they had in mind, their essay established a theological justification for ascribing this role to Marxism.

In doing so, they reinforced the tendency among progressive Catholics to treat Marxism as a "science" rather than a political ideology or a metaphysical system. Montuclard, for instance, attributed his support for a socialist economy entirely to "the point of view of economic science."[93] By rejecting Marxist economics out of hand, he warned, the Church was in danger of repeating the same mistake it had made long ago in rejecting the findings of Galileo. If Montuclard and the "progressive Christians" leaned on the distinction between spiritual and temporal affairs, then, this was because they believed that an objective reading of history and political economy would lead Christians to embrace socialism. But Catholics like Fessard denied that it was possible to distinguish theory from practice, science from metaphysics, the natural from the supernatural, in the way these progressives claimed. For Fessard, Marxism was not just a science; it was something closer to a religion, with its own ethics, anthropology, and philosophy of history. And this necessarily brought it into conflict with Christian values.

In 1949, the Vatican weighed in. The Holy Office issued a decree banning Catholics from joining Communist parties and excommunicating anyone who defended or propagated communism.[94] This decree effectively made the position of the "progressive Christians" untenable and the UCP disbanded soon thereafter. But the controversy over Christian progressivism had substantially clarified the theological stakes of the debate over the possibility of Catholic-communist dialogue. Increasingly, those who argued for some form of Catholic engagement with the left justified their position by appealing to the principles of Thomism, which scrupulously distinguished the natural from the supernatural order and safeguarded the autonomy of temporal affairs. These Catholics presented Marxism as a neutral scientific tool—one that Catholics could apply to socioeconomic questions without subscribing to its atheism. In doing so, Montuclard argued, Catholics were simply imitating Aquinas himself. If "Thomas Aquinas did not deem the materialism . . . of the pagan Aristotle to be incompatible with Christian revelation," he reasoned, "how could we call ourselves Catholics if we claimed that no point of convergence was possible between Christ's revelation and a historical movement in which 800 million men are engaged?"[95]

From the Working-Class Apostolate to the Theology of Labor

The choice appeared to be between a model that drew a sharp distinction between spiritual and temporal affairs, and one that avoided this sort of dualism but attributed a purely negative, critical role to theology in relation to political ideologies. Both, it should be noted, sought to avoid directly politicizing the faith. But for some Catholics, such as Chenu, neither of these approaches seemed entirely satisfactory. If the experience of the spiritual resistance had inspired de Lubac's circle to develop new theological approaches to the sacraments, the Church, and Catholic teaching on Judaism, Chenu's work with the Mission de France and the worker-priests inspired him to develop a more robust theological engagement with economic questions and the spiritual significance of matter. And once again, he turned to the resources of the Thomist tradition to make sense of these experiences. In a series of articles from the late 1940s and early 1950s, Chenu sought to develop a theology of labor that would speak to the profound changes in social and economic life over the past two centuries—one that could incorporate the insights of Marxism without falling prey to its atheism. In the process, he articulated an alternative to both Fessard's approach and that of the progressive Christians. Striking a middle path between them, he sought to preserve the Thomist respect for the autonomy of temporal affairs without bifurcating the natural and supernatural orders. If human affairs had become increasingly independent of religious institutions and referents, Chenu came to believe, this was itself a sign of God's grace.

Chenu began by taking the Church to task for its reaction to the industrial revolution and the new "civilization of labor" that it had inaugurated. Clinging to an idealized model of a pre-industrial economy, he argued, gave the Church few resources with which to make sense of the contemporary world. Instead of railing against the development of mechanized production, Catholics should approach the economic changes of the past two hundred years as a positive step in human development—one that revealed the spiritual dignity of labor. This dignity derived from the very essence of what it meant to be human, Chenu explained; through our labor, we come to resemble the creator God in whose image we are made, and even to participate in his act of creation by placing our imprint on nature and "humanizing" it. Here, Chenu fused theology with the contemporary vocabulary of Marxist humanism. What Marxism had gotten right was the idea that labor should be a humanizing force; by working on the natural world, humans come to recognize themselves in the product of their labor and form bonds of solidarity. But capitalism had transformed labor into a force for alienation. It was the dehumanization of labor—not the seductions of communism—that lay at the origins of proletarian unbelief, Chenu insisted. "To the very extent that man alienated himself through his labor, he lost God at the same time as he lost himself," the Dominican explained. "Labor could no longer have a religious meaning because it no longer had a human meaning."[96] Chenu therefore sought to develop a theology that would recover the spiritual and humanizing function of labor.

Central to this theology of labor was a new appreciation for the spiritual dignity of matter. It is because human beings are both body and soul, Chenu argued, and because these two entities are "consubstantial" in the human person, that economic affairs necessarily have a role to play in the history of salvation. "Matter is *in* the very definition of man," he insisted; "it is not the fragile and compromising support, the passing receptacle for another more definitive life." In a "total economy of salvation," even the material dimension of human life is saved.[97] If Marxist materialism erred by reducing spiritual affairs to material forces, Chenu warned that Christians were just as guilty of embracing "a 'spiritualism' that prudishly relegates physical realities and material concerns to the basement of the soul and the dependent variable of history."[98] Here, Chenu drew on the work of the Jesuit paleontologist Teilhard de Chardin, who had woven theology together with physics, biology, and geology to recover the spiritual dignity of matter. Like Teilhard, Chenu insisted that spiritual life and salvation history had to be anchored in the material conditions of life on earth. And this meant that biology, technology, the natural world, and economic structures should be viewed, not as constraints on human freedom and transcendence, but as their very condition of possibility. "Everything in man, including his contemplation and his freedom, is rooted in a physical organism," Chenu insisted.[99] And consequently, "man, including his freedom, is rooted in nature and its determinisms."[100] In this way, Chenu sought to reconcile material determinism with human freedom and spiritual life so as to elaborate a distinctively Catholic form of materialism.

In order to square this circle, the Dominican sought to affirm the autonomy of the natural order without cutting it off from the supernatural. To do this, he turned for inspiration to Thomas Aquinas, who had salvaged the autonomous value of nature from an Augustinian tradition that disparaged the things of this world. But Aquinas had done so without separating nature and grace either, stressing that grace does not impose itself on nature, but rather perfects and transforms it from within. Through "the dialectic of nature and grace," Chenu explained, grace progressively builds up the internal resources of nature so that it can become autonomous and self-sufficient in its own order. This meant that every aspect of human life was the "material for grace," including the modern industrial economy and the "civilization of labor." But it also meant that economic affairs possessed their own internal laws and should be understood and valued on their own terms. While "it is certainly not a supreme end . . . as Marxism believes," Chenu concluded, "labor and the civilization of labor is worthy in itself."[101] Here, the Dominican endorsed the idea of a "profane Christendom," which Maritain had first advanced in *Integral Humanism*. Like Maritain, Chenu believed that it was a testament to the spiritual progress of humankind that social, economic, and political institutions had emancipated themselves from clerical tutelage and become "an order of values that has reached its maturity."[102]

Chenu viewed the advent of an industrial economy as part of this broader process by which humans progressively achieve greater freedom and self-sufficiency in the natural order. For the great medievalist, this process had begun with the upheavals of twelfth-century Europe—including the advent of new agricultural technologies, the rise of cities, and the birth of mendicant orders such as the Dominicans—all of which found their theological expression in the work of Aquinas, with its emphasis on reason, nature, and earthly affairs.[103] For Chenu, this twelfth-century revolution marked "the beginning of the modern era" because it revealed the "eminent dignity" of temporal affairs and launched the march toward greater human freedom in political, economic, and intellectual life.[104] He believed that his own society was passing through a comparable transformation, as a result of the rise of an industrial economy. If the immediate effect of industrialization had been the exploitation of the proletariat, Chenu insisted that it also contained "the resources for a liberation" because it had given rise to a new collective consciousness grounded in the solidarity of labor.[105] The rise of industry thus constituted a further step in the historical trend toward freedom and autonomy in temporal affairs, a trend that also implied autonomy from religious authority. "Thanks to the extraordinary boom in science and technology with industrial civilization," Chenu explained, "desacralization has accelerated, conferring to knowledge, culture, social life, and the least of our activities, their internal consistency, without involving any explicit reference to the divine." And this led Chenu to the remarkable conclusion that, "whereas atheism requires from us a refusal, secularization can receive a certain consent," since "this evolution favors a just consciousness of the dignity of man and society."[106] The secularization of European life, on this reading, was itself a sign of spiritual progress.

Here we can see how far Chenu's approach had diverged from that of the Jesuits associated with the *nouvelle théologie*. That both continued to look to Teilhard de Chardin as a model is a testament to the extent to which both remained committed to overcoming the division between the supernatural and natural orders, Church and world, spirit and matter. But if the Jesuits tended to place the accent on the first element in each couplet, Chenu instead emphasized the second. And this had everything to do with his Thomism. As with Maydieu, Serrand, and the "progressive Christians," Chenu looked to Aquinas to underscore the dignity and autonomy of worldly matters. But whereas they simply disarticulated spiritual and temporal affairs, Chenu argued that the self-sufficiency of political, economic, and intellectual life was *itself* the sign of the presence of grace secretly at work within it. His work thus marked a further step in the diversification of twentieth-century Thomism. Chenu's effort to revalue nature and earthly affairs without splitting them off from the supernatural would find an echo in the work of transcendental Thomists like Karl Rahner, and later on, liberation theologians. But the fact that he remained anchored in the Thomist tradition, with its emphasis on the autonomy of nature, while his French Jesuit counterparts turned instead to St. Paul and the Church Fathers, may help to explain the different positions they took on political and economic matters. This becomes clearer when we examine how Chenu translated his theological vision into new forms of left-wing political engagement after 1949.

La Quinzaine and the Politics of Peace

By 1949, these internal French Catholic debates had once again been overtaken by international events. That year, the North Atlantic Treaty brought NATO into existence, with France as a founding member, while the creation of the Federal Republic of Germany (FRG) and the German Democratic Republic (GDR) formalized the division between West and East Germany, and the Communist revolution in China added an entirely new dimension to the Cold War. Perhaps most ominously, 1949 saw the Soviet Union detonate its first atomic bomb, while the United States stepped up its efforts to develop a thermonuclear weapon. But it was the arrest and show trial of Cardinal József Mindszenty by the Soviet-backed regime in Hungary—soon followed by similar persecutions in Poland and other Soviet satellite states—that caused the greatest consternation in Rome.[107] In July, the Holy Office issued its decree against communism, which forbade Catholics from professing, defending, or supporting communism under pain of excommunication. But the condemnation did not bring an end to the Catholic left in France. Instead, as in 1947, the hardening of Cold War divisions brought some Catholics into line but also radicalized others.

After 1949, this activism was driven by a new set of commitments, including anticolonialism and, above all, the campaign against nuclear weapons. The peace movement might seem like an uncontroversial program for Catholics to support, but what made it controversial in the 1950s was that it was very much a communist-led project backed by Moscow. Under the leadership of the French nuclear physicist and communist Frédéric Joliot-Curie, the World Peace Council launched a massive petition against nuclear armament in March 1950, three months before the outbreak of the Korean War. Known as the Stockholm Appeal, it was signed by nearly 275 million people, including the entire adult population of the Soviet Union and high-profile artists and intellectuals such as Pablo Picasso, W. E. B. Du Bois, Marc Chagall, and Pablo Neruda. But it also attracted support from many left-leaning Catholics. A number of French Catholics, such as André Mandouze and the "red priest" Jean Boulier, had attended the first congress of the peace movement in Poland, where they forged connections with a vigorous Catholic left organized around the journal *Dziś i Jutro*.[108] Following the launch of the Stockholm Appeal, a number of these French Catholics issued their own manifesto calling on Catholics to sign the petition. Led by Henri Desroches, a Dominican member of Économie et humanisme, "Christians against the Atomic Bomb" garnered forty-six signatures, including all the usual suspects: Chenu, Boisselot, Féret, Jacques Hollande (the superior of the Mission de Paris), Boulier, Montuclard, Lacroix, Mandouze, and many others associated with the Catholic left. While most Catholics supported the principle of nuclear disarmament, however, many were wary of throwing their weight behind a movement so clearly identified with the Soviet Union and the Communist Party.[109]

Chenu was sensitive to this problem as well, but he was convinced that the cause of peace was a just and a Christian one, and that it was necessary to put aside ideological differences in order to achieve it.[110] For Chenu, this decision reflected a broader battle within the Church between an older Christendom model, which viewed any movement beyond the Church with suspicion, and the new missionary movements that strove to "plant themselves in new communities, situations, and aspirations that are not Christian" by "throwing into this fermenting human dough the yeast of the Gospel."[111] To partisans of the first model, the Church was the true guarantor of peace and any effort to promote it outside the aegis of Christian institutions was therefore suspect. But those who embraced a missionary Church "do not believe that the Church is soiled by the use of means that are good in themselves, when they are accidentally mixed in with a historical context that men have rendered impure."[112] The goals of the Stockholm Appeal were objectively good in themselves, even if the intentions behind them were not. Consequently, Chenu threw his energies into the peace movement and related projects, such as the campaigns against German rearmament and the war in Indochina, which he forcefully condemned in a 1953 speech to the Committee of Study and Action for the Peaceful Resolution of the War in Vietnam.[113]

The peace movement breathed new life into a Catholic left hit hard by the condemnation of 1949. It inspired the creation of a new publication called *La Quinzaine* in 1950, which took over the position left vacant by the UCP and attracted veterans of various other Catholic movements on the left. Though the journal claimed not to hew to a particular ideology or provide any political directives, its editorial line was driven by a commitment to working-class solidarity. It advocated for the Catholic and communist-dominated trade unions to forge a united front—

something vigorously opposed by the French hierarchy. But perhaps the two governing positions of the new journal were its commitment to the peace movement and its anticolonialism. Unlike most Catholics, the editors of *La Quinzaine* opposed the French Union, which had been established under the Constitution of the Fourth Republic in order to integrate the metropole and overseas territories into a single political structure and offset growing demands for local autonomy within the empire. By the early 1950s, the French were battling the Viet Minh in Indochina and struggling to maintain control over Morocco and Tunisia. *La Quinzaine* was one of the most forceful critics of colonialism within the French Church at the time and supported independence for the overseas territories.[114] But its editors also recognized that it would be "impossible to make the Christian masses share this position." They therefore limited themselves to decrying the economic exploitation of France's overseas territories and the government's efforts to limit the extension of democratic rights to the *indigènes*. The governing line for the journal, they decided, must be "respect in France and in the overseas territories for democratic freedoms and the rights of man; support for the progressive possibilities and intentions within the constitution of the French Union."[115] Throughout the 1950s, the "colonial question" would become a central preoccupation in progressive Catholic circles, and they would go on to play a key role in the resistance to the Algerian War.[116]

Given Chenu's role in the peace movement and his opposition to colonialism, it is perhaps not surprising that he became the official theological advisor to *La Quinzaine*. He wrote several articles under the alias "Apostolus" on topics ranging from the war in Indochina to economic questions and the peace movement.[117] But his most significant contribution was to articulate the journal's position on the relationship between religion and politics. In both internal communications to the staff and published articles, Chenu sought to chart a middle course between a "confusion" of the temporal and spiritual orders and "a complete separatism between planes."[118] This position reflected his theological commitment to defending the autonomy of the natural order without bifurcating nature and grace. On the one hand, Chenu insisted that Christian political engagement could, and should, take inspiration from faith. "Man does not live his life in separate rooms," he reasoned, as if it were possible for people to be "Christians in one room, enjoying their faith, their religious practices, their solidarity in the Christian community, and political men on the other side of the door."[119] Politics necessarily involved moral questions, which meant that it could never be fully disentangled from religion. And yet, Chenu insisted that Christians could not simply "deduce their political options from the Gospel" either.[120] He therefore distinguished between three kinds of political statements: "general principles" prescribed by the faith (such as the freedom of the person and the exigencies of communal life), less binding "directives," and finally, "concrete options" that were entirely beyond the purview of the Church. In such matters, Christians had to make their own political decisions.[121]

In taking this position, Chenu was deeply sensitive to the long history of clerical intervention in European politics. He therefore insisted on the need to approach political and economic realities "according to their proper value, their goal, and their laws" and to uphold "the autonomy of profane economic, social, and political action," which lay beyond the "technical competency" of the Church.[122] To support this position, Chenu appealed once again to Aquinas, who had affirmed the autonomous value of human affairs against an Augustinian tradition that conflated religion and politics. Chenu firmly rejected this Christendom model, which he associated with Augustinianism. Instead of striving "to draw economic, social, political, and temporal realities toward the Church," Chenu encouraged Catholics to "go out and plant themselves in the profane world, in the non-Christian world."[123] For, as St. Thomas had shown, the progressive development of human freedom and worldly autonomy was itself the sign of God's grace. "The advance of Christian thought is achieved through the increasingly precise autonomy of the political," he told the staff of *La Quinzaine*. It was therefore crucial that they justify the political positions they took in its pages on political rather than religious grounds.[124] This did not mean that their faith was irrelevant to their engagement, but that it should serve as "a kind of internal lucidity" and "rarely intervene directly" in their political choices.[125] Even as Chenu sought to chart a "middle path" between confusion and separation, then, his characteristically Thomist emphasis on the autonomy of temporal affairs ultimately brought him closer to Thomists like Maydieu and Serrand than Jesuits like Fessard.[126]

Chenu also had good political reason to stress the autonomy of political affairs from clerical intervention. In the first place, doing so allowed him to defend the legitimacy of Catholic engagement with the left in the aftermath of the Vatican decree against communism. But Chenu also had another aim. If he and so many other progressive French Catholics stressed the distinction between faith and politics, this was also because they sought to purge the Church of its long-standing entanglement with the political right. Again and again they called out the Church's historical opposition to democracy, its complicity with capitalism, and its open support for the Americans in the Cold War as so many instances of the illegitimate politicization of the faith. In 1950, for instance, Congar penned a fierce critique of right-wing "integrists" within the Church, whose politics he blamed on a theological suspicion of human agency and the autonomy of the natural order. At issue, Congar explained, was "a particular way of conceiving the 'supernatural,'" which led these Catholics to "combat . . . even healthy manifestations of nature and the human subject."[127] Dominicans such as Congar and Chenu thus found in the Thomist argument for the autonomy of the natural order ammunition for their battle against the Catholic right.

In this way, the Thomist vision of the internal consistency and autonomy of the natural order, in which political, economic, and social life takes place, became the foundation for a distinctively Catholic left in postwar France. It allowed theologians like Chenu to maintain the independence of political affairs from ecclesiastical intervention and to critique the politicization of Catholicism in the service of the right without thereby suggesting that faith had nothing to contribute to political life. This does not mean that theologians like Chenu and Congar simply instrumentalized Thomism in the service of their politics. Instead, Thomism was the grid through which they made sense of their own experiences, such as their involvement with the worker-priests, the peace movement, and the increasingly polarized climate of the Cold War. And these experiences in turn led them to reformulate their Thomist theology in such a way as to grant the things of this world an autonomous value without cutting them off from the supernatural. Doing so allowed them to argue for the social and political significance of the faith, without giving the Church hierarchy the authority to dictate the political choices of the faithful.

The bishops sensed the danger in this logic. In 1952, the Assembly of Cardinals and Archbishops, sounding rather like Fessard, rebuked *La Quinzaine* for drawing "a radical separation between the spiritual and the profane" and encouraging "its readers to lay claim to complete autonomy on the civic and social plane in relation to the directives of the Church." "Is this not just an unexpected return to the *'politique d'abord'* [of the Action française]," the bishops asked?[128] As with the conflict over the AF, what worried the bishops about *La Quinzaine*'s position was not just that it undermined the role of faith in politics, but that it specifically undermined the authority of the Church to pronounce on these questions. In the process, it threatened the entire tradition of Social Catholicism—from Catholic Action, to Catholic social teaching, to confessional parties. By suggesting that "it is up to each person to decide, according to his conscience, what line of conduct to adopt in this domain," and that there is no "superior criterion beyond individual reflection by which to judge the legitimacy of an engagement on the social plane," the bishops accused *La Quinzaine* of opening the door to radical subjectivism in social and political life.[129] If Christians could make decisions about such questions in light of their own faith, rather than the way this faith was interpreted by the hierarchy, then what role would remain for the Church in public life?

Reclaiming the Political

By the mid-1950s, Church authorities had taken measures to shut down almost all the postwar experiments of the Catholic left. After two official warnings from the French bishops, *La Quinzaine* was shuttered, while the worker-priests were forced out of the factories and their Dominican supporters sanctioned (see Chapter 7). But despite the frequent parallels drawn between the Catholic left and the AF, the outcome of the postwar conflict turned out to be quite different. Whereas the condemnation of Maurras inspired a deep suspicion of politics among Catholic theologians and philosophers, essays by Chenu and Daniélou from the 1950s suggest that the controversy over the Catholic left instead opened the way for a new effort to reclaim the political as a legitimate space for Catholic engagement—an effort that would continue to bear fruit in the 1960s and 1970s with the rise of political and liberation theology. What the two theologians took from the travails of the Catholic left was the need to clarify the Church's relationship to politics. A comparison between their approaches reveals the points of convergence as well as the significant differences between the way the Jesuits and the Dominicans envisioned the role of Catholicism in public life.

On the fundamentals, they tended to agree. Both sought some kind of "happy medium between an outdated identification and a condemnable separation" of religion and politics.[130] But the lesson that Chenu drew from the postwar experiments of the Catholic left was the need for Catholics to overcome their suspicion of politics and claim a rightful place for themselves in the political order. Chenu acknowledged that "politics" was a fundamentally ambiguous term, one that encompassed everything from "a concern for the common good of the City—one of the highest human values!—all the way to the combative choices of parties and the corruption . . . of human life by the ambitions and ravages of the pursuit of power."[131] Given the specific history of the French Church—its long-standing entanglement with the state and with the forces of reaction—it was only natural that many French Catholics had developed a deep suspicion of all forms of political Catholicism. But Chenu thought this backlash had gone too far. He sought to distinguish politics (la politique)—the grubby domain of ambition and party politics— from the much broader and loftier domain of the political (la réalité politique), which he defined as "the total dimension of participation in the construction of the City and the world."[132] This was the domain in which the terrestrial common good would be achieved, and Catholics had a responsibility to contribute to it. It was something larger than the machinations of parties and politicians—a set of principles that included the dignity of labor, the need for peace, and the right to self-determination for colonial peoples. For Chenu, the great achievement of the postwar experiments of the Catholic left was to teach Catholics to respect the "supreme dignity" of this political order and reclaim their rightful place within it.

Daniélou also took away from these disputes the need for a clearer definition of the relationship between the Church and the political order. Like Chenu, he sought to chart a middle path between the tendency to conflate faith and politics, and a strict separation of spheres.[133] He likewise distinguished between those positions that flowed necessarily from Catholic teaching and the areas in which Catholics were free to make their own political choices. The first of these, the Jesuit argued, was the realm of "properly Christian politics," and the principles it prescribed were absolutely binding.[134] For Daniélou, the most important of these was the freedom to spread the Gospel, and, in a clear dig at the communists, he insisted that Catholics could not work with any party or regime that denied this freedom or defined the human person in ways that were incompatible with Christian anthropology. But Daniélou also insisted that other principles were equally "non-negotiable" from a Catholic perspective, including the right to work, respect for the dignity of colonial subjects, and the need to limit the power of money in contemporary society. Daniélou thus distanced himself from both the Catholic left and the anticommunist hierarchy, arguing that "a Christian cannot work toward the advent of Marxism" but also "cannot remain complicit in the current injustice."[135] If the Church was well within its rights to condemn Catholics who had embraced communism, it also had to show the same rigor against those who violated its social and economic teaching. "The day a priest refuses communion to a boss who fails gravely in his social obligations," he concluded, "the seriousness of the rupture between the Church and the established disorder would become concretely apparent."[136]

This reference to the "established disorder"—a term first coined by Mounier in the 1930s to disparage the decadence of the Third Republic—highlights the distance that separated Daniélou's vision of Catholic politics from that of Chenu. For the Dominican, it was crucial to affirm the autonomy of the political order and work within the existing structures of social, economic, and political life—including the structures of working-class solidarity. But from the Jesuit's perspective,

> the great error of contemporary Christian politicians is that they accept to situate themselves within the existing order, whether this be the liberal or the communist order. And from the moment this has been accepted, Christianity necessarily becomes ineffective, because it has lost its essential resource. Christian politics must therefore consist first and foremost in a refusal of what Mounier called the established disorder, whatever form it takes.[137]

Jesuits like Daniélou, Fessard, and de Lubac thus clung to the logic of refusal that had informed their resistance activities during the war. The role of Christian politics, they believed, was to critique the existing political order—whether right or left—from the perspective of Christian principles. But such a critical model was not enough for Chenu and the Catholic left. They wanted to build something more positive, even if this approach came with the risk of collaboration and compromise.

Yet the fact that both Daniélou and Chenu used the word "politics" to describe what they were doing signaled an important shift. It was the first sign that French theologians were beginning to move beyond their long-standing suspicion of politics, especially since the backlash against Maurras's *"politique d'abord."* Ultimately, both priests sought to carve out a public role for the Church that would avoid the extremes of "excessively separating" or "too narrowly identifying" religion and politics. And Chenu would no doubt have agreed with Daniélou that the domain of Catholic politics was "neither that of private morality, nor that of pure politics."[138] In making this claim, both sought to chart a middle course between the clericalization of politics they associated with an outdated Christendom model and the privatization of religion in modern liberal polities. The Dominicans found inspiration for their approach in Thomas Aquinas, who had affirmed the autonomy and dignity of the temporal order and emancipated it from clerical tutelage. But for the Jesuits, Catholic politics was defined above all by its refusal to compromise with the structures of secular politics, whatever they might be—a critical and eschatological model they found in the works of the Church Fathers. And this led them to adopt a very different position on the dominant political challenges of the day. It is to this model that we turn next.

CHAPTER SIX

The Drama of Atheist Humanism and the Politics of History

In 1948, Gaston Fessard offered his own contribution to the postwar "humanism" debate at a conference on "Humanism and Existentialism" that was attended by many of the leading lights of French intellectual life. In his talk, Fessard asserted that Christianity alone could overcome the contradictions of atheist humanism in both its Marxist and existentialist guises.[1] But he made it clear that Christianity did not oppose these philosophies in equal measure. "Faced with the opposition between Marxist Humanism and atheist existentialism," the Jesuit explained, Christianity "aims to establish a true humanism and *to give existentialism free rein.*"[2] It was not a question of articulating a Christian alternative to both Marxism and existentialism, then, but of deploying and perfecting the insights of existentialism in the service of Christianity. For, despite the fame and prestige enjoyed at the time by Jean-Paul Sartre, Fessard insisted that existentialism need not be an atheist philosophy. In fact, he maintained, atheist existentialism was only a recent deviation from what was first and foremost a religious philosophy.

The Jesuit was not the only person to make this claim. He was but one representative of a vibrant Christian existentialist tradition in France, which has received considerably less attention from historians than the atheist existentialism of Sartre and his colleagues at *Les Temps modernes.*[3] And yet, in his map of postwar French intellectual life, Jean Daniélou identified Christian existentialism as one of the two dominant strands of Catholic thought in this period—the other being the "humanist socialism" discussed in the previous chapter.[4] Daniélou associated Christian existentialism above all with the work of Gabriel Marcel, who had become Fessard's spiritual disciple in 1934, and with the newly established journal *Dieu vivant,* to which Daniélou served as theological advisor. Far from an exclusively Catholic movement, it was an ecumenical project drawing together Protestant disciples of Karl Barth or Oscar Cullmann and Russian Orthodox philosophers and theologians, many of whom had fled the Bolshevik Revolution for Paris. What united these disparate strands of Christian existentialism, Daniélou argued, was their shared focus on "eschatological expectation, with its triple character of a judgment taken by God upon every human reality, the transfiguration of man and the cosmos through the Resurrection, and the gathering together of all men in the unity of Christ."[5]

This emphasis on eschatology was the defining feature of the theological engagement with existentialism on the part of the Jesuits associated with the *nouvelle théologie.* It allowed them to correct the limitations that they perceived in existential phenomenology by integrating its insights on the individual subject into the broader framework of salvation history, conceived above all as a social affair. They believed that such an existential eschatology, because it was "oriented more fully toward a consideration of the social and historical," could more effectively answer the challenge of Marxism.[6] But it also served as a counterpoint to the main Catholic humanism of the day—the Thomist anthropology that underwrote Jacques Maritain's theory of human rights. In opposition to a static vision of human nature grounded in natural law, which provided the foundation for the emerging Catholic discourse on human rights, Jesuits such as Fessard, Daniélou, and de Lubac instead articulated a dynamic anthropology. Like the existentialists, they defined the human being not as an essence, but as a process—one driven by a negativity or lack that was constitutive of human nature itself. For the Jesuits, however, this lack was the very call of the divine at the heart of human nature. Such an approach refused the neo-Thomist distinction between the natural and supernatural ends of human life, a theological difference with important implications for contemporaneous debates about human rights and the Church's relationship to projects such as the Universal Declaration of Human Rights (UDHR).

The Jesuits' contribution to the postwar debate on humanism was thus the logical extension of the counter-political stance they had adopted during the war, and the same was true of their postwar reflections on the problem of history. They continued to look to eschatology as a critical reminder that all temporal institutions and political projects were ultimately only provisional, but now they directed their critical energies against the left rather than the right. Rejecting the linear notion of time that informed both liberalism and Marxism, they instead privileged the discontinuous temporality common to Christian eschatology and existentialism. By inscribing the eschatological event at the heart of the historical present, they reminded Christians of the need to be both engaged in, and critical of, the institutions and projects of temporal life. When taken together, this existential eschatology and the theological anthropology that went along with it constituted a theological rejoinder to both liberalism and Marxism. Rather than addressing these ideologies at a more overtly political level, however, Fessard, de Lubac, and Daniélou sought to undermine the anthropology and the philosophy of history on which they relied. This was, in other words, a paradigmatic case of counter-politics.

The story of the theological vision articulated by these priests reveals just how porous was the boundary between theology and mainstream philosophy in twentieth-century France.[7] Crucially, this influence did not operate in one direction alone. Even before the heyday of existentialism, Catholic theologians had been key contributors to the interwar revival of Hegelian philosophy. And secular philosophers such as Sartre, Maurice Merleau-Ponty, Georges Bataille, and Alexandre Kojève were keenly aware of contemporaneous developments in Catholic thought and often oriented their own work in relation to them. Recovering the role that Catholic theologians played in these debates thus has crucial implications for the study of twentieth-century French thought. But it also reframes our understanding of Catholic theology. It allows us to situate de Lubac's *Surnaturel,* which is usually interpreted through the lens of internal theological debates about Thomism and Augustinianism, in the context of the postwar engagement with human rights and existentialism.[8] Doing so demonstrates the value of adopting an approach to contextualization that is both temporally intensive and temporally extensive—one that balances the immediate historical context in which theology is produced with the much older tradition in which it is embedded.

Hegel Resurrected

To understand the postwar debate between Catholics and secular philosophers, we must first return to the 1930s, when French thought rediscovered Hegel. This was the moment when French philosophy shook off the weight of academic neo-Kantianism, with its abstract and atemporal form of reasoning.[9] This was still the dominant approach when Alexandre Kojève—a Russian émigré who had studied with Karl Jaspers—took over the Hegel seminar at the École Pratique des Hautes Études in 1933. Filtered through Kojève's idiosyncratic interpretation, Hegel provided French philosophers with a vision of human consciousness as socially and historically constituted—one that did not exist for all time as a fixed nature, but was progressively *made* in the act of encountering other beings and working on the world. What Hegel offered, in other words, was an anthropology conceived as *anthropogenesis*. As a result, the Hegelian revival became the crucible in which most of the postwar developments in French philosophy, from Marxism and existentialism to psychoanalysis and post-structuralism, were forged. Indeed, the attendance list for Kojève's seminar reads like a "who's who" of postwar French thought: from avant-garde writers such as Georges Bataille and Raymond Queneau to the psychoanalytic theorist Jacques Lacan, as well as leading French philosophers such as Maurice Merleau-Ponty, Raymond Aron, Emmanuel Levinas, and Éric Weil.

What is less often recalled, however, is the role that Catholics played in the Hegelian renaissance. Though the standard reference work on French Hegelianism mentions him only in passing, one name appears more frequently than virtually any other on the list of those who attended Kojève's seminar between 1933 and 1939: Gaston Fessard.[10] Indeed, when Kojève selected two people to offer a response during the final session of his seminar, one of these was Fessard. "Amongst my listeners," Kojève told him, "you were, without any doubt, one of the most competent and perhaps the only one who, like me, took the [*Phenomenology of Spirit*] 'seriously.'"[11] Nor was Fessard the only Catholic drawn to Hegel in this period. He was simply the most famous of a group of Catholic Hegelians who were disenchanted with the ahistorical rationalism of Thomist philosophy, a group that also included the Jesuits Henri Rondet and Henri Niel. That historians have often overlooked these figures owes much to the tendency to read French Hegelianism through the lens of subsequent developments in Marxist and existentialist thought, and therefore, to miss the theological questions at the heart of the Hegelian revival.[12] I argue instead that the central conflict in French Hegelianism was between theistic and atheistic interpretations of Hegel—a dispute with significant political implications, which set the terms for the postwar debate on humanism. In other words, the twentieth-century French reception of Hegel in many ways reiterated the battle between "Left" and "Right" Hegelians a century earlier.[13]

No two figures exemplified these competing positions better than Fessard and Kojève. As one of his students put it, Kojève's reading of Hegel was "the intellectual *ménage à trois* of Hegel, Marx and Heidegger."[14] Above all, Kojève concerned himself with the problem of recognition, which he viewed as the key to anthropogenesis. It led him to fixate on Hegel's master-slave dialectic, elevating it from a passing phase in Hegel's phenomenology to the very lynchpin of human history. What drives this process, Kojève believed, is the human desire for recognition from another being who is desirous of the very same recognition. The process of becoming a fully self-conscious human being is therefore inescapably social. But it is also necessarily violent, because these competing desires for recognition cannot initially be squared. Consequently, "the 'first' anthropogenetic action takes the form of a fight: a fight to the death . . . for the sake of 'recognition' by the adversary."[15] Only the combatant willing to sacrifice the animal part of his nature, his very instinct for survival, can master his opponent, whereas the combatant who chooses self-preservation over freedom is relegated to the status of a slave. And yet, the slave paradoxically emerges from the conflict in a better position than the master, who has risked his life for something that "is not recognition properly so-called" because it is granted under duress and is not mutual.[16] Moreover, the master now depends on the labor of the slave, and thus lacks the tool with which the slave can succeed where the master has failed. This tool is the ability to work, for "in transforming the World by this work, the Slave transforms himself, too, and thus creates the new objective conditions that permit him to take up once more the liberating Fight for recognition."[17] Consequently, Kojève concluded, "laborious Slavery . . . is the source of all human, social, historical progress. History is the history of the working Slave."[18]

The political implications of this statement were not lost on Kojève's audience, and his account of the master-slave dialectic was widely interpreted as an allegory for the class struggle, especially after the 1947 publication of Raymond Queneau's notes on the seminar. Historians, too, have tended to portray Kojève as a Marxist reader of Hegel. But Stefanos Geroulanos has recently drawn attention to Kojève's debt to the Orthodox theologian Vladimir Solovyov, and indeed, when one examines Kojève's own writing (rather than Queneau's second-hand report), religious and theological questions take center stage.[19] What they reveal is a man who conceived of himself as the inheritor of the "Left" or "Young" Hegelian tradition, who was locked in a struggle against Hegel's Catholic interpreters.

In the 1930s, the most famous of these interpreters was Gaston Fessard. The Jesuit's lifelong interest in Hegel dated to 1926, and he attributed it in part to his "disappointment" with the neo-scholastic philosophy that he had been taught at Jersey.[20] What attracted Fessard to Hegel was something that was missing from this philosophy: a "sense of the historical and sociological development of all things."[21] In the 1930s, then, Catholic and secular philosophers shared a growing realization "that time and history penetrate all knowledge, natural as well as supernatural." This new historical consciousness, Fessard believed, placed Hegel's Catholic readers "in a situation analogous to that which Saint Thomas experienced when Arab philosophy introduced him to Aristotle." Just as Aquinas had distinguished the "elements of truth" in Aristotle from the "errors" of the Arab commentators, Fessard wished to do the same for Hegel.[22] He sought to "return to the source" behind the distortions of subsequent interpreters—in this case, Marx and the Left Hegelians—in order to reconcile Hegelianism with Catholic theology. By doing for Hegel what Thomas had done for Aristotle, Fessard hoped to develop a "new dogmatic synthesis" that would "render Christianity useful to contemporary man."[23]

To do this, Fessard "corrected" the limitations of Hegel's dialectic with the Jew-Gentile dialectic that he derived from St. Paul (see Chapter 2). For the Jesuit, the addition of this second dialectic added a vertical dimension to the anthropocentric (and rather violent) account of the emergence of human consciousness based on the struggle between master and slave. The Pauline dialectic raised this encounter beyond a purely immanent struggle for recognition between human beings and endowed Christ—who had reconciled Jew and Gentile in his person—with a central role in the drama of anthropogenesis. Fessard had first elaborated the Jew-Gentile dialectic in his 1930s works *Pax Nostra* and *La main tendue*, and these works also occasioned his first dispute with Kojève. The two men had been in contact since 1934, when each discovered that the other was working on a French translation of the *Phenomenology of Spirit*. Although Fessard had initially hoped that the two might collaborate on the project, it soon became clear that their radically divergent interpretations of the text would make any such partnership impossible.[24] In any case, Fessard's superiors, who were troubled by the pantheist and historicist thrust of Hegel's thought, soon put a stop to his efforts to publish on the subject.[25]

These differences first became apparent when Kojève reviewed the two works in which Fessard elaborated his distinctive synthesis of Hegel and St. Paul. Although it was never published, the review revealed the main point of contention between the two philosophers: the relationship between Hegelianism and Christianity. Kojève read Fessard's work as a transparent bid to draw "modern man" back into the arms of the Church by "making Catholicism profit from the philosophical efforts of Hegel and Marx," a move Kojève could not allow to go unchallenged. Writing from a "'Hegelian' and 'Marxist,' which is to say, atheist" perspective, Kojève subtly shifted the terms of Fessard's Jew-Gentile dialectic in order to turn Fessard's argument on its head. It was Hegel and Marx, Kojève argued, who had overcome the dialectical opposition between "the Gentile thesis and the Judeo-Christian (or 'bourgeois') *antithesis*" by establishing a "post-Christian *synthesis* . . . that is essentially atheist and irreligious."[26] This conflation of Marx and Hegel was characteristic of Kojève's Left Hegelian approach, whereas Fessard sought to distinguish Hegel from Marx in order to make Hegel safe for theology.

Fessard got his chance to reply when Kojève invited Fessard and Raymond Aron to offer a public response during the final session of his Hegel seminar. Aron and Fessard had become close during the seminar, bonding over their shared distaste for the Marxist commitments that they perceived as coloring Kojève's interpretation.[27] What they objected to, in particular, was his account of Hegel's phenomenology as a closed anthropological circle in which humans could achieve absolute knowledge and build a "universal, homogeneous state," understood by many of Kojève's interpreters as a reference to Marx's classless society. While Fessard embraced this as a worthwhile goal, he insisted that it could not be achieved on earth and through human agency alone. Instead, he identified the ideal of the universal, homogeneous state with the mystical body of Christ and insisted that the Incarnation was the indispensable precondition for achieving absolute knowledge. In this sense, divine agency did not "suppress man's freedom," as Kojève assumed; instead, it was precisely what made our transcendence of the given world possible.[28] Although by no means the only readings of Hegel in circulation at the time, by 1939, it was clear that two very different interpretations had emerged in France—one atheist; the other theist. And they rather strikingly echoed the politico-theological disputes between Right and Left Hegelians in nineteenth-century Germany.

This battle for Hegel's soul reemerged with even greater force after the war, in the context of the humanism debate among Marxists, Catholics, and existentialists. The immediate trigger was the publication of Fessard's anticommunist tract, *France, Take Care Not to Lose Your Freedom,* which Kojève reviewed in 1946. Even though the two philosophers diverged in their interpretation of Hegel, they could still agree that Marxism was atheist through and through. Kojève in fact praised Fessard for his deep understanding of Marxism, which he thought far exceeded that of the communists themselves. "If he had wished," Kojève mused, "the author would certainly be by far the best theorist of Marxism in France."[29] But he could not allow Fessard "to exploit the Hegelian discovery of the dialectic in the service of Christianity" and of anticommunism.[30] In response to Fessard's claim that the atheism of the Marxist philosophy of history led it into an insuperable contradiction, Kojève retorted that "the dialectic is bound to finitude" and to "the decisive, definitive, and irreducible value of historical action."[31] It precluded, by definition, the idea of Christ's resurrection and the transhistorical claims of Christian doctrine. "The notion of a Christian or theological dialectic is therefore a contradiction in terms," Kojève concluded.[32] And while he conceded that Hegel's anthropology "maintain[ed] the fundamental categories of Christian theology," Kojève insisted that it transferred these properties from God to man. In this way, he presented Hegel as a Feuerbachian *avant-la-lettre,* who had recognized that "theology was always an unconscious anthropology."[33]

Kojève further clarified the political stakes of this dispute in a lengthy review essay on the work of another Catholic Hegelian, Henri Niel. Once again, Kojève identified Hegel's relationship to religion as the crux of the disagreement, which manifested itself in the very different ways that Niel and Kojève approached the Hegelian corpus. Against Kojève's emphasis on the violent master-slave dialectic, Niel privileged the "dialectic of love" that results in the birth of a child; against Kojève's concern with the problem of recognition, Niel stressed the role of mediation, which finds its highest expression in Christ. Like many theistic accounts of Hegel, Niel's shifted the focus from the *Phenomenology* to Hegel's later work, which allowed for a more robustly metaphysical interpretation of the Hegelian system.[34] In contrast, Kojève insisted that "the evolution of

Hegel's thought ends at the moment he discovers (in 1800) the dialectic of Recognition."[35] This was crucial because the master-slave dialectic constituted only one, very early stage in the development of consciousness traced in the *Phenomenology*. And yet, in order to deploy it in the service of revolutionary politics, Kojève had to argue that it was *the* fundamental conflict of human history. Indeed, he insisted that it marked the birth of political life, "because the man who is recognized by others in his human dignity and reality, is by that very fact recognized politically: he is a Citizen [*Bürger*] of the State formed by those who recognize him and whom he recognizes in turn."[36] Only when this form of recognition becomes universal can history come to an end. At this point, "man will be perfectly satisfied by the fact of being a recognized citizen of a *universal and homogeneous State,* or, if one prefers, a classless society encompassing the whole of humanity."[37]

That Kojève offered the clearest expression of his own politics in an article devoted to refuting Catholic Hegelianism indicates that theology and politics were just as intertwined for Hegel's twentieth-century interpreters as they were for his nineteenth-century disciples. On the one hand, the communist press and "progressive Christians" presented Fessard's Catholic Hegelianism as the "theology of the R.P.F. [Rassemblement du peuple français]," linking it to Charles de Gaulle's newly formed center-right party.[38] On the other, Kojève's reading of Hegel paved the way for the rise of existential Marxism. This led Kojève to argue that all political and intellectual developments since the death of Hegel were ultimately reducible to the quarrel between Right and Left Hegelianism, of which his own dispute with the Catholic Hegelians was a case in point. If Hegel's death paved the way for the emergence of "a Hegelian left and right," he explained, "that is also *all* there has been since Hegel."[39] But the battle would ultimately be decided in the realm of practical action. The stakes could not be higher, he insisted, "for it may well be that the future of the world . . . depends in the final analysis on the way in which one interprets today the writings of Hegel."[40]

Fessard got a chance to respond to this challenge in 1947, when he reviewed the newly published text of Kojève's Hegel seminar alongside Jean Hyppolite's doctoral thesis on the *Phenomenology*.[41] While Fessard chided Hyppolite for "refus[ing] to choose between the Hegelian right and left," the Jesuit devoted the bulk of his energies to refuting Kojève.[42] Once again, it was Kojève's vision of "a perfectly and consciously atheist Hegel" that elicited the Jesuit's ire, but it was clear that this was no longer just a dispute between rival Hegelianisms. Instead, Fessard suggested that the postwar drama of atheist humanism, in both its Marxist and existentialist guises, could be traced to Kojève's atheist misreading of Hegel. By insisting "that the radical finitude of man alone explains human history," Kojève had made Hegel "not only Feuerbachian and Marxist, but also Heideggerian *avant-la-lettre.*" And yet, Fessard insisted that Kojève's efforts to "Marxicize" Hegel were ultimately self-defeating, because "if it is true that Hegel was already 'Marxist,' then all of the critiques that Marx directed against Hegel lose their meaning." The Jesuit was only too happy to note that many Marxists had repudiated Kojève's "pseudo-Marxist existentialist" reading of Hegel for this very reason and rallied instead behind a theistic interpretation.[43] But it was not enough to demonstrate that Hegel's philosophy was open to God; Fessard also sought to "correct" the limitations of what was, after all, a *Protestant* philosophy with his own Jew-Gentile dialectic.[44] Fessard, in other words, responded to Kojève's attempts to "Marxicize" Hegel by "Catholicizing" him.

The struggle for the soul of Hegelianism in the 1930s thus set the terms for the postwar encounter between Marxism, existentialism, and Catholicism. This was not only because Kojève wove insights from both Marx and Heidegger into his reading of Hegel. Above all, it was the religious question that provided the element of continuity between the two moments—a question that twentieth-century French thought had itself inherited from nineteenth-century Germany. Fessard made this clear in an unpublished essay that explained how postwar Marxism and existentialism had emerged from the bosom of interwar Hegelianism. "Historically, it was the interpretation of [Hegel's] religious philosophy that caused the Hegelian school to rupture into its two branches—right and left," he explained. "Today it is once again the same question that is at the center of all these problems."[45] But if the battle for Hegel's soul had begun to die down by 1947, the battle for the soul of existentialism was still going strong.

The Battle for the Soul of Existentialism

On October 29, 1945, Jean-Paul Sartre made his entry into the postwar humanism debate. Before a packed audience at the Club Maintenant, he announced that existentialism, too, was a humanism. The immediate context for the speech was the strong showing by socialists, communists, and Christian democrats at the polls eight days earlier.[46] Sartre's famous talk was therefore not simply an attempt to articulate an existentialist humanism over and against both its Marxist and Catholic counterparts; it was also an intervention in the politico-theological conflicts of postwar France. It marked the beginning of Sartre's increasing concern to align existentialism with the left and against Catholicism, which would find its fullest expression in his *Critique of Dialectical Reason* (1960).[47] In other words, it was the opening salvo in a postwar battle for the soul of existentialism that mirrored the ongoing conflict within French Hegelianism, pitting atheist existentialists against their Christian counterparts.

In his speech, Sartre responded to both the Marxist and Catholic critiques of existentialism. The first charged him with articulating an individualist, "bourgeois philosophy" that consigned the human being to "a state of quietism and despair," while Catholics like Jeanne Mercier took issue with his amoral and pessimistic view of human nature.[48] In response to his Marxist critics, Sartre denounced rigid historical materialism for reducing the human being to an object devoid of agency, while also dispensing with the liberal notion that humans are "essences" defined by an unchanging human nature. Instead, Sartre argued that "man is constantly in the making" and is "nothing more than the sum of his actions."[49] In order to offset the Marxist critique that such a philosophy imprisoned individuals within their own subjectivity, Sartre maintained that individual freedom was bound up with a collective project of human liberation. "In creating the man each of us wills ourselves to be," he explained, we also "create an image of man as we think he ought to be."[50] Consequently, he concluded, "I am obliged to will the freedom of others at the same time as I will my own."[51] In making this argument, Sartre held out the possibility that existentialism could be reconciled with the political goals of the communists, if not their materialist philosophy.[52]

His true target, then, was less the communists than the Catholics, and Catholic existentialism in particular. Sartre acknowledged the existence of two rival strands of existentialism: a religious one indebted to Kierkegaard and represented by such figures as Karl Jaspers and Gabriel Marcel, and an atheist one inspired by Nietzsche and Heidegger. And yet, he insisted that only the second strand was authentically existentialist. Religious belief was absolutely incompatible with the core existentialist principle that humans are fully free and responsible for their choices, unconstrained by any external agency or predetermined moral code. For Sartre, in other words, religion was the archetypal form of "bad faith."

Because Sartrean existentialism has become so canonical, it has often been assumed that existentialism, at least in postwar France, was an atheist philosophy first and foremost.[53] But the very fact that Sartre needed to make this argument should give us pause, and indeed, historians have increasingly begun to attend to the powerful strain of religious phenomenology in France, which in fact predated Sartrean existentialism.[54]

As Edward Baring has shown, the prewar French engagement with phenomenology and existential philosophy was almost entirely dominated by Catholics, and in particular by the "Philosophie de l'Esprit" group that formed around René le Senne and Louis Lavelle.[55] But above all, it was Gabriel Marcel whose name became synonymous with Christian existentialism. A Catholic convert, Marcel broke with idealist philosophy to devote his attention to the concrete problem of human existence. His *Journal métaphysique*—published in 1927, the same year as Heidegger's *Being and Time*—eschewed systematic thinking in order to explore the "ontological mystery" that reveals the limits of human understanding. Following Kierkegaard, Marcel found in human finitude, not the despair, nihilism, and absurdity that Sartre deduced from it, but a source of hope and faith in a supra-human agency. And where Sartre approached the relationship between human beings as one of mutual objectification and conflict, Marcel discovered in the human encounter with the divine the grounds for "our capacity to open ourselves to others" in a mutually enriching way.[56] In 1932, Marcel launched a study circle at his home, where many of the leading lights of postwar French thought were introduced to phenomenology.[57] Its participants included not just religious philosophers such as Emmanuel Levinas and Nikolai Berdyaev, but also Sartre, de Beauvoir, and Merleau-Ponty. Given the existence of this robust Christian existentialist tradition, when Sartre announced in 1945 that existentialism was incompatible with religious faith, Emmanuel Mounier retorted that "historically, existentialism is more often synonymous with Christian philosophy, transcendence, and humanism, than atheism and despair."[58] And to prove this, he drew an "existentialist tree" that emphasized the philosophy's religious genealogy and confined Sartrean atheism to a single, isolated branch (see Figure 6.1).

The specifically theological engagement with existential phenomenology in France likewise predated Sartre. As early as 1932, the Société thomiste, led by Maritain and Chenu, devoted its annual study day to phenomenology. This was the first conference on phenomenology to be held outside Germany, and it attracted an international roster of guests

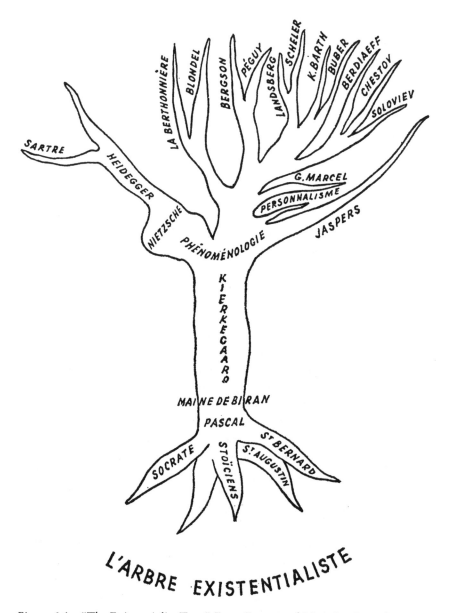

Figure 6.1 "The Existentialist Tree." From Emmanuel Mounier, *Introduction aux existentialismes* (Paris: Denoël, 1947). *Credit:* © Éditions Denoël, 1947.

including Edith Stein, Alexandre Koyré, and Étienne Gilson.[59] That same year, Yves de Montcheuil published an article in the *Nouvelle revue théologique* on the phenomenology of René le Senne. His friend Gaston Fessard soon followed suit, devoting two long essays to the philosopher, whose *Obstacle et valeur* he dubbed "the first work of French phenomenology."[60] Fessard himself drew inspiration from many of the branches of the "existentialist tree," having spent his years at Jersey reading Augustine, Bergson, and Blondel and writing his thesis on Maine de Biran. In 1934, he came into contact with another branch of this tree when Jean Wahl introduced him to Gabriel Marcel. Following his conversion in 1929, Marcel had initially been drawn to Maritain's circle, but he grew increasingly dissatisfied with the group's Thomism. "I will never be able to subscribe to such a philosophy," he complained to Fessard in 1934, for its "fundamental lack of humility, peremptory and pedantic doctrinalism exasperate me."[61] That same year, Marcel asked Fessard to become his spiritual director, and thus was born a very close intellectual and spiritual friendship that lasted until the Jesuit's death in 1978. Fessard envisioned Marcel as the heir to a specifically French phenomenological tradition derived from Blondel, Biran, and Pascal.[62] This was also the tradition with which Fessard identified, and he looked to existentialism to breathe new life into Catholic thought by restoring "youth and a new vigor to the most traditional of views."[63]

Fessard's own postwar engagement with existentialism was framed by the context of Sartre's speech at the Club Maintenant. Precisely because Sartre had sought to identify existentialism with atheism, just as Kojève had done with Hegel ten years earlier, the Jesuit approached this as yet another politico-theological conflict between an atheist philosophy and its Catholic counterpart. Despite the tension between Sartre and the PCF, Fessard did not hesitate to draw a connection between atheist existentialism and atheist communism in order to discredit both. As he explained it, "After being born in Germany at the very moment when the crest of the Hitlerian wave was preparing to submerge everything," the very same atheist existentialism "appears today *chez nous* at the crest of the communist wave."[64] What Fessard was referring to here was Heidegger's infamous involvement with the Nazi Party, and he did not hesitate to suggest that Heidegger's nihilism had played directly into the hands of the Nazis by inducing people "to recognize Hitler as their savior and cheerfully sacrifice their finitude to him." Fessard was convinced that

Sartre's philosophy was now doing for communism what Heidegger's had done for fascism. Sartre's "nauseous vision of the world" had simply crystallized the contradictions within the Marxist philosophy of history, something Fessard attributed to their shared atheism.[65]

Catholics like Fessard instead looked to Kierkegaard, the father of Christian existentialism, for a solution to the impasses of Sartre's philosophy. Unlike Sartre, Kierkegaard took the absurdity of human existence as a point of departure rather than an endpoint. For the Danish philosopher, "this 'absurd' was the means to a fulfillment of the Promise which exceeded all that his reason could imagine" and required a leap of faith like the one Abraham took when he agreed to the "absurd" demand to sacrifice his son.[66] Jean Daniélou likewise treated Sartrean existentialism as a wayward strain that kept only the negative elements of Kierkegaard's philosophy—a sense of despair untransfigured by faith.[67] It was only because Sartre viewed the relationship between God and man as a question of sovereignty that he perceived existentialism as incompatible with faith. But Daniélou insisted that Sartre's atheism was not warranted by his own existentialist premises. As Kierkegaard had shown, to "reject the primacy of essence over existence" was not "to deny that *an* Existence precedes our existence."[68] What Sartre had failed to recognize was that human freedom and divine agency were not mutually exclusive; that "the God of Christianity, far from being an obstacle to human freedom, is the living source of all profound spiritual liberty."[69] Daniélou thus approached Sartre's philosophy as a deviation from the authentic existentialist tradition represented by people like Gabriel Marcel or Karl Barth.

Both Sartre and his Catholic critics could agree, then, that the primary division within postwar existentialist thought was a religious one, albeit with important political consequences. These political stakes became clear in the course of an exchange between Daniélou and Maurice Merleau-Ponty. In fact, the exchange did not even start as a disagreement over phenomenology. It began when Merleau-Ponty intervened in Daniélou's quarrel with the communist intellectual Pierre Hervé. Although he had initially been drawn to Marcel's Christian existentialism, by 1945, Merleau-Ponty was firmly in the atheist camp.[70] In these years before his break with Sartre and his disillusionment with revolutionary politics, Merleau-Ponty was a pioneer in the effort to square existentialist philosophy with Marxism. In his response to Daniélou, he therefore attacked the Church on both political and philosophical grounds. Merleau-Ponty argued that Christianity was fundamentally torn between the logic of transcendence and the logic of incarnation, between the religion of the Father and that of the Son.[71] The former devalued the world and any effort to transform it. But the Incarnation changed all this by introducing the divine into the fallen world and redeeming it as the theater of human action. "The political ambiguity of Christianity," Merleau-Ponty argued, stemmed from the opposition between these two logics: "in line with the Incarnation, it can be revolutionary. But the religion of the Father is conservative."[72] And yet, Merleau-Ponty was at pains to show that, for the Christian, the logic of the Father invariably took precedence over that of the Son. "Faith" always trumped "good faith" because it bound believers to unchanging principles and prevented them from making a free political choice based on the concrete needs of the moment. Remarkably, Merleau-Ponty insisted that communism did not necessarily imply the same sort of "bad faith" because it allowed greater space for critique and personal choice.

In his response to Merleau-Ponty, Daniélou did not dispute the affinity between atheist existentialism and Marxism, but he denied that either remained true to the principles of existentialism. He attributed Sartre and Merleau-Ponty's "*gauchissement*" (a term denoting both a movement to the left and a distortion) of the existentialist tradition to "influences that have nothing to do with existentialism itself and instead relate, much like Marx's atheism, to the old tradition of Feuerbach."[73] Daniélou also pointed out that Merleau-Ponty's argument for the incompatibility between existentialism and faith was based on the mistaken assumption that Christianity rested on a theology of essences, such as Thomism. In fact, the Jesuit retorted, "there is a Christian existentialism that refuses, just like non-Christian existentialism, the primacy of essence over existence; of nature over freedom."[74] This tradition understood that the "Christian condition is not a nature but a vocation," one that depends upon a "freely-made decision" to respond to the call of the divine and play "a historical role in the establishment of his Kingdom."[75] When viewed from this "eschatological perspective," the conflict that Merleau-Ponty identified between incarnation and transcendence melted away in favor of a recognition that "God made himself man only in order to make man God."[76] "For the Christian," Daniélou concluded, "transcendence and incarnation are part of a single order of reality, which is radically opposed to the political reality." Merleau-Ponty had failed to grasp this fact because he had emptied "religious reality . . . of its own content and assimilated [it] to political reality by virtue of purely formal analogies."[77] He had wrongly assumed that one could translate theological principles directly into political terms.

Daniélou thus used his response to Merleau-Ponty not just to discredit atheist existentialism, but also to elaborate a coded theological critique of Thomism. There were important reasons for him to do so in 1946, for Thomist philosophers were also trying to appropriate the mantle of existentialism. In fact, as Edward Baring has shown, neo-scholastic Thomists were among the earliest interlocutors of Husserl, Heidegger, and Scheler and were largely responsible for spreading phenomenology beyond its German birthplace to Europe and the Americas.[78] Marcel, Fessard, and Daniélou were not just competing with atheist existentialists, then; they were also responding to Thomists like Maritain, who claimed that "Thomism is the only authentic existentialism."[79] Étienne Gilson made a similar argument. "Thomism is not *another* existential philosophy; it is the *only* one," he insisted, for it was already "a doctrine centering upon existence at a time when the existential philosophers were not yet born."[80]

What these philosophers had in mind when they labeled Thomism an "existentialism," however, differed substantially from the meaning that Marcel and the *nouveaux théologiens* ascribed to the term. These Thomists did not seek to lay claim to the existentialist tradition that descended from Pascal and Kierkegaard. "The 'existentialism' of St. Thomas is utterly different from that of the 'existentialist' philosophies propounded today," Maritain insisted, and Gilson agreed that it was difficult to link Thomism to the Kierkegaardian tradition because of the Danish philosopher's aversion to systematic thought.[81] Instead, Gilson and Maritain presented Thomism as an *alternative* to the modern existentialist tradition in both its theist and atheist guises. Gilson, for instance, thought that Thomism could provide a healthy antidote to the excesses of modern existentialism, including its dubious emphasis on nonrational ways of knowing, subjective experience, and the primacy of existence over essence. Maritain concurred, noting that modern existentialism had lost its way when it abandoned all "intelligible nature or essence."[82] These philosophers wished not so much to rescue the modern existentialist tradition from its atheist deviation, as Daniélou and Fessard did, but rather to replace the entire edifice with a Thomist one. The "new theologians" were at pains to point this out, presenting themselves as the authentic heirs to the existentialist tradition, above and beyond both its atheist and Thomist misinterpreters.[83]

The Catholic debate over Heidegger's phenomenology crystallized these theological divisions. Initially, as Fessard's remarks in *France, Take Care Not to Lose Your Freedom* attest, French Catholics tended to identify Heidegger and Sartre as the leading exponents of atheist existentialism, even though Heidegger's first forays into phenomenology were in fact framed by his engagement with neo-scholasticism.[84] But Heidegger's 1947 "Letter on Humanism," in which the philosopher famously distanced himself from Sartrean existentialism, changed all this. Not only did the "Letter" reject the anthropocentrism of Sartre's thought, which was distasteful to many Catholics; it also opened the way for a possible theistic reading of Heidegger's phenomenology. Disavowing the atheist position of Sartre and company as "rash" and "an error in procedure," Heidegger placed new philosophical weight on the concept of the "holy" [*das Heilige*] and increasingly characterized his own position as "waiting for God."[85] Thomists such as Gilson remained profoundly skeptical, however, alienated as they were by Heidegger's nonrational, esoteric style and his commitment to moving beyond metaphysics.[86]

The reaction of the Jesuit theologians was rather different. Fessard and de Lubac had, in fact, helped to introduce Heidegger to a French Catholic audience in 1940, when they published an overview of his work by the German theologian Karl Rahner in the journal they coedited.[87] Indeed, Fessard assisted with the translation of the "Letter on Humanism" into French, and the experience led him to a qualified reconsideration of Heidegger's views.[88] Henri Bouillard, a fellow Jesuit associated with the *nouvelle théologie* and an authority on Barth and Heidegger, took an even more generous stance. He paid a visit to the German philosopher's home in Todtnauberg in 1947, where they discussed their shared admiration for the work of Maurice Blondel (Heidegger had read both Yves de Montcheuil's and Bouillard's work on Blondel).[89] The meeting convinced Bouillard that Heidegger's philosophy was neither nihilist nor necessarily atheist.

Bouillard reported that the philosopher was anxious to dispel the misconceptions associated with the atheist reading of his work. Their conversation persuaded the Jesuit that Heidegger's account of "being-towards-death" [*Sein zum Tode*] did not constitute "a nihilist philosophy," but simply acknowledged that man is "a being who has a relationship to death." The Jesuit then asked Heidegger point-blank whether "Being" in his framework designated God, to which the philosopher replied that "Being is absolute and unconditioned," but that philosophy is incapable of determining whether it is God because such things can only be known through revelation. Bouillard agreed that "the proof of God is not philosophical, but theological" and concluded that Heidegger's attitude toward religion had been misunderstood. "Heidegger is not an atheist," the Jesuit reported; he does not "oppose theology as such, but only a 'naturalist theology'" such as scholasticism. Bouillard concluded that atheist interpreters like Sartre, as well as Protestant theologians such as Rudolf Bultmann, had "totally misunderstood" Heidegger because they read his thought in anthropological terms—a misreading Bouillard attributed to the current humanist vogue and the fact that Heidegger had "expressed his metaphysics in a psychological language."[90] In fact, the goal of his philosophy was "to penetrate beyond mere consciousness, beyond psychology and ethics, to Being."[91] Bouillard emerged from the meeting convinced that Heidegger's philosophy offered important resources for Catholic theology, just as Fessard had argued that Hegelianism could be recuperated from its atheist interpreters.

Theological Anthropology and Human Rights

We are now better poised to understand how the *nouveaux théologiens* mobilized existentialist insights to develop their own Christian anthropology, which they conceived in opposition to both Marxist humanism and atheist existentialism. But their vision of the Christian "New Man" also differed in important respects from the Thomist account of human nature that underwrote the emerging Catholic discourse on human rights, which, as historians have begun to show, played a significant role in the development of an international human rights framework after the war.[92] The theological anthropology articulated by de Lubac, Fessard, and Daniélou instead shared much with existentialism—notably, the idea that the human subject is not a fixed essence, but instead constitutes itself through an ongoing process of transcendence, or negation. For the "new theologians," this negativity was nothing other than the desire to see God, which is written into human nature itself. Such an anthropology refused the distinction between the natural and supernatural ends of human life that made it possible for Maritain to cooperate with non-Christians on secular human rights projects. Instead, the Jesuits articulated a vision of human nature that was much more difficult to inscribe in the categories of secular law. In this sense, their theological anthropology was yet another plank in their ongoing counter-political project—one that rather remarkably anticipated some of the critiques of human rights now customarily mobilized by the left.

Phenomenology offered these Jesuits a useful set of resources for a theological anthropology that could compete with Thomism. What the existentialists had understood, Fessard believed, was that human life is not be defined by a shared essence or nature, as Thomist anthropology conceived it, but by "the freedom that raises [humans] above all of nature."[93] The fundamental insight of existentialism was to grasp the dynamic, temporal quality of the human person, who "ceaselessly overcomes what he is" in each free choice he makes. But Fessard transformed this existentialist understanding of human freedom as a constant process of transcendence and self-overcoming into a warrant for a very different kind of transcendence. "This transcendence of the spirit in relation to itself," he argued, is what "grounds and safeguards the true transcendence of God in relation to man."[94] In and through each free act, we not only create ourselves, but also draw nearer to God.

For Fessard, then, the process of "becoming-human" through each freely chosen act was inseparable from what Kierkegaard had called the process of "becoming-Christian." This argument had two crucial implications. First, it bound Fessard's anthropology to an eschatology. The process of becoming-human could not come to an end until the end of history, when the Second Coming would resolve the Jew-Gentile dialectic that was driving the process of becoming-Christian.[95] It also meant that human life within history could only be a dynamic process of "becoming-Christian," and never one of "being-Christian." As Kierkegaard had shown, "We never *are*—in the full sense of the word—Christian, but must always *become it*."[96] Only when history itself came to an end could one fully *be* Christian, and this eschatological horizon structured all of human existence within time. The second implication of Fessard's identification between becoming-human and becoming-Christian was that human freedom and divine agency were in no way incompatible, as atheist humanism presumed. As Fessard explained it, Christ is "the origin of the free act by which, in temporalizing myself, I respond to his call and thus achieve authentic personhood."[97] Grace, in other words, was the true source of human freedom. Daniélou made a similar argument in his exchange with the communist intellectual Pierre Hervé. Whereas Marxists approached man and God as competing sovereigns, Daniélou insisted that "the acceptance of God in no way destroys the greatness of man."[98] It is a petty humanism indeed, he remarked, that is driven by resentment of God's power.

Implicit in this theological anthropology was a sense that human beings are never fully in possession of themselves. It was sometimes difficult to distinguish this vision from the antihumanism that began to gather steam in French thought, especially after the publication of Heidegger's "Letter on Humanism."[99] This became clear during the 1944 "Discussion on Sin" between Jean Daniélou and the ex-Surrealist (and ex-Catholic) writer Georges Bataille. The ensuing discussion brought together the leading lights of postwar French thought—Sartre, de Beauvoir, Merleau-Ponty, Albert Camus, Gabriel Marcel, Maurice Blanchot, Pierre Klossowski, Jean Paulhan, Michel Leiris, Maurice de Gandillac, Jean Hyppolite, Louis Massignon, and Marcel Moré—and was eventually published in *Dieu vivant*.[100] The discussion focused on a talk in which Bataille undertook a Nietzschean "transvaluation" of the problem of sin. Bataille argued that by wounding the self and breaking down the boundaries of self-sufficiency, sin in fact makes possible a radical form of communication between self and other. The state of openness and self-annihilation achieved by the sinner is similar to that of the mystic, he argued, but ultimately exceeds it. Whereas the mystic takes refuge in the logic of salvation and the closure of the divine, the sinner "leaves the wound gaping."[101]

In response, Daniélou sought to show that Bataille's account of self-annihilation was not quite as incompatible with Christianity as he thought. In the first place, the Jesuit denied that mystics achieve anything like the self-possession and spiritual comfort that Bataille imagined. "No one is less comfortable than the mystic," he argued, who "realizes in ecstasy that total decentering of self which is effectively what we are all tending towards, and which renders one totally communicable to others."[102] Nor was this state of disaggregation peculiar to the mystic. In fact, Daniélou agreed with Bataille that all of us achieve something like this through sin, but for different reasons. For the Jesuit, it was because sin established a "tragic duality" within the soul, alienating it from itself and revealing the illusion of self-possession, that it paradoxically opened the way for grace.[103] But sin was not the only way to achieve this; sanctity also required a "total dispossession" of the self.[104] Daniélou thus sought to show that faith was by no means incompatible with the radical self-rending that Bataille sought. In fact, this self-laceration was the very condition for union with the divine. The debate thus revealed the unexpected affinity between a certain Augustinian strain in postwar Catholic theology and the antihumanist tenor of some secular philosophy at the time.

This affinity found its most robust theological expression in the work of Henri de Lubac. In a 1947 talk, he explained that the problem with atheist humanism was that it tended to reduce the human being to an object—a "deadly negation" that had opened the way for totalitarianism—whereas the defining feature of human existence was precisely that which eluded objectification.[105] "Those who say to us: here is man, never show us anything but the traces of man's passage," he insisted, echoing the classic existentialist dictum that man is "the being which is what it is not and is not what it is."[106] Instead, de Lubac endorsed the work of Christian existentialists such as Marcel and Jaspers, who had broken with "stifling objectivism" to recover the indispensable role of mystery in human life. Like the existentialists, de Lubac insisted that human nature was defined above all by a wound or lack. But far from being "an obstacle to [our] greatness," he argued that this "wound" at the heart of human nature "is, on the contrary, the intolerable sign of it."[107] It is the call of the divine within us, which prevents us from ever being satisfied with purely terrestrial structures. From de Lubac's perspective, this eschatological call accounted for both the negativity or lack at the heart of human life as well as its unique dignity, because it was precisely what raised humans above the level of a thing.

De Lubac articulated the theological rationale for this anthropology in *Surnaturel*, the controversial book that helped to elicit the eventual condemnation of the *nouvelle théologie*. If *The Drama of Atheist Humanism* laid out de Lubac's critique of atheist humanism, *Surnaturel* offered a theological alternative to it. Here, de Lubac argued against the theory—which was central to neo-Thomism—of a hypothetical state of "pure nature" in which human nature would be ordered to a purely natural end. De Lubac traced the origins of this concept to early modern scholastics who had imported Aristotelian categories into Catholic theology. Initially, the idea of "pure nature" had been introduced as a purely abstract tool to facilitate theological discussion, a "convenient fiction" rather like the idea of a "state of nature" in political theory.[108] Its primary function had been to safeguard the gratuity of grace—the principle that grace is a gift freely bestowed by God and in no way owed to humans—by demonstrating that grace is not built into the definition of human nature;

that it is at least possible to conceive of human life in purely natural terms. But the effect of this intellectual exercise was to treat grace as something external and "super-added" onto an already complete human nature. Consequently, de Lubac argued, "pure nature" had slowly hardened from a mere fiction into a descriptor of *actual* human existence, underwriting a sharp theological distinction between the natural and supernatural ends of human life. Henceforth, an entire sphere of human action—political, ethical, intellectual, social—would be conceived in purely natural terms, without reference to a supernatural end. Thus, de Lubac concluded, the "pure nature" theory had become an "unconscious accomplice" in the secularization of European life.[109]

Through a painstaking genealogy of this theological development, de Lubac sought to show that the concept of "pure nature" marked a significant departure from the teachings of the Church Fathers and St. Thomas himself, who instead affirmed that humans are created with a desire for the beatific vision that inheres within our very nature. By placing this desire at the foundation of what it means to be human, de Lubac pointed once again to the constitutive lack at the heart of human nature. "This desire is in us, yes, but it is not of us," he explained. "Or rather, it is so much in us that it *is* us, but we do not belong to ourselves. Our own nature is not our own. And because the truth of our being is to be, in a sense, alienated from ourselves, we awaken to ourselves by feeling ourselves *bound*."[110] Such an anthropology evidently repudiated the liberal vision of the autonomous self. But once again, de Lubac envisioned the negativity at the heart of human nature as the very source of human dignity, as that which raises us above every other element of the natural order and indicates that we are made to participate in divine life.[111] It is also what makes it impossible to conceive of human life in purely natural terms. The desire for the beatific vision, de Lubac explained, while it "is essentially in our nature and expresses its foundation," is also "something of God," and this means that "there can be only one end for man: the supernatural end."[112] Contemporary Thomist theologians had lost sight of this, de Lubac believed. Because they remained beholden to the notion of a "pure nature," they tended to overemphasize the distinction between the natural and supernatural ends of the human person and the concomitant autonomy of the natural order.

To draw out the political implications of this anthropology, it is worth contrasting it with the theory of human rights advanced at the time by philosophers such as Jacques Maritain, which bore all the markers of the

Thomist approach de Lubac opposed. As we have seen, Maritain developed his natural law–based theory of rights during the war, and in 1947, he got the opportunity to put this theory into practice thanks to his involvement in a UNESCO report on the philosophical grounds for human rights, which was supposed to prepare the way for the Universal Declaration on Human Rights (UDHR).[113] Maritain recalled that the biggest challenge in these discussions was how to arrive at a list of rights that would be acceptable to people from a variety of religious and intellectual traditions. As he famously put it, "We agree about the rights but on the condition that no one asks us why."[114] To overcome this problem, Maritain argued that it was necessary to draw "a sharp and clear distinction" between the set of rights to be enshrined in such a declaration and "the *theoretical justifications,* the conceptions of the world and of life, the philosophical or religious creeds" that informed them. Bracketing these sorts of theoretical differences would allow "men possessing quite different, even opposite metaphysical or religious outlooks" to agree on a common charter, "provided that they similarly revere, perhaps for quite diverse reasons, truth and intelligence, human dignity, freedom."[115] In this way, Catholics and nonbelievers, liberals and conservatives, could put aside their differences and work together to secure the protection of human rights around the world.

What made Maritain's approach possible was a distinctively Thomist understanding of human nature. As we have seen, Maritain derived his account of human rights from the natural law inscribed on every human heart. Because natural law decrees that humans are ordered to certain ends by virtue of their very nature as human beings, Maritain argued, they are necessarily owed the right to fulfill these ends. Human rights are thus required "by what the nature of man is, and is cut out for . . . by virtue of which certain things like life, work, freedom are due to the human person."[116] Crucially, this argument presupposed a distinction between the natural and supernatural ends of human life, because Maritain was of course *not* suggesting that humans have a right to grace. Maritain's argument for human rights thus rested on the natural ends of human life and not, or at least not directly, on grace and salvation. And this was critical because it allowed him to argue that both Christians and non-Christians could apprehend these rights and appreciate their binding force, since natural law was intelligible without the aid of revelation. Consequently, human rights could serve as the shared *"civic or secular* faith" for a modern, pluralist society because, even though the true source and justification for these rights came from God, they were intelligible to all human beings by virtue of their humanity.[117]

Much like the position advanced by many "progressive Christians" (see Chapter 5), Maritain's argument thus relied on a typically Thomist distinction between the natural and supernatural ends of human life in order to safeguard the autonomy of temporal affairs. But it was precisely this distinction which de Lubac had rejected in *Surnaturel*. From the Thomist perspective, then, the difficulty with de Lubac's anthropology was that it abolished the distinction that secured the autonomy and integrity of *both* the natural and supernatural orders. By denying that human life possessed a distinct natural end alongside its supernatural one, de Lubac seemed to compromise, not only the gratuity of grace—the more common charge leveled against him—but *also* human freedom and the autonomy of the natural order.[118] For Maritain, as for the Catholic left, the great virtue of the Thomist system was precisely that it allowed for a realm of human affairs possessing its own integrity apart from any religious referent or ecclesiastical authority. But by defining human life exclusively in terms of its supernatural end, the Jesuit seemed to deny any autonomous value to the wide range of human activities, including politics, that were performed with a purely natural end in view. He had thus undermined the basis for Maritain's human rights discourse, as well as for the Catholic left.

Even though de Lubac did not address the question of human rights explicitly in *Surnaturel,* his argument thus had important implications for the postwar debate on Christianity and human rights—implications that his contemporary disciples have drawn out more explicitly. By placing the supernatural at the heart of human nature, De Lubac's anthropology made it difficult to bracket the theological grounds for human rights in order to work with nonbelievers on their practical implementation, as Maritain sought to do. And this made his vision much more difficult to square with nonconfessional projects such as the UDHR or the European Convention on Human Rights. Maritain's anthropology allowed for a vision of human rights that, although it derived from Catholic theology, did not require any reference to the supernatural and could thus be encoded in a secular legal framework. But this vision rested on a distinction between the natural and supernatural ends of human life, which de Lubac could not accept. To disentangle human nature from its supernatural end in this way, he argued, was to degrade rather than empower it by amputating man "from his transcendent finality and the superior faculties by which he is constituted . . . in the image of God."[119] It was to reduce him to a mere *"political animal* [for whom] laws, ordinances, magistracies are made," whereas the characteristic feature of the supernatural was that it lay "outside the categories of law."[120] What endowed human life with dignity, from this perspective, was precisely that which eluded the political and could not be codified into law.

In making this claim, de Lubac partly anticipated the biopolitical critique of human rights that is now usually advanced by scholars on the left such as Talal Asad and Wendy Brown. Often working in a Foucauldian tradition, these scholars argue that human rights do not constitute a neutral or protective instrument, but in fact underwrite forms of political and institutional power and produce a certain kind of rights-bearing subject.[121] Though there is no indication that de Lubac opposed human rights per se—at least when these were framed in explicitly and unequivocally Christian terms, as they were in the pages of *Témoignage chrétien*—the anthropology he developed in *Surnaturel* suggests a wariness of the kind of subject that secular rights projects such as the UDHR presupposed, and of the way they gave institutions like the state or the United Nations the power to define human life.[122] By placing the supernatural at the heart of human nature and articulating a dynamic, antifoundationalist anthropology, he insisted that the defining feature of human life was precisely what could not be rendered into secular law. And this perhaps explains why many of the leading architects of the biopolitical critique of human rights today are de Lubac's contemporary theological disciples.[123]

There were many forms of Catholic anthropology in the late 1940s, in other words, and not all of them were necessarily compatible with postwar efforts to institutionalize human rights in constitutional and international law. But we should also avoid overstating the differences between Maritain and de Lubac, for both remained deeply suspicious of the prevailing liberal rights model, which they associated with the eigtheenth-century declarations. As we have seen, Maritain was highly critical of the way the liberal rights tradition privileged individual over social rights and robbed human rights of their objective foundation in the natural law—a critique recently reiterated by Benedict XVI.[124] De Lubac's theological anthropology was similarly premised on a rejection of the liberal, agentive subject, for he and his fellow Jesuits envisioned dependence on God as the very foundation of human freedom. These concerns would continue to inform the Catholic response to human rights, even after the Church embraced them more fully in the 1960s.[125]

Existential Eschatology and the Politics of History

By now it should be clear that within the postwar debates among Christians, Marxists, and existentialists, the "humanism" question was invariably bound up with the problem of time. For Marxists and existentialists, as much as for the "new theologians," human nature was a process rather than a thing, and the postwar debate on humanism was thus necessarily *also* a debate about the structure of historical time. The connection between these two questions was clear in the theological anthropology articulated by de Lubac, Fessard, and Daniélou, for whom the eschatological horizon of history defined what it meant to be human. By yoking anthropology to eschatology, these theologians sought to avoid the individualist premises of Sartrean (and, indeed, Kierkegaardian) existentialism. If each individual possesses an inalienable desire for the divine, de Lubac explained, that is because "a Future is being prepared in which all are called to collaborate" and because "the salvation of each is a function of the salvation of all."[126] Defining human nature in eschatological terms thus allowed these theologians to anchor the individual's relationship to God in the collective history of human salvation. Doing so, they believed, would provide a more effective weapon against the Marxist philosophy of history and those who sought to reconcile it with Catholic theology. By merging the insights of existentialism with the resources of eschatology, they sought to develop an alternative to the linear, unidirectional account of time that informed both Marxist and liberal philosophies of history.

De Lubac and his friends were not the only ones with the end of the world on their mind in these years. Despite the relief of the Liberation, many Europeans found little reason to rejoice given the catastrophic destruction of the war, the onset of a new global conflict between the two world powers, and the threat of nuclear annihilation. In the late 1940s, then, the End Times seemed far from remote to many Christians. No publication expressed this sensibility better than *Dieu vivant*. It was the brainchild of two Catholic laymen—Marcel Moré and Louis Massignon—and Jean Daniélou. Massignon was a Catholic convert and influential scholar of Islam whose vision of a shared Abrahamic tradition would help to shape the Second Vatican Council's teaching on non-Christian religions.[127] Moré had initially been drawn to *Esprit* and Christian Democracy, but as with de Lubac's circle, the war convinced him of the need to correct the excessive Catholic concern for "incarnation" with a renewed attention to the eschatological dimension of the faith.[128] This insight grew out of the regular meetings that Moré hosted at his home during the war, which brought together Catholics, secular intellectuals, Protestants, and Orthodox theologians such as Vladimir Lossky and Nikolai Berdyaev.[129] It was at one of the meetings that the famous "discussion on sin" between Bataille and Daniélou took place. These interconfessional meetings were the crucible out of which *Dieu vivant* emerged in 1945. Although the editors were Catholic, the committee was deliberately ecumenical, and included a Protestant (Pierre Burgelin), an Orthodox theologian (Lossky), a secular intellectual (Jean Hyppolite), and a Catholic (Marcel). In addition, a "vigilance committee" staffed by Catholic clergy was tasked with ensuring the journal's compliance with Church teaching.[130] It was headed by Daniélou, who served as the journal's official "theological advisor."[131]

The mission of *Dieu vivant*, as explained in its opening editorial, was twofold: to foster ecumenical dialogue and to advance "an eschatological conception of Christianity."[132] Invoking the specters of Nazism, communism, and capitalism, the editorial announced the creation of *Dieu vivant* "at a moment which makes one think of the darkest pages of the Apocalypse."[133] Echoing the language of *Témoignage chrétien*, the editors of *Dieu vivant* insisted that "the battle we must wage today is above all spiritual."[134] Its target would be the "great idolatry of our times": atheist humanism.[135] Even though it was the product of anti-Christian ideologies, the editors warned that this "dubious" humanism had been aided and abetted by the current enthusiasm for "incarnation" within the Church.

The problem, the editors argued, was that the Church had lost sight of its eschatological roots. The early Christians had lived as if the Parousia were imminent, but when several centuries had passed and it had not arrived, the Church "entered into relations with the State" in order to "render its existence less precarious."[136] Thus began the long era of Constantinian Christianity, when the Church "relied upon political and social institutions" for its security, growing comfortable in what was meant to be only a temporary earthly home. As a result, Christianity had degenerated into "nothing more than a social structure."[137] It was this

"penchant for Constantinianism," the editors believed, that led contemporary Catholics to "seek salvation in social institutions, to aspire to
peace and happiness here below." Here, the editors likely had in mind
both Christian Democrats and the Catholic left (even though, as we have
seen, many "progressives" were just as critical of Constantinian Christianity). These Catholics, the editors complained, had forgotten that "it
is not by political and social means that the 'Revelation' of Christ is accomplished."[138] But the secularization of modern political institutions
had, fortunately, liberated the Church to return to the critical role it had
played in relation to worldly power before it threw in its lot with the
Roman Empire. By recovering the eschatological mind-set of the early
Christians, the editors of Dieu vivant hoped that the Church would
once again become a thorn in the side of secular ideologies and social
structures. In order to do this, though, Christians had to give up the
comforting notion that the apocalypse was a distant event set off in the
remote future and realize that "the End Times have begun, that they
began with the Resurrection of Christ."[139]

In order to transform their relationship to the institutions of this world,
in other words, Christians had to divest themselves of a characteristically
secular notion of time. This vision of time as a linear series of moments
proceeding from past to future in an unbroken chain—what Walter Benjamin famously called "homogeneous, empty time"—was the basis for
both liberal and Marxist accounts of history.[140] But the time of eschatology resisted this logic. "Considered from an eschatological perspective," the editors of Dieu vivant explained, "the instant is not a mere
passage between the past and the future, but the living presence of eternity."[141] The eschatological event is not locked in some distant future to
be passively awaited; nor does it require a retreat from the drama of
human history, because "eschatological time is already inserted into our
historical time."[142] In fact, they argued, it actually heightens our responsibilities in the here and now, because "true eschatology is the present
life of the Christian and demands from him a total engagement."[143] This
was precisely the temporal logic that had informed the resistance activities of de Lubac, Fessard, and Montcheuil during the war. They had appealed to the eschatological vision of the mystical body of Christ as a
means to relativize human political projects such as the National Revolution, but also to prevent attentisme—the temptation to retreat from
one's temporal responsibilities. To do this, they had invoked the nonlinear

structure of salvation history, which is omnipresent in each moment of linear time, arguing that the *actuality* of the eschatological future underwrites the responsibilities of the Christian in the present. *Dieu vivant* thus represented the logical extension of the counter-political eschatology that de Lubac's circle had developed to steer Catholics away from collaboration with Vichy and the Germans. Only now it was redeployed to steer Catholics away from collaboration with communists.

In articulating its critique of the Marxist theory of history, the journal found itself drawn into the orbit of that other great force in postwar French intellectual life: existentialism. The influence was evident in the presence of high-profile Christian existentialists such as Marcel on the journal's committee, but also in the content of its articles. *Dieu vivant* devoted at least sixteen articles to existentialist philosophy (and only two to Marxism), focusing on a wide range of authors, from Kierkegaard and Nietzsche to Sartre and Camus.[144] Evidently, the focus was on Christian, or at least theistic, existentialism. In order to counteract the dominance of Sartre and the *Temps modernes* crew, *Dieu vivant* published translations of German articles on religious existentialism by Karl Jaspers, Martin Buber, Karl Barth, and Erik Peterson, as well as a discussion of the theistic implications of Heidegger's philosophy involving Marcel, Merleau-Ponty, Bataille, Gandillac, Wahl, and Koyré.[145]

The journal's opening mission statement drew a direct connection between eschatological temporality and the insights of existentialism, on the grounds that both opposed "the myth of progress" and the chimera of earthly salvation at the heart of the Marxist philosophy of history.[146] Fessard clarified the link between eschatology and existentialism in a subsequent issue of *Dieu vivant*. As he explained it, "The Christian who awaits the Parousia and the philosopher of the absurd can agree on at least one thing: they emphasize the image of discontinuity that history affords."[147] Louis Massignon echoed this sentiment. "For men of the absolute," he proclaimed, "there is—and let us call this our Christian existentialism—only the present."[148] But *Dieu vivant* also presented Christian eschatology as a necessary complement and corrective to the existentialist tradition. Without it, existentialism would degenerate into an impotent nihilism, reducing history to a "vain game of equally illusory 'projects.'"[149] Only by grasping the eschatological end that gives meaning to these earthly endeavors could one establish an effective alternative to the misguided progressivism of both liberals and the Catholic left.

Fessard made this case in an article published in the eighth issue of *Dieu vivant,* which intervened in a growing debate among French Catholics on the theology of history. Distinguishing "philosophies of existence," which stressed historical discontinuity, from "philosophies of essences," which privileged historical continuity, the article constituted an elaborate rejoinder to both the Marxist philosophy of history and that of Thomists like Charles Journet, Jacques Maritain, and Henri-Marie Féret.[150] A close friend of Chenu and Congar, Féret was part of the Dominican branch of the *nouvelle théologie* and an advisor to the worker-priests. In a work published in 1943, he had turned to the Book of Revelation for clues to God's historical plan and developed an account of the stages of history leading up to the apocalypse.[151] Prior to this final conflagration, Féret predicted that there would be a thousand-year reign of Christian civilization on earth when earthly society would progressively come to embody the values of the Gospel. In this way, the Dominican sought to elaborate a theological answer to the Marxist philosophy of history—one that would endow human historical striving and the struggle to build a more just society with a role in the history of salvation. In the face of "false messianisms" capable of inspiring political action on a mass scale, Féret insisted that Christians must be able to provide their own account of "the historical evolution in which [Christians] must insert their action."[152]

Although Féret initially sat on the theological advisory committee for *Dieu vivant,* both Fessard and his former teacher Joseph Huby (also a Jesuit) took the Dominican to task in the pages of the journal for departing from its eschatological vision. Huby responded by invoking the journal's distinctive account of time, conceived not as a linear succession of events but as the presence of the end of history within each historical moment. "The task of Revelation," he wrote, "is not to inform us about the 'progressive development' of the Church and the 'successive stages' of this development, but to make us grasp through faith the contemporaneity of the Judgment of God to the events of history, the presence of eternity at the heart of historical time."[153] Fessard also chastised Féret for looking to scripture to predict the future out of a misplaced "jealousy" for the Marxist philosophy of history. He suggested that Thomists were particularly vulnerable to this temptation because of the ahistorical bent of Thomist philosophy.[154] A true theology of history, Fessard insisted, does not consist in determining the future stages of history but in developing an ontology based on *"the structures of human historical being."*[155]

What Fessard had in mind here were the "existential attitudes" he had derived from his combined reading of Hegel and St. Paul, which formed the basis for his dynamic anthropology. They included the Jew-Gentile dialectic, which drove the process of "becoming-Christian," and the master-slave dialectic, which had been so central to Fessard's analysis of the Pétain regime. But now Fessard added a third couplet, the "man-woman" dialectic, which he likewise derived from Galatians 3:28.

The man-woman dialectic took on a crucial role in Fessard's critique of Marxism in particular. Given the centrality of the master-slave dialectic to Kojève's Marxist reading of Hegel, Fessard's own reliance on the master-slave dialectic as the primary motor of social and political life left him with few resources to combat the Marxist theory of history. Beginning in the late 1940s, he therefore introduced the idea of the man-woman dialectic, which interacted with the master-slave dialectic to explain both the genesis of social life out of the family unit and the possibility of forms of governance based on reciprocity rather than force.[156] Whereas the master-slave dialectic was driven by violence, the man-woman dialectic transmuted this violence into love. And it did so through the model of the conjugal bond, with the reproductive union of maternity and paternity engendering a new principle in social and political life: fraternity. Here, once again, we glimpse the foundational role that heterosexual love and gender difference played in twentieth-century Catholic political thought. Whatever their differences, Catholic intellectuals from Fessard to Teilhard de Chardin and from Chenu to Léopold Sédar Senghor all agreed that the complementarity of the heterosexual couple was the model for social and political life writ large—a view they shared with many secular republicans.[157]

The man-woman dialectic gave Fessard a weapon against those who deployed the master-slave dialectic to justify the principle of class struggle and the need for violent revolution. But it also served a broader role in Fessard's counter-politics, allowing him to argue that the divisions of earthly life could not be fully overcome until the end of time. This was because, while the political and economic conflicts governed by the master-slave dialectic were properly historical, and thus might one day come to an end, the division between man and woman was "natural," or more precisely, it was the nexus between nature and society.[158] "Having originated at the first moment of history," Fessard argued, "this opposition cannot be definitively overcome until the last." And consequently, "the same must be true of the other oppositions" of the social and political order.[159] What the ubiquity of gender difference revealed, for Fessard, was the impossibility of ever fully overcoming social conflicts within historical time, just as the spiritual division within and between persons (the Jew-Gentile dialectic) would not be resolved until Christ came again. The class struggle, in other words, could not come to an end within history.

But Fessard did not want to suggest that it was useless for humans to strive to create a better world here on earth. Because the dialectics that structured social and political life interacted with the Jew-Gentile dialectic driving the history of salvation, Fessard argued that social and political divisions could be progressively overcome here on earth through the process of "becoming-Christian." By "bearing witness to the New Man [Christ] who lives in him," the Christian "is capable of overcoming here and now both the political and religious divisions of the international order and of guiding humanity onto the path by which they can be effectively surmounted within history."[160] Fessard thus sought to hold together two temporalities: the linear, continuous time of historical becoming and the discontinuous time of eschatology. The Hegelian and the existentialist in Fessard might seem at odds here, but he sought to balance both in order to combat Marxist millenarianism without devaluing the responsibilities of temporal engagement. This was precisely the same balancing act that *Témoignage chrétien* had tried to strike during the war, rejecting both collaboration and *attentisme*. But for people like Féret, this approach no doubt seemed like a cop-out. It offered too little encouragement to those seeking to building a more just and equitable society and few practical solutions to the material problems confronting the working class.[161]

What both of these theologians were grappling with was how to respond to the Marxist critique of Christianity as a bourgeois ideology that devalued the struggle for justice and equality in this world by promising redemption in the next. How could theologians furnish a Christian justification for striving to build a better world within history without secularizing salvation in the process? For Dominicans like Féret and Chenu, the solution was to incarnate Catholicism in the earthly movements and institutions working to promote social justice. But the Jesuits maintained that the Church had to remain at arm's length from the institutions of this world because it occupied a fundamentally different temporality. As Daniélou explained, Christianity and human history were bound together by a paradox. "On the one hand, Christianity falls within history. It emerged at a particular moment in the sequence of historical events," which meant that Christians could not simply withdraw from earthly struggle and dismiss this world as irredeemably fallen. "But on the other hand," Daniélou continued, "history falls within Christianity: all secular history is included in sacred history, as both a part and a preparation."[162] And this meant that Christianity could not be yoked to any passing social or political form. Because it occupies both the time of human history and the time of the Kingdom, Daniélou concluded, Christianity "always requires both an incarnation and a detachment." As the sacrament through which "the thing that is beyond history is already present and exists in historical time," the Church's role was to be *engaged* but *independent* and *critical* vis-à-vis the institutions of temporal life—a role the Jesuit hoped it could finally rediscover now that the age of "Constantinianism" was coming to an end.[163]

History as Critique

One of the aims of *Dieu vivant* was to introduce religious thinkers whose work was not widely known or available in French. One of them was the German theologian Erik Peterson, who became a regular contributor to both *Dieu vivant* and *Recherches de science religieuse*, the theological journal edited by de Lubac and Fessard.[164] Peterson, who had converted to Catholicism in 1930, is perhaps most famous for his dispute with Carl Schmitt on the subject of political theology. In *Monotheism as a Political Problem*, which was published in 1935, Peterson turned to the Church Fathers in order to show how the theology of the trinity precluded the politico-theological analogy that Schmitt drew between monotheism and political sovereignty.[165] But Peterson went even further, arguing that the eschatological vocation of the Church meant that the very concept of a Christian political theology was a contradiction in terms. This was because the time of eschatology was not the time of political institutions and could never be identified with any earthly political formation. Consequently, as Augustine had insisted, Christians would always be both insiders and outsiders to any political community.

What Peterson shared with Daniélou, Fessard, and de Lubac was a keen awareness of the politics of time. All of them were opposed to any effort to translate theological concepts into political, legal, or socioeconomic ones—whether on the right (Schmitt), center (Maritain), or left (Féret). And all of them found in the time of eschatology a key resource to combat the logic of political theology in its various guises. Crucially, however, they did not view eschatology as an *apolitical* force, but rather as a *counter-political* one—something that required an engagement with, rather than a retreat from, the demands of temporal life. It did so for two reasons. First, as de Lubac never ceased to reaffirm, salvation was an inescapably social affair, and this truth could not leave the structures of temporal life untouched.[166] Second, these theologians adhered to a sacramental vision of time that did not place the eschatological event outside of history or in some ever-receding future, but at the very heart of the historical present. In his book on the paradoxes of Christianity, a portion of which appeared in *Dieu vivant,* de Lubac argued that "eternity, which is beyond the future, is not exterior to the present, as the future is."[167] Eschatology therefore "does not tear us away from the present," but instead binds us to it even more closely than "those who only contemplate an earthly future . . . for this future as such is entirely exterior to the present."[168] For de Lubac and the architects of *Dieu vivant,* eschatological time—by which the "past" of the Incarnation and the "future" of the Parousia are sacramentally present in each moment of historical time—offered a powerful rejoinder to modern historicism. And they were keenly aware that the problem of history was a political problem. Like Walter Benjamin, they turned to the nonlinear "now-time" of eschatology in order to articulate a critique of the linear, progressive time that underwrote secular political projects.[169]

But this "homogeneous, empty time" is also the time of the historian. This was something Benjamin understood, and thus his "Theses on the Concept of History" also functioned as a critique of historical empiricism—the notion that the past is an object that is temporally remote from the present and capable of being known as such. Instead, Benjamin invited the historian to attend to the way in which certain moments from the past suddenly become recognizable and contemporaneous to the historian's present, when "what has been comes together with the now in a flash to form a constellation," unleashing critical and transformative possibilities that had previously been foreclosed.[170] De Lubac, Daniélou, and Fessard certainly did not share Benjamin's revolutionary politics, but their work was nevertheless alive to precisely these sorts of "constellations." In their effort to resist the logic of political theology and divest the Church of its longstanding entanglement with the powers of this world, the Jesuits ceaselessly returned to the historical past of the early Church. The memory of a small, beleaguered Church surrounded by heathens seemed strangely contemporary at a moment when the Church found itself beset by the forces of secularization. Moreover, because the Church Fathers had been the first to grapple with how to secure the Church's independence from the temporal authorities (in this case, the Roman Empire), their work seemed strangely topical. This was precisely why Peterson turned to these sources for theological ammunition in his dispute with Carl Schmitt.

As we shall see in Chapter 7, the notion that the teaching of the Church Fathers possessed uncanny affinities with modern thought, and indeed seemed somehow *more* contemporary than the scholastic theology that had succeeded it, was a key premise of the French Jesuits' commitment to *ressourcement*. Consequently, "returning to the sources" was never just an antiquarian project; it was also animated by the present political and theological concerns of its authors. *Corpus Mysticum,* for instance, was more than an attempt to recover the Eucharistic ecclesiology of St. Paul and the Church Fathers. It was also a theological critique of scholasticism and a political critique of the tendency to conflate the communal impulse at the heart of Catholicism with collectivist political projects. *Surnaturel* took a similar genealogical approach, using the tools of historical scholarship to demonstrate how scholastic theology had deviated from the teachings of Aquinas and the Church Fathers, introducing innovations that left the contemporary Church vulnerable to the forces of secularization. Although ostensibly about the very distant past of the Catholic tradition, both these books were more properly about the historical present in which de Lubac was writing. They were, to use a contemporary term, "histories of the present," which deployed the tools of historical genealogy to interrogate how the present state of the Church had come to be and to knock the feet of his contemporary theological opponents out from under them.[171]

This approach is strangely in tune with the more recent post-structuralist critique of historicism, which was embraced by Anglo-American historians who took the "linguistic turn" in the 1980s and 1990s. And indeed, one of de Lubac's closest disciples—even, for a period of time, his next of kin—was the Jesuit psychoanalytic theorist and historian Michel de Certeau, who would become a favorite resource for these historians.[172] For de Lubac, it should be recalled, the Catholic tradition was a living thing; even its oldest resources were not locked in a dead historical past, but could be recovered and reactivated at any moment. Consequently, they could never be fully grasped with the tools of historicism.

The editors of *Dieu vivant* echoed this sentiment, proclaiming that "the true past, far from being an inert object, only acquires its true meaning and full structure through the present engagements of the concrete man oriented towards the future."[173]

Herein lies the connection between the Jesuits' vision of *ressourcement* and their critique of political ideologies that relied on a linear or progressive theory of history. Both these projects presupposed a sacramental, nonlinear model of time defined by the contemporaneity of both the past history of the Church and the future of eschatological fulfillment. History, conceived in this way, was a crucial resource for the critique of progressivist political theologies.[174] But it was also a tool to dethrone neo-scholastic theology from the privileged position it occupied in the contemporary Church, on the grounds that it was both too modern and not modern enough: too modern, because it had departed from the traditional formulations of the Church Fathers and of Aquinas himself; not modern enough, because the categories in which neo-scholastic theology was formulated now seemed out of step with modern thought. This was what Bouillard sought to demonstrate in *Conversion et grâce chez saint Thomas d'Aquin,* by disentangling Aquinas's theology of grace from the outdated Aristotelian categories in which he and his commentators had expressed it.[175] In addition to its function as a resource for political and theological critique, however, the *ressourcement* project could also be interpreted as an implicit critique of the centralized structures of Church authority. And this was ultimately what sealed its fate.

CHAPTER SEVEN

The Death and Resurrection of the
Nouvelle Théologie

In April 1946, Jean Daniélou published an article titled "The Present Orientation of Religious Thought." Though it was ostensibly a panorama of postwar French Catholic intellectual life, the article was widely viewed as nothing less than a "manifesto" for a "new theology."[1] Indeed, these fifteen pages inadvertently provided the spark for the greatest theological conflict to rock the Church since the Modernist Crisis at the turn of the century. By the mid-1950s, both the Jesuit and Dominican architects of the *nouvelle théologie* had been stripped of their teaching and editorial positions, condemned by the Vatican, and sent into exile. But their time in the wilderness would be short-lived. Just ten years later, they would serve as leading theological advisors at the Second Vatican Council—a landmark event in the life of the Church and European history more broadly.

Daniélou's article linked the developments in postwar French thought that the previous two chapters have traced to the theological project known as *ressourcement*—the effort to return to the early sources of the Catholic tradition, which had been overshadowed by the dominance of neo-scholasticism.[2] The French Jesuits had spearheaded the retrieval of the Church Fathers in particular with their series *Sources chrétiennes* and *Théologie.* The first of these, which was launched by Daniélou and de Lubac in 1942, published translations and new editions of lesser-known works by the Greek and Latin Fathers of the Church. The second, edited by Henri Bouillard and the Jesuits of the Fourvière scholasticate in Lyon, published contemporary works of theology inspired by the patristic sources, including de Lubac's *Corpus Mysticum* and *Surnaturel,* as well as works by Fessard, Daniélou, Yves de Montcheuil, and Bouillard.[3] Dominicans such as Chenu and Congar, meanwhile, undertook a parallel effort of *ressourcement* by recovering the teachings of the "historical Thomas" behind the accretions of neo-scholasticism, and both projects dovetailed with broader movements of liturgical and biblical renewal.[4] But while the Dominicans remained firmly anchored in the Thomist tradition, the Jesuits sought to break the virtual monopoly that Thomism had achieved over Catholic orthodoxy. No "one man, one school, one country, one religious order can provide all of the notes that compose the great concert of the Church," de Lubac insisted, in a dig at both Aquinas and his Dominican champions.[5]

In his 1946 "manifesto," Daniélou made a somewhat counterintuitive argument about the value of *ressourcement*. He argued that going back to the earliest sources of the Catholic tradition would paradoxically enable Catholics to better "respond to the experiences of the modern soul" by engaging with contemporary philosophies such as Marxism and existentialism.[6] Thomism was singularly ill-equipped to perform this task, the Jesuit argued, because the questions and categories at the heart of modern thought—questions of subjectivity and of history—were "foreign to Thomism." Not only did it have "no place for history," but "by defining reality in terms of essences rather than subjects, it [had lost] sight of the dramatic world of persons . . . which transcend all essence and are distinguished only by existence."[7] Although it predated scholasticism by nearly a thousand years, the work of the Church Fathers seemed, to Daniélou, to be far more contemporary. What made their work seem like "the most modern nourishment for the men of today" was the central place it accorded to history and the social dimension of the faith.[8] It was, paradoxically, by returning to the ancient sources of the Catholic tradition, then, that Catholic theology could be brought into dialogue with the modern world. This effort to "modernize" by returning to the sources would eventually become the guiding principle behind the Second Vatican Council.

Daniélou's argument that a commitment to *ressourcement* was inextricable from the desire to bring theology into dialogue with modern thought is crucial to understanding both the condemnation of the *nouvelle théologie* and its eventual rehabilitation. What bound together these two apparently contradictory impulses for the Jesuits was a common suspicion of neo-scholasticism—what Daniélou called "bastardized Thomism"—which they had struggled against since their student days at Jersey.[9] The campaign against the *nouvelle théologie* therefore drew support from a range of different theologians who often shared little more than a commitment to the preeminent status of Thomas Aquinas. This helps to explain why the Dominicans associated with the movement were less directly targeted by the encyclical *Humani Generis,* although they would have their own difficulties with Rome a few years later when they were caught up in the controversy over the worker-priests. It is therefore crucial not to conflate the two condemnations. They corresponded to the two distinct movements of renewal in postwar French Catholicism that are traced in Chapters 5 and 6, and the Jesuits' and Dominicans' shared travails with Rome did nothing to lessen the theological and political differences between them. Indeed, these tensions would reappear at Vatican II, where de Lubac, Daniélou, Chenu, and Congar helped to enshrine the key tenets of the *nouvelle théologie* in the documents of the council. Their different visions of the relationship between the Church and the modern world would go on to set the terms for the theological disputes of the postconciliar Church.

The *Nouvelle Théologie* in Crisis

Rumors of a condemnation began almost as soon as the war ended. By the end of 1945, the whispers reached de Lubac and his friends: a campaign was being waged in Rome against the so-called new theology emanating from the Jesuit scholasticate of Fourvière in Lyon. The man rumored to be behind this campaign was none other than the Dominican Father Réginald Garrigou-Lagrange—erstwhile mentor to Maritain and Chenu, longtime partisan of the Action française (AF), and a staunch Pétainist. From his position at the Angelicum pontifical university in Rome, it appeared that Garrigou-Lagrange was busily gathering reports on the activities of several French Jesuits with a view to a denunciation. And to make matters worse, he had the ear of the pope. De Lubac quickly shared the news with his friend Fessard. "The Dominican integrist party," he reported, "is spreading the word that we at Fourvière are a hotbed of modernism."[10]

In 1947, Garrigou-Lagrange dropped his "atomic bomb" on this group—an article titled "Where Is the New Theology Going?"[11] Although the term "new theology" had initially been coined in 1942 to refer to works by the Dominicans Chenu and Charlier, Garrigou-Lagrange used it instead to designate a group of Jesuits that included de Lubac,

Fessard, Daniélou, Montcheuil, Bouillard, and Teilhard de Chardin.[12] The Dominican treated the movement as nothing less than a frontal assault on the foundations of the faith. It had sacrificed the very possibility of metaphysical truth to the vagaries of historicism and subjectivism, such that "the true is no longer *that which is* but *that which becomes and changes constantly.*"[13] Garrigou blamed this misguided view on the fact that these theologians had strayed from the path of Thomism and fallen under the spell of modern philosophies such as Hegelianism and existentialism. In answer to the question, "Where is the new theology going?," then, Garrigou concluded: "It is returning to modernism."[14] And just as the turn-of-the-century conflict over Catholic Modernism had ended in papal condemnation, Garrigou-Lagrange was calling for nothing less against the *nouvelle théologie*.

When Pius XII handed down *Humani Generis* in 1950, it closely echoed Garrigou-Lagrange's critique, and it is very likely that the Dominican had a hand in drafting it.[15] Although the document did not refer by name to the *nouvelle théologie,* it was clear who and what the pope had in mind:

> In theology some want to . . . bring about a return in the explanation of Catholic doctrine to the way of speaking used in Holy Scripture and by the Fathers of the Church. . . . Moreover, they assert that when Catholic doctrine has been reduced to this condition, a way will be found to satisfy modern needs, that will permit of dogma being expressed also by the concepts of modern philosophy, whether of immanentism or idealism or existentialism or any other system. Some more audacious affirm that this can and must be done, because they hold that the mysteries of faith are never expressed by truly adequate concepts but only by approximate and ever changeable notions. . . . Wherefore they do not consider it absurd, but altogether necessary, that theology should substitute new concepts in place of the old ones in keeping with the various philosophies which in the course of time it uses as its instruments.[16]

This was simultaneously an attack on the project of *ressourcement* and on the effort to bring theology into dialogue with modern philosophy. And as with Garrigou-Lagrange, the pope's central objection concerned the intrusion of historical thinking into theology.

The challenge of history took two somewhat different forms. In the first place, there was the influence of modern philosophies of becoming and historical change—from Hegelianism and Marxism to existentialism and evolution—which seemed to threaten the immutable truths of dogma. Although one might expect that Pius XII, the great Cold Warrior, was particularly concerned about Marxism, the bulk of his encyclical was instead directed against a different enemy: "the new erroneous philosophy which . . . has assumed the name of existentialism, since it concerns itself only with existence of individual things and neglects all consideration of their immutable essences" (§6). That the encyclical fixated on existentialism in particular had everything to do with its influence, as we have seen, on the work of the Jesuits associated with the *nouvelle théologie*. These theologians had adopted existentialism's historicism and contempt for the value of reason, the pope charged, which led them to dismiss Thomism as "only a philosophy of immutable essences," whereas "the contemporary mind must look to the existence of things and to life, which is ever in flux" (§32). Here, Pius had in mind not just the work of Christian existentialists, but also the evolutionary theory of Teilhard de Chardin. And to those who sought to distinguish a legitimate Christian existentialism from the atheist variant associated with Sartre, the encyclical made it clear that both forms of existentialism, "whether atheistic or simply the type that denies the validity of the reason in the field of metaphysics," were equally unacceptable (§32).

But the pope was also concerned about the way theologians like Bouillard and de Lubac applied the tools of historical scholarship to the Catholic tradition. As with Pius X's condemnation of Modernism in 1907, Pius XII worried that the project of *ressourcement* risked undermining the authority of the magisterium along with the privileged status of Thomism. Against demands for theological pluralism, he affirmed that "the method of Aquinas is singularly preeminent . . . for bringing truth to light" (§31). While it was possible to fine-tune this system and "prudently enrich it with the fruits of progress," he made clear that "never may we overthrow it . . . or regard it as a great, but obsolete, relic" (§30). But the pope readily perceived that the *nouvelle théologie*'s appeal to the authority of scripture and of the Church Fathers also implicitly challenged the authority of the Vatican, "which gives such authoritative approval to scholastic theology" (§18). In response, the encyclical reaffirmed that the teaching authority of the Church was the true guardian of the "deposit of faith" revealed in scripture and the tradition. And as proof of the Jesuits' insubordination, the encyclical alluded to certain documents that were circulating without *imprimatur* and infecting the minds of the youth and laity (§13).

In part, then, this was a dispute over the nature and distribution of authority within the Church. The mysterious allusion to "writings intended for private circulation" no doubt referred to the numerous unpublished essays by Teilhard de Chardin, which had long circulated in manuscript form because of their author's publication ban. It was also likely a reference to an essay by Yves de Montcheuil on the Eucharist that expressed reservations about the Aristotelian categories in which the doctrine of transubstantiation was formulated.[17] According to de Lubac, these were informal notes dating back to Montcheuil's student days and not intended for public consumption, but of course Montcheuil was no longer alive to explain himself.[18] It was Garrigou-Lagrange who had first drawn attention to these "typewritten pages that are circulating (some since 1934) among the clergy, seminarians, and Catholic intellectuals," which he claimed were exposing young people to dangerous ideas that threatened the very foundations of their faith.[19] For Garrigou-Lagrange, these texts were evidence of a full-scale assault on the system of ecclesiastical censorship, and thus on hierarchical authority within the Church. This obsession with "typewritten pages" very clearly recalled the struggle over the clandestine resistance newspaper *Témoignage chrétien,* which the French bishops had denounced as the work of "theologians without a mandate" because it was published without imprimatur. Church authorities in Rome had not forgotten this act of disobedience, and it was no coincidence that the Jesuits behind the spiritual resistance were also those targeted by the campaign against the *nouvelle théologie.* The Roman authorities sensed in both these enterprises a spirit of insubordination that threatened the centralized structures of Church hierarchy—an independence of spirit they associated above all with the French Church.

But this was not just a dispute over ecclesiastical authority, pitting French Catholics against their Roman counterparts (many of whom were themselves French). It was also a theological quarrel over the status of Thomism—one that split the French Church itself. In fact, the "Fourvière Affair" began as an internal French dispute when two Dominican disciples of Jacques Maritain, Marie-Michel Labourdette and Marie-Joseph Nicolas, launched a blistering critique of the "Fourvière School" in the

Revue thomiste in 1946. In this "school," the authors included de Lubac, Daniélou, Bouillard, Fessard, Teilhard de Chardin, and Hans Urs von Balthasar, whom they accused of undermining the privileged status of Thomism. Maritain himself agreed, having encouraged Labourdette to publish his "declaration of war," and he also believed that Garrigou-Lagrange was "terribly right," even though he deplored Garrigou's polemical tone.[20] Maritain and his friend Charles Journet were concerned that the Jesuits had dispensed with the rational categories of Thomism in favor of a "return to the Greek Fathers," on the one hand and, "on the other hand, a formulation that would borrow from the register of Hegel and existentialism."[21] Indeed, critics increasingly framed the conflict over the *nouvelle théologie* not just as a dispute between patristic theology and Thomism, but as a choice between *Hegel* and St. Thomas. Labourdette accused the Jesuits of "abandoning Thomism, pure and simple, to adopt the central principles of Hegel," while Garrigou-Lagrange likened Teilhard de Chardin's philosophy to a "Hegelian evolutionism" that was "Christian in name only."[22] This notion of a "Hegel–St. Thomas conflict" quickly became a fixture of the critical literature on the *nouvelle théologie,* even though only one of the Jesuits under scrutiny (Fessard) had expressed much interest in Hegel.[23]

Even Congar and Chenu, who were facing their own difficulties with Rome, were sympathetic to some of the concerns raised by their Dominican confrères. They certainly shared the Jesuits' commitment to *ressourcement* and its historical methodology, to ecumenical dialogue, and to the social dimension of Catholicism. But the status of Thomism remained a significant sticking point. As Chenu explained, his position on "the situation of 'scholasticism' in Christian thought" converged with "the critique of [his] brothers at the *Revue thomiste,*" even if he abhorred their prosecutorial tone.[24] Congar expressed a similar sentiment in his review of *Corpus Mysticum,* where he took issue with de Lubac's "critique of scholasticism in favor of a symbolic theology in the manner of the Fathers."[25] The Dominican was at pains to distinguish de Lubac's approach from his own *ressourcement* project, which remained firmly Thomist. For while he shared the Jesuit's desire to "return beyond the baroque theology" of the sixteenth-century commentators, Congar preferred to linger upon Aquinas and Bonaventure, whereas de Lubac privileged a much earlier moment.[26] Congar therefore could not condone de Lubac's "relativization, by means of historical criticism, of the so upright, so humble, so rigorous work . . . of St. Thomas Aquinas."[27] Despite their stark political and theological differences with integrists like Garrigou-Lagrange, then, Chenu and Congar echoed some of the concerns of their Dominican confrères, even if they deplored the way these critics had impugned the Jesuits' orthodoxy.

It was ultimately the Roman authorities who benefited from these differences between the Jesuits and Dominicans, as each group accused the other of providing ammunition to their enemies in Rome and provoking a condemnation. After Fessard published a vigorous critique of Henri Desroches (a Dominican priest affiliated with Économie et humanisme) for his Marxist sympathies, a number of Dominicans accused Fessard of mounting a "police operation" against their brother. No dialogue was possible, they complained, between a Hegelian like Fessard and Catholics who were faithful to the Thomist tradition.[28] De Lubac, for his part, expressed frustration that Congar's critical review of *Corpus Mysticum* had appeared "at the peak of a very violent and very unjust campaign to which everyone will think that . . . you are adding the weight of your authority."[29] It fell to a layperson, Jean Lacroix, to point out that these internal divisions within the French Church only played into the hands of their mutual enemies. Writing to the editor of *Études* in 1949, Lacroix warned that "such a polemic could have disastrous consequences for both sides." The Dominicans would "be suspected of 'communizing'" and the Jesuits of being "Hegelians and partisans of a 'nouvelle théologie,'" with the result that "this most authentically Christian and most liberating work will be threatened, restricted or stopped."[30] But at a moment when both sides were consumed by their own troubles with Rome, these words fell on deaf ears.

Just as Lacroix predicted, both groups soon fell victim to disciplinary measures imposed by their superiors in Rome. In 1950, de Lubac was forced to step down from his teaching post at the Catholic University of Lyon and his editorial functions at *Recherches de science religieuse*.[31] A similar fate befell his colleague Pierre Ganne and four professors at Fourvière—Henri Rondet, Émile Delaye, Alexandre Durand, and Henri Bouillard—even though most of them (with the exception of Bouillard) had scarcely been mentioned in the polemics against Fourvière. In addition, de Lubac was sent into exile—first to Paris, then Tunisia, and then to a remote convent in the French Alps.[32] He was forbidden from publishing on theological questions and three of his books—*Corpus Mysticum, Connaissance de Dieu,* and *Surnaturel*—were removed from circulation, along with several works by Montcheuil, Daniélou, and Bouillard. Fessard seems to have emerged from the Fourvière Affair relatively unscathed, apart from being relieved of his position on the board of *Recherches*. Teilhard, for his part, was sent into exile in New York, where he died in 1955. Although these disciplinary measures were taken by the Jesuit superior general, the impetus for them almost certainly came from the Vatican.[33]

By the mid-1950s, the Roman authorities had turned their attention from the French Jesuits to the Dominicans. The context for the new round of sanctions was less *Humani Generis* and the crisis over the *nouvelle théologie* than the Cold War and the crackdown on the French Catholic left. At the end of 1950, Desroches left the Dominican order. In 1953, several works by Maurice Montuclard were placed on the Index of Forbidden Books and he was stripped of the priesthood—a move soon followed by the official condemnation of the group he had founded, Jeunesse de l'Église.[34] At the same time, the French bishops were taking measures to rein in the worker-priests and the internal missionary movement. In 1952, they replaced the superior of the Mission de France with a new superior tasked with bringing the seminary under greater episcopal oversight. Then, in 1954, the French bishops ordered the worker-priests out of the factories, but roughly two-thirds of them refused to submit.[35] Because of their ties to Dominicans such as Chenu, Féret, and Congar, suspicion soon shifted onto these theologians. It certainly did not help that Chenu published his prominent defense of the worker-priests after they were sanctioned, fueling suspicion that "the soul of the resistance to the decisions of the Holy See was Dominican."[36] As a result, the Dominican master general relieved Congar, Chenu, Féret, and Boisselot of their teaching and editorial functions and sent them away from Paris.[37] Under severe pressure to "clean house," he took the further unprecedented step of firing the three provincial superiors of the Dominican order in France. According to Chenu, the Vatican had threatened to take matters into its own hands and revise the Constitution of the order. The master general therefore asked Chenu and his brothers to accept the disciplinary measures because the very autonomy of the order was at stake.[38]

Coming on the heels of *Humani Generis* and the sanctions against the Jesuits, these events sent shockwaves through France. In *Le Figaro*, François Mauriac called for a "new Concordat" in order to protect the autonomy of the French Church from Vatican overreach. Hubert Beuve-Méry, founder and editor of *Le Monde*, complained that an excessive fear of communism had led the Vatican to return to "the most questionable methods of the Inquisition."[39] As with the Jesuit condemnation, the campaign against the French Dominicans was waged through secretive means that struck many as uncomfortably similar to the techniques used by totalitarian regimes to silence internal critics. Chenu decried the use of the very same "police procedures" and "Gestapo behavior" that Church officials roundly condemned when they were deployed on the other side of the Iron Curtain. Congar, too, complained bitterly about the "mania for secret denunciations in Rome" and "whispered criticisms, of which the person they concern never receives a clear and frank explanation," nor an opportunity "to defend or at least explain himself."[40] So incensed was he by these tactics that, in a small act of defiance, Congar apparently urinated on the outer wall of the Holy Office during a visit to Rome.[41]

Despite the similar timing and tactics involved in the campaigns against the Jesuits and Dominicans, it is important not to conflate the two condemnations. It is certainly true that they were driven by similar concerns about authority and change within the Church, and both were part of a broader effort by the Roman Curia to rein in the perceived excesses of the French Church. Not even Maritain was immune from this campaign, though he managed to escape formal censure.[42] But while *Humani Generis* and the Fourvière Affaire were directed primarily against the Catholic theological engagement with contemporary philosophy, the condemnation of the Dominicans was inextricable from the backlash against the Catholic left.[43] To be sure, political questions were not the only driving force behind the sanctions. Congar had already been censured in 1952 for his book *True and False Reform in the Church,* and there was some speculation that the references to "irenism" in *Humani Generis* might be directed against his ecumenical writings.[44] But the common denominator among the Dominicans who were targeted in 1954 was their involvement with the Catholic left. This was not lost on commentators at the time. The sanctions against the Dominicans were widely perceived as a political campaign orchestrated by right-wing clerical forces—what one writer described as a "cabal of old fascist prelates and new McCarthyite prelates."[45] For many observers, the crackdown on the Dominicans was proof that the Church had definitively sided with the forces of capitalism in the Cold War.

The 1950s were thus a long and difficult time in the wilderness for the French Church, bringing an end to one of the richest periods of renewal and experimentation. But while the Roman authorities were waging their campaign against the *nouvelle théologie* in France, the movement was gathering steam beyond its borders.[46] This was particularly the case in Germany, Switzerland, and the Low Countries, where a new generation of theologians raised on the works of Congar, Chenu, and de Lubac was coming into its own. Some of them had studied with the French masters after the war, when young priests and seminarians from all over the world flocked to the country. They included the Belgian Dominican Edward Schillebeeckx, who learned from Chenu to read theology with a historian's eye.[47] Schillebeeckx would go on to become an influential figure at the Second Vatican Council, where he served as a theological advisor to the Dutch bishops. Others read the classic works of the *nouvelle théologie* in translation. A young Joseph Ratzinger read the German translation of de Lubac's *Catholicism* in 1949 and the book made a profound impression on the future pope, shaping his understanding of the faith and the Fathers.[48] Like Schillebeeckx, Ratzinger would become a key player at Vatican II. Many more of the leading theologians of the twentieth century, from Karl Rahner to Hans Urs von Balthasar, were greatly affected by their reading of the French Jesuits and Dominicans and helped to popularize their works beyond France. Thus, at the very moment when the original architects of the *nouvelle théologie* were being silenced or exiled, a second generation was beginning to emerge beyond France's borders that would ensure its lasting legacy.

Perhaps more significantly, the *nouvelle théologie* was also attracting a growing following beyond Europe. Between the 1930s and the 1960s, waves of Catholic students from Africa, Asia, and Latin America flocked to France, where they became engaged in the major currents of French Catholic thought. Among them were liberation theologians such as Gustavo Gutiérrez, who studied with Henri de Lubac in the 1950s, as well as architects of the Negritude movement such as Alioune Diop and Léopold Sédar Senghor.[49] A celebrated poet and politician, Senghor served in the Constituent Assembly of the Fourth Republic and would go on to become the first president of independent Senegal in 1960. In the late 1950s, he became particularly taken with the ideas of Teilhard de Chardin, which had finally begun to appear in print after the Jesuit's death in 1955 and quickly attracted a diverse following of politicians, eco-feminists, liberation theologians, and UN functionaries.

Senghor believed that Teilhard's work could provide theological support for the project of Negritude—the effort to promote the values of

"Negro-African civilization" long disparaged by Europeans.[50] Senghor found in Teilhard's Catholic materialism an alternative to the atheist and Eurocentric materialism of Marx, one he hoped could inform a distinctively African socialism attentive to the spiritual dimension of human life. He also found inspiration in Teilhard's theory of evolution, which posited that human life on earth was converging in such a way as to preserve the distinct identities of the persons and cultures it joined together. As we have seen, this theory was based on Teilhard's personalist conviction that "*union differentiates;* in every organized whole, the parts perfect and fulfill themselves."[51] For Senghor, this principle meant that Africans did not have to choose between remaining true to their own values and contributing to the global "Civilization of the Universal" because this civilization in fact depended on the complementarity of distinct racial and cultural groups.[52] Indeed, he insisted that such typically "African" values as religion and community were needed to save Europe from its own particularism. This personalist vision went hand in hand with Senghor's political commitment to federalism, which he conceived as an alternative to the model of decolonization based on national independence. Although his efforts ultimately came to naught, Senghor worked hard to promote the establishment of a postcolonial federation in which metropolitan France and its overseas territories would join together as equal partners deriving mutual benefit from the symbiosis of their cultures.[53]

The growing influence of the *nouvelle théologie* among Catholics like Senghor and Gutiérrez was critical to securing its lasting legacy, for the face of the Church was changing dramatically in these years. Between the end of World War II and the beginning of the Second Vatican Council, European empires crumbled and a wealth of new states came into being across the Global South. In 1954, at the very same moment when the tensions between the French Church and Rome were at their peak, the humiliating defeat of French forces at Dien Bien Phu brought an end to the French colonial presence in Indochina and an uprising broke out in Algeria. The conflict rapidly escalated into a bloody war that attracted international condemnation for the French forces' use of torture and even brought down the Fourth Republic in 1958.[54] By 1960, the territories of West and Central Africa had gained their independence and, six months before the opening of the Second Vatican Council, the Evian Accords brought an independent Algeria into existence. Decolonization represented a profound challenge for the Church, which had been slow to develop an indigenous clergy in the territories of the French Empire.[55] But the indigenous churches of Africa and Asia would become increasingly central to the life of the Church as the demographic heart of the Catholic faith shifted to the Global South after the 1960s.

The Tide Turns: The *Nouvelle Théologie* at Vatican II

It was not until the death of Pius XII in 1958—just days after the crisis over the Algerian War brought France's Fifth Republic into being—that the frosty relations between Rome and the French Church began to thaw. Pius was succeeded by John XXIII, who had been nuncio to France at the time of *Humani Generis,* and in a highly symbolic gesture, one of the first acts of the newly elected pope was to make a substantial contribution to *Sources chrétiennes*—the centerpiece of the Jesuits' *ressourcement* project. On January 25, 1959, the new pope took the most significant step of his papacy when he announced the convocation of an ecumenical council—what would become known as Vatican II. The following year, he established a set of preparatory commissions to oversee the production of draft documents that would be discussed and voted on at the council. In August 1960, Henri de Lubac opened *La Croix* to read the list of theologians chosen to serve on the Preparatory Theological Commission. To his astonishment, he found his own name listed there, alongside that of Yves Congar.[56]

This gesture indicated that the new pope considered the affair of the *nouvelle théologie* to be closed. But not everyone shared this view. Cardinal Alfredo Ottaviani, who had long been a forceful critic of the *nouvelle théologie,* now presided over the Preparatory Theological Commission in his capacity as Secretary of the Holy Office. In response to the pope's initial call for proposals about what the council should address, Ottaviani suggested that it expand on *Humani Generis* by explicitly condemning the errors of relativism, immanentism, existentialism, and evolutionism and by defending "scholastic theology against the hidden assaults of the New Theology."[57] De Lubac's efforts on the commission were thus an exercise in frustration as he was constantly having to defend himself and Teilhard de Chardin against the enemies of the *nouvelle théologie.*[58]

De Lubac's experience on the Theological Commission indicates how much the preparatory phase of the council and the draft documents that emerged from it remained bound to the theological approach that had dominated the Church since the nineteenth century and which de Lubac, Congar, and Chenu had spent their careers combating. The draft texts (known as "schemata") remained firmly anchored in a neo-scholastic framework, with its ahistorical, legalistic, deductive style of reasoning.[59] This was particularly evident in *De Ecclesia,* the schema on the Church. Prepared by Sebastian Tromp and longtime critic of the *nouvelle théologie,* Marie-Rosaire Gagnebet, the text stressed the hierarchical and juridical nature of the Church. But it was also true of the documents on revelation and the deposit of faith, which treated revelation as a body of propositional knowledge about God.[60] In fact, the second of these documents included a new formula for the profession of faith that would have Catholics proclaim: "I also condemn and reject whatever is condemned and rejected in those Councils [Trent and Vatican I] and in Encyclicals, namely in *Pascendi* and *Humani generis.*"[61] The text even included a direct condemnation of two positions that de Lubac had advanced in his work, which prompted the Jesuit to threaten to resign from the commission.[62]

Events took a dramatic turn when the roughly 2,400 "council fathers" gathered in Rome in October 1962 to debate the schemata. In a surprising twist, the draft documents drew sharp criticism from a number of the bishops and were sent back to the commissions to be rewritten. Behind this revolt was a new generation of theologians who had been influenced by the *nouvelle théologie* and who came to the council as official advisors (*periti*) to the council fathers. A memorandum signed by Cardinal Josef Frings of Cologne, for instance, demanded that the conciliar documents "not be treatises in a scholastic style . . . but should instead speak the language of Holy Scripture and the holy Fathers of the Church."[63] But the true author of the memo was actually the cardinal's *peritus* Joseph Ratzinger—the future Benedict XVI—whose work bore the indelible imprint of the *nouvelle théologie.* Ratzinger was one of several theologians who had penned critiques of the schemata in the lead-up to the council and even circulated alternative drafts. The most significant of these alternative proposals came from Dutch, Belgian, and German theologians steeped in the *nouvelle théologie,* such as Schillebeeckx, Pieter Smulders, Gérard Philips, Karl Rahner, and Ratzinger himself.[64] Even before voting began in late 1962, then, some of the most prominent critics of neo-scholasticism were shopping around alternatives to the documents that Ottaviani's commission had prepared.

The turning point came on November 20, 1962, when voting began on *De Fontibus*, the schema on the sources of revelation. Cardinal Achille Liénart of Lille was the first to vote. He rejected the schema for its "frigid" language and reliance on "Scholastic arguments," a sentiment soon echoed by several other council fathers.[65] With the vote locked in a stalemate, John XXIII decided to set up a new commission to redraft the text. Ten days later, the discussion of *De Ecclesia* followed a similar path. Bishop Émile-Joseph De Smedt of Bruges denounced the schema for its "triumphalism," "clericalism," and "juridicism," while Cardinal Frings complained that the document cited virtually no patristic or medieval sources.[66] With the first session of the council drawing to a close, the document was pulled from consideration and sent back to the Doctrinal Commission, where it was reworked by a seven-person subcommission that drew on the work of Gérard Philips, Karl Rahner, Jean Daniélou, and Yves Congar. The effect of these early votes was to break Ottaviani's control over the commission and allow the leading voices of the *nouvelle théologie* to play a key role in rewriting the central doctrinal pronouncements of the council. The significance of this moment was not lost on the Jesuit journal *Études,* which proclaimed that, "with the vote on November 20, the era of the Counter-Reformation has come to an end.'"[67]

The clearest evidence of the influence of the *nouvelle théologie* at the Second Vatican Council was the contribution that its leading architects made to crafting specific documents. Although Marie-Dominique Chenu was not named as an official *peritus*, he put his stamp on the proceedings as advisor to Bishop Claude Rolland of Antsirabé, Madagascar—a former student of his at Le Saulchoir. Chenu seems to have played a particularly important role in the discussion of "Schema 13," which became the Pastoral Constitution on the Church in the Modern World (*Gaudium et Spes*).[68] Henri de Lubac and Jean Daniélou were also involved in these discussions and served on the subcommission that drew up sections 19–22, which dealt with the problem of atheism.[69] Section 21 in particular echoed their counter-political vision when it taught that "a hope related to the end of time does not diminish the importance of intervening duties but rather undergirds the acquittal of them with fresh incentives."[70] In addition to his work on *Gaudium et Spes,* Daniélou also worked on *Lumen Gentium* (The Dogmatic Constitution on the Church) and played a pivotal role in drafting *Dei Verbum* (The Dogmatic Constitution on

Divine Revelation). After the initial schema was voted down, Archbishop Gabriel-Marie Garrone of Toulouse tasked him with writing a new prologue, which would lay the groundwork for the first six sections of *Dei Verbum*.[71] Along with Smulders, Ratzinger, and Rahner, Daniélou helped to reorient the council's teaching on revelation toward a more inclusive, sacramental, and historical vision.

But few theologians played a more integral role than Yves Congar, who helped draft no fewer than eight of the council's sixteen documents, including three of its four constitutions.[72] The ecumenical language adopted by the council is perhaps the greatest testament to Congar's influence. It appears, for instance, in *Lumen Gentium*, for which Congar wrote initial drafts of Chapter 1 and parts of Chapter 2.[73] Chapter 1 affirmed that the "one, holy, catholic and apostolic" Church "*subsists* in the Catholic Church," rather than being strictly identical with it, and acknowledged that "many elements of sanctification and of truth are found outside of its visible structure."[74] Section 16 went even further, affirming that salvation was not beyond the reach of those "who through no fault of their own do not know the Gospel of Christ or His Church" or "have not yet arrived at an explicit knowledge of God." This more inclusive vision of salvation was further developed in the Decree on the Missionary Activity of the Church (*Ad Gentes*), the first chapter of which Congar described as "my work from A to Z."[75] It affirmed that "whatever truth and grace are to be found among the nations" not yet touched by the Gospel constitute "a sort of secret presence of God."[76] The idea that salvation could extend to people outside the visible borders of the Church was a significant innovation of the council and testifies to Congar's "ubiquitously influential" role there.[77]

Beyond the direct role that its architects played in drafting the documents themselves, the *nouvelle théologie* also had a more indirect influence on the council, via the many theologians and bishops who took inspiration from it. It found expression in the council's vision of the Church, which marked a shift away from the hierarchical and juridical ecclesiology of neo-scholasticism in favor of the sacramental, horizontal, and communal vision advanced by theologians such as Congar and de Lubac. *Lumen Gentium* enshrined two models in particular. It described the Church as the "people of God," a formulation indebted to Congar that downplayed the distinction between the clergy and the laity, between Catholics and non-Catholics.[78] But the document also presented the Church as the "body of Christ," adopting the Eucharistic ecclesiology that de Lubac had recovered in *Corpus Mysticum*.[79] Section 3, for instance, echoed de Lubac's claim that the Eucharist makes the Church: "In the sacrament of the Eucharistic bread, the unity of all believers who form one body in Christ is both expressed and brought about" (§3). And it also adopted de Lubac's emphasis on the communal dimension of the Eucharistic celebration, through which "all of us are made members of His Body" and "severally members one of another" (§7).

The most significant impact that the *nouvelle théologie* had on the council, however, manifested itself the broader spirit and tone of the documents. We see this especially in the theological methodology they adopted—what Chenu called their "inductive" approach—which gave new prominence to the role of history in the life of the Church.[80] It was most clearly on display in *Gaudium et Spes*. Rather than beginning with eternal principles or Church teaching, the document broke new ground by proceeding from an examination of the contemporary historical situation and interpreting the Church's mission in light of the "signs of the times." This meant acknowledging that the Church was "an historical reality" and that changing circumstances called for new pastoral approaches (GS§44). It meant finally endorsing the use of historical criticism in biblical studies (DV§12). And it even meant acknowledging that, in some cases, doctrine itself could change, as documents such as *Nostra Aetate* and *Dignitatis Humanae*—the most controversial documents of the council—reversed centuries of Catholic teaching on Judaism and religious freedom.[81]

In the case of *Nostra Aetate,* the council expanded on the arguments that Catholic critics of anti-Semitism had made during the Second World War. Like the Lyon theologians who led the spiritual resistance in France, the document stressed the Jewish roots of Christianity—the fact that Jesus and his disciples were Jews—and anchored its analysis in Paul's Letter to the Romans. It stressed that the arrival of Christ had not abrogated God's covenant with the Jews since "[God] does not repent of the gifts He makes or of the calls He issues."[82] This meant that "the Jews should not be presented as rejected or accursed by God," as traditional anti-Judaism maintained, since "God holds the Jews most dear for the sake of their Fathers" (§4). The document also explicitly condemned anti-Semitism and rejected the notion that the Jews were somehow to blame for the death of Christ, although earlier drafts of the text contained a more forceful repudiation of the charge of deicide.[83] But *Nostra Aetate* also went considerably further than the wartime critics of anti-Semitism in breaking with the heritage of anti-Judaism. Whereas the Lyon theologians had continued to approach Judaism through the framework of Christianity and to look forward to the eventual conversion of the Jews, *Nostra Aetate* abandoned this language of conversion in favor of a much vaguer hope for the eschatological union of all peoples at the end of time. This led some commentators to hail the document as a "Copernican revolution in Catholic thinking about the Jewish religion and people."[84] And yet, it is equally important to point out that the document made no mention of the Holocaust, nor did it offer an apology for the long history of anti-Semitism within the Church. Indeed, since the end of the war, the Vatican had been conspicuously silent on the subject of the Holocaust and of its own response to the murder and persecution of Jews during the war.[85]

The council's teaching on religious freedom represented perhaps the clearest break with the past teaching of the Church. As we have seen, the nineteenth-century popes had firmly rejected the "absurd and erroneous" principle of religious liberty on the grounds that other religions were false and only truth had rights.[86] In the very different context of the Cold War, with Catholics facing persecution under the communist regimes of Eastern Europe, *Dignitatis Humanae* broke with centuries of Church teaching by affirming religious freedom as a basic human right.[87] This move was part of the council's broader adaptation to political modernity, which led it to endorse democracy, the separation of Church and state, and human rights. Abandoning once and for all the logic of the Constantinian era, the council affirmed that "the Church and the political community in their own fields are autonomous and independent," even as it also rejected the liberal principle that religion ought to be confined to the private sphere (GS§76, §43). In a similar way, the Declaration on Religious Freedom embraced one of the key tenets of liberal democracy, but without endorsing the liberal justification for it. Appealing instead to natural law, the document insisted that "the right to religious freedom has its foundation not in the subjective disposition of the person, but in his very nature" (DH§2). Because humans were "endowed with reason and free will" by their creator, they had to embrace the truth of the Gospel freely and without coercion. In addition to invoking natural law, the Declaration also mined scripture and the Church Fathers for evidence "that man's response to God in faith must be free" (DH§10). Such evidence was crucial because it allowed the document to claim that it was simply reaffirming a principle long maintained by the Catholic tradition, even as it quite clearly departed from previous Church teaching. The appeal to *ressourcement* thus cushioned what many considered to be the most significant legacy of *Dignitatis Humanae:* its tacit admission that the doctrine of the Church develops and changes.[88]

The council's teaching on Judaism and religious freedom clearly reflected the concern to bring the Church "up to date" with the modern world, in keeping with the central watchword of Vatican II: *aggiornamento.* But the fact that these innovations were justified by appealing to scripture and the Church Fathers is an indication that the council was equally committed to returning to the sources of the tradition. Here we can glimpse perhaps the most profound effect of the *nouvelle théologie* on Vatican II. The spirit of *ressourcement,* which theologians such as de Lubac, Congar, and Daniélou had done so much to promote, runs like a red thread through the conciliar documents. The texts called on Catholics to steep themselves in the biblical sources of the faith, which were the "soul of all theology," as well as promoting the patristic *ressourcement* pioneered by de Lubac, Congar, and Daniélou.[89] References to the patristic sources peppered the council documents, and priests in particular were encouraged to anchor themselves in the study of the Greek and Latin Fathers of the Church.[90] Embracing *ressourcement* in turn transformed the very style and language of the council documents. As John O'Malley has persuasively shown, the texts of Vatican II departed dramatically from the juridical, abstract language of scholastic disputation that had dominated previous councils, encyclicals, and of course the early draft documents. Instead, they adopted the "pastoral" style of the Church Fathers. This "epideictic" language was more literary than legalistic, more spiritual than intellectual, and more inclusive than analytic. It placed the accent on dialogue and engagement rather than prescription and condemnation. Nor were these stylistic choices ancillary to the substantive changes wrought by Vatican II; on the contrary, they reflected and communicated the spirit of the council.[91]

It might seem that such calls for a return to the sources would be at odds with the council's mission to bring the Church "up to date" with modern life. And yet, the principles of *ressourcement* and *aggiornamento* were closely bound together in the documents of Vatican II, just as they had been for the *nouvelle théologie.* The Decree on the Adaptation and Renewal of Religious Life, for instance, explained that "the adaptation and renewal of the religious life includes both the constant return to the sources of all Christian life . . . and their adaptation to the changed conditions of our time."[92] *Aggiornamento* and *ressourcement* were mutually reinforcing, in other words, just as Daniélou had argued in his 1946 "manifesto" that returning to the Church Fathers would paradoxically bring Catholic thought closer to the concerns of modern intellectual life. In fact, as we have seen, the logic of *ressourcement* underwrote some of the most important innovations of the council, from the teaching on religious freedom to the principle of episcopal collegiality.[93] O'Malley therefore concludes that *ressourcement* was "the most traditional yet potentially the most radical" of the various approaches to change invoked at Vatican II.[94] Rather than imagining the council as part of an ongoing and incremental process of development that would require only a continuation in the same direction, the call to return to the sources arguably implied a more radical form of change.[95] After all, it was precisely this logic that the Protestant reformers had invoked five centuries earlier. And indeed, the changes wrought by the council would have been unthinkable to most Catholics only a few years earlier.

The Church and the Modern World

This is not to suggest that there was no tension at all between the imperatives of *ressourcement* and *aggiornamento*. In fact, after their initial victory against the wardens of neo-scholasticism, significant fissures began to emerge among the partisans of the *nouvelle théologie* at the council. These fractures were in many ways the logical extension of the divisions that had emerged between the Dominican and Jesuit *nouveaux théologiens* after the war, and they came to the surface when the council turned to debating the all-important question of the relationship between the Church and the modern world.

On the eve of the council, Chenu had been concerned that the meeting might degenerate into a narrow squabble over internal Church affairs. To preempt this, he spearheaded a campaign to publish an opening "Message to the World" that would signal the council's commitment to addressing the world beyond its borders and engaging in a fruitful dialogue with modernity. Congar supported the project wholeheartedly, and with the help of prelates such as Cardinal Liénart, they managed to put the issue on the agenda.[96] In the course of the subsequent debate, Chenu's draft was substantially revised—as he put it, "they dipped my baby in holy water!"—but the end result nevertheless conveyed his core concerns.[97] Addressing itself to all people of good will, the message called on "all men to work along with us in building up a more just and brotherly city in this world."[98] The Church thereby signaled its commitment, not just to Catholic issues, but also to "whatever concerns the dignity of man, whatever contributes to a genuine community of people."[99] This opening message would set the terms for one of the most important legacies of Vatican II: a dramatic transformation in the Church's attitude to the modern world. It found expression in the all-important Pastoral Constitution on the Church in the Modern World (*Gaudium et Spes*), known in draft form as "Schema 13." It was during the debates over this document that the first cracks began to appear between "progressive" theologians such as Chenu, Congar, Schillebeeckx, Karl Rahner, and Hans Küng and a group that included de Lubac and Daniélou, as well as the future Popes John Paul II (Karol Wojtyła) and Benedict XVI (Joseph Ratzinger).

For Chenu's group, as we might expect from their history of engagement with the left, the priority was to open the Church up to the modern world by acknowledging the value of extraecclesial ideas and movements. In September 1964, Schillebeeckx gave a lecture that ruffled a few feathers, in which he suggested that the world outside the Church was already implicitly Christian because God's grace was at work within it, albeit in a hidden way.[100] This line of thinking drew on the theology of incarnation that Dominicans like Chenu had been developing since the 1930s, with its emphasis on the value of nature and human history, and it found expression in *Gaudium et Spes* as well. For Chenu, it was particularly significant that the title of the Pastoral Constitution referred to the "Church *in* the Modern World" rather than the "Church *and* the Modern World." The implication was that "the Church and the world are not two juxtaposed societies, with a border over which one might quarrel or sign concordats." Instead, the Church "*is* the world, inasmuch as it is taken up by the Christian economy."[101] Chenu thus credited the document with overcoming the traditional devaluation of nature and worldly affairs that he attributed to the heritage of Augustinianism.[102]

This approach was met with suspicion from those more attuned to the eschatological model advanced by the French Jesuits. Along with Ratzinger, Wojtyła, and Daniélou, de Lubac thought that existing drafts of the document conveyed an overly optimistic view of secular modernity. He worried that inflating the spiritual significance of the world in even its most secular, modern manifestations would lead to the "atrophy of

Figure 7.1   Marie-Dominique Chenu consulting with colleagues at the Second Vatican Council, November 1963. *Credit:* Archives de la Province dominicaine de France.

the supernatural" and devalue the Church's evangelical mission.[103] In June 1964, de Lubac wrote to several committee members to express his concerns about the way Schema 13 was taking shape. Without naming names, he complained that some theologians had interpreted the need to open up to the modern world in such a way as to allow the Church "to be invaded by it."[104] So concerned were they to demonstrate the Church's willingness to engage with modernity that they risked neglecting the truths of the Christian faith, without which all human life is meaning-less. He worried that nonbelievers would interpret this as "a concession rooted in weakness, as the expression of an inferiority complex with re-spect to the 'world.'"[105] The problem, he insisted, was not that the text was too bold or went too far, but that it did not go far enough. It lacked the "apostolic audacity" to engage with the world on its own terms, with a "boldness that alone has a chance of reaching people of our age."[106] De Lubac reiterated these concerns in an October letter to Cardinal Léger of Montreal, who promised to bring them up during the upcoming general debate.[107] Once again, de Lubac complained that the document "lack[ed] spiritual density." Such "silences or timidities in the schema about the eternal vocation of man," he feared, would only encourage people to turn away from the faith rather than invigorate it.[108]

The debate over *Gaudium et Spes* thus revealed an emerging split within the group that had successfully sidelined Ottaviani's anti-reformist faction in 1962. It pitted Thomists who tended to embrace the value of worldly affairs against Augustinians who took a more critical view and sought to recall the centrality of the supernatural; the logic of incarnation against the demands of eschatology.[109] In this way, it reproduced precisely the postwar divisions among French theologians outlined in the previous chapters.

Such tensions would only grow more acute in the years following the council, as these rival factions competed to lay claim to its legacy. Both groups grappled with the same problem: how to bridge the divide between the Church and the modern world without reducing one to the other. Chenu insisted that Vatican II should be interpreted "prophetically," as a starting point for further reflection rather than a fixed set of teachings. By taking its cue from the "signs of the times," he urged, the council necessarily "call[ed] for its own overcoming" in light of changed circumstances; it was an invitation to "permanent invention."[110] This meant looking outside the Church and making use of the resources of the secular social sciences, just as Thomas Aquinas had incorporated Greek thought. Daniélou and de Lubac firmly rejected this approach. They warned that treating Vatican II as a starting point for something new risked betraying the council and hastening the process of secularization. De Lubac still worried, just as he had in the 1930s and 1940s, about the risk of reducing the Church to a sociological or political entity like any other.[111] He also remained deeply suspicious of the social sciences because they treated the human being as a scientific object—a position that resembled contemporaneous critiques by post-structuralist philosophers such as Michel Foucault.[112] Whereas Chenu and Schillebeeckx stressed the positive value of modernity, Daniélou and de Lubac insisted on the need to resist those aspects of the modern world that were contrary to the spirit of Christ.[113]

These differences came to a head in the quarrel over *Concilium,* a new international journal that was created in the 1960s to promote the spirit of Vatican II. It was staffed by many of the leading theologians of the day, including de Lubac, Johann Baptist Metz, Congar, Rahner, Schillebeeckx, and Küng. But only a year into its existence, de Lubac and Daniélou began to have grave doubts about the journal's direction. In November 1965, de Lubac resigned from the editorial board on the grounds that "the orientation of the Journal did not correspond to what its title had led me to expect."[114] These concerns were shared by Ratzinger and Hans Urs von Balthasar, and together they launched a rival journal called *Communio* in 1972, in order to advance their competing interpretation of the council's legacy. In this way, the internal differences within the *nouvelle théologie* hardened into the "progressive" and "conservative" blocs of the postconciliar Church.

But these familiar labels are in some ways misleading. Just as the French Jesuits had accused the postwar Catholic left of reviving arguments once marshaled by the old Catholic right, de Lubac believed that there was a hidden kinship between neo-scholasticism and the "progressive" voices at the council. Their "new integrism," as he called it, was simply the latest iteration of the old scholastic theory of "pure nature" that evacuated the supernatural from the natural order.[115] Both positions, de Lubac maintained, unwittingly played into hands of the forces of secularization and both were equally modern. The "new 'modernity'" embraced by theologians such as Schillebeeckx had simply replaced the "petrified modernity" of neo-scholasticism.[116] Absent from both was a sense of the indissoluble bond between tradition and renewal, of a "true *aggiornamento*" rooted in the rich soil of *ressourcement.*[117] This was the genuine legacy of Vatican II, de Lubac believed. "*There is no aggiornamento without a traditional spirit, and there is no traditional spirit without aggiornamento,*" he explained. "Only in a more complete faithfulness to the tradition can one obtain the renewal that is always necessary. And in this renewal, and only in it, is found complete faithfulness to the tradition."[118] The commitment to "update" the Church and fidelity to tradition were thus mutually reinforcing for de Lubac. Only by balancing the two could the Church engage with modernity without capitulating to it.

This is what makes it so difficult to label de Lubac a "conservative" or "progressive" and indicates the limits of such categories in making sense of theology. He himself always refused the choice between these alternatives, on the grounds that the Catholic tradition could not be identified "either with a conservative spirit or a revolutionary one."[119] When he opposed those who argued for the need to "adapt" the Church to the modern world at Vatican II, he was reiterating the same line of critique that he had used against Catholic supporters of Vichy during the war. It was then that he and his friends had first turned away from the logic of incarnation and adaptation, precisely because of the way some Catholics had used it to justify their support for Pétain. In the postwar period, the Jesuits had turned this same argument against the Catholic left. When situated in this longer history, de Lubac's critique of the "progressive" interpretation of Vatican II looks less like a conservative backlash than the product of a much earlier turn from incarnation to eschatology, which emerged from the crucible of wartime occupation.

This perhaps explains why he has been a favorite, not only of so-called conservative popes such as John Paul II and Benedict XVI, but also of Pope Francis, who paid tribute to his fellow Jesuit in one of the few books he wrote before becoming pope:

> There are those that seek to compromise their faith for political alliances or for a worldly spirituality. One Catholic theologian, Henri de Lubac, says that the worst that can happen to those that are anointed and called to service is that they live with the criteria of the world instead of the criteria that the Lord commands. . . . The worst that can happen in the priestly life is to be worldly.[120]

Here we see how the counter-political vision developed by French Jesuits such as Fessard and de Lubac continues to inform the worldview of the current pope.[121] This is a testament to the distance traveled since the condemnation of the *nouvelle théologie* in the 1950s. By the 1990s, Daniélou, Congar, and de Lubac had all been elevated to the rank of cardinal and the rehabilitation of the *nouvelle théologie* was truly complete. But the political and theological differences that emerged between the Dominicans and Jesuits in the wake of World War II and underwrote their different responses to the council remain alive and well. They continue to inform how the Church grapples with its relationship to the modern world, as it seeks to strike the right balance between adaptation and refusal—between being in the world and rising above it.

Epilogue

The face of the Catholic Church changed dramatically in the years following the Second Vatican Council. European churches began to see their pews empty out and vocations drop off sharply, while the demographic center of the Church increasingly shifted to the Global South. With secularization eroding the institutional power of Catholicism in its historic heartland, it seemed that the Church's days as a powerful force in European politics were finally at an end.

And yet, this diagnosis appears to have been premature. As early as the 1990s, the sociologist José Casanova observed that, despite ecclesiastical disestablishment and declining rates of religious belief and practice, religion had by no means receded into the private sphere. Indeed, pointing to examples such as the Solidarity movement in Poland and liberation theology in Latin America, he argued that religion was actually undergoing a process of "deprivatization" and reasserting itself in the public sphere.[1] The events of the past twenty years—from the growing power of the religious right in America, to the attacks of 9/11 and the "war on terror," to the recent surge of Christian populism in Eastern Europe—have only confirmed the fact that religion remains a powerful political force today. This has led some scholars to declare that we are living in a "post-secular" age and has inspired a renewed interest in the public role of religion among philosophers, anthropologists, sociologists, political scientists, historians, and theologians.[2] In light of this development, the questions raised by the *nouvelle théologie* about the relationship between theology and politics, the history of secularization, and the limits of secularism seem as timely as ever. In what follows, I draw out a few of the ways in which these theologians anticipated, foreshadowed, or directly influenced recent debates about the role of religion in public life, both within and beyond the Church.

Reclaiming the Political: Liberation Theology and Radical Orthodoxy

As decolonization brought a raft of new states into existence following World War II, Catholic theologians began to grapple with how to decolonize the theology and structures of the Church itself. Vatican II helped galvanize these efforts, and in the wake of the council, theologians across Latin America, Africa, and Asia began to transform Catholic theology to reflect the values, priorities, and concerns of Catholics in these regions. Perhaps the most significant expression of this new orientation was the rise of liberation theology in Latin America, which undertook to write theology from the perspective of the poor and the oppressed.[3]

Although liberation theologians inhabited a very different world from the one that had birthed the *nouvelle théologie* at the beginning of the twentieth century, they nevertheless drew inspiration from the French Jesuits and Dominicans. Liberation theologians found in their work a model capable of overcoming the separation between the natural and supernatural orders and endowing the struggle for social justice with redemptive value. But they were also determined to go beyond where their French predecessors, who had always claimed to remain at arm's length from politics, stopped short. Such a position had made sense in early twentieth-century France, given the long historical association there between Catholicism and counterrevolution. This history led Catholics such as de Lubac, Congar, Chenu, and Maritain to defend the autonomy of the political order from Church intervention, even as they sought to preserve a role for Catholicism in the newly secular public sphere. How they variously negotiated this double imperative and the new forms of theological politics to which it gave rise has been the subject of this book. But theologians writing since the 1960s were not bound by these same constraints. While they built on the central insights of the *nouvelle théologie,* they also moved beyond it to reclaim a robust political role for theology. In the process, they made explicit something that remained only implicit in the work of their French precursors—the fact that theology can still be politically powerful even when it disavows politics.

In the middle decades of the twentieth century, close links between the French and Latin American churches ensured that the ideas of Maritain, Mounier, Lebret, Chenu, de Lubac, and Teilhard de Chardin circulated widely throughout the region.[4] One of the earliest beneficiaries of these networks was Jacques Maritain, who developed a loyal Latin American following after his first visit to South America in 1936. His disciples Alceu Amoroso Lima, Rafael Caldera, and Eduardo Frei Montalva would go on to lead Christian Democratic movements in Brazil, Venezuela, and Chile, respectively.[5] But Maritain's influence would soon be eclipsed among a new generation of Latin American theologians who found themselves drawn to the *nouvelle théologie* instead. They included Gustavo Gutiérrez, who studied psychology at Louvain in the early 1950s before coming to the Catholic University of Lyon, where he was mentored by de Lubac. Indeed, almost all the leading liberation theologians studied in Europe in the 1940s and 1950s, when the controversy over the *nouvelle théologie* was at its peak: Juan Luis Segundo in Paris and Belgium, Hugo Assmann in Münster, Leonardo Boff in Munich, and Enrique Dussel in Paris and Münster.[6] Here, they were exposed to the ideas of the leading European theologians and philosophers of the day. But when they sought to apply these principles to the needs of their own communities in Peru or Brazil, for instance, many found that the solutions proposed by even the most progressive of European theologians fell short. What was needed was a new approach to theology, one that would be appropriate to the Latin American context.

The story of Gustavo Gutiérrez illustrates how liberation theologians drew on the insights of the *nouvelle théologie* while seeking to move beyond its limitations. In 1971, Gutiérrez published his programmatic statement of the aims of liberation theology, *A Theology of Liberation*, in which he explained how the movement fit into the history of Catholic theology. Like most of the figures in this book, Gutiérrez rejected the "Christendom" model that had long defined Church-state relations and embraced the separation of Church and state. But he also rejected the "New Christendom" model advanced by Jacques Maritain, which he associated with both Catholic Action and Christian Democracy. The problem with this model, for Gutiérrez, was its reliance on a "distinction of planes" that separated spiritual from temporal affairs, the role of the clergy from that of the laity, in order to secure the autonomy of the temporal order from ecclesiastical interference. Such a model reduced the temporal role of the Church to one of moral suasion; it was to be the "soul" and conscience of society—an approach that found expression in the Catholic Action movements that Latin America had inherited from Europe.[7]

While the New Christendom had marked an important step forward in the context of a European Church still coming to grips with the legacy of the French Revolution, Gutiérrez argued that it had now come to serve the forces of reaction instead. It was particularly ill-suited to the deeply unequal societies of Latin America, where secularization had not yet penetrated and the Church retained substantial social capital. In this context, the Church's claim to remain above politics only served to reinforce the entrenched power of economic and political elites by allowing it to wash its hands of any responsibility for redressing the deep imbalances of wealth and power. "Under these circumstances," he asked, "can it honestly be said that the Church does not interfere in 'the temporal sphere'? Is the Church fulfilling a purely religious role when by its silence or friendly relationships it lends legitimacy to a dictatorial and oppressive government?"[8] In this context, the claim to remain above politics was itself a political choice in favor of the status quo. "Concretely, in Latin America," Gutiérrez concluded, "the distinction of planes model has the effect of concealing the real political option of a large sector of the Church—that is, support for the established order."[9]

Given the inadequacies of Maritain's model, the Peruvian theologian turned to the *nouvelle théologie* for an alternative. Among others, he singled out the work of Henri de Lubac and Yves de Montcheuil, who had done so much to overcome the Thomist distinction between the natural and supernatural orders on which the "distinction of planes" model was premised. In particular, he cited de Lubac's *Surnaturel,* which had punctured the theory of pure nature and the notion that human life possessed a natural end distinct from its supernatural vocation. "This affirmation of the single vocation to salvation," Gutiérrez argued, "allows us to break out of a narrow, individualist viewpoint and see with more Biblical eyes that human beings are called to meet the Lord insofar as they constitute a community." In addition to foregrounding the social nature of salvation, he argued, such a model "gives religious value in a completely new way to human action in history," revealing that "the building of a just society has worth in terms of the Kingdom."[10] Gutiérrez thus adopted the eschatological language that was so pervasive in the work of the French Jesuits, and which had also been taken up by the German po-

litical theologian Johann Baptist Metz.[11] But he insisted that this eschatological perspective should lead beyond a critique of existing structures
and anchor a commitment to changing these structures through concrete
praxis. In this sense, Gutiérrez drew on, but considerably radicalized, the
position of the French Jesuits. In other words, he transformed it from a
counter-politics into a politics proper.

But the Peruvian also drew on the work of the French Dominicans
and articulated certain positions that seemed much closer to their efforts
to revalue the world. Like Chenu, he insisted that the modern world
was a world "come of age," as Dietrich Bonhoeffer had put it, and no
longer dependent on clerical tutelage.[12] The natural and social sciences no
longer relied on theology and humans had become conscious of themselves as agents of history and architects of their own destiny. In fact,
Gutiérrez went so far as to suggest that secularization "is a process which
not only coincides perfectly with a Christian vision of human nature, of
history, and of the cosmos; it also favors a more complete fulfillment of
the Christian life insofar as it offers human beings the possibility of
being more fully human."[13] In other words, secularization was itself an
expression of Christianity and something to be valued. In making this
argument, the Peruvian echoed Chenu's claim that the growth of human
freedom and autonomy was itself a sign of the presence of grace. Like
Chenu and the German theologian Karl Rahner, Gutiérrez sought to move
beyond the traditional ecclesiocentrism of the Church by affirming the
value of the world outside its borders.

In this way, Gutiérrez wove the two strands of the *nouvelle théologie*
back together, fusing the very different insights of the Dominicans and
the Jesuits in his effort to overcome the limitations of Maritain's "distinction of planes" model. But the demands of his own Latin American
context also led him beyond his European forebears. While both the Dominicans and the Jesuits had resisted the privatization of religion in
favor of an engaged theology, they also insisted that it was not their job
as theologians to prescribe political solutions or engage directly in political affairs. Yet, as Gutiérrez pointed out, theology continued to have
political effects, even when it claimed not to engage in politics. As fellow
liberation theologian Juan Luis Segundo put it, "Every theology is political, even one that does not speak or think in political terms."[14] But
this did not mean that one could simply deduce one's political stance directly from theology. While liberation theologians modeled their politics
on the preference that Jesus had shown for the poor and the oppressed,

they also insisted that theology and revelation alone were not sufficient to prescribe public policy. It was therefore necessary for Catholics to look beyond theology and draw on the insights of social science—whether it be Marxist theory or, as was more often the case, the dependency theory of Andre Gunder Frank.[15]

Liberation theologians thus offered a critical corrective to the *nouvelle théologie,* revealing how its disavowal of politics was itself deeply political. In the process, they put their finger on the central tension within the counter-political project: the difficulty of being *in* but not *of* the secular public sphere; of maintaining a public role for the Church without binding it to a political project or ideology. The particular needs and concerns of the Latin American context allowed theologians like Gutiérrez to move well beyond where the *nouvelle théologie* had stopped and to draw out political implications that remained only implicit in the European context.

A very similar argument has been made more recently by Anglo-American theologians associated with the radical orthodoxy movement, such as John Milbank and William Cavanaugh. They have turned to the *nouvelle théologie* for resources to develop a postliberal theology that resists the dominant formations of modern political life: the state and the market.[16] In doing so, they have criticized theologians such as de Lubac for failing to draw out the full political implications of their theology. Cavanaugh understands why de Lubac failed to do so. Given how many Catholics of his day were drawn to the Action française and Vichy, Cavanaugh acknowledges that it was only natural for the Jesuit to be suspicious of any effort to politicize theology, even as he also rejected the liberal account of religion as a private matter of individual faith. Caught as he was in this two-front battle against the privatization of religion and its politicization, de Lubac could not fully lean into the political implications of his theology. But as a result, Cavanaugh argues that de Lubac unwittingly reinforced the distinction between religion and politics that was central to the founding mythology of the modern state—the notion that the state had saved Europe from the wars of religion by confining religion to the private sphere.[17] Instead, radical orthodoxy aims to break the state's monopoly on the definition of politics. According to one theologian associated with the movement, "politics and the designation 'political' do not in the first instance refer to the machinations and deceits of the state and party officials, but to the social arrangement of bodies, the organization of human communities (the root meaning of 'polity' or 'politics')." Considered from this perspective, "all theology is always already political."[18]

Postliberal theologians thus share the liberation theologians' recognition that theology is necessarily political. Like Gutiérrez, they reject Maritain's distinction of planes model and look to the *nouvelle théologie* for resources to overcome the artificial separation between theology and politics.[19] But they also differ markedly from their Latin American counterparts in their attitude toward secular institutions and ideas. Whereas liberation theologians wanted to open the Church to the world beyond its borders, radical orthodoxy seeks to reconquer the world for the Church. Whereas liberation theology drew on the resources of the social sciences, Milbank and his colleagues resist the colonization of theology by secular reason.[20] Rebuking Christians on both the right and left who simply adopt the logic of secular institutions, they look to the Church as the primary locus of political life. In doing so, they take their cue from the patristic tradition represented by the French Jesuits, while liberation theologians remained somewhat closer to the spirit of Dominicans such as Chenu.

But despite their differences, both these movements share a capacious understanding of the political—one that does not limit it the business of statecraft. They recall Chenu's efforts to reclaim a political role for Catholicism by distinguishing the grubby arena of party politics from the broader domain of the political, conceived as "the total dimension of participation in the construction of the City and the world."[21] Gutiérrez envisioned the political in similarly broad terms, as the effort to construct "a society in which people can live in solidarity," while Cavanaugh defines it as the configuration of bodies in space and time.[22] Both acknowledge that the political is first and foremost about building a community in historical time, and this is precisely what ensures that theology still has something to say on the subject. It seems crucial to maintain this wider understanding of the political if we are to fully grasp the political power, not just of religious ideas, but of a whole host of other institutions and ideas that are frequently treated as lying outside the realm of politics proper, from art and aesthetics to ideas about nature, time, and the body.

But the history recounted in this book also shows that the interaction between theology and politics is fraught with risk. In a modern context in which Church and world, religion and politics, the natural and the supernatural have become disarticulated, the effort to overcome these divisions always runs the risk of reducing one term to the other. In the effort to open the Church to the world, as liberation theology tries to do, one runs the risk of naturalizing the supernatural and diluting the specificity and critical power of theology. Even more concerning, however, is the way radical orthodoxy's tendency to absorb the world into the Church risks devaluing extra-ecclesial realities, leaving little space for those outside the Church. These risks may well explain why the *nouveaux théologiens* worked so hard to steer between these two alternatives. They sought to bridge the divide between Church and world, between theology and politics, but without reducing one to the other. In charting a course between "confusion" and "separation," they recognized that an irreducible tension would always remain between the demands of the faith and those of politics—a lesson worth remembering in the age of resurgent Christian nationalism. They remind us that religion and politics can never be fully disarticulated, even as they must not simply be conflated.

Theology and Post-Secular Thought

The legacy of the *nouvelle théologie* is not confined to the field of Catholic theology, however, in part because of the renewed interest that theology has attracted in recent decades from philosophers, political theorists, anthropologists, and historians. This resurgence is evident in the "theological turn" in continental philosophy, led by philosophers such as Jean-Luc Marion.[23] It is likewise evident in the newfound interest in St. Paul among leftist philosophers such as Alain Badiou, Slavoj Žižek, and Giorgio Agamben, who have found new inspiration for a post-Marxist revolutionary politics in Paul's eschatological vision.[24] In part, this theological turn may be explained by historical factors such as the end of the Cold War or the renewed interest in secularization and political theology since 9/11. But it may also have to do with the affinities between Catholic antimodernism and secular postmodernism—their shared suspicion of the modern cult of universal reason, the transcendental subject, and historical progress—which help to explain the newfound interest in premodern thought on the part of postmodern philosophers.[25] To be sure, not everyone has embraced the theological turn in continental thought.[26] And yet, even robust defenders of the secular Enlightenment tradition such as Jürgen Habermas have acknowledged that religion has not disappeared from European public life, and indeed, that it might

have important normative resources to contribute to securing democratic structures.[27]

This has led to a renewed interest in secularization theory and the historical relationship between theology and politics. Of course, these were
precisely the same questions that concerned theologians and philosophers
such as de Lubac, Fessard, Chenu, and Maritain, and it is rather striking
how closely their work anticipated contemporary discussions and, in some
cases, even helped to shape them. In his celebrated study of medieval political theology, *The King's Two Bodies,* the historian Ernst Kantorowicz
turned to de Lubac's *Corpus Mysticum* to understand how developments
in medieval ecclesiology opened the way for secular states to appropriate
the concept of the mystical body to hallow their own institutions.[28]
Through the influence of Kantorowicz, this account was then taken up by
French philosophers such as Marcel Gauchet and Claude Lefort in the
1980s and incorporated into their own accounts of secularization and the
origins of political modernity.[29] In this way, de Lubac's work indirectly
became a key resource for political theorists seeking to understand how
modern political formations, such as the nation-state and democratic legitimacy, emerged from the bosom of medieval theology. For instance, de
Lubac's argument about how developments in scholastic theology paved
the way for the secularization of European life was adopted by secular
philosophers seeking to show how Christianity became "*a religion for
departing from religion.*"[30] While the Jesuit had used this argument to
discredit his contemporary theological opponents, it could thus also be
taken up by secular political theorists seeking to secure the legitimacy of
modern democratic institutions—a testament to the way secularization
theory can be deployed to serve both theological and secular ends.

The influence of the *nouvelle théologie* on secularization theory is perhaps most directly evident in the work of the Canadian philosopher
Charles Taylor. In a recent interview, Taylor recalls how he was exposed
to the works of de Lubac, Chenu, and Congar as a Catholic coming of
age in the 1950s, and when asked to list the five books that have formed
his intellectual outlook, one of the works he selected was a biography of
Congar.[31] Taylor goes into some detail about his admiration for the *nouvelle théologie,* crediting these theologians with restoring an ecumenical
and historical sensibility to Catholic theology—a deep sense of how faith
is formed by the "signs of the times," such that no particular culture or
period can claim to represent the privileged expression of Christian

revelation. The *nouveaux théologiens* understood that *ressourcement* was bound up with modernizing the Church, that the "ability to connect with the Christian faith of another age can help us to relate to our own," Taylor explains, which allowed them to open the Church up to the modern world while also remaining critical of modernity's shortcomings.[32] This same sensibility informs Taylor's own magisterial account of secularization in *A Secular Age*. His argument about the rise of exclusive humanism and the "buffered self" is remarkably similar to de Lubac's critique of atheist humanism, and like the Jesuit, Taylor is also highly attentive to the ways in which Christianity itself has been complicit in the process of secularization. His own diagnosis that something is missing from the modern world, that it can't quite fulfill the natural human yearning for transcendence, seems to presuppose a vision of human nature that is similar to the theological anthropology of the *nouvelle théologie*.[33] And like the mid-century French Jesuits, this vision is informed both by Taylor's own faith and by his engagement with developments in secular philosophy such as Hegelianism and Heideggerian phenomenology.

The *nouvelle théologie* also seems to have anticipated certain aspects of the critique of secularism and liberalism that has been articulated by scholars on the secular left working in a Foucauldian tradition, such as Talal Asad, Saba Mahmood, and Wendy Brown. These anthropologists, sociologists, political theorists, and historians have shown that secularism does not entail the absence of religion from public life or state neutrality with regard to religion. Instead, it constitutes a positive ideology in its own right, by which the state seeks to manage religion and police the public forms it can assume.[34] These scholars point to the French state's recent efforts to restrict the wearing of Muslim head coverings as evidence of this ideology, which endows the state with the power to decide what constitutes a religious sign and which religions can be recognized publicly—an exercise that tends to privilege Christianity over minority religions such as Islam.[35] This contemporary critique of secularism often goes hand in hand with a broader critique of liberalism and associated ideas of human rights and the agentive liberal subject. It has yielded a critical reevaluation of human rights and religious freedom in particular by scholars seeking to show how rights discourses have variously reinforced the logic of neoliberalism, the marginalization of underrepresented groups, or the power of the state over human life (biopolitics).[36]

Such scholarship is a reminder of the forms of power and exclusion that often lurk behind the emancipatory claims of liberal ideas and insti-

tutions. As such, the contemporary scholarship on secularism has reiterated many of the critiques of liberalism that were raised nearly a century
ago by the Catholic theologians in this book. As we have seen, these
priests were keenly attuned to the dangers of overweening state power,
the limits of liberal accounts of agency and selfhood, and the biopolitics
of human rights—albeit for very different reasons than those that inspire
contemporary scholars on the secular left. Whereas scholars working in
the Asadian tradition often attribute the violence and exclusion produced
by contemporary secularism in part to its genealogical debt to Christianity, these theologians instead blamed the very exclusion of Christianity from public life.[37] Nevertheless, both arrive at a similar critique
of the limitations of modern secular liberalism, which perhaps explains
the remarkable convergence between the post-secular left and those contemporary heirs to the *nouvelle théologie*—theologians associated with
radical orthodoxy. This convergence is clear from the favorable references
to Milbank's work that pepper Asad's *Formations of the Secular,* as well
as Cavanaugh's frequent appeals to Asad.[38]

What should we make of the surprising parallels between radical orthodoxy and the secular left? In the first place, they are evidence of the
continuing ways in which religious thought tends to defy the logic of right
and left. They also testify to the extent to which theology and the secular disciplines continue to speak to each other in productive but often
unacknowledged ways. This interaction is certainly not without risk. As
some observers have pointed out, secular scholars should be careful that
in adopting the critique of secularism advanced by radical orthodoxy they
do not play into the hands of an exclusionary Christianity.[39] As we have
seen, there is little place in this theology for an appreciation of the independent value of non-Christian religions or intellectual traditions that
emerge from beyond the Church, a difficulty that was already apparent in
de Lubac and Fessard's tendency to conflate the mystical body of Christ
with the human race. This is a very real danger, and it is certainly worth
asking whether the Catholic critique of secularism can be disentangled
from the religious commitments that inform it, just as de Lubac and Fessard questioned whether the political goals of the communists could be
disentangled from their atheism.

And yet, these theologians still have much to teach us about the ongoing role of religion in public life. Faced with the dramatic events of the
twentieth century, the *nouveaux théologiens* struggled with how to
bring their faith to bear on the dominant political, economic, and social

challenges confronting their world. The key question they grappled with was how to carve out a public role for Catholicism in a secular, pluralist society. How could they articulate an account of the human person and the common good that could speak to nonbelievers as well as believers? Could Catholics work with secular (or even atheist) movements and institutions to advance their goals, and could Catholic theology incorporate the insights of modern philosophy while remaining faithful to its tradition? How could the Church be in the world and contribute to building a more just society without being reduced to the rank of the powers of this world? When did the Pauline duty to obey the established temporal authority yield to the spiritual duty to resist an unjust regime? These were far from abstract questions for these priests. Their answers were forged in the crucible of war, exile, and condemnation, and in the case of Yves de Montcheuil, ultimately cost him his life. These questions remain just as relevant today as they did in the 1940s. At the very least, the story of how Catholic theologians grappled with them can help us to understand how and why religion continues to play such a powerful role in public life. At best, it may point us in the direction of a more reflexive and inclusive form of secularism—one that opens itself up to self-questioning rather than erecting itself as a replacement religion.

Whatever one's position on secularism and the public role of religion, it is clear that there has been, and continues to be, far more traffic between theology and the secular disciplines than the historiography of European thought suggests. Nor is it necessary, as Carl Schmitt believed, to look back to the early modern past to understand theology's continuing political and intellectual effects.[40] There are much more recent antecedents to the current theological turn among European and North American scholars. As the history narrated in this book has shown, theology and secular thought have interacted and engaged with one another for much of the twentieth century, and we should not be surprised that they continue to do so today. If contemporary philosophers, historians, and social scientists have turned to theology for insights, it is perhaps because secular and religious thought have never been as separate as we might expect.[41] What the notion of a "turn" to theology obscures, in other words, is the extent to which it has been part of the history of European thought all along.

ABBREVIATIONS

NOTES

ACKNOWLEDGMENTS

INDEX

ABBREVIATIONS

ACA	Assemblée des Cardinaux et Archevêques de France
ACJF	Association catholique de la jeunesse française
AF	Action française
AFCJ	Archives françaises de la Compagnie de Jésus
APDF	Archives de la Province dominicaine de France
CAEHL	Centre d'Archives et d'Études Cardinal Henri de Lubac
CEJRM	Cercle d'Études Jacques et Raïssa Maritain
CFTC	Confédération française des travailleurs chrétiens
CGT	Confédération générale du travail
JAC	Jeunesse agricole catholique
JC	Jeunesse communiste
JEC	Jeunesse étudiante chrétienne
JECF	Jeunesse étudiante chrétienne féminine
JOC	Jeunesse ouvrière chrétienne
LOC	Ligue ouvrière chrétienne
MPF	Mouvement populaire des familles
MRP	Mouvement républicain populaire
NATO	North Atlantic Treaty Organization
PCF	Parti communiste français
RPF	Rassemblement du peuple français
SFIO	Section française de l'Internationale ouvrière
STO	Service du travail obligatoire
UCP	Union des chrétiens progressistes
UDHR	Universal Declaration of Human Rights
UNESCO	United Nations Educational, Scientific and Cultural Organization

NOTES

Introduction

1. Jean Liouville, "Jersey," in *Les établissements des jésuites en France depuis quatre siècles,* vol. 2, ed. Pierre Delattre, 840–42 (Wetteren, Belgium: Imprimerie De Meester Frères, 1953).

2. See Christian Sorrel, *Le catholicisme français de la Séparation à Vatican II* (Paris: Karthala, 2020), part 1; Maurice Larkin, *L'Église et l'État en France. 1905: La crise de la séparation* (Toulouse: Privat, 2004); Christian Sorrel, *La République contre les congrégations: Histoire d'une passion française (1899–1914)* (Paris: Cerf, 2003); Jacqueline Lalouette, *La République anticléricale: XIXe–XXe siècles* (Paris: Seuil, 2002); Émile Poulat, *Liberté, laïcité: La guerre des deux France et le principe de la modernité* (Paris: Cerf, 1987).

3. Patrick Cabanel, "Le grand exil des congrégations enseignantes au début du XXe siècle: L'exemple des jésuites," *Revue d'histoire de l'Église de France* 81 (January–June 1995): 207–8.

4. On the pan-European "culture wars," see Christopher Clark and Wolfram Kaiser, eds., *Culture Wars: Catholic-Secular Conflicts in Nineteenth-Century Europe* (Cambridge: Cambridge University Press, 2003); Nicholas Atkin and Frank Tallett, *Priests, Prelates and People: A History of European Catholicism since 1750* (New York: Oxford University Press, 2003); David Kertzer, *The Kidnapping of Edgardo Mortara* (New York: Vintage, 1997); Todd Weir, *Secularism and Religion in Nineteenth-Century Germany: The Rise of the Fourth Confession* (Cambridge: Cambridge University Press, 2014).

5. See Owen Chadwick, *A History of the Popes, 1830–1914* (Oxford: Oxford University Press, 1998), 215–72.

6. This explains why histories of twentieth-century Catholic politics often focus on the laity. See, for example, James Chappel, *Catholic Modern: The Challenge of Totalitarianism and the Remaking of the Church* (Cambridge, MA: Harvard University Press, 2018); Susan B. Whitney, *Mobilizing Youth: Communists and Catholics in Interwar France* (Durham, NC: Duke University Press, 2009); and the literature on Christian Democracy cited below.

7. Recent work on Christian Democracy includes Carlo Invernizzi Accetti, *What is Christian Democracy? Politics, Religion, and Ideology* (Cambridge:

Cambridge University Press, 2019); Chappel, *Catholic Modern*, chaps. 4 and 5; Maria Mitchell, *The Origins of Christian Democracy: Politics and Confession in Modern Germany* (Ann Arbor: University of Michigan Press, 2012); Émile Perreau-Saussine, *Christianity and Democracy: An Essay in the History of Political Thought* (Princeton, NJ: Princeton University Press, 2012); Wolfram Kaiser, *Christian Democracy and the Origins of the European Union* (Cambridge: Cambridge University Press, 2007); Michael Gehler and Wolfram Kaiser, eds., *Christian Democracy in Europe since 1945* (London: Routledge, 2004); Thomas Kselman and Joseph A. Buttigieg, eds., *European Christian Democracy: Historical Legacies and Comparative Perspectives* (Notre Dame, IN: Notre Dame University Press, 2003). On Catholics and human rights discourse, see Sarah Shortall and Daniel Steinmetz-Jenkins, eds., *Christianity and Human Rights Reconsidered* (Cambridge: Cambridge University Press, 2020); Marco Duranti, *The Conservative Human Rights Revolution: European Identity, Transnational Politics, and the Origins of the European Convention* (New York: Oxford University Press, 2017); Samuel Moyn, *Christian Human Rights* (Philadelphia: University of Pennsylvania Press, 2015). On the Catholic engagement with the left, see Piotr Kosicki, *Catholics on the Barricades: Poland, France, and "Revolution," 1891–1956* (New Haven, CT: Yale University Press, 2018); Denis Pelletier and Jean-Louis Schlegel, eds., *À la gauche du Christ: Les chrétiens de gauche en France de 1945 à nos jours* (Paris: Seuil, 2012); Phillippe Chenaux, *L'Église catholique et le communisme en Europe, 1917–1989: De Lénine à Jean-Paul II* (Paris: Cerf, 2009); Gerd-Rainer Horn, *Western European Liberation Theology: The First Wave, 1924–1959* (Oxford: Oxford University Press, 2008); Gerd-Rainer Horn, *Left Catholicism, 1943–1955: Catholics and Society in Western Europe at the Point of Liberation* (Leuven, Belgium: Leuven University Press, 2001). The literature on the Church and the right is vast, but see especially Giuliana Chamedes, *A Twentieth-Century Crusade: The Vatican's Battle to Remake Christian Europe* (Cambridge, MA: Harvard University Press, 2019); Chappel, *Catholic Modern;* Paul Hanebrink, *In Defense of Christian Hungary: Religion, Nationalism, and Anti-Semitism, 1890–1944* (Ithaca, NY: Cornell University Press, 2006); John F. Pollard, *The Papacy in the Age of Totalitarianism, 1914–1958* (Oxford: Oxford University Press, 2014), chaps. 4, 7, and 9; David Kertzer, *The Pope and Mussolini: The Secret History of Pius XI and the Rise of Fascism in Europe* (New York: Random House, 2014); Hubert Wolf, *Pope and Devil: The Vatican's Archives and the Third Reich* (Cambridge, MA: Belknap / Harvard University Press, 2010).

8. A new generation of scholars has begun to more seriously consider the ways in which Catholic thought and politics seem to defy the logic of right and left. See especially Chappel, *Catholic Modern* and Kosicki, *Catholics on the Barricades.*

9. See especially Chappel, *Catholic Modern.*

10. See especially Chamedes, *A Twentieth-Century Crusade.* The roundtable on Chappel's book in H-Diplo is perhaps the best illustration of the debate between Chappel and Chamedes: https://networks.h-net.org/node/28443/discussions/2854877/roundtable-xx-9-james-chappel-catholic-modern-challenge.

11. See, for instance, Eric Hobsbawm and Terence Ranger, eds., *The Invention of Tradition* (Cambridge: Cambridge University Press, 2014).

12. See Gerald McCool, *Nineteenth-Century Scholasticism: The Quest for a Unitary Method* (New York: Fordham University Press, 1989).

13. See Jacques Prévotat, *Les catholiques et l'Action française: Histoire d'une condamnation, 1899–1939* (Paris: Fayard, 2001), 441–48; Michael Sutton, *Nationalism, Positivism, and Catholicism: The Politics of Charles Maurras and French Catholics, 1890–1914* (Cambridge: Cambridge University Press, 1982). On the specifically Dominican context, see André Laudouze, *Dominicains français et Action française, 1899–1940: Maurras au couvent* (Paris: Éditions Ouvrières, 1989), chaps. 5–7. On the Jesuit side, see Peter Bernardi, *Maurice Blondel, Social Catholicism, and Action Française: The Clash over the Church's Role in Society during the Modernist Era* (Washington, DC: Catholic University of America Press, 2009).

14. Jacques Maritain, *Humanisme integral: Problèmes temporels et spirituels d'une nouvelle chrétienté* (Paris: Aubier, 1936), 314. Emphasis in original.

15. See Jacques Maritain, *Les droits de l'homme et la loi naturelle* (New York: Éditions de la Maison Française, 1942); Jacques Maritain, *Christianisme et démocratie* (New York: Éditions de la Maison Française, 1943); John P. Hittinger, "Jacques Maritain and Yves R. Simon's Use of Thomas Aquinas and His Legacy," in *Thomas Aquinas and His Legacy,* ed. David M. Gallagher, 149–72 (Washington, DC: Catholic University of America Press, 1994); Moyn, *Christian Human Rights,* chap. 2.

16. Gerd-Rainer Horn makes much of this debt in *Left Catholicism,* 24–30. See also Philippe Chenaux, *L'Église catholique et le communisme,* 196–204.

17. It is important to note that the term *"nouvelle théologie"* was developed by the movement's critics and was repudiated by most of the figures usually associated with it. Nevertheless, it has become the standard scholarly term of reference, which is why I have chosen to use it in this book.

18. Henri de Lubac, *Surnaturel: Études historiques* (Paris: Lethielleux, 2010 [1946]), 153; Henri de Lubac, *Catholicisme: Les aspects sociaux du dogme* (Paris: Cerf, 1938), 242. De Lubac returned to this argument often: see Joseph Komonchak, "Theology and Culture at Mid-Century: The Example of Henri de Lubac," *Theological Studies* 51 (1990): 579–602.

19. De Lubac, "Le pouvoir de l'Église en matière temporelle," *Revue des sciences religieuses* 12, no. 3 (1932): 343, 346.

20. On this history, see Michael Wilks, *The Problem of Sovereignty in the Later Middle Ages* (Cambridge: Cambridge University Press, 1963). De Lubac sought to challenge this association in "Political Augustinianism?," reprinted in *Theological Fragments,* trans. Rebecca Howell Balinksi, 235–86 (San Francisco: Ignatius, 1989).

21. On *Témoignage chrétien,* see Renée Bédarida, *Les armes de l'esprit: Témoignage chrétien, 1941–1944* (Paris: Éditions Ouvrières, 1977). On the spiritual resistance more broadly, see Bernard Comte, *L'honneur et la conscience: Catholiques français en résistance, 1940–1944* (Paris: Éditions de l'Atelier, 1998); Étienne Fouilloux, *Les chrétiens français entre crise et liberation* (Paris: Seuil, 1997), esp. 108–13, 133–45.

22. Henri de Lubac, *Mémoire sur l'occasion de mes écrits* (Namur, Belgium: Culture et Vérité, 1989), 147–48.

23. "Neither right nor left" is how 1930s personalism has frequently been described. See Jean-Louis Loubet del Bayle, *Les non-conformistes des années trente: Une tentative de renouvellement de la pensée politique française* (Paris: Seuil, 1969).

24. In developing this framework, I have drawn on the insights of Saba Mahmood, *Politics of Piety: The Islamic Revival and the Feminist Subject* (Princeton, NJ: Princeton University Press, 2005); William Cavanaugh, *Theopolitical Imagination* (London: T&T Clark, 2002); William Cavanaugh, *Torture and Eucharist: Theology, Politics, and the Body of Christ* (Malden, MA: Blackwell, 1998).

25. Étienne Gilson, *Le philosophe et la théologie* (Paris: Vrin, 2005 [1960]), 178. On this internal diversity, see Gerald McCool, *From Unity to Pluralism: The Internal Evolution of Thomism* (New York: Fordham University Press, 1989).

26. Most of the classic intellectual histories of twentieth-century France make little mention of Catholic theology, even when they do mention developments in Catholic philosophy. See, for instance, Mark Poster, *Existential Marxism in Postwar France: From Sartre to Althusser* (Princeton, NJ: Princeton University Press, 1975); Michael Roth, *Knowing and History: Appropriations of Hegel in Twentieth-Century France* (Ithaca, NY: Cornell University Press, 1988); Gary Gutting, *French Philosophy in the Twentieth Century* (Cambridge: Cambridge University Press, 2001); Ethan Kleinberg, *Generation Existential: Heidegger's Philosophy in France, 1927–1961* (Ithaca, NY: Cornell University Press, 2005). This has recently begun to change, however. See especially Stefanos Geroulanos, *An Atheism That Is Not Humanist Emerges in French Thought* (Stanford, CA: Stanford University Press, 2010), and Edward Baring, *Converts to the Real: Catholicism and the Making of Continental Philosophy* (Cambridge, MA: Harvard University Press, 2019). There has also been excellent work on the crucial role that Jewish thought has played in European intellectual history, including Ethan Kleinberg, *Emmanuel Levinas's Talmudic Turn: Philosophy and Jewish Thought* (Stanford, CA: Stanford University Press, 2021); Benjamin Lazier, *God Interrupted: Heresy and the European Imagination between the World Wars* (Princeton, NJ: Princeton University Press, 2009); Samuel Moyn, *The Origins of the Other: Emmanuel Levinas between Revelation and Ethics* (Ithaca, NY: Cornell University Press, 2005); Peter E. Gordon, *Rosenzweig and Heidegger: Between Judaism and German Philosophy* (Berkeley, CA: University of California Press, 2003).

27. This point has been beautifully made in Brenna Moore, *Kindred Spirits: Friendship and Resistance at the Edges of Modern Catholicism* (Chicago: University of Chicago Press, 2021).

28. See, for instance, Jon Kirwan, *An Avant-garde Theological Generation: The Nouvelle Théologie and the French Crisis of Modernity* (Oxford: Oxford University Press, 2018); Hans Boersma, *Nouvelle Théologie and Sacramental Ontology: A Return to Mystery* (Oxford: Oxford University Press, 2009); Gabriel Flynn and Paul D. Murray, eds., *Ressourcement: A Movement for Renewal in Twentieth-Century Catholic Theology* (Oxford: Oxford University Press, 2012). Mettepen-

ningen and Fouilloux instead treat the two groups somewhat more separately: Jürgen Mettepenningen, *Nouvelle Théologie—New Theology: Inheritor of Modernism, Precursor of Vatican II* (London: T&T Clark, 2010); Étienne Fouilloux, *Une Église en quête de liberté: La pensée catholique française entre modernisme et Vatican II (1914–1962)* (Paris: Desclée de Brouwer, 1998).

29. A case in point is Hent de Vries and Lawrence E. Sullivan, eds., *Political Theologies: Public Religions in a Post-Secular World* (New York: Fordham University Press, 2006). Of its thirty-five essays, two appear to be by theologians.

30. Carl Schmitt, *Political Theology: Four Chapters on the Concept of Sovereignty,* trans. George Schwab (Chicago: University of Chicago Press, 2005). Works in this vein include James Simpson, *Permanent Revolution: The Reformation and the Illiberal Roots of Liberalism* (Cambridge, MA: Belknap/Harvard University Press, 2019); Devin Singh, *Divine Currency: The Theological Power of Money in the West* (Stanford, CA: Stanford University Press, 2018); Gil Anidjar, *Blood: A Critique of Christianity* (New York: Columbia University Press, 2014); Larry Siedentrop, *Inventing the Individual: The Origins of Western Liberalism* (Cambridge, MA: Harvard University Press, 2014); Giorgio Agamben, *The Kingdom and the Glory: For a Theological Genealogy of Economy and Government* (Stanford, CA: Stanford University Press, 2011); Michael Allen Gillespie, *The Theological Origins of Modernity* (Chicago: University of Chicago Press, 2008); Gil Anidjar, "Secularism," *Critical Inquiry* 33 (Autumn 2006): 52–77; Amos Funkenstein, *Theology and the Scientific Imagination from the Middle Ages to the Sixteenth Century* (Princeton, NJ: Princeton University Press, 1986).

31. For a similar argument, see Jonathan Sheehan, *The Enlightenment Bible: Translation, Scholarship, Culture* (Princeton, NJ: Princeton University Press, 2007).

32. Mahmood, *Politics of Piety,* 194.

33. Mahmood, *Politics of Piety,* 35.

34. Jürgen Habermas, "'The Political': The Rational Meaning of a Questionable Inheritance of Political Theology," in *The Power of Religion in the Public Sphere,* ed. Eduardo Mendieta and Jonathan VanAntwerpen (New York: Columbia University Press, 2011), 26. Where Habermas differs from Rawls is in applying the translation proviso only to the realm of policy-making and not to the public sphere more broadly. Habermas has also increasingly begun to acknowledge that there may be truth contents in religion that are not susceptible to this sort of translation. On this evolution in his thinking, see Peter Gordon, "Critical Theory between the Sacred and the Profane," *Constellations* 23, no. 4 (2016): 466–81. The logic of translation is also implicit in Carl Schmitt's famous theory that "all significant concepts of the modern theory of the state are secularized theological concepts" (Schmitt, *Political Theology,* 36).

35. Gaston Fessard, "Révolution et persécution" (1938), AFCJ, Fonds Gaston Fessard, 19.1/a/3, p. 11.

36. See, for instance, Talal Asad, "Trying to Understand French Secularism," in de Vries and Sullivan, eds., *Political Theologies,* 494–526; Joan Scott, *The Politics of the Veil* (Princeton, NJ: Princeton University Press, 2007).

1. Exile Catholicism

1. After training at a novitiate and then a juniorate, Jesuits had to undertake three years of philosophical study and four years of theology . A "scholasticate" is the generic name for various the institutions where they completed these studies.

2. Henri de Lubac, *Mémoire sur l'occasion de mes écrits* (Namur, Belgium: Culture et Vérité, 1989), 12. This particular quote refers to de Lubac's experiences at Ore Place in England, where he moved to undertake his theological studies after completing his studies at Jersey, but the sentiment holds just as well for his experience at Jersey, as this chapter makes clear.

3. Marie-Dominique Chenu, *Un théologien en liberté: Jacques Duquesne interroge le Père Chenu* (Paris: Le Centurion, 1975), 27.

4. On the association between Catholicism and counterrevolution, see especially Joseph Byrnes, *Catholic and French Forever: Religious and National Identity in Modern France* (University Park: Pennsylvania State University Press, 2005); Raymond Jonas, *France and the Cult of the Sacred Heart: An Epic Tale for Modern Times* (Berkeley: University of California Press, 2000), 54–118; Darrin McMahon, *Enemies of Enlightenment: The French Counter-Enlightenment and the Making of Modernity* (Oxford: Oxford University Press, 2001).

5. The literature on *laïcité* is vast. See especially Philippe Portier, *L'État et les religions en France. Une sociologie historique de la laïcité* (Rennes: Presses Universitaires de Rennes, 2016); Jean Baubérot, *Histoire de la laïcité* (Paris: Presses Universitaires de France, 2013); Jean-Marie Mayeur, *La question laïque: XIXe–XXe siècle* (Paris: Fayard, 1997); Émile Poulat, *Liberté, laïcité: La guerre des deux France et le principe de la modernité* (Paris: Cerf, 1987).

6. On the Jesuit colleges, see John W. Padberg, *Colleges in Controversy: The Jesuit Schools in France from Revival to Suppression, 1815–1880* (Cambridge, MA: Harvard University Press, 1969).

7. On the conflicts over schooling, see James McMillan, "'Priest Hits Girl': On the Front Lines of the War of the Two Frances," in *Culture Wars: Catholic-Secular Conflicts in Nineteenth-Century Europe,* ed. Christopher Clark and Wolfram Kaiser, 77–101 (Cambridge: Cambridge University Press, 2003); André Lanfrey, *Sécularisation, séparation et guerre scolaire: Les catholiques français et l'école, 1901–1914* (Paris: Cerf, 2003). On the school's significance in republican ideology, see Eugen Weber, *Peasants into Frenchmen: The Modernization of Rural France, 1870–1914* (Stanford, CA: Stanford University Press, 1976).

8. Jules Ferry, quoted in "Note sur l'état actuel de la législation et sur les précédents administratifs relatifs aux autorisations des Congrégations, Communautés ou Associations religieuses d'hommes ou de femmes," AFCJ, Fonds C-PA: Documents historiques sur la Compagnie, 555.

9. On this longer history, see Dale Van Kley, *The Jansenists and the Expulsion of the Jesuits from France, 1757–1765* (New Haven, CT: Yale University Press, 1975); Dale Van Kley, *Reform Catholicism and the International Suppression of the Jesuits in Enlightenment Europe* (New Haven, CT: Yale University Press, 2018). On anti-Jesuit sentiment in France more broadly, see Geoffrey Cu-

bitt, *The Jesuit Myth: Conspiracy Theory and Politics in Nineteenth-Century France* (Oxford: Clarendon, 1993).

10. *Journal officiel de la République française,* March 29, 1880, 1, 2.

11. Christian Sorrel, *La République contre les congrégations: Histoire d'une passion française (1899–1914)* (Paris: Cerf, 2003), 44–45.

12. Leo XIII, *Au milieu des sollicitudes* (February 16, 1892), §14. This and all subsequent references to papal encyclicals and Vatican documents, unless otherwise noted, are taken from the Vatican website: www.vatican.va.

13. See Philip Nord, "Three Views of Christian Democracy in Fin-de-Siècle France," *Journal of Contemporary History* 19, no. 4 (October 1984): 713–27; Jeanne Caron, *Le Sillon et la démocratie chrétienne, 1894–1910* (Paris: Plon, 1967).

14. See Maurice Larkin, *Church and State after the Dreyfus Affair: The Separation Issue in France* (London: MacMillan, 1974); Ruth Harris, "The Assumptionists and the Dreyfus Affair," *Past & Present* 194 (February 2007): 175–211.

15. Articles 13–18. On the 1901 law, see *Associations et champ politique. La loi de 1901 à l'épreuve du siècle,* ed. Claire Andrieu, Gilles Le Béguec, and Danielle Tartakowsky (Paris: Sorbonne, 2001).

16. "Déclaration des provinciaux de la Compagnie de Jésus en France" (1 October 1901), AFCJ, Fonds C-PA, 575.

17. These passages come from a speech given by the Jesuit Provincials at a meeting of French religious on how to respond to the law, AFCJ, Fonds C-PA, 575.

18. Text in Sorrel, *La République contre les congrégations,* 238–40.

19. See J. P. Daughton, *An Empire Divided: Religion, Republicanism, and the Making of French Colonialism, 1880–1914* (Oxford: Oxford University Press, 2006).

20. Talal Asad, "Trying to Understand French Secularism," in *Political Theologies: Public Religions in a Post-Secular World,* ed. Hent de Vries and Lawrence Sullivan, 494–526 (New York: Fordham University Press, 2006); Joan Scott, *The Politics of the Veil* (Princeton, NJ: Princeton University Press, 2007), 99–102. Such arguments often draw on Carl Schmitt's claim that the "sovereign is he who decides on the exception" (*Political Theology: Four Chapters on the Concept of Sovereignty,* trans. George Schwab [Chicago: University of Chicago Press, 2005], 5).

21. Théophile Delcassé, quoted in Sorrel, *La République contre les congrégations,* 207.

22. The precise number is difficult to ascertain, but both Christian Sorrel and Patrick Cabanel put it around 30,000. See Sorrel, *La République contre les congrégations,*183; Patrick Cabanel and Jean-Dominique Durand, eds., *Le grand exil des congrégations religieuses françaises, 1901–1914* (Paris: Cerf, 2005), 11.

23. Patrick Cabanel, "Le grand exil des congrégations enseignantes au début du XXe siècle: L'exemple des jésuites," *Revue d'histoire de l'Église de France* 81, no. 206 (January–June 1995): 207–8.

24. See Sofie Leplae, "'La Belgique envahie': L'immigration des religieux français en Belgique, 1900–1914," in Cabanel and Durand, eds., *Le grand exil,* 244–56.

25. Cabanel, "Le grand exil des congrégations enseignantes," 189. On the logistics of exile, see Sorrel, *La République contre les congregations*, 183–223.

26. Bishop of Southwark to P. Labrosse, 10 July 1901, AFCJ, Fonds C-PA, 575.

27. Provincial of England to the Provincial of Paris, 11 October 1879, AFCJ, Fonds Jersey, EJe 11. See also Jean Liouville, "Jersey," in *Les établissements des jésuites en France depuis quatre siècles*, vol. 2, ed. Pierre Delattre, 841 (Wetteren, Belgium: Imprimerie De Meester Frères, 1953).

28. Liouville, "Jersey," 843. The internal journal of the British Society of Jesus, *Letters and Notices,* also contains many references to these tensions. See, for instance, "Jersey," *Letters and Notices* 85 (July 1885); "Jersey—with the French Jesuits," *Letters and Notices* 84 (April 1884).

29. See "Le Moniteur à l'Étranger," *Le Moniteur universel,* September 11, 1881, AFCJ, Fonds Jersey, EJe 13.

30. For the text of the bill, see AFCJ, Fonds Jersey, EJe 12.

31. Untitled article, *Jersey Observer,* April 21, 1883, AFCJ, Fonds Jersey, EJe 13.

32. Liouville, "Jersey," 850. The text of the law is reproduced in Fonds Jersey, AFCJ, EJe 11. See also "French Religious Orders: Is Another Invasion Pending?" *Jersey Evening Post,* May 12, 1902, AFCJ, Fonds Jersey, EJe 11.

33. Dossier on the fiftieth anniversary of the Maison Saint-Louis, AFCJ, Fonds Jersey, EJe 13.

34. Louis Rosette, "Hastings," in Delattre, ed., *Les établissements des jésuites en France,* 803; Jean-Claude Dhôtel, *Histoire des jésuites en France* (Paris: Desclée de Brouwer, 1991), 72. The Jesuit Provincial of England recommended that the French Jesuits exclude British boys from their college so as not to compete with local schools.

35. Leplae, "'La Belgique envahie,'" 251–53.

36. Georges Chantraine, *Henri de Lubac,* tome II: *Les années de formation (1919–1929)* (Paris: Cerf, 2009), 616.

37. Quoted in Rosette, "Hastings," 807.

38. Étienne Fouilloux, *Une Église en quête de liberté: La pensée catholique française entre modernisme et Vatican II (1914–1962)* (Paris: Desclée de Brouwer, 1998), 106. A 1922 report on the state of teaching at Jersey bears this out. It complained about Modernist tendencies and an insufficient teaching of Thomas Aquinas: "Simple notes sur l'état d'enseignement à Jersey," 21 October 1922, Fonds Jersey, AFCJ, EJe 12.

39. Chenu, *Un théologien en liberté,* 45.

40. Patrick Cabanel also comments in passing that the "healthy dépaysement" of exile was a source of renewal for some orders that had become inward-looking and complacent (*Le grand exil,* 18).

41. Ambroise Gardeil, "Soixante-dix ans d'études et d'exodes," *L'Année dominicaine* 50 (1910): 84.

42. Joseph A. Komonchak, "Theology and Culture at Mid-Century: The Example of Henri de Lubac," *Theological Studies* 51, no. 4 (1990): 579.

43. On the pan-European "culture wars," see Clark and Kaiser, eds., *Culture Wars*; Roger Aubert, *The Church in the Age of Liberalism,* trans. Peter Becker (New York: Crossroad, 1981); Nicholas Atkin and Frank Tallett, *Priests, Prelates and People: A History of European Catholicism since 1750* (New York: Oxford University Press, 2003), 120–88.

44. See Gary Lease, "Vatican Foreign Policy and the Origins of Modernism," in *Catholicism Contending with Modernity: Roman Catholic Modernism and Anti-Modernism in Historical Context,* ed. Darrell Jodock, 31–55 (Cambridge: Cambridge University Press, 2000), 50–1.

45. On Vatican I and the consolidation of papal power, see John O'Malley, *Vatican I: The Council and the Making of the Ultramontane Church* (Cambridge, MA: Belknap/Harvard University Press, 2018); Owen Chadwick, *A History of the Popes, 1830–1914* (Oxford: Oxford University Press,1998), chap. 5.

46. Leo XIII, *Aeterni Patris* (August 4, 1879), §24. On the Thomist revival, see especially Gerald A. McCool, *Nineteenth-Century Scholasticism: The Quest for a Unitary Method* (New York: Fordham, 1989).

47. Edward Baring, *Converts to the Real: Catholicism and the Making of Continental Philosophy* (Cambridge, MA: Harvard University Press, 2019), 28–53.

48. On the Modernist Crisis, see Gabriel Daly, *Transcendence and Immanence: A Study in Catholic Modernism and Integralism* (Oxford: Clarendon Press, 1980); Jodock, *Catholicism Contending with Modernity;* Émile Poulat, *Histoire, dogme et critique dans la crise moderniste* (Paris: Casterman, 1962); David Schultenover, *A View from Rome: On the Eve of the Modernist Crisis* (New York: Fordham, 1993); Marvin O'Connell, *Critics on Trial: An Introduction to the Catholic Modernist Crisis* (Washington, DC: Catholic University of America, 1994).

49. Alfred Loisy, *L'Évangile et l'Église* (Paris: Picard, 1902).

50. Blondel's precise relationship to Catholic Modernism is much debated. Although he escaped formal censure during the Modernist Crisis and vehemently disagreed with some of the leading Modernists, his work nevertheless addressed many of the central Modernist themes.

51. Pius X, *Pascendi Dominici Gregis* (September 8, 1907), §39.

52. Jodock, ed., *Catholicism Contending with Modernity,* 6–8, summarizes the disciplinary measures.

53. Pius X, *Pascendi Dominici Gregis,* §42.

54. Quoted in Daly, *Transcendence and Immanence,* 205.

55. Jürgen Mettepenningen, *Nouvelle Théologie—New Theology: Inheritor of Modernism, Precursor of Vatican II* (London: T&T Clark, 2010), 24.

56. See Michael Sutton, *Nationalism, Positivism and Catholicism: The Politics of Charles Maurras and French Catholics, 1890–1914* (Cambridge: Cambridge University Press, 1982), chaps. 4 and 5.

57. Sorrel, *La République contre les congrégations,* 211; Dominique Avon and Philippe Rocher, *Les jésuites et la société française, XIXe-XXe siècles* (Toulouse: Privat, 2001), 111. For the numbers from the Maison Saint-Louis, see AFCJ, Fonds Jersey, EJe 12.

58. Annette Becker, *War and Faith: The Religious Imagination in France, 1914–1930,* trans. Helen McPhail (New York: Berg, 1998).

59. On these priests, see Anita Rasi May, *Patriot Priests: French Catholic Clergy and National Identity in World War I* (Norman: Oklahoma University Press, 2018).

60. Quoted in Jon Kirwan, *An Avant-garde Theological Generation: The Nouvelle Théologie and the French Crisis of Modernity* (Oxford: Oxford University Press, 2018), 104.

61. Quoted in Henri de Lubac, *Trois jésuites nous parlent: Yves de Montcheuil 1899–1944, Charles Nicolet 1897–1961, Jean Zupan 1899–1968* (Paris: Lethielleux, 1980), 63; quoted in Étienne Fouilloux, *Yves de Montcheuil: Philosophe et théologien jésuite (1900–1944)* (Paris: Médiasèvres, 1995), 14.

62. Robert Hamel to Henri de Lubac, 21 December 1923, CAEHL, 3794. These Jesuits frequently invoked the category of "generation" to describe what distinguished them from their teachers at Jersey. Jon Kirwan applies this generational analysis to the *nouvelle théologie* in *Avant-garde Theological Generation.* On the concept of a "generation of 1914," see also Robert Wohl, *The Generation of 1914* (Cambridge, MA: Harvard University Press, 1979).

63. This was Étienne Gilson's characterization (*Lettres de M. Étienne Gilson addressées au P. Henri de Lubac et commentées par celui-ci,* ed. Jacques Prévotat [Paris: Cerf, 1986], 155). See also de Lubac's annotations in Maurice Blondel and Auguste Valensin, *Correspondance,* vol. 3, ed. Henri de Lubac (Paris: Aubier-Montaigne, 1965), 165; Avon and Rocher, *Les jésuites et la société française,* 105.

64. De Lubac, *Mémoire sur l'occasion de mes écrits,* 67.

65. See, for instance, Robert Hamel to Henri de Lubac, 1 November 1923 and 20 February 1924; de Lubac to Hamel, 28 February 1924, AFCJ, Fonds de Lubac, 42 / 1. Two unsigned reports from 1915 to 1922 lamented that the students at Jersey were able to complete their entire philosophical formation without having read anything by Thomas Aquinas (AFCJ, Fonds Jersey, EJe 12).

66. This statement comes from a 1919 investigation of the state of philosophical teaching in the order, quoted in Chantraine, *Henri de Lubac,* 121.

67. De Lubac, *Mémoire sur l'occasion de mes écrits,* 40. For instance, see Robert Hamel to Henri de Lubac, 6 May 1924, AFCJ, Fonds de Lubac, 42/1.

68. Gaston Fessard to Henri de Lubac, 15 October 1923, AFCJ, Fonds Fessard, 73/A.

69. The texts of these presentations and de Lubac's notes on the ensuing discussions are in AFCJ, Fonds de Lubac, 52. De Lubac described the activities of the group to his mother on December 1, 1921, quoted in Chantraine, *Henri de Lubac,* 163. See also Avon and Rocher, *Les jésuites et la société française,* 147.

70. De Lubac himself later recognized the importance of his rector's solicitude: "Through a praiseworthy exception, some of our masters at the time, who were generally strict in what they excluded from our reading, allowed us, though without encouraging us, to study the thought of the philosopher from Aix [Blondel]" (*Mémoire sur l'occasion de mes écrits,* 15).

71. Fouilloux, *Yves de Montcheuil,* 13.

72. "Réponse aux objections du P. Gabriel Picard, Recteur," AFCJ, Fonds Fessard, 1/1. The full text of the *"esquisse"* is in the same dossier.

73. Henri de Lubac to Gaston Fessard, 21 January 1924, AFCJ, Fonds Fessard, 73/B.

74. Gaston Fessard, *La méthode de réflexion chez Maine de Biran* (Paris: Bloud et Gay, 1938). The book was initially slated for publication in the *Archives de philosophie,* but Picard and Descoqs blocked it because of their concerns about the text's orthodoxy. See Henri de Lubac to Gaston Fessard, 6 February 1924, AFCJ, Fonds Fessard, 73/B.

75. De Lubac later recalled that at Jersey, he "had been marked down as a Thomist (of a Thomism, it is true, revitalized by Maréchal and Rousselot). At the time this was called 'not holding the doctrines of the Society [of Jesus]'" (de Lubac, *Mémoire sur l'occasion de mes écrits,* 147).

76. On the influence of these figures on the *nouvelle théologie* see Hans Boersma, *Nouvelle Théologie and Sacramental Ontology: A Return to Mystery* (Oxford: Oxford University Press, 2009), 62–85; Kirwan, *Avant-garde Theological Generation,* 92–95, 108–9.

77. Yves de Montcheuil to Henri de Lubac, 9 November 1925, CAEHL, 48913.

78. Henri de Lubac to Gaston Fessard, 20 August 1924, AFCJ, Fonds Fessard, 73/B.

79. Yves de Montcheuil to Henri de Lubac, 16 September 1923, CAEHL, 48887.

80. "Esquisse nature et surnaturel," AFCJ, Fonds Fessard, 1/1.

81. As in the case of Rousselot and Maréchal, the group got hold of these manuscripts through Auguste Valensin, who was a friend of Teilhard and had studied with him at Jersey twenty years earlier (see Chantraine, *Henri de Lubac,* 322). De Lubac recalled the formative influence the geologist had on his work in *Mémoire sur l'occasion de mes écrits,* 103–12. For Hamel's take on Teilhard, see Robert Hamel to Henri de Lubac, 21 December 1923, CAEHL, 3794.

82. Maurice Blondel, *Action: Essay on a Critique of Life and a Science of Practice,* trans. Oliva Blanchette (Notre Dame, IN: University of Notre Dame Press, 1984 [1893]), 314–29.

83. Blondel, *The Letter on Apologetics, and History and Dogma,* trans. Alexander Dru and Illtyd Trethowan (London: Harvill, 1964 [1896; 1904]), 151–52.

84. Quoted in Fouilloux, *Yves de Montcheuil,* 19.

85. Auguste Valensin and Yves de Montcheuil, *Maurice Blondel* (Paris: Gabalda, 1934). The publication of this book coincided with one of the periodic waves of anti-Blondelian sentiment in Rome, which caused some trouble for Montcheuil. See Fouilloux, *Yves de Montcheuil,* 69–78, and the documents in AFCJ, Fonds Montcheuil, HMo 51/1. On de Lubac's debt to Blondel, see Antonio Russo, *Henri de Lubac: Teologia e dogma nella storia. L'influsso di Blondel* (Rome: Studium, 1990); Fouilloux, *Une Église en quête de liberté,* 174–81.

86. Robert Hamel to Henri de Lubac, 17 April 1924, CAEHL, 3819.

87. Henri de Lubac, "Apologetique et théologie," *Nouvelle revue théologique* 57 (May 1930): 364.

88. De Lubac, "Apologetique et théologie," 366.

89. Henri de Lubac, *Catholicisme: Les aspects sociaux du dogme* (Paris: Cerf, 1938), 242.

90. Robert Hamel to Henri de Lubac, 23 November 1923, CAEHL, 3785.

91. Henri de Lubac to Gaston Fessard, 10 May 1924, AFCJ, Fonds Fessard, 73/B.

92. Henri de Lubac to Yves de Montcheuil, 1926 or 1927 (undated), CAEHL, 48781. De Lubac made a similar argument to Montcheuil, 23 September 1925, CAEHL, 48777.

93. Robert Hamel to Henri de Lubac, 1 November 1923, CAEHL, 3779.

94. Henri de Lubac to Robert Hamel, 10 November 1923, CAEHL, 3782.

95. See especially Henri de Lubac to Gaston Fessard, 26 April 1936, AFCJ, Fonds Fessard, 73/2.

96. Henri de Lubac to Yves de Montcheuil, 1926 or 1927 (undated), CAEHL, 48781.

97. Henri de Lubac to Yves de Montcheuil, 1 January 1925, CAEHL, 48737.

98. Robert Hamel to Henri de Lubac, 29 April 1926, CAEHL, 3903.

99. This is borne out by the work of historical sociologists like Michael Farrel, who shows that friendship groups play an important role in spurring innovation when a group of novices within a particular discipline feels alienated from the dominant paradigm and established authorities in their field. See *Collaborative Circles: Friendship Dynamics and Creative Work* (Chicago: University of Chicago Press, 2001), 268. On the role of friendship in the development of religious thought, see William Young, *Uncommon Friendships: An Amicable History of Modern Religious Thought* (Eugene, OR: Cascade, 2009); Brenna Moore, "Friendship and the Cultivation of Religious Sensibilities," *Journal of the American Academy of Religion* 83, no. 2 (2015): 437–64; Brenna Moore, *Kindred Spirits: Friendship and Resistance at the Edges of Modern Catholicism* (Chicago: University of Chicago Press, 2021).

100. Henri de Lubac to Gaston Fessard, 30 August 1935, AFCJ, Fonds Fessard, 73/2.

101. Chenu, *Un théologien en liberté*, 42.

102. This method was guided above all by the work of the school's founder on the scriptural sources of theology. Chenu described Gardeil's *Le donné révélé et la théologie* as "the breviary of theological method" for Le Saulchoir. Also crucially influential were Fathers Pierre Mandonnet, a historian of medieval philosophy, and Marie-Joseph Lagrange, a biblical scholar and pioneer of historical criticism. See Fouilloux, *Une église en quête de liberté*, 124–48; Jean-Pierre Jossua, "Le Saulchoir: Une formation théologique replacée dans son histoire," *Cristianesimo nella storia* 14 (1993): 99–124.

103. Chenu, *Un théologien en liberté*, 38–39.

104. Jacques Le Goff's tribute to Chenu the historian is appended to his June 1954 letter in APDF, Fonds Marie-Dominique Chenu (V772), General Correspondence, 1948–1954. See also Josep Ignasi Saranyana, "Marie-Dominique Chenu," in *Rewriting the Middle Ages in the Twentieth Century*, vol. 1, ed. Jaume Aurell and Francisco Crosas, 183–93 (Turnhout, Belgium: Brepols, 2005).

105. See André Duval, "Aux origines de 'l'Institut historique d'études thomistes' du Saulchoir (1920 et ss): Notes et documents," *Revue des Sciences philosophiques et théologiques* 75, no. 3 (July 1991): 423–48.

106. Yves Congar, *Une passion: L'unité. Réflexions et souvenirs, 1929–1973* (Paris: Cerf, 1974), 11. On Chenu and Le Saulchoir, see Janette Gray, "Chenu and Le Saulchoir: A Stream of Catholic Renewal," in *Ressourcement: A Movement of Renewal in Twentieth-Century Catholic Theology,* ed. Gabriel Flynn and Paul D. Murray, 205–18 (Oxford: Oxford University Press, 2012); Étienne Fouilloux, "Deux écoles françaises de théologie au XXe siècle. Le Saulchoir et Fourvière," *Gregorianum* 29, no. 4 (2011): 768–80.

107. Quoted from a presentation Chenu gave on the methods and goals of Le Saulchoir in 1936, which became the basis for his book on the subject, APDF, Fonds Chenu (V772), 3/2. Emphasis added.

108. Chenu, for instance, provoked the ire of his superiors by stocking the communist newspaper *L'Humanité* at Le Saulchoir. See APDF, Fonds Chenu (V772), 5.

109. Henri de Lubac, "Causes internes de l'atténuation et de la disparition du sens du sacré," in *Theologie dans l'histoire II: Questions disputées et résistance au nazisme* (Paris: Desclée de Brouwer, 1990), 22. Emphasis added.

2. From Royalism to the Mystical Body of Christ

1. Henri de Lubac to Robert Hamel, 13 May 1925, AFCJ, Fonds de Lubac, 42/1.

2. The dominance of the AF at Jersey is borne out by a 1930 report on the "État d'esprit du Scolasticat de Fourvière," reprinted in Georges Chantraine, *Henri de Lubac,* tome II: *Les années de formation (1919–1929)* (Paris: Cerf, 2009), 618. Support for the AF was particularly strong in the Dominican order. See André Laudouze, *Dominicains français et Action française, 1899–1940: Maurras au couvent* (Paris: Éditions Ouvrières, 1989).

3. Robert Hamel to Henri de Lubac, 16 March 1926, CAEHL, 3898–99. Emphasis added.

4. See Zeev Sternhell, *Neither Right nor Left: Fascist Ideology in France* (Berkeley: University of California Press, 1986); Jean-Louis Loubet del Bayle, *Les non-conformistes des années trente: Une tentative de renouvellement de la pensée politique française* (Paris: Seuil, 1969).

5. I use the term *totalitarianism* here as an actor's category rather than an empirical descriptor of the relationship between communism and Nazism. On the role that Catholics played in the genesis of totalitarianism theory, see James Chappel, "The Catholic Origins of Totalitarianism Theory in Interwar Europe," *Modern Intellectual History* 8, no. 3 (2011): 561–90; Udi Greenberg, *The Weimar Century: German Emigrés and the Ideological Foundations of the Cold War* (Princeton, NJ: Princeton University Press, 2014), chap. 3. On Maritain's influence on human rights theory, see Samuel Moyn, "Personalism, Community, and the Origins of Human Rights," in *Human Rights in the Twentieth Century,* ed. Stefan-Ludwig Hoffmann, 85–106 (Cambridge: Cambridge University Press, 2011);

Samuel Moyn, *Christian Human Rights* (Philadelphia: University of Pennsylvania Press, 2015), chap. 2.

6. For a somewhat similar use of this term and one that is deeply indebted to theologians like de Lubac, see William Cavanaugh, *Theopolitical Imagination* (London: T&T Clark, 2002), 46–52.

7. The title of this section is quoted in Jacques Prévotat, *Les catholiques et l'Action française: Histoire d'une condamnation, 1899–1939* (Paris: Fayard, 2001), 445.

8. Charles Maurras, *La démocratie religieuse: Le dilemme de Marc Sangnier, La politique religieuse, l'Action française et la religion catholique* (Paris: Nouvelle librairie nationale, 1921), 13.

9. Yves Simon, *The Road to Vichy, 1918–1939,* trans. James A. Corbett and George J. McMorrow (Lanham, MD: University Press of America, 1988 [1942]), 42.

10. On the relationship between Thomism and the AF, see Prévotat, *Les catholiques et l'Action française,* 441–48. On the specific role of the Dominicans, see Laudouze, *Dominicains français et Action française,* chaps. 5–7. On Descoqs's attitude to the AF, see Peter Bernardi, *Maurice Blondel, Social Catholicism, and Action Française: The Clash Over the Church's Role in Society During the Modernist Era* (Washington, D.C.: Catholic University of America Press, 2009). On Garrigou-Lagrange, see Richard Peddicord, *The Sacred Monster of Thomism: An Introduction to the Life and Legacy of Reginald Garrigou-Lagrange, O.P.* (South Bend, IN: St. Augustine's Press, 2005), esp. 88–93.

11. Charles Maurras, quoted in Michel Fourcade, "Feu la modernite? Maritain et les maritainismes," PhD dissertation, Université Paul Valéry (Montpellier III), 1999, 242. Consulted at the Cercle d'Études Jacques et Raïssa Maritain (CEJRM).

12. Reported in Henri Massis, *Maurras et notre temps* (Paris: La Palatine, 1951), 169. On Maurras's quarrels with Blondel and Laberthonnière, see Michael Sutton, *Nationalism, Positivism and Catholicism: The Politics of Charles Maurras and French Catholics, 1890–1914* (Cambridge: Cambridge University Press, 1982), chaps. 4 and 5.

13. This dispute is the subject of Bernardi, *Maurice Blondel, Social Catholicism, and Action Française.*

14. Marcel Breton [Maurice Blondel], "Les conclusions d'une expérience personelle," in "Un grand débat catholique et français," *Cahiers de la nouvelle journée* 10 (Paris: Bloud et Gay, 1927): 201. Blondel also made this point in his 1909–1910 exchange with Descoqs, which was republished as *Une alliance contre nature: Catholicisme et intégrisme. La Semaine sociale de Bordeaux, 1910* (Brussels: Lessius, 2000).

15. Maurras, *Le dilemme de Marc Sangnier,* 18; see also Carl Schmitt, *Roman Catholicism and Political Form,* trans. G. L. Ulmen (Westport, CT: Greenwood Press, 1966 [1923]).

16. Pedro Descoqs, *À travers l'oeuvre de M. Maurras* (Paris: Beauchesne, 1911), 192, 195. Maurras himself had made the same point in *Le dilemme de Marc Sangnier,* 6.

17. Descoqs, "Un cas de conscience," quoted in Bernardi, *Maurice Blondel, Social Catholicism, and Action Française,* 225.

18. Piux XI to Cardinal Andrieu, 5 September 1926, *Acta Apostolicae Sedis* vol. 18 (Vatican City: Typis Polyglottis Vaticanis, 1926), 385.

19. Quoted in Laudouze, *Dominicains français et Action française,* 100.

20. Consultation on the condemnation organized by the professors of the Institut Catholique de Toulouse, quoted in Laudouze, *Dominicains française et Action française,* 90.

21. Breton [Blondel], "Les conclusions d'une expérience personelle," 205.

22. See Frédéric Gugelot, *La conversion des intellectuels au catholicisme en France (1885–1935)* (Paris: CNRS, 1998). On the role of the Maritains in this revival, see Stephen Schloesser, *Jazz Age Catholicism: Mystic Modernism in Postwar Paris, 1919–1933* (Toronto: University of Toronto Press, 2005); Brenna Moore, *Sacred Dread: Raïssa Maritain, the Allure of Suffering, and the French Catholic Revival (1905–1944)* (Notre Dame, IN: Notre Dame University Press, 2012).

23. Quoted in Fourcade, "Feu la modernité?," 232.

24. Quoted in Fourcade, "Feu la modernité?," 235.

25. See Jacques Maritain, *Une opinion sur Charles Maurras et le devoir des catholiques* (Paris: Plon, 1926); Pedro Descoqs to Yves de la Brière, 9 January 1927, AFCJ, Fonds C-PA, 613/4.

26. Jacques Maritain to Charles Journet, 9 September 1926, *Journet–Maritain Correspondance,* vol. 1 (Fribourg: Éditions Universitaires Fribourg, 1984), 406.

27. *Pourquoi Rome a parlé* (Paris: Spes, 1927), *Le joug du Christ* (Paris: Spes, 1928), and *Clairvoyance de Rome* (Paris: Spes, 1929).

28. Maritain, *Primauté du spirituel,* OC, vol. 3 (Fribourg and Paris: Éditions Universitaires Fribourg/Éditions Saint-Paul, 1984), 803. On the origins of "indirect power," see Stefania Tutino, *Empire of Souls: Robert Bellarmine and the Christian Commonwealth* (Oxford: Oxford University Press, 2010).

29. Charles Journet, "La pensée thomiste et le 'pouvoir indirect,'" *La Vie intellectuelle* 2 (April 15, 1929): 633. Emphasis in original.

30. Journet, "La pensée thomiste," 659. Emphasis in original.

31. Pedro Descoqs, *À travers l'oeuvre de Charles Maurras* (Paris: Beauchesne, 1911), 137, 138. See also Bernardi, *Maurice Blondel, Social Catholicism, and Action Française,* 253–55.

32. Gaston Fessard to Henri de Lubac, 22 November 1948, AFCJ, Fonds Fessard, 73/3.

33. Henri de Lubac, "Le pouvoir de l'Église en matière temporelle," *Revue des sciences religieuses* 12 (July 1932): 337. The article was a rejoinder to the book-length version of the Journet article cited above: Charles Journet's *La juridiction de l'Église sur la Cité* (Paris: Desclée de Brouwer, 1931).

34. De Lubac, "Pouvoir de l'Église," 342.

35. De Lubac, "Pouvoir de l'Église," 342–43. Emphasis in original.

36. De Lubac, "Pouvoir de l'Église," 343–44.

37. De Lubac, "Pouvoir de l'Église," 346.

38. De Lubac, "Pouvoir de l'Église," 352.

39. De Lubac, "Pouvoir de l'Église," 349.

40. Piux XI to Cardinal Andrieu, 384.

41. Martin Conway, *Catholic Politics in Europe, 1918–1945* (London: Routledge, 1997), 5.

42. Quoted in Gerd-Rainer Horn, *Western European Liberation Theology: The First Wave (1924–1959)* (Oxford: Oxford University Press, 2008), 41.

43. On Catholic Action in Italy, see Giuliana Chamedes, *A Twentieth-Century Crusade: The Vatican's Battle to Remake Christian Europe* (Cambridge, MA: Harvard University Press, 2019), 111–18; Mario Casella, *L'azione cattolica nell'Italia contemporanea (1919–1969)* (Rome: Ave, 1992). On the tensions with Mussolini over Catholic Action, see David Kertzer, *The Pope and Mussolini: The Secret History of Pius XI and the Rise of Fascism in Europe* (New York: Random House, 2014), 55–56, 158–64, 303–12, 329–31.

44. Quoted in Horn, *Western European Liberation Theology,* 43.

45. On this early variant of Social Catholicism, see Paul Misner, *Social Catholicism in Europe: From the Onset of Industrialization to the First World War* (New York: Crossroad, 1991); Jean-Marie Mayeur, *Catholicisme social et démocratie chrétienne: Principes romains, expériences françaises* (Paris: Cerf, 1968); Bernardi, *Maurice Blondel, Social Catholicism, and Action Française,* chap. 1.

46. On the interwar Belgian context more broadly, see Martin Conway, "Building the Christian City: Catholics and Politics in Inter-War Francophone Belgium," *Past & Present* 128 (August 1990): 117–51.

47. On the development of the JOC, see especially Paul Debès and Émile Poulat, *L'appel de la J.O.C., 1926–1928* (Paris: Cerf, 1986); Susan B. Whitney, *Mobilizing Youth: Communists and Catholics in Interwar France* (Durham, NC: Duke University Press, 2009).

48. Quoted in Michel Launay, "La J.O.C. dans son premier développement," in *La J.O.C.: Regards d'historiens,* ed. Pierre Pierrard, Michel Launay, and Roland Trempé (Paris: Éditions Ouvrières, 1984), 43.

49. Whitney, *Mobilizing Youth,* 104.

50. Joseph Cardijn, quoted in Whitney, *Mobilizing Youth,* 99.

51. For an excellent account of the vision of femininity promoted by the JOCF, see Whitney, *Mobilizing Youth,* chap. 4.

52. Philip Nord, "Catholic Culture in Interwar France," *French Politics, Culture & Society* 21, no. 3 (Fall 2003): 9; James Chappel, *Catholic Modern: The Challenge of Totalitarianism and the Remaking of the Church* (Cambridge, MA: Harvard University Press, 2018), 121.

53. Chamedes, *A Twentieth-Century Crusade,* 178–183, 199–201. On Vatican anticommunism in this period, see chapter 5 of the same monograph. For an overview of Catholic politics in the 1930s more broadly, see Conway, *Catholic Politics in Europe,* 47–77.

54. Maurice Thorez, Address on Radio-Paris, April 17, 1936, reprinted in *L'Humanité,* April 18, 1936, 8.

55. See, for instance, "La position du parti communiste après la victoire du Front populaire," *L'Humanité,* May 10, 1936. On the Catholic response, see Francis J. Murphy, "*La Main Tendue*: Prelude to Christian-Marxist Dialogue in France, 1936–

1939," *Catholic Historical Review* 60, no. 2 (July 1974): 255–70; Piotr Kosicki, *Catholics on the Barricades: Poland, France, and "Revolution," 1891–1956* (New Haven, CT: Yale University Press, 2018), 50–59; René Rémond, *Les crises du catholicisme en France dans les années trente* (Paris: Cana, 1979), chap. 7.

56. Robert Honnert, "Foi et révolution," *Europe* 161 (May 15, 1936): 55, 57.

57. John Hellman, "French 'Left-Catholics' and Communism in the Nineteen-Thirties," *Church History* 45, no. 4 (December 1976): 507–23.

58. Gaston Fessard to Pierre Vaillant-Couturier, in Gaston Fessard, *La main tendue: Le dialogue catholique-communiste est-il possible?* (Paris: Grasset, 1937), 32.

59. Fessard, *La main tendue, 12n1.*

60. Gaston Fessard, "La main tendue . . . ? Ce que M. Thorez a omis de dire aux communistes et aux catholiques," *La Croix,* November 3, 1937.

61. Fessard, "La main tendue . . . ? Réponse à un chrétien révolutionnaire," *Études* 229 (December 1936): 762.

62. See *Gabriel Marcel–Gaston Fessard: Correspondance, 1934–1971,* ed. Henri de Lubac, Marie Rougier, and Michel Sales (Paris: Beauchesne, 1985), 137; Hellman, "French 'Left-Catholics' and Communism in the Nineteen-Thirties," 523. The key work that introduced these texts to French audiences was Auguste Cornu, *Karl Marx, l'homme et l'oeuvre* (Paris: Librairie Félix Alcan, 1934). On the reception of the young Marx, see Tony Judt, *Marxism and the French Left: Studies on Labour and Politics in France, 1830–1981* (Oxford: Clarendon Press, 1986), 179–81.

63. On Catholic readings of the young Marx, see David Curtis, *The French Popular Front and the Catholic Discovery of Marx* (Hull, UK: University of Hull Press, 1997).

64. Fessard, *La main tendue,* 112.

65. Fessard, *La main tendue,* 145.

66. Fessard, *La main tendue,* 33.

67. Fessard, "La main tendue . . . ? Ce que M. Thorez a omis de dire aux catholiques."

68. Pius XI, *Divini Redemptoris* (March 19, 1937), §58.

69. Pius XI, *Divini Redemptoris,* §66.

70. Pius XI, *Mit brennender Sorge* (March 14, 1937), §§10–11.

71. See, for instance, Étienne Fouilloux, *Les chrétiens français entre crise et liberation, 1937–1947* (Paris: Seuil, 1997), chap. 1; Giuliana Chamedes, "The Vatican, Nazi-Fascism, and the Making of Transnational Anti-communism in the 1930s," *Journal of Contemporary History* 51, no. 2 (2015): 283–87.

72. See Joseph Komonchak, "Returning from Exile: Catholic Theology in the 1930s," in *The Twentieth Century: A Theological Overview,* ed. Gregory Baum, 35–48 (Maryknoll, NY: Orbis, 1999); Kirwan, *An Avant-garde Theological Generation: The Nouvelle Théologie and the French Crisis of Modernity* (Oxford: Oxford University Press, 2018), chap. 6.

73. For a conservative reading of Maritain, see Moyn, *Christian Human Rights,* chap. 2; Carlo Invernizzi Accetti, *What is Christian Democracy? Politics, Religion, and Ideology* (Cambridge: Cambridge University Press, 2019),

passim. For a more liberal reading, see John Hittinger, *Liberty, Wisdom, and Grace: Thomism and Democratic Political Theory* (Lanham, MD: Lexington Books, 2002), chap. 3; John T. McGreevy, *Catholicism and American Freedom: A History* (New York: Norton, 2003), chap. 7.

74. John Hellman stresses the links between the Ordre nouveau circle and the anti-Hitler faction within National Socialism in *The Communitarian Third Way: Alexandre Marc's Ordre Nouveau, 1930–2000* (Montreal: McGill-Queen's University Press, 2002); see also Marco Duranti, "The Holocaust, the Legacy of 1789 and the Birth of International Human Rights Law: Revisiting the Foundation Myth," *Journal of Genocide Research* 14, no. 2 (June 2012): 174–80. Hellman also stresses Mounier's links to Vichy and fascism in *The Knight-Monks of Vichy France: Uriage, 1940–1945* (Montreal: McGill-Queen's University Press, 1993), and *Emmanuel Mounier and the New Catholic Left, 1930–1950* (Toronto: University of Toronto Press, 1983). Contrast the literature that instead emphasizes Mounier's role as a leading voice of the Resistance and the Catholic left, such as Michael Kelly, *Pioneer of the Catholic Revival: The Ideas and Influence of Emmanuel Mounier* (London: Sheed and Ward, 1979); Michel Winock, *Histoire politique de la revue "Esprit," 1930–1950* (Paris: Seuil, 1975).

75. Jacques Maritain, *Humanisme intégral: Problèmes temporels et spirituels d'une nouvelle chrétienté* (Paris: Aubier, 1936), 144.

76. Maritain, *Humanisme intégral,* 152.

77. Maritain, *Humanisme intégral,* 175. Emphasis in original.

78. Maritain, *Humanisme intégral,* 176. Emphasis in original.

79. This distinction was developed by the German personalist Max Scheler. See Edward Baring, *Converts to the Real: Catholicism and the Making of Continental Philosophy* (Cambridge, MA: Harvard University Press, 2019), chap. 8.

80. Maritain, *Humanisme intégral,* 175–89.

81. Maritain, *Humanisme intégral,* 177.

82. Maritain, *Humanisme intégral,* 317.

83. Maritain, *Humanisme intégral,* 314. Emphasis in original.

84. Maritain, *Humanisme intégral,* 220. Emphasis in original.

85. Chappel, "Catholic Origins of Totalitarianism Theory," 569–70.

86. Maurice Blondel, "Les équivoques du 'personnalisme,'" *Politique* 8, no. 3 (March 1934): 193–205.

87. See the description in Kelly, *Pioneer of the Catholic Revival,* chap. 2.

88. See Hellman, *Communitarian Third Way;* Christian Roy, *Alexandre Marc et la jeune Europe, 1904–1944: L'Ordre nouveau aux origines du personnalisme* (Nice: Presses d'Europe, 1998).

89. See especially Pierre Teilhard de Chardin, "Esquisse sur un univers personnel" (1936), AFCJ, Fonds Pierre Teilhard de Chardin, T. TdC 8/3; Pierre Teilhard de Chardin, *Le Phénomène humain* (Paris: Seuil, 1955).

90. Teilhard de Chardin, *Le Phénomène humain,* 263.

91. Teilhard de Chardin, "Essai sur la personne" (undated, circa 1936), AFCJ, Fonds Teilhard de Chardin, T.TdC 8/3, p. 4.

92. This development coincided with the rise of what James Chappel calls a "fraternal" Catholic approach to marriage and the family, which stressed conjugal love over reproduction. See Chappel, *Catholic Modern,* 115–23. On the mid-century origins of Catholic teaching on gender complementarity, see Mary Anne Case, "The Role of the Popes in the Invention of Complementarity and the Vatican's Anathematization of Gender," *Religion and Gender* 6, no. 2 (2016): 155–72; Prudence Allen, "Man-Woman Complementarity: The Catholic Inspiration," *Logos* 9, no. 3 (2006): esp. 91–96. Allen stresses the pioneering role of the Catholic personalist philosophers Dietrich von Hildebrand and Edith Stein in particular.

93. See, for instance, Teilhard de Chardin, "L'Éternel féminin," reprinted in Henri du Lubac, *The Eternal Feminine: A Study on the Poem of Teilhard de Chardin,* trans. René Hague (New York: Harper & Row, 1971).

94. Quoted in Jean-Yves Calvez, *Chrétiens penseurs du social: Maritain, Mounier, Fessard, Teilhard de Chardin, de Lubac (1920–1940)* (Paris: Cerf, 2002), 128, 127. On the political implications of Teilhard's work, see Pierre-Louis Mathieu, *La pensée politique et économique de Teilhard de Chardin* (Paris: Seuil, 1969).

95. Teilhard de Chardin, "Essai sur la personne," 3.

96. Quoted in Calvez, *Chrétiens penseurs du social,* 131.

97. Kirwan, *Avant-garde Theological Generation,* 144–53, 166–90.

98. See, for instance, the exchange between Gaston Fessard and Teilhard de Chardin, AFCJ, Fonds Fessard, 48/D.

99. Henri de Lubac, *Catholicisme: Les aspects sociaux du dogme* (Paris: Cerf, 1938), 43.

100. De Lubac, *Catholicisme,* 45.

101. This point is echoed by Yves de Montcheuil, *Aspects de l'Église* (Paris: Cerf, 1949), 32–44.

102. Yves Congar, *Chrétiens désunis, principes d'un oécunémisme catholique* (Paris: Cerf, 1937).

103. Henri de Lubac, *Catholicisme,* ix.

104. De Lubac, *Catholicisme,* 83.

105. Henri Rondet, "Église et corps mystique," *Aider* (December 1943), in AFCJ, Fonds Henri Rondet, 10/8.

106. De Lubac, *Catholicisme,* 237.

107. De Lubac, *Catholicisme,* 238–39. De Lubac is quoting Philippe de Régis here.

108. De Lubac, *Catholicisme,* 257.

109. De Lubac, *Catholicisme,* 267.

110. De Lubac, *Catholicisme,* 257.

111. De Lubac, *Catholicisme,* 281.

112. De Lubac, *Catholicisme,* 13–14.

113. Pedro Descoqs, "Individu et personne," *Archives de philosophie* 14 (1938): 40, 44. The immediate target of Descoqs's critique was Gaston Fessard's *Pax Nostra,* but his words apply equally well to de Lubac's *Catholicism.*

114. Gaston Fessard, *Pax Nostra: Examen de conscience international* (Paris: Grasset, 1936), 44.

115. Frédéric Louzeau, *L'Anthropologie sociale du Père Gaston Fessard* (Paris: Presses Universitaires de France, 2009), 415–19.

116. See Romans 11:15–32.

117. Michael Sutton, "Jews and Christians in Vichy France: New and Renewed Perspectives," *French Politics, Culture & Society* 35, no. 3 (2017): 122–23.

118. Fessard, *Pax Nostra,* 309–10.

119. For an overview of notable works, see J. Eileen Scully, "The Theology of the Mystical Body of Christ in French Language Theology, 1930–1950," *Irish Theological Quarterly* 58 (1992): 58–74.

120. Horn, *Western European Liberation Theology,* 72–76; Palémon Glorieux, "L'Action catholique et l'enseignement dogmatique," *La Vie intellectuelle* 28 (1934): 357–81; Joseph Cardijn, "La mystique de la J.O.C.," *La Vie spirituelle* 38 (1934): 319.

121. Yves Congar, *Lay People in the Church: A Study for a Theology of Laity,* trans. Donald Attwater (London: Chapman, 1963), 54–55.

122. Yves Congar, "Une conclusion théologique à l'Enquête sur les raisons actuelles de l'incroyance," *La Vie intellectuelle* 37 (1935): 224.

123. Yves Congar, "Bulletin de théologie," *Revue des sciences philosophiques et théologiques* 23 (1934): 685.

124. On Congar's ecclesiology, see Gabriel Flynn, *Yves Congar's Vision of the Church in a World of Unbelief* (Aldershot, UK: Ashgate, 2004).

125. Marie-Dominique Chenu, "Dimension nouvelle de la Chrétienté," *La Vie intellectuelle* 53 (December 25, 1937): 325–51. On the retreats, see Chenu, "La J.O.C. au Saulchoir," *L'Année dominicaine* (May 1936): 190–93.

126. Chenu, "Dimension nouvelle," 327, 329.

127. Chenu, "Dimension nouvelle," 338.

128. Chenu, "Dimension nouvelle," 339.

129. Chenu, "Dimension nouvelle," 331. Emphasis added.

130. Chenu, "Dimension nouvelle," 347.

131. Chenu, "Dimension nouvelle," 344.

132. See Gerald A. McCool, *From Unity to Pluralism: The Internal Evolution of Thomism* (New York: Fordham University Press, 1989); Fouilloux, *Une Église en quête de liberté,* 109–48.

133. Étienne Gilson, *Le philosophe et la théologie* (Paris: Vrin, 2005 [1960]), 178.

134. The best overview of the *ressourcement* project remains Gabriel Flynn and Paul Murphy, eds. *Ressourcement: A Movement for Renewal in Twentieth-Century Catholic Theology* (Oxford: Oxford University Press, 2011).

135. Chenu also distinguished his approach from Maritain's. See Marie-Dominique Chenu, *Un théologien en liberté: Jacques Duquesne interroge le Père Chenu* (Paris: Le Centurion, 1975), 81–85.

136. Yves de Montcheuil, "La liberté et la diversité dans l'unité," quoted in Renée Bédarida, "Le Père Pierre Chaillet: De la théologie de Möhler à la Résis-

tance," in *Spiritualité, théologie et résistance: Yves de Montcheuil, théologien au maquis du Vercors,* ed. Pierre Bolle and Jean Godel (Grenoble: Presses Universitaires de Grenoble, 1987), 59.

137. Henri Rondet, "L'Église totalitaire" (1934), AFCJ, Fonds Rondet, 12 / 5.

138. Rondet, "L'Église totalitaire," 4.

139. Rondet, "L'Église totalitaire," 16.

140. Rondet, "L'Église totalitaire," 8.

141. Congar formulated this term much later in *Jalons pour une théologie du laïcat* (1953), but it accurately describes the vision presented here.

142. Cardijn, "La Mystique du J.O.C.," 319.

143. See especially John Connelly, *From Enemy to Brother: The Revolution in Catholic Teaching on the Jews* (Cambridge, MA: Harvard University Press, 2012), 71–78.

144. The literature on Pius XII is vast, but perhaps the most balanced account is Robert Ventresca, *Soldier of Christ: The Life of Pope Pius XII* (Cambridge, MA: Harvard University Press, 2013). See also the second half of Chamedes, *A Twentieth-Century Crusade;* Frank J. Coppa, *The Life and Pontificate of Pope Pius XII: Between History and Controversy* (Washington, D.C.: Catholic University of America Press, 2013); Philippe Chenaux, *Pie XII: Diplomate et pasteur* (Paris: Cerf, 2003).

3. Fighting Nazism with the "Weapons of the Spirit"

1. Yves de Montcheuil to Henri de Lubac, 3 July 1940, CAEHL, 48934.

2. Philippe Pétain, "Appel du 25 juin 1940 (mardi)," in *Discours aux Français: 17 juin 1940–20 août 1944,* ed. Jean-Claude Barbas (Paris: Albin Michel, 1989), 66.

3. See Robert Paxton, *Vichy France: Old Guard and New Order, 1940–1944* (New York: Columbia University Press, 2001), 138–39, 142–43.

4. Quoted in Paxton, *Vichy France,* 149.

5. Philippe Pétain, "Message du 10 octobre 1940 (jeudi)," in *Discours aux Français,* 89. These principles are most clearly expressed in Pétain's *Principes de la communauté,* his answer to the 1789 Declaration of the Rights of Man and Citizen, which is reprinted in the same volume, 363–5.

6. On the regime's gender and family policy, see Francine Muel-Dreyfus, *Vichy and the Eternal Feminine: A Contribution to a Political Sociology of Gender,* trans. Kathleen A. Johnson (Durham, NC: Duke University Press, 2001); Miranda Pollard, *Reign of Virtue: Mobilizing Gender in Vichy France* (Chicago: University of Chicago Press, 1998). On Vichy anti-Semitism, see Michael Marrus and Robert Paxton, *Vichy France and the Jews* (New York: Basic Books, 1981); Serge Klarsfeld, *Vichy-Auschwitz: Le rôle de Vichy dans la solution finale de la question juive en France, 1942* (Paris: Fayard, 1983–1985); Laurent Joly, *Vichy dans la "solution finale": Histoire du Commissariat général aux questions juives, 1941–1944* (Paris: Grasset, 2006). On the limits of Vichy anti-Semitism, see Daniel

Lee, *Pétain's Jewish Children: French Jewish Youth and the Vichy Regime, 1940–1942* (Oxford: Oxford University Press, 2014).

7. An army of social scientists, doctors, and hygienists descended on Vichy to lend their "expertise" to the task of regenerating the ailing national body. See Julian Jackson, *France: The Dark Years, 1940–1944* (Oxford: Oxford University Press, 2001), 327; Philip Nord, *France's New Deal: From the Thirties to the Postwar Era* (Princeton, NJ: Princeton University Press, 2010), 115–30.

8. See, for instance, Pétain's "Message du 24 décembre 1940 (mardi)," in *Discours aux Français*, 102–3. Paxton refers to Pétain as a "paternal substitute for politics" (*Vichy France*, 186).

9. Muel-Dreyfus, *Vichy and the Eternal Feminine*, 5. Other historians have also pointed to the role that other ostensibly apolitical discourses, such as aesthetics, played in fascist ideology. See, for instance, David Carroll, *French Literary Fascism: Nationalism, Anti-Semitism, and the Ideology of Culture* (Princeton, NJ: Princeton University Press, 1995); Sandrine Sanos, *The Aesthetics of Hate: Far-Right Intellectuals, Antisemitism, and Gender in 1930s France* (Stanford, CA: Stanford University Press, 2012). Jean-Pierre Azéma likewise presents the National Revolution as, above all, a cultural revolution that drew from both left and right. See Azéma, "Vichy, l'héritage maudit," *L'Histoire* 162 (January 1993): 102–107.

10. Zeev Sternhell, *Neither Right nor Left: Fascist Ideology in France*, trans. David Maisel (Berkeley: University of California Press, 1986), 229, 287–93; John Hellman, *Knight-Monks of Vichy France: Uriage, 1940–1945* (Montreal: McGill-Queen's University Press, 1993), passim; On "non-conformism," see also Jean-Louis Loubet del Bayle, *Les non-conformistes des années trente: Une tentative de renouvellement de la pensée politique française* (Paris: Seuil, 1969).

11. Muel-Dreyfus, *Vichy and the Eternal Feminine*, 44.

12. Paxton, *Vichy France*, 150. See also W. D. Halls, *Politics, Society and Christianity in Vichy France* (Oxford: Berg, 1995), 87–92.

13. On the regime's policy on the *congrégations*, see Michèle Cointet, *L'Église sous Vichy, 1940–1945: La repentance en question* (Paris: Perrin, 1998), chaps. 2 and 3. On religious education under Vichy, see Paxton, *Vichy France*, 150–52; Nicholas Atkin, *Church and Schools in Vichy France, 1940–1944* (New York: Garland, 1991).

14. See Fouilloux, *Les chrétiens français entre crise et libération, 1937–1947* (Paris: Seuil, 1997), 123–4; Paxton, *Vichy France*, 186; Cointet, *L'Église sous Vichy*, chap. 1.

15. Mgr. Martin, Bishop of Puy and Louis Cruvillier, quoted in Renée Bédarida, *Les catholiques dans la guerre, 1939–1945: Entre Vichy et la Résistance* (Paris: Hachette, 1998), 72, 71.

16. Gabriel Marcel to Gaston Fessard, 24 August 1940, in *Gabriel Marcel—Gaston Fessard, Correspondance (1934–1971)*, ed. Henri de Lubac, Marie Rougier, and Michel Sales (Paris: Beauchesne, 1985), 190.

17. Quoted in Cointet, *L'Église sous Vichy*, 25. See also Sylvie Bernay, *L'Église de France face à la persécution des juifs, 1940–1944* (Paris: CNRS, 2012), 247.

18. Réginald Garrigou-Lagrange to Jacques Maritain, 25 March 1941, quoted in Étienne Fouilloux, *Une Église en quête de liberté: La pensée catholique fran-*

çaise entre modernisme et Vatican II (1914–1962) (Paris: Desclée de Brouwer, 1998), 113.

19. Garrigou-Lagrange to Maritain, quoted in Fouilloux, *Une Église en quête de liberté*, 113. See also Jacques Maritain to Réginald Garrigou-Lagrange, 12 December 1946, in *Oeuvres complètes de Jacques et Raïssa Maritain*, vol. 9 (Fribourg, Switzerland: Éditions Universitaires Fribourg, 1990), 1103–4.

20. The Vatican nuncio to Vichy expressed this suspicion to his superior at the Vatican Secretariat of State. See Mgr. Valerio Valeri to Cardinal Maglione, 30 September 1941, in *Actes et documents du Saint Siège relatifs à la seconde guerre mondiale*, vol. 8 (Vatican City: Vatican Library, 1974), 296. See also Henri de Lubac, *Résistance chrétienne à l'antisémitisme: Souvenirs 1940–1944* (Paris: Fayar, 1988), 94. For Gillet's role in the Vatican negotiations with Maurras, see André Laudouze, *Dominicains français et Action française, 1899–1940: Maurras au couvent* (Paris: Éditions Ouvrières, 1989), chap. 11.

21. On these conflicting appropriations of Péguy, see Jackson, *France: The Dark Years*, 4–6; Carroll, *French Literary Fascism*, chap. 2.

22. Paul Doncoeur, "Péguy et la Révolution," *Cité nouvelle* 24 (25 January 1942), quoted in Philippe Rocher, "*Cité Nouvelle*, 1941–1944: Les jésuites entre incarnation et eschatologie," *Chrétiens et sociétés* 2 (1995): para. 86: https://journals.openedition.org/chretienssocietes/149. The book in question was Paul Doncoeur, *Péguy, la révolution et le sacré* (Lyon: l'Orante, 1942). De Lubac penned a vigorous critique of this work. See Henri de Lubac, *Résistance chrétienne au nazisme,* ed. Renée Bédarida and Jacques Prévotat (Paris: Cerf, 2006), 319–20.

23. See John Hellman, *Emmanuel Mounier and the New Catholic Left, 1930–1950* (Toronto: University of Toronto Press, 1981), 158–87.

24. On Vichy corporatism, see Jean-Pierre Le Crom, *Syndicats, nous voilà! Vichy et le corporatisme* (Paris: Éditions Ouvrières, 1995).

25. For a different reading of the politics of "presence," see Vesna Drapac, *War and Religion: Catholics in the Churches of Occupied Paris* (Washington, D.C.: Catholic University of America Press, 1998).

26. See John Hellman, "Emmanuel Mounier: A Catholic Revolutionary at Vichy," *Journal of Contemporary History* 8, no. 4 (1973): 3–23. For a more sympathetic interpretation, see Michael Kelly, *Pioneer of the Catholic Revival: The Ideas and Influence of Emmanuel Mounier* (London: Sheed and Ward, 1979), 91–97. On Jeune France, see Philip Nord, "Pierre Schaeffer and Jeune France: Cultural Politics in the Vichy Years," *French Historical Studies* 30, no. 4 (2007): 685–709.

27. Quoted in Jackson, *France: The Dark Years,* 344; see also Bédarida, *Les catholiques dans la guerre,* 59.

28. Quoted in Rocher, "*Cité Nouvelle*," para. 11.

29. Quoted in Muel-Dreyfus, *Vichy and the Eternal Feminine,* 56.

30. For this figure, see Thomas Kselman, "Catholicism, Christianity, and Vichy," *French Historical Studies* 23, no. 3 (Summer 2000): 518. W. D. Halls notes large discrepancies in wartime membership numbers, with some placing the figure closer to 700,000 (Halls, *Politics, Society and Christianity,* 288).

31. On Catholic Action and Vichy, see Bédarida, *Les catholiques dans la guerre,* 72–76; Nicholas Atkin, "*Ralliés* and *résistants*: Catholics in Vichy France,

1940–44," in *Catholicism, Politics and Society in Twentieth-Century France,* ed. Kay Chadwick (Liverpool: Liverpool University Press, 2000), 99; Halls, *Politics, Society and Christianity,* 287–310.

32. Quoted in Bédarida, *Les catholiques dans la guerre,* 52. De Lubac advances a much more positive reading of this document in his memoir, *Résistance chrétienne à l'antisémitisme,* 78–79. On the bishops' relationship to the Vichy government, see also Jacques Duquesne, *Les catholiques français sous l'Occupation,* 2nd ed. (Paris: Grasset, 1986), 39–60, 244–56, 273–87, 320–53; Jackson, *France: The Dark Years,* 268–71; Cointet, *L'Église sous Vichy,* 28–38; Atkin, *"Ralliés and résistants,"* 100, 106–7.

33. See Halls, *Politics, Society and Christianity,* 82–83.

34. Gaston Fessard, "Note sur la situation actuelle de l'Église de France," November 1944; "La théorie du 'Prince-Esclave' et 'Le rôle de l'Episcopat français sous l'occupation,'" 1 July 1945, AFCJ, Fonds Gaston Fessard, 3/22.

35. Gaston Fessard, *Pax Nostra: Examen de conscience international* (Paris: Grasset, 1936); Gaston Fessard, *Épreuve de force: Réflexions sur la crise internationale* (Paris: Bloud et Gay, 1939); see also Michèle Aumont, *Philosophie sociopolitique de Gaston Fessard, S.J., "Pax Nostra"* (Paris: Cerf, 2004).

36. Gaston Fessard, "Conférence de Vichy," 15 December 1940, in *Au temps du prince-esclave: Écrits clandestins, 1940–1945,* ed. Jacques Prévotat (Paris: Critérion, 1989), 40.

37. Fessard, "Conférence de Vichy," 41.

38. Fessard, "Conférence de Vichy," 41, n2.

39. Fessard, "Conférence de Vichy," 43–44.

40. Fessard, "Conférence de Vichy," 52.

41. Fessard, "Conférence de Vichy," 42, 52.

42. Fessard, "Conférence de Vichy," 46n5. In the original sermon, this passage was much more explicit in forbidding any collaboration between Catholics and the "opposing mystiques of Race and Class," which are "each as false as the other" and tend to reduce human history to that of "beasts" or "ants." Fessard, "Conférence de Vichy," 45–46.

43. Fessard, "Conférence de Vichy," 47.

44. Gaston Fessard, "Custos, quid de nocte?," 27 December 1940, in *Au temps du prince-esclave,* 59.

45. Fessard, "Custos, quid de nocte?," 59, 60.

46. Fessard, "Conférence de Vichy," 50–51.

47. Fessard, "Custos, quid de nocte?," 59. Emphasis added.

48. See, for instance, Hellman, *Knight-Monks of Vichy France,* 6–7, 50–51, 55–56. Hellman nevertheless notes that de Lubac was rather less enthusiastic about Pétain than many at Uriage.

49. Henri de Lubac, "Explication chrétienne de notre temps," 1 October 1941, in *Résistance chrétienne au nazisme,* 128.

50. De Lubac, "Explication chrétienne de notre temps," 131. Emphasis in original.

51. De Lubac, "Explication chrétienne de notre temps," 132. Remarkably, the word "totalitarianism" managed to pass the censor.

52. De Lubac, "Explication chrétienne de notre temps," 132. See Eric Voegelin, *Political Religions,* trans. T. J. DiNapoli and E. S. Easterly (Lewiston, NY: Mellen Press, 1986); Raymond Aron, *The Dawn of Universal History: Selected Essays from a Witness of the Twentieth Century,* trans. Barbara Bray, ed. Yair Reiner (New York: Basic Books, 2002), 161–202.

53. De Lubac, "Explication chrétienne de notre temps," 143.

54. De Lubac, "Explication chrétienne de notre temps," 141.

55. De Lubac, "Explication chrétienne de notre temps," 143.

56. De Lubac, "Explication chrétienne de notre temps," 144.

57. De Lubac, "Explication chrétienne de notre temps," 136.

58. Yves de Montcheuil, "Dieu et la vie morale," *Construire* 6 (1941), reprinted in *Mélanges théologiques* (Paris: Aubier, 1951), 144. Gabriel Marcel, Jean Lacroix, and Emmanuel Mounier authored a similar critique of the education reforms titled "Dieu à l'école," in the February 1941 issue of *Esprit.*

59. De Montcheuil, "Dieu et la vie morale," 148–49, 155–56.

60. De Montcheuil, "Dieu et la vie morale," 149. Emphasis added.

61. Victor Dillard to Henri de Lubac, 12 December 1941, AFCJ, Fonds Henri de Lubac, 21. Desbuquois also refused to publish the article in *Cité nouvelle.* See Gustave Desbuquois to Henri de Lubac, 14 December 1941, AFCJ, Fonds de Lubac, 21.

62. Henri de Lubac, "Lettre à mes supérieurs," 25 April 1941, AFCJ, Fonds de Lubac, 21.

63. De Lubac, "Lettre à mes supérieurs," 9.

64. De Lubac, "Lettre à mes supérieurs," 10.

65. Norbert de Boynes (Assistant General) to the Jesuits of France, 12 July 1941, AFCJ, Fonds Henri de Lubac, 21, p. 2.

66. De Boynes to the Jesuits of France, 4.

67. De Boynes to the Jesuits of France, 5–6.

68. Henri de Lubac to Joseph du Bouchet (Provincial of Lyon), 24 July 1941, AFCJ, Fonds Henri de Lubac, 21, p. 3.

69. Henri de Lubac to Joseph du Bouchet, p. 3.

70. Pierre Chaillet, *L'Autriche souffrante* (Paris: Bloud et Gay, 1939), 120. On Chaillet's role in the resistance, see Renée Bédarida, *Pierre Chaillet: Témoin de la résistance spirituelle* (Paris: Fayard, 1988); Kathleen Harvill-Burton, *Le nazisme comme religion: Quatre théologiens déchiffrent le code religieux nazi (1932–1945)* (Lévis, Canada: Presses de l'Université de Laval, 2006), chap. 5.

71. Pierre Chaillet to Yves Congar, 20 August 1936, APDF, Fonds Yves Congar (V-832), 500; Yves Congar, quoted in Renée Bédarida, "Le Père Pierre Chaillet: De la théologie de Möhler à la Résistance," in *Spiritualité, théologie et résistance: Yves de Montcheuil, théologien au maquis du Vercors,* ed. Pierre Bolle and Jean Godel (Grenoble: Presses Universitaires de Grenoble, 1987), 52.

72. Pierre Chaillet, "La liberté de L'Église," *La Vie intellectuelle* 57 (June 1938): 182.

73. Chaillet, "La liberté de L'Église," 172, 173.

74. Chaillet, "La liberté de L'Église," 187.

75. Pierre Chaillet, "Rapport du Père Chaillet, S.J. sur Témoignage Chrétien et l'Amitié Chrétienne—1941–1942," AFCJ, Fonds Pierre Chaillet, 1/1.

76. Chaillet, "Rapport du Pere Chaillet, S.J." See also the account in Renée Bédarida, *Les armes de l'esprit: Témoignage chrétien (1941–1944)* (Paris: Éditions Ouvrières, 1977), 52–53; Bernard Comte, "Jésuites lyonnais résistants," in *Les jésuites à Lyon: XVIe–XXe siècle,* ed. Étienne Fouilloux and Bernard Hours (Lyon: ENS Éditions, 2005), 199.

77. On the logistics, see Bédarida, *Les armes de l'esprit,* chaps. 4, 5, 11, esp. 277.

78. Bédarida, *Les armes de l'esprit,* 288.

79. Gaston Fessard, "France, prends garde de perdre ton âme," in *Au temps du prince-esclave,* 70.

80. Fessard, "France, prends garde," 67. Emphasis in original.

81. Fessard, "France, prends garde," 74.

82. Fessard, "France, prends garde," 79.

83. Fessard, "France, prends garde," 84.

84. Fessard, "France, prends garde," 92.

85. Anon. [Pierre Chaillet], "Témoignage chrétien," *Cahiers du Témoignage chrétien* 1 (November 1941), in *Cahiers et Courriers clandestins du Témoignage chretien, 1941–1944,* vol. 1, integral reedition in facsimile (Paris: Renée Bédarida and Adrien Nemoz, 1980), 28.

86. Anon. [Pierre Chaillet], "Collaboration et fidelité," *Cahiers du Témoignage chrétien* 10–11 (October–November 1942), reprinted in *La résistance spirituelle, 1941–1944: Les Cahiers clandestins du Témoignage chrétien,* ed. François and Renée Bédarida (Paris: Albin Michel, 2001), 190.

87. Anon. [Pierre Chaillet], "Collaboration et fidelité," 190.

88. Anon., "Défi," *Cahiers du Témoignage chrétien* 13–14 (January–February 1943), in *La résistance spirituelle,* 221. This information came from the Polish Cardinal Hlond, who had fled Poland for France during the war.

89. Anon. [Pierre Chaillet], "Défi," 222, 216.

90. Anon., "Antisémites," *Cahiers du Témoignage chrétien* 6–7 (April–May 1942), reprinted in *La résistance spirituelle,* 119. The author was most likely Chaillet.

91. The ACA communiqué on *Témoignage chrétien* appeared in *La Croix,* April 10, 1943; quoted in de Lubac, *Résistance chrétienne au nazisme,* 420.

92. Anon. [Henri de Lubac], "Le scandale de la vérité," *Courriers du Témoignage chrétien* 3 (September 1943), reprinted in *La résistance spirituelle,* 358.

93. Yves de Montcheuil, "Collaboration," undated, AFCJ, Fonds Yves de Montcheuil, H Mo 55, p. 3. This passage, along with many of Montcheuil's resistance writings, were published posthumously in *l'Église et le monde actuel* (Paris: Éditions du Témoignage chrétien, 1945), 102.

94. Chaillet explained in the November 1944 issue of *Témoignage chrétien*: "on the level of thought and action . . . L'Amitié chrétienne and *Témoignage chrétien* were, under the occupation, the active symbols of this unity" (Bédarida, *Les armes de l'esprit,* 131). On Amitié chrétienne and other Christian rescue efforts, see Robert Gildea, *Fighters in the Shadows: A New History of the French Resis-*

tance (Cambridge, MA: Belknap / Harvard University Press, 2015), 180–204; Susan Zuccotti, *Père Marie-Benoît and Jewish Rescue: How a French Priest Together with Jewish Friends Saved Thousands During the Holocaust* (Bloomington, IN: University of Indiana Press, 2013).

95. Chaillet, "Rapport," 4.

96. Bédarida, *Les armes de l'esprit*, 132–33.

97. Chaillet, "Rapport," 4; De Lubac also praises her efforts in *Résistance chrétienne à l'antisémitisme*, 151.

98. Gildea, *Fighters in the Shadows*, 183.

99. This episode is reported in Chaillet's "Rapport," 5; Bédarida, *Les armes de l'esprit*, 134; Gildea, *Fighters in the Shadows*, 196.

100. Bédarida, *Les armes de l'esprit*, 135–36; Gildea, *Fighters in the Shadows*, 197; Service des Émissions vers l'Étranger, report, "L'Homme du jour: Le Père Chaillet," 15 January 1946, AFCJ, Fonds C-PA: Documents historiques sur la Compagnie, 619.

101. This is reported in the list of Jesuits mobilized, incarcerated, deported, or killed during the war, AFCJ, Fonds C-PA, 618. D'Ouince was incarcerated from March to April 1944.

102. For these figures, see François and Renée Bédarida, eds., *La résistance spirituelle*, 400–404.

103. François and Renée Bédarida, eds., *La résistance spirituelle*, 404.

104. Joseph Chaine, Henri de Lubac, Louis Richard, and Joseph Bonsirven, *Israël et la foi chrétienne* (Fribourg: Éditions de la Librairie de l'Université de Fribourg, 1942), 7; Anon. [Pierre Chaillet], "Collaboration et fidelité,' 190.

105. Anon. [Henri de Lubac], "L'antisémitisme et la conscience chrétienne," *Cahiers du Témoignage chrétien*, VI–VII (April–May 1942), reprinted in *Résistance chrétienne au nazisme*, 361–62.

106. Yves de Montcheuil, "La loi d'amour, insatisfaction du chrétien," *Cité nouvelle*, 33 (June 10, 1942), quoted in Rocher, "*Cité nouvelle*," para. 108.

107. De Lubac, "Un nouveau 'front' religieux," in *Israël et la foi chrétienne*, 18, 20.

108. De Lubac, *Résistance chrétienne à l'antisémitisme*, 20n4.

4. The Theoretical Foundations of the Spiritual Resistance

1. Yves de Montcheuil, "Dangers d'une fausse critique de l'individualisme," undated, AFCJ, Fonds Yves de Montcheuil, H Mo 55.

2. Yves de Montcheuil, "Problèmes posés par les tendances nouvelles de l'état," undated, AFCJ, Fonds Montcheuil, H Mo 55.

3. Montcheuil, "Problèmes posés."

4. On the origins of this text, see de Lubac, *Résistance chrétienne au nazisme*, ed. Renée Bédarida and Jacques Prévotat, 196–200 (Paris: Cerf, 2006). Both the 1942 and 1946 versions of the text are reprinted in this volume, and unless otherwise noted, all citations refer to the 1942 version.

5. De Lubac, "Fondements religieux du nazisme et du communisme," 202. De Lubac here quotes Marx's claim that "the critique of religion is the first condition of all critique."

6. De Lubac, "Fondements religieux du nazisme et du communisme," 202.

7. De Lubac, "Fondements religieux du nazisme et du communisme," 235.

8. This distinction is articulated by Richard Steigmann-Gall in "Nazism and the Revival of Political Religion Theory," *Totalitarian Movements and Political Religions* 5, no. 3 (December 2004): 376–96. Examples of the "political religions" discourse include Fritz Stern, *The Politics of Cultural Despair: A Study in the Rise of the Germanic Ideology* (Berkeley: University of California Press, 1974); Hans Maier, *Politische Religionen: Die totalitären Regime und das Christentum* (Freiburg: Herder, 1995). More recent scholarship tends to focus on the interaction between Nazism and Christianity, exemplified by the German Christian movement. See Doris Bergen, *Twisted Cross: The German Christian Movement in the Third Reich* (Chapel Hill, NC: University of North Carolina Press, 1996); Susannah Heschel, *The Aryan Jesus: Christian Theologians and the Bible in Nazi Germany* (Princeton, NJ: Princeton University Press, 2008). On the Christian commitments of Nazi Party leaders, see Steigmann-Gall, *The Holy Reich: Nazi Conceptions of Christianity, 1919–1945* (Cambridge: Cambridge University Press, 2003).

9. De Lubac, "Fondements religieux du nazisme et du communisme," 228.

10. De Lubac, "Fondements religieux du nazisme et du communisme," 229.

11. De Lubac, "Fondements religieux du nazisme et du communisme," 229.

12. Charles Journet, "Résistance" (November 12, 1943), reprinted in *Exigences chrétiennes en politique* (Paris: Egloff, 1945), 409–16; Henri de Lubac, "Collaboration et service de travail obligatoire," *Courrier du Témoignage chrétien* 1 (May 1943), reprinted in *La résistance spirituelle, 1941–1944: Les Cahiers clandestins du Témoignage chrétien*, ed. François and Renée Bédarida (Paris: Albin Michel, 2001), 342. Emphasis in original. The relevant passages from the *Summa Theologica* on tyranny are II–II, q.64, a.3; Ia, q.81, a.3, ad.2; II–II, q.42, a.2; and on unjust laws, I–II, q.96, a.4.

13. Quoted in Henri de Lubac, *Mémoire sur l'occasion de mes écrits* (Namur, Belgium: Culture et Vérité, 1989), 240.

14. See Nicholas Atkin, "*Ralliés* and *résistants*: Catholics in Vichy France, 1940–44," in *Catholicism, Politics and Society in Twentieth-Century France*, ed. Kay Chadwick (Liverpool: Liverpool University Press, 2000), 109; W. D. Halls, *Politics, Society, and Christianity in Vichy France* (Oxford: Berg, 1995), 311–14.

15. Henri de Lubac, "Service obligatoire du travail," *Courriers du Témoignage chrétien* 1 (May 1943), reprinted in *La résistance spirituelle*, 348.

16. Halls, *Politics, Society, and Christianity*, 165–74.

17. Quoted in Halls, *Politics, Society, and Christianity*, 169.

18. "Exigences de la Libération," *Cahiers du Témoignage chrétien* 26–27 (May 1944), reprinted in *La résistance spirituelle*, 309–12.

19. The occasion was the publication of a collaborationist pamphlet by a prominent professor at the Institut Catholique in Paris, which had received the imprimatur of the archdiocese of Paris. This angered Fessard, and Suhard invited

him to submit his own views on the subject, but Fessard never received a response to his treatise.

20. See Gaston Fessard, "Révolution et persécution" (1938), AFCJ, Fonds Gaston Fessard, 19.1/a/3.

21. Gaston Fessard, "La conscience catholique devant la défaite et la révolution," undated, AFCJ, Fonds Fessard, 2/17, pp. 32–33.

22. Fessard, "La conscience catholique," 36.

23. Fessard, "La conscience catholique," 107.

24. Fessard, "La conscience catholique," 108. Emphasis in original.

25. Fessard instead treats the consent of the governed as a *sign* of legitimacy rather than its source. See Fessard, "La conscience catholique," 9; Jacques Maritain, *Christianisme et démocratie* (New York: Éditions de la Maison Française, 1943), esp. 58 and 79–80.

26. Philippe Pétain, "Appel du 20 juin 1940," in *Discours aux Français: 17 juin 1940–20 août 1944*, ed. Jean-Claude Barbas (Paris: Albin Michel, 1989), 60.

27. Francine Muel-Dreyfus, *Vichy and the Eternal Feminine: A Contribution to a Political Sociology of Gender,* trans. Kathleen A. Johnson (Durham, NC: Duke University Press, 2001), 283. On the regime's gender politics, see also Miranda Pollard, *Reign of Virtue: Mobilizing Gender in Vichy France* (Chicago: University of Chicago Press, 1998).

28. Muel-Dreyfus, *Vichy and the Eternal Feminine,* 43–44.

29. The literature on the "feminization" of religion is vast. See especially Caroline Ford, *Divided Houses: Religion and Gender in Modern France* (Ithaca, NY: Cornell University Press, 2005); Suzanne Desan, *Reclaiming the Sacred: Lay Religion and Popular Politics in Revolutionary France* (Ithaca, NY: Cornell University Press, 1990), 197–216; Suzanne Kaufman, *Consuming Visions: Mass Culture and the Lourdes Shrine* (Ithaca, NY: Cornell University Press, 2005).

30. "Le christianisme a-t-il dévirilisé l'homme?" *Jeunesse de l'Église* 2–3 (1943–1944); Louis Beirnaert, *Pour un christianisme de choc* (Paris: Éditions de l'Orante, 1942); see also Emmanuel Mounier, *L'affrontement chrétien* (Neuchâtel: Éditions de Baconnière, 1945).

31. Henri de Lubac, "Le combat spirituel," *Cité nouvelle* 65 (December 25, 1943), reprinted in *Résistance chrétienne au nazisme,* 346, 347.

32. Yves de Montcheuil, "La force," reprinted in *L'Église et le monde actuel* (Paris: Éditions du Témoignage chrétien, 1945), 90.

33. De Lubac, "Le combat spirituel," 349–50.

34. Montcheuil, "La force," 87.

35. Montcheuil, "La force," 88, 87.

36. For the list of *Témoignage chrétien* militants, which includes ten women and twenty men, see AFCJ, Fonds Henri de Lubac, 5. On the role of women in Amitié chrétienne, see Renée Bédarida, *Les armes de l'esprit: Témoignage chrétien (1941–1944)* (Paris: Éditions Ouvrières, 1977), 129–30; Robert Gildea, *Fighters in the Shadows: A New History of the French Resistance* (Cambridge, MA: Belknap/Harvard University Press, 2015), 180–204.

37. Saba Mahmood, *Politics of Piety: The Islamic Revival and the Feminist Subject* (Princeton, NJ: Princeton University Press, 2005); Brenna Moore, *Sacred*

Dread: Raïssa Maritain, the Allure of Suffering, and the French Catholic Revival (1905–1944) (Notre Dame, IN: University of Notre Dame Press, 2013).

38. Jules Isaac, *L'enseignement du mépris* (Paris: Fasquelle, 1962).

39. Saul Friedlander's notion of "redemptive anti-Semitism" is an important case in point: see *Nazi Germany and the Jews,* vol. 1, *The Years of Persecution (1933–1939)* (New York: HarperCollins, 1997). See also Uriel Tal, *Religious and Anti-Religious Roots of Modern Anti-Semitism* (New York: Leo Baeck Institute, 1971); Heschel, *The Aryan Jesus.* A similar dynamic played out in the case of Fascist Italy's racial laws. See David Kertzer, *The Pope and Mussolini: The Secret History of Pius XI and the Rise of Fascism in Europe* (New York: Oxford University Press, 2014), 309, 313.

40. John Connelly, *From Enemy to Brother: The Revolution in Catholic Teaching on the Jews, 1933–1965* (Cambridge, MA: Harvard University Press, 2012), 23, 127.

41. Connelly, *From Enemy to Brother,* 146.

42. Quoted in Brenna Moore, "Philosemitism under a Darkening Sky: Judaism in the French Catholic Revival (1900–1945)," *Catholic Historical Review* 99, no. 2 (2013): 272n27.

43. This has led some to label Bloy an anti-Semite. See, for instance, Pierre Birnbaum, *Antisemitism in France: A Political History from Léon Bloy to the Present* (New York: Oxford University Press, 1992).

44. Jacques Maritain, *L'impossible antisémitisme* (Paris: Desclée de Brouwer, 1994). On Jacques and Raïssa Maritain's critique of anti-Semitism, see Richard Francis Crane, *The Passion of Israel: Jacques Maritain, Catholic Conscience, and the Holocaust* (Scranton, PA: University of Scranton Press, 2010); Moore, *Sacred Dread,* chap. 3.

45. Maritain called, for instance, for a "pluralist and personalist" regime that would respect religious freedom (Maritain, *L'impossible antisémitisme,* 97).

46. Jacques Maritain, *L'impossible antisémitisme,* 78.

47. See, for instance, Brian Porter-Szücs, *Faith and Fatherland: Catholicism, Modernity, and Poland* (Oxford: Oxford University Press, 2011), 273–328; John Connelly, *From Enemy to Brother.*

48. Julian Jackson, *France: The Dark Years, 1940–1944* (Oxford: Oxford University Press, 2001), 150; chap. 15. On Vichy anti-Semitism, see especially Michael Marrus and Robert Paxton, *Vichy France and the Jews* (New York: Basic Books, 1981). Daniel Lee also reveals that there were limits to the regime's anti-Semitic campaign, especially when it conflicted with other policy priorities. See *Pétain's Jewish Children: French Jewish Youth and the Vichy Regime, 1940–1942* (Oxford: Oxford University Press, 2014).

49. Jackson, *France: The Dark Years,* 151–52.

50. On the Commissariat, see Laurent Joly, *Vichy dans la "solution finale": Histoire du Commissariat général aux questions juives, 1941–1944* (Paris: Grasset, 2006).

51. The first protests came from Bishop Jules-Géraud Saliège in Toulouse and Bishop Pierre-Marie Théas in Montauban in August 1942. On the Holocaust in France, see Susan Zuccotti, *The Holocaust, The French, and the Jews* (Lincoln:

University of Nebraska Press, 1999); Serge Klarsfeld, *Vichy-Auschwitz: Le rôle de Vichy dans la solution finale de la question juive en France* (Paris: Fayard, 1983–85).

52. See Marrus and Paxton, *Vichy France and the Jews;* Jackson, *France: The Dark Years,* 355–61.

53. "Rapport au maréchal Pétain de Léon Bérard," 2 September 1941, reprinted in *Le Monde juif,* October 1946, 2.

54. "Rapport au maréchal Pétain," 3. The relevant passage from the *Summa* is IIa IIae, q.10, a.9–12.

55. "Rapport au maréchal Pétain," 4.

56. See Valerio Valeri to Cardinal Maglione, 30 September 1941, in *Actes et documents du Saint Siège relatifs à la seconde guerre mondiale,* vol. 8 (Vatican City: Vatican Library, 1974), 296.

57. Henri de Lubac, *Résistance chrétienne à l'antisémitisme: Souvenirs 1940–1944* (Paris: Fayard, 1988), 96.

58. Joseph Chaine, Henri de Lubac, Louis Richard, and Joseph Bonsirven, *Israël et la foi chrétienne* (Fribourg: Éditions de la Librairie de l'Université de Fribourg, 1942), 152. The author of these lines was de Lubac (see Bédarida, *Les armes de l'esprit,* 119n20). This claim has since been discredited by historians who have pointed to the blood purity laws of medieval Spain. See David Nirenberg, "Was There Race before Modernity? The Example of 'Jewish' Blood in Late Medieval Spain," in *The Origins of Racism in the West,* ed. Miriam Eliav-Feldon, Benjamin Isaac, and Joseph Ziegler, 232–64 (Cambridge: Cambridge University Press, 2009).

59. Chaine et al., *Israël et la foi chrétienne,* 153. The author here is de Lubac.

60. Charles Journet, "Antisémitisme," *Nova et vetera* (July–September 1941), reprinted in *Exigences chrétiennes en politique,* 162–64.

61. For an excellent overview, see Bernard Comte, "Conscience catholique et persécution antisémite: L'engagement de théologiens lyonnais en 1941–1942," *Annales. Histoire, Sciences Sociales* 48, no. 3 (May–June, 1993): 635–54.

62. Henri de Lubac, *Catholicisme: Les aspects sociaux du dogme* (Paris: Cerf, 1938), 128. He also argued that Christianity owes its social model of salvation to Judaism (33).

63. Bonsirven's most significant works include *Sur les ruines du Temple: Le Judaïsme après Jésus-Christ* (Paris: Grasset, 1928); *Les idées juives au temps de Notre-Seigneur* (Paris: Bloud et Gay, 1934); *Juifs et chrétiens* (Paris: Flammarion, 1936); *Exégèse rabbinique et exégèse paulinienne* (Paris: Beauchesne, 1939).

64. "Draft of a Declaration of the Catholic Theology Faculty of Lyons," 17 June 1941, reprinted in De Lubac, *Résistance chrétienne à l'antisémitisme,* 70. Emphasis added.

65. De Lubac has a rather more charitable reading of the reasoning of these colleagues and superiors, in *Résistance chrétienne à l'antisémitisme,* 62, 77–79. For a less charitable reading, see Atkin, "*Ralliés* and *résistants,*" 108.

66. Chaine et al., *Israël et la foi chrétienne,* 153. The author here is de Lubac.

67. See Bergen, *Twisted Cross,* 143–54.

68. De Lubac, "Un nouveau front religieux," in *Israël et la foi chrétienne,* 31.

69. Chaine et al., *Israël et la foi chrétienne*, 151–52. The author here is de Lubac.

70. Chaine et al., *Israël et la foi chrétienne*, 8.

71. Victor Fontoynont, "La destinée du peuple juif," *Rencontres* 4 (December 1941), reprinted in "Les théologiens lyonnais et la persécution contre les juifs," *Les Cahiers de l'Institut Catholique de Lyon*, 25 (1994): 31. The relevant passage from Paul is Romans 11:29.

72. Fontoynont, "La destinée du peuple juif," 29. Fontoynont here paraphrases Romans 11:12–15.

73. Fontoynont, "La destinée du peuple juif," 30.

74. Fontoynont, "La destinée du peuple juif," 32.

75. Louis Richard, "La question juive et la foi chrétienne," October 1942, quoted in Comte, "Conscience catholique et persécution antisémite," 652–53.

76. They included Dietrich von Hildebrand, Karl Thieme, and Johann Oesterreicher. See Connelly, *From Enemy to Brother,* chaps. 4–6 and 8.

77. Samuel Moyn, *Christian Human Rights* (Philadelphia: University of Pennsylvania Press, 2015); Marco Duranti, *The Conservative Human Rights Revolution: European Identity, Transnational Politics, and the Origins of the European Convention* (New York: Oxford University Press, 2017).

78. See especially Moyn, *Christian Human Rights,* 8; Duranti, *Conservative Human Rights Revolution,* chaps. 6 and 7.

79. I have made this argument in greater detail in Sarah Shortall, "Theology and the Politics of Christian Human Rights," *Journal of the History of Ideas* 79, no. 3 (July 2018): 445–60.

80. Jacques Maritain, "On the Philosophy of Human Rights," in *Human Rights: Comments and Interpretations,* ed. UNESCO (London: Wingate, 1949), 77.

81. Maritain, *Les droits de l'homme et la loi naturelle* (New York: Éditions de la Maison Française, 1942),114.

82. Maritain, *Les droits de l'homme,* 85–86.

83. On Maritain's contribution, see *Human Rights: Comments and Interpretations,* introduction and 72–77; Moyn, *Christian Human Rights,* chap. 2; Shortall, "Theology and the Politics of Christian Human Rights," 449–51.

84. Pierre Chaillet, "Histoire clandestine du *Témoignage chrétien,*" November 11, 1944, quoted in Renée Bédarida, *Pierre Chaillet: Témoin de la résistance spirituelle* (Paris: Fayard, 1988), 170–71.

85. Anon. [Henri de Lubac], "L'antisémitisme et la conscience chrétienne," *Cahiers du Témoignage chrétien* 6–7 (April–May 1942), reprinted in *La résistance spirituelle,* 144.

86. Quoted in Renée Bédarida, *Les armes de l'esprit,* 122. This is based on 1 Corinthians 12:26.

87. See Paul Hanebrink, *In Defense of Christian Hungary: Religion, Nationalism, and Antisemitism, 1890–1944* (Ithaca, NY: Cornell University Press, 2006), 170–80; Piotr Kosicki, "Masters in Their Own Home or Defenders of the Human Person? Wojciech Korfanty, Anti-Semitism, and Polish Christian Democracy's Illiberal Rights-Talk," *Modern Intellectual History* 14, no. 1 (2017): 99–130.

88. De Lubac, *Catholicisme*, 2.

89. See Connelly, *From Enemy to Brother*, 67–78.

90. Karl Adam, *The Spirit of Catholicism*, trans. Dom Justin McCann (New York: Crossroad, 1997), 36–37.

91. Karl Adam, "Deutsches Volkstum und katholisches Christentum," *Theologisches Quartalschrift* 114 (1933): 58–59. I have adopted Robert Krieg's translation in *Karl Adam: Catholicism in German Culture* (Notre Dame, IN: Notre Dame University Press, 1992), 119.

92. See the discussion in Robert Krieg, *Catholic Theologians in Nazi Germany* (New York: Continuum, 2004), 164–70.

93. Louis Bouyer, "Où en est la théologie du corps mystique?" *Revue des sciences religieuses* 22 (1948): 326.

94. Bouyer, "Où en est la théologie du corps mystique?," 326.

95. Pius XII, *Mystici Corporis Christi* (June 29, 1943), §31.

96. Henri de Lubac, *Corpus mysticum: L'Eucharistie et l'Église au Moyen Âge. Étude historique* (Paris: Cerf, 2009 [1949]), 104.

97. De Lubac, *Corpus mysticum*, 129. The political implications of this argument are well conveyed in Brian Hollon, *Everything Is Sacred: Spiritual Exegesis in the Political Theology of Henri de Lubac* (Cambridge: James Clark, 2010), 54–71.

98. Ernst Kantorowicz, *The King's Two Bodies: A Study in Mediaeval Political Theology* (Princeton, NJ: Princeton University Press, 1997), 193–232. Kantorowicz makes his debt to de Lubac explicit in 194n4.

99. De Lubac, *Corpus mysticum*, 293.

100. Henri de Lubac, "Communauté chrétienne et communion sacramentelle," 1942, reprinted in de Lubac, *Corpus mysticum*, 397.

101. Henri de Lubac, "Fondements religieux du nazisme et du communisme," 289. This quote comes from the 1946 version of the text, but de Lubac makes the same point in the 1942 version (228).

102. Henri de Lubac, "La portée sociale de la messe. Rapport présénté aux Journées nationales de Lyon," April 1942, reprinted in de Lubac, *Corpus mysticum*, 390.

103. Yves de Montcheuil, "La présence réelle," AFCJ, Fonds Fessard, 4/21bis, pp. 2–3.

104. Fessard, "Conférence de Vichy," 15 December 1940, in *Au temps du prince-esclave: Écrits clandestins, 1940–1945*, ed. Jacques Prévotat (Paris: Critérion, 1989), 50.

105. See Giorgio Agamben, *Homo Sacer: Sovereign Power and Bare Life*, trans. Daniel Heller-Roazen (Stanford, CA: Stanford University Press, 1998); William Cavanaugh, *Torture and Eucharist: Theology, Politics, and the Body of Christ* (Oxford: Blackwell, 1998).

106. Cavanaugh, *Torture and Eucharist*, 229, 17.

107. Yves de Montcheuil, "Communisme," *Courriers du Témoignage chrétien* 5 (November 1943), reprinted in *La résistance spirituelle*, 370.

108. Montcheuil, "Communisme," 370.

109. Quoted in Bédarida, *Les armes de l'esprit*, 173.

110. *Courriers du Témoignage chrétien,* 13 (August 1944), quoted in Bédarida, *Les armes de l'esprit,* 269.

111. Jean Lacroix, "Les catholiques et la politique," *Esprit* (June 1945): 71.

112. Gaston Fessard, "Avant-propos pour les Cahiers de la IVe République," in *Au temps du prince-esclave,* 127.

5. The Postwar Catholic Engagement with the Left

1. Henri de Lubac, *Le drame de l'humanisme athée* (Paris: Spes, 1945), 10.

2. See Michael Kelly, *The Cultural and Intellectual Rebuilding of France after the Second World War* (New York: Palgrave Macmillan, 2004), 127–54; Edward Baring, "Humanist Pretensions: Catholics, Communists, and Sartre's Struggle for Existentialism in Postwar France," *Modern Intellectual History* 7, no. 3 (2010): 581–609; Stefanos Geroulanos, *An Atheism That Is Not Humanist Emerges in French Thought* (Stanford, CA: Stanford University Press, 2010), 209–21.

3. Naville made this comment in response to Sartre's famous attempt to appropriate the language of humanism in the service of existentialism. It is quoted in Jean-Paul Sartre, *Existentialism Is a Humanism,* trans. Carol Macomber (New Haven, CT: Yale University Press, 2007), 62.

4. On Marxist humanism, see Mark Poster, *Existential Marxism in Postwar France: From Sartre to Althusser* (Princeton, NJ: Princeton University Press, 1975), chap. 2. Leading examples of Marxist humanism include Henri Lefebvre, *Le matérialisme dialectique* (Paris: Alcan, 1939) and Georges Friedmann, *Machine et humanisme* (Paris: Gallimard, 1946).

5. See the account of the Catholic and Marxist critiques of existentialism in Jonathan Judaken, "Sisyphus' Progeny: Existentialism in France," in *Situating Existentialism: Key Texts in Context,* ed. Jonathan Judaken and Robert Bernasconi, 91–98 (New York: Columbia University Press, 2012).

6. Pierre Hervé, *La libération trahie* (Paris: Grasset, 1945), 62, quoted in Baring, "Humanist Pretensions," 587.

7. Jean Daniélou, "La vie intellectuelle en France: Communisme, existentialisme, christianisme," *Études* 246 (July–August 1945): 249.

8. Daniélou, "La vie intellectuelle en France," 249–50. I prefer this term to "Left Catholicism," which Gerd-Rainer Horn uses to designate the range of Catholic intellectual, apostolic, and political movements broadly oriented to the left. See "Left Catholicism in Western Europe in the 1940s," in *Left Catholicism, 1943–1955: Catholics and Society in Western Europe at the Point of Liberation, 1943–1955,* ed. Gerd-Rainer Horn and Emmanuel Gerard, 13–44 (Leuven: KADOC/Leuven University Press, 2001). The difficulty with this approach is that it tends to treat these phenomena as part of a single movement, obscuring the considerable diversity of approaches and perspectives. This is why I prefer the more generic term "Catholic left," although it still has the disadvantage of relying

upon secular political categories. In the absence of a better term—"progressivism," for instance is too narrowly associated with the Union des chrétiens progressistes—I have chosen to use this term anyway, while also highlighting the continuities between the prewar Catholic right and postwar Catholic left and stressing the specifically theological and pastoral roots of the Catholic engagement with the left.

9. Daniélou, "La vie intellectuelle," 251.

10. One important exception was the Thomist philosopher Étienne Gilson, who briefly represented the MRP in the Conseil de la République. On his involvement with the MRP, see Florian Michel, *Étienne Gilson: Une biographie intellectuelle et politique* (Paris: Vrin, 2018), 229–43. On Christian Democracy, see Carlo Invernizzi Accetti, *What is Christian Democracy? Politics, Religion and Ideology* (Cambridge: Cambridge University Press, 2019); James Chappel, *Catholic Modern: The Challenge of Totalitarianism and the Remaking of the Church* (Cambridge, MA: Harvard University Press, 2018), chaps. 4 and 5; Jan-Werner Müller, "Towards a New History of Christian Democracy," *Journal of Political Ideologies* 18, no. 2 (2012): 243–55; Maria Mitchell, *The Origins of Christian Democracy: Politics and Confession in Modern Germany* (Ann Arbor: University of Michigan Press, 2012); Wolfram Kaiser, *Christian Democracy and the Origins of the European Union* (Cambridge: Cambridge University Press, 2007); Thomas Kselman and Joseph A. Buttigieg, eds., *European Christian Democracy: Historical Legacies and Comparative Perspectives* (Notre Dame, IN: Notre Dame University Press, 2003).

11. On this point, see also Piotr Kosicki, *Catholics on the Barricades: Poland, France, and "Revolution," 1891–1956* (New Haven, CT: Yale University Press, 2018*).*

12. Henri de Lubac, *Mémoire sur l'occasion de mes écrits* (Namur, Belgium: Culture et Vérité, 1989), 147–48.

13. The crisis was precipitated by Pietro Parente, "Nuove tendenze teologiche," *L'Osservatore Romano* (February 9–10, 1942), 1. See Étienne Fouilloux, "Le Saulchoir en procès (1937–1942)," in *Une école de théologie: Le Saulchoir,* ed. Giuseppe Alberigo, 37–59 (Paris: Cerf, 1985).

14. Gaston Fessard, *France, prends garde de perdre ta liberté* (Paris: Éditions du Témoignage Chrétien, 1946), 9.

15. Fessard, *France, prends garde,* 11, 10.

16. Fessard, *France, prends garde,* 21.

17. Karl Marx, "Economic and Philosophic Manuscripts of 1844," in *The Marx-Engels Reader,* ed. Robert Tucker (New York: Norton, 1978), 84.

18. Fessard, *France, prends garde,* 132. Fessard is here quoting René Maublanc, the editor of the communist journal *La Pensée.*

19. As Edward Baring shows, the creation of the Cominform in 1947 forced the PCF to move away from its earlier embrace of Marxist humanism toward a more "scientific" materialism. See "Humanist Pretensions:," 601–604. On the longer history of these tensions in the PCF, see William S. Lewis, *Louis Althusser and the Traditions of French Marxism* (Lanham, MD: Lexington, 2005), chaps. 5

and 6; Tony Judt, *Marxism and the French Left* (Oxford: Oxford University Press, 1986), chap. 4.

20. Fessard, *France, prends garde*, 135.

21. Fessard, *France, prends garde*, 136.

22. Fessard, *France, prends garde*, 144.

23. Fessard, *France, prends garde*, 156.

24. Fessard, *France, prends garde*, 166.

25. Fessard, *France, prends garde*, 271.

26. André Mandouze, *Mémoires d'outre-siècle*, vol. 1: *D'une résistance à l'autre* (Paris: Éditions Viviane Hamy, 1998), 157.

27. André Mandouze, "Notes à l'usage de quelques Pères sur la question du communisme," undated, AFCJ, Fonds Gaston Fessard, 3.24/2. On the nature of these divisions, see also Gaston Fessard to Pierre Chaillet, 20 November 1945, AFCJ, Fonds Fessard, 3.24/2.

28. Quoted in Frank Emmanuel to Gaston Fessard, 16 November 1945, AFCJ, Fonds Fessard, 3.24/2.

29. Mandouze, "Notes à l'usage de quelques Pères."

30. Gaston Fessard, "Réflexions sur la note à l'usage de quelques Pères de A. Mandouze," AFCJ, Fonds Fessard, 3.24/2.

31. Mandouze, *Mémoires d'outre-siècle*, 158.

32. See Darcie Fontaine, *Decolonizing Christianity: Religion and the End of Empire in France and Algeria* (Cambridge: Cambridge University Press, 2016), 20–21, 49–50, 123–28.

33. Quoted in Renée Bédarida, *Pierre Chaillet: Témoin de la résistance spirituelle* (Paris: Fayard, 1988), 265–66.

34. On the postwar evolution of *Témoignage chrétien*, see Étienne Fouilloux, "Les cinq étapes de 'Témoignage chrétien,'" *Vingtième Siècle. Revue d'histoire* 125 (January-March 2015): 3–15.

35. Emmanuel Mounier, "Récents critiques du communisme," *Esprit* 10 (October 1946): 476.

36. These reservations were shared by Daniélou and Chaillet (see Bédarida, *Pierre Chaillet*, 261–62). They led to a particularly bitter quarrel between Fessard and de Lubac: see Frédéric Louzeau, "Gaston Fessard et Henri de Lubac: Leur différend sur la question du communisme et du progressisme chrétien (1945–1950)," *Revue des sciences religieuses* 84, no. 4 (2010): 517–43. But both de Lubac and Daniélou still closely echoed Fessard's critique of Marxist humanism in their own work. See, for instance, Henri de Lubac, "La recherche d'un Homme Nouveau," in *Affrontements mystiques* (Paris: Éditions du Témoignage Chrétien, 1950), 2–92; Jean Daniélou, *Dialogues avec les marxistes, les existentialistes, les protestants, les juifs, l'hindouisme* (Paris: Le Portulan, 1948), 31–95.

37. De Lubac, "La recherche d'un Homme Nouveau," 60, 59.

38. Henri Godin and Yvon Daniel, *La France, pays de mission?* (Paris: Éditions Abeille, 1943), 129. Emphasis in original.

39. Godin and Yvon Daniel, *La France, pays de mission?*, 129.

40. "Compte rendu de la visite des Pères Lévesque, Perrot, et Giboin à Son Éminence le Cardinal Liénart," 30 May 1952, APDF, Fonds Marie-Dominique

Chenu (V-772), 7. The missionaries selected locations where more than 20 percent of the population was unbaptized.

41. Horn, *Western European Liberation Theology: The First Wave (1924–1959)* (Oxford: Oxford University Press, 2008), 243.

42. Godin and Daniel, *France, pays de mission?*, 18.

43. Marie-Dominique Chenu, *Un théologien en liberté: Jacques Duquesne interroge le Père Chenu* (Paris: Le Centurion, 1975), 134–38.

44. See François Leprieur, *Quand Rome condamne: Dominicains et prêtres-ouvriers* (Paris: Cerf, 1989), 215–17. On Chenu's role in these institutions, see the contributions by L. Augros and J. Hollande in *L'hommage différé au Père Chenu* (Paris: Cerf, 1990), 25–37.

45. Chenu, *Un théologien en liberté*, 133.

46. Chenu, *Un théologien en liberté*, 136.

47. Marie-Dominique Chenu, "L'Église missionaire," *L'actualité religieuse dans le monde* 8 (1953), in APDF, Fonds Chenu (V-772), 8.

48. On the worker-priests, see Émile Poulat, *Naissance des prêtres-ouvriers* (Paris: Casterman, 1965); Oscar Arnal, *Priests in Working-Class Blue: The History of the Worker-Priests (1943–1954)* (New York: Paulist Press, 1986); Horn, *Western European Liberation Theology*, chap. 5; René Poterie and Louis Jeusselin, eds., *Prêtres-ouvriers: 50 ans d'histoire et de combats* (Paris: L'Harmattan, 2001).

49. Quoted in Philippe Chenaux, *L'Église catholique et le communisme*, 191.

50. See Oscar Arnal, "The 'Témoignages' of the Worker-Priests and the 'Main Tendue' to Communism (1943–1954)," *French Historical Studies* 13, no. 4 (1984): 529–55.

51. Quoted in Leprieur, *Quand Rome comdamne*, 11; Chenu, *Un théologien en liberté*, 158.

52. Marie-Dominique Chenu, "Le sacerdoce des prêtres-ouvriers," *La Vie intellectuelle* (February 1954): 176.

53. Chenu, "Le sacerdoce des prêtres-ouvriers," 176. Emphasis in original.

54. Chenu, *Un théologien en liberté*, 153.

55. Chenu, "Le sacerdoce des prêtres-ouvriers," 181.

56. Yves Congar, "L'avenir des prêtres-ouvriers," *Témoignage chrétien* (September 25, 1953): 1.

57. On the tensions between the missionary *équipes* and parish clergy, see "Compte rendu de la visite des Pères Lévesque, Perrot, et Giboin."

58. Congar, "L'avenir des prêtres-ouvriers," 1.

59. Chenu, *Un théologien en liberté*, 147.

60. Arnal cites several such examples in "A Missionary 'Main Tendue,'" 538–43. The following account is greatly indebted to his analysis.

61. Arnal, "A Missionary 'Main Tendue,'" 544.

62. Quoted in Arnal, *Priests in Working-Class Blue*, 151.

63. On the MPF, see Bruno Duriez, "Left-Wing Catholicism in France from Catholic Action to the Political Left: The *Mouvement Populaire des Familles*," in Horn and Gerard, *Left Catholicism*, 64–90; Horn, *Western European Liberation Theology*, chap. 4; Denis Pelletier and Jean-Louis Schlegel, eds., *À la gauche du*

Christ: Les chrétiens de gauche en France de 1945 à nos jours (Paris: Seuil, 2012), 142–27, 163–66.

64. The best work on this group remains Denis Pelletier, *Économie et humanisme: De l'utopie communautaire au combat pour le tiers monde, 1941–1966* (Paris: Cerf, 1996).

65. On Vichy corporatism and Perroux's role in particular, see Philip Nord, *France's New Deal: From the Thirties to the Postwar Era* (Princeton, NJ: Princeton University Press, 2010), 38–39, 94–100, 113–14; James Chappel, *Catholic Modern*, 87–79.

66. Giuliana Chamedes, "The Catholic Origins of Economic Development after World War II," *French Politics, Culture, and Society* 33, no. 2 (2015): 55–76.

67. Paul VI, *Populorum Progressio* (March 26, 1967), esp. §14. On Lebret, see also Lydie Garreau, *Louis-Joseph Lebret, précurseur de Vatican II (1897–1966)* (Paris: L'Harmattan, 2011).

68. See Nord, *France's New Deal*.

69. On the "progressive Christians," see Yvon Tranvouez, *Catholiques et communistes: La crise du progressisme chrétien, 1950–1955* (Paris: Cerf, 2000); Tranvouez, *Catholicisme et société dans la France du XXe siècle: Apostolat, progressisme et tradition* (Paris: Karthala, 2011), 137–53, 171–86; Philippe Chenaux, *L'Église catholique et le communisme en Europe (1917–1989)* (Paris: Cerf, 2009), 181–204.

70. André Mandouze, "Prendre la main tendue," *Les chrétiens et la politique* (Paris: Éditions du Temps Présent, 1948), 41. On Mandouze's relationship to the UCP, see his *Mémoires d'outre-siècle*, 188–94.

71. André Mandouze, "Rome ou Moscou?," quoted in *Mémoires d'outre-siècle*, 189.

72. Mandouze, "Prendre la main tendue," 71.

73. Emmanuel Mounier, "Les chrétiens progressistes," *Esprit* (November 1948): 744.

74. Emmanuel Mounier to Gaston Fessard, 22 January 1949, reprinted in *Études* 260 (January 1949): 392. On the political evolution of *Esprit*, see Michel Winock, *Histoire politique de la revue Esprit (1930–1950)* (Paris: Seuil, 1975); Goulven Boudic, *Esprit, 1944–1982: Métamorphoses d'une revue* (Paris: IMEC, 2005).

75. On Jeunesse de l'Église, see Thierry Keck, *Jeunesse de l'Église, 1936–1955: Aux sources de la crise progressiste en France* (Paris: Karthala, 2004). On Althusser's involvement, see Yann Moulier Boutang, *Louis Althusser: Une biographie*, vol. 1 (Paris: Grasset, 1992), 276–341.

76. Maurice Montuclard, "Église et partis," in *Les chrétiens et la politique*, 169.

77. Quoted in Gaston Fessard, "Le christianisme des chrétiens progressistes," *Études* 260 (January 1949): 74, 76.

78. Fessard, "Le christianisme des chrétiens progressistes," 75.

79. Fessard, "Le christianisme des chrétiens progressistes," 90.

80. Fessard, "Le christianisme des chrétiens progressistes," 90; Gaston Fessard to Henri de Lubac, 22 November 1948, AFCJ, Fonds Fessard, 73/3.

81. Fessard, "Le christianisme des chrétiens progressistes," 77. Emphasis in original.

82. Fessard, "Le christianisme des chrétiens progressistes," 78.

83. Fessard, "Le christianisme des chrétiens progressistes," 81.

84. On Maydieu, see Tranvouez, *Catholiques et communistes,* chap. 11. Serrand, writing under the pseudonym "Christianus," was the primary editorialist for *La Vie intellectuelle.*

85. Fessard, "Le christianisme des chrétiens progressistes," 82–83.

86. A. J. Maydieu and A. Z. Serrand, "À propos des chrétiens progressistes," *La Vie intellectuelle* (March 1949): 207–8.

87. Maydieu and Serrand, "À propos des chrétiens progressistes," 217.

88. Maydieu and Serrand, "À propos des chrétiens progressistes," 216.

89. Maydieu and Serrand, "À propos des chrétiens progressistes," 212.

90. Maydieu and Serrand, "À propos des chrétiens progressistes," 212.

91. Maydieu and Serrand, "À propos des chrétiens progressistes," 213.

92. Maydieu and Serrand, "À propos des chrétiens progressistes," 216.

93. Jeunesse de l'Église to Cardinal Guerry, 15 May 1953, APDF, Fonds Chenu (V-772), General Correspondence, 6.

94. See *Acta Apostolicae Sedis,* vol. 41 (Vatican City: Typis Polyglottis Vaticanis, 1949), 334.

95. Jeunesse de l'Église to Cardinal Guerry, 3.

96. Marie-Dominique Chenu, *Pour une théologie du travail* (Paris: Seuil, 1955), 28. This essay was first published in *Esprit* in 1952.

97. Chenu, *Pour une théologie du travail,* 29, 30.

98. Marie-Dominique Chenu, "Réflexions chrétiens sur la vérité de la matière," *Esprit* (May-June 1948), reprinted in Chenu, *La parole de Dieu,* vol. 2: *L'Évangile dans le temps* (Paris: Cerf, 1964), 448.

99. Marie-Dominique Chenu, "Matérialisme et spiritualisme," *Économie et humanisme* (March–April, 1948), reprinted in *Parole de dieu,* 464.

100. Chenu, "Le devenir social" (1947), reprinted in *Pour une théologie du travail,* 104. This was originally a talk that Chenu delivered at the 1947 Semaine sociale.

101. Chenu, *Pour une théologie du travail,* 36, 35.

102. Chenu, *Pour une théologie du travail,* 37.

103. Chenu took up this theme in a number of essays. In addition to the article cited below, see "St. Dominique et le communisme," *La Vie intellectuelle* 52 (October 10, 1937): 31–34; "La condition humaine du prêtre au moyen âge," *Esprit* (December 1959): 725–28.

104. Chenu, "Le devenir social," 89.

105. Chenu, "Le devenir social," 101.

106. Chenu, *Un théologien en liberté,* 171–72.

107. On the Vatican reaction to these cases, see Giuliana Chamedes, *A Twentieth-Century Crusade: The Vatican's Battle to Remake Christian Europe* (Cambridge, MA: Harvard University Press, 2019): 241–48; Chenaux, *L'Église catholique et le communisme,* 205–36; Peter Kent, *The Lonely Cold War of Pius XII* (Montreal: McGill-Queen's University Press, 2002), chap. 18.

108. Kosicki, *Catholics on the Barricades*, 178–88.

109. René d'Ouince laid out these concerns in "Les catholiques et l'Appel de Stockholm," *Études* 266 (July-August 1950): 106–20. On the Catholic response to the Stockholm Appeal, see Chenaux, *L'Église catholique et le communisme*, 182–190; Kosicki, *Catholics on the Barricades*, chap. 8.

110. Chenu, *Un théologien en liberté*, 162–65.

111. Marie-Dominique Chenu, "Chretienté ou mission? À propos des 'Mouvements de la paix,'" *La Vie intellectuelle* (June 1950), reprinted *Parole de Dieu*, 255, 256. While *Vie intellectuelle* did not sign onto the Stockholm Appeal, the journal printed Chenu's defense alongside its own demurral.

112. Chenu, "Chretienté ou mission?," 258.

113. See the letters (including from Joliot-Curie) and invitations in APDF, Fonds Chenu (V-772), 7 and 8; Sabine Rousseau, *La colombe et le napalm: Des chrétiens français contre les guerres d'Indochine et du Vietnam, 1945–1975* (Paris: CNRS, 2002), 91.

114. See Rousseau, *La colombe et le napalm*, 68–70.

115. "La Quinzaine: Position et projets" (report for Bishop Feltin, dated 1951), APDF, Fonds Chenu (V-772), 7.

116. Darcie Fontaine singles out the role of the "progressive Christians" and the Mission de France in particular (*Decolonizing Christianity*, esp. 20–21, 70–91, 125–34). On Catholic opposition to the war in Indochina, see Rousseau, *La colombe et le napalm*.

117. See, for instance, "La vérité contre l'amour," *La Quinzaine* 2 (December 1950): 1–2; "La paix chrétienne," *La Quinzaine* 12 (May 1951): 16; "Notre conscience n'accepte pas la guerre du Viet Nam pour défendre la 'civilisation chrétienne,'" *La Quinzaine* 56 (May 1953): 7.

118. "1er Congrès de 'la Quinzaine.' Rapport du R. P. Chenu," APDF, Fonds Chenu (V-772), 7.

119. Apostolus [Chenu], "Le chrétien engagé et le prêtre," *La Quinzaine* (October 15, 1952), APDF, Fonds Chenu (V-772), 7; Chenu, "Dossier politique," APDF, Fonds Chenu (V-772), 8, p. 10.

120. Apostolus [Chenu], "Le chrétien engagé et le prêtre."

121. Chenu, "1er Congrès de 'la Quinzaine.'"

122. Chenu, "Le chrétien engagé et le prêtre."

123. Chenu, "Dossier politique," 26.

124. Chenu, "1er Congrès de 'la Quinzaine.'"

125. Chenu, "1er Congrès de 'la Quinzaine.'"

126. Hans Boersma points out that despite Chenu's incarnational theology and his critique of the separation between the natural and supernatural orders, his work sometimes appeared "to reintroduce a certain dualism through the back door," largely because of his classically Thomist commitment to the autonomy of the natural order. See *Nouvelle Théologie and Sacramental Ontology: A Return to Mystery* (Oxford: Oxford University Press, 2009), 144–48. Joseph Komonchak has made similar observations, noting Chenu's frequent appeals to the principle of autonomy and showing how this approach was at odds with de Lubac's. See "Returning from Exile: Catholic Theology in the 1930s," in *The Twentieth*

Century: A Theological Overview, ed. Gregory Baum, 35–48 (Maryknoll, NY: Orbis, 1991).

127. Yves Congar, "Mentalité de 'droite' et intégrisme," *La Vie intellectuelle* (June 1950): 656–57.

128. "Avis de l'A.C.A. sur la Quinzaine," appended to letter from Cardinal Feltin to Jacques Chatagner, 25 November 1952, APDF, Fonds Chenu (V-772), General Correspondence, Dossier "Condemnation de *Quinzaine.*"

129. "Avis de l'A.C.A. sur la Quinzaine."

130. Marie-Dominique Chenu, "L'Église fait-elle de la politique?," *La Quinzaine* 29 (February 15, 1952): 16.

131. Chenu, "L'Église fait-elle de la politique?," 16.

132. Marie-Dominique Chenu, "'Civique' ou 'politique'?" (June 15, 1958), reprinted in *Parole de Dieu,* 614, 612.

133. Jean Daniélou, "Religion et politique" (undated, but likely from the 1950s), AFCJ, Fonds Jean Daniélou, H Dan 47/1, p. 1.

134. Daniélou, "Religion et politique," 7.

135. Daniélou, "Religion et politique," 13

136. Daniélou, "Religion et politique," 11.

137. Daniélou, "Religion et politique," 5.

138. Daniélou, "Religion et politique," 12.

6. The Drama of Atheist Humanism and the Politics of History

1. Fessard presentation notes, Conference on Humanism and Existentialism, Institut d'études italiennes, 27 October 1948, AFCJ, Fonds Gaston Fessard, 4/23bis.

2. Fessard presentation notes. Emphasis added.

3. See, for instance, Gary Gutting, *French Philosophy in the Twentieth Century* (Cambridge: Cambridge University Press, 2001), whose section on existentialism includes chapters on Sartre, de Beauvoir, and Merleau-Ponty. Mark Poster's *Existential Marxism in Postwar France: From Sartre to Althusser* (Princeton, NJ: Princeton University Press, 1975), and Ethan Kleinberg's *Generation Existential: Heidegger's Philosophy in France, 1927–1961* (Ithaca, NY: Cornell University Press, 2005) likewise devote little space to the Catholic engagement with existentialism and phenomenology.

4. Jean Daniélou, "La vie intellectuelle en France: Communisme, existentialisme, christianisme," *Études* 246 (July–August 1945): 249–50.

5. Jean Daniélou, "La vie intellectuelle en France," 251.

6. Fessard presentation notes.

7. In this respect, my work builds on Edward Baring, *Converts to the Real: Catholicism and the Making of Continental Philosophy* (Cambridge, MA: Harvard University Press, 2019), and Stefanos Geroulanos, *An Atheism That Is Not Humanist Emerges in French Thought* (Stanford, CA: Stanford University Press, 2010).

8. Much of the recent theological scholarship on *Surnaturel* is written from a Thomist perspective and criticizes de Lubac's thesis. See Lawrence Feingold, *The*

Natural Desire to See God According to St. Thomas Aquinas and His Inter-preters (Ave Maria, FL: Sapientia, 2010); Steven A. Long, *Natura Pura: On the Recovery of Nature in the Doctrine of Grace* (New York: Fordham University Press, 2010). A more balanced account is *Surnaturel: A Controversy at the Heart of Twentieth-Century Thomistic Thought,* ed. Serge-Thomas Bonino, trans. Robert Williams and Matthew Levering (Ave Maria, FL: Sapientia, 2009). For an Augustinian reading, see David Grummett, "De Lubac, Grace, and the Pure Nature Debate," *Modern Theology* 31, no. 1 (January 2015): 123–46. My own view aligns with Grummett's, but I also believe that de Lubac's Augustinianism was modified by the influence of his reading of the Greek Fathers and by contemporary intellectual developments in France. On the influence of the Greek Fathers in particular, see John Milbank, *The Suspended Middle: Henri de Lubac and the Debate Concerning the Supernatural* (Grand Rapids, MI: Eerdmans, 2005), 16.

9. See Gutting, *French Philosophy,* 40–48; Kleinberg, *Generation Existential,* 5–6; Vincent Descombes, *Modern French Philosophy,* trans. L. Scott-Fox and J. M. Harding (Cambridge: Cambridge University Press, 1980), 9.

10. Michael Roth, *Knowing and History: Appropriations of Hegel in Twentieth-Century France* (Ithaca, NY: Cornell University Press, 1988), 43, 84, 96. Fessard is likewise overlooked in the more recent study by Bruce Bauch, *French Hegel: From Surrealism to Postmodernism* (New York: Routledge, 2003). The exception to this rule is Geroulanos, *An Atheism That Is Not Humanist,* esp. 146–55.

11. Alexandre Kojève to Gaston Fessard, 26 June 1935, in *Gabriel Marcel–Gaston Fessard: Correspondance (1934–1971),* ed. Henri de Lubac, Marie Rougier, and Michel Sales (Paris: Beauchesne, 1985), 84.

12. See, for instance, Poster, *Existential Marxism,* chap. 1; Kleinberg, *Generation Existential,* chap. 3.

13. On the role of theological questions in nineteenth-century Hegelianism, see Warren Breckman, *Marx, the Young Hegelians, and the Origins of Radical Social Theory: Dethroning the Self* (Cambridge: Cambridge University Press, 1999); John Edward Toews, *Hegelianism: The Path Toward Dialectical Humanism, 1805–1941* (Cambridge: Cambridge University Press, 1980). On the role of theology in twentieth-century Hegelianism, see Peter Eli Gordon, *Rosenzweig and Heidegger: Between Judaism and German Philosophy* (Berkeley: University of California Press, 2003), chap. 2.

14. Aimé Patri, quoted in Poster, *Existential Marxism,* 34.

15. Alexandre Kojève, *Introduction to the Reading of Hegel,* ed. Allan Bloom, and trans. James H. Nichols (New York: Basic Books, 1969), 11–12.

16. Kojève, *Introduction to the Reading of Hegel,* 19.

17. Kojève, *Introduction to the Reading of Hegel,* 29.

18. Kojève, *Introduction to the Reading of Hegel,* 20.

19. Geroulanos, *An Atheism That Is Not Humanist,* chap. 3.

20. For Fessard's account of his introduction to Hegel, see "Originalité de la philosophie de Hegel et sa signification actuelle" (1947), AFCJ, Fonds Fessard,

29/G, p. 1; see also Michel Sales, *Gaston Fessard (1897–1978): Génèse d'une pensée* (Brussels: Culture et Vérité, 1997), 121.

21. Fessard, "Originalité de la philosophie de Hegel," 6.

22. Fessard, "Originalité de la philosophie de Hegel," 8. Sales makes much of this analogy in *Gaston Fessard (1897–1978)*, 120–21.

23. Fessard, "Originalité de la philosophie de Hegel," 8; Gaston Fessard, "Hegel, peut-il être baptisé?" (1961), AFCJ, Fonds Fessard, 19.1/b, p. 12.

24. See Gaston Fessard to Henri de Lubac, 23 July 1934, and 8 November 1934, AFCJ, Fonds Fessard, 73/C. On Fessard's differences with Kojève, see also Ana Petrache, *Gaston Fessard, un chrétien de rite dialectique?* (Paris: Cerf, 2017), 50–53, 98–101.

25. See the letters from Fessard's superior and the ecclesiastical censor concerning a commentary on Hegel that Fessard had authored in 1930, AFCJ, Fonds Fessard, 29/E; Gaston Fessard, *Hegel, le christianisme et l'histoire*, ed. Michel Sales (Paris: Presses Universitaires de France, 1990), 9n4. This volume includes many of the writings on Hegel that Fessard was unable to publish during his lifetime.

26. Kojève's review is reprinted in *Gabriel Marcel–Gaston Fessard*, 510–11. Emphasis in original.

27. See Raymond Aron, *Mémoires* (Paris: Julliard, 1983), 523; *Gabriel Marcel–Gaston Fessard*, 84n4.

28. Fessard, "Notes préparatoires, à une intervention au cours de la dernière 'Leçon' d'A. Kojeve à l'École des Hautes Études" (May 1939), Fonds Fessard, 29/E, p. 6.

29. Alexandre Kojève, "Christianisme et communisme," *Critique* 3–4 (1946): 308.

30. Kojève, "Christianisme et communisme," 308.

31. Kojève, "Christianisme et communisme," 308–9

32. Kojève, "Christianisme et communisme," 309.

33. Alexandre Kojève, "Hegel, Marx et le christianisme," *Critique* 3–4 (1946): 345.

34. Fessard similarly privileged Hegel's *Logic* over the *Phenomenology*: see Fessard, "Notes préparatoires."

35. Kojève, "Hegel, Marx et le christianisme," 351.

36. Kojève, "Hegel, Marx et le christianisme," 353.

37. Kojève, "Hegel, Marx et le christianisme," 356. The precise nature of Kojève's politics has been much debated. For a persuasive argument against reading Kojève as a Marxist, see Geroulanos, *An Atheism That Is Not Humanist Emerges in French Thought*, chap. 3. Whatever the idiosyncrasies of Kojève's own politics and vision of the end of history, it seems clear that at the very least many of his contemporaries perceived him as a Marxist.

38. Jean Verlhac and Maurice Caveing, "Une opération R.P.F.: L'article du R. P. Fessard," *Position* (March 1949), in AFCJ, Fonds Fessard, 5/28.

39. Kojève, "Hegel, Marx et le christianisme," 365.

40. Kojève, "Hegel, Marx et le christianisme," 366.

41. Jean Hyppolite, *Genèse et structure de la Phénoménologie de l'esprit de Hegel* (Paris: Aubier, 1946).

42. Gaston Fessard, "Deux interprètes de la Phénoménologie de Hegel: Jean Hyppolite et Alexandre Kojève," *Études* 255 (December 1947): 369.

43. Fessard, "Deux interprètes de la Phénoménologie de Hegel," 370, 370n1. In the second and third instances, Fessard is quoting a recent communist critique of Kojève.

44. Fessard argued that Protestant subjectivism had prevented Hegel from effecting a true synthesis between the subjective and objective—something only the Catholic idea of the mystical body of Christ could achieve. See Fessard, "Pourquoi je ne suis pas hégélien," 17 January 1958, AFCJ, Fonds Fessard, 19/1/b; Fessard, "Hegel, peut-il être baptisé?"; Sales, *Gaston Fessard*, 122.

45. Gaston Fessard, "Hegel et la philosophie contemporaine," AFCJ, Fonds Fessard, 29/3, 11.

46. Edward Baring, "Humanist Pretensions: Catholics, Communists, and Sartre's Struggle for Existentialism in Postwar France," *Modern Intellectual History* 7, no. 3 (2010): 582–83.

47. On Sartre's political evolution, see Poster, *Existential Marxism;* Thomas Flynn, *Sartre and Marxist Existentialism* (Chicago: University of Chicago Press, 1984).

48. Jean-Paul Sartre, *Existentialism Is a Humanism,* trans. Carol Macomber (New Haven, CT: Yale University Press, 2007), 17. On the Marxist critique, see Poster, *Existential Marxism,* 109–34. The Catholic response is exemplified by Jeanne Mercier, "Le ver dans le fruit," *Études* 244 (February 1945): 232–49.

49. Sartre, *Existentialism Is a Humanism,* 52, 37.

50. Sartre, *Existentialism Is a Humanism,* 24.

51. Sartre, *Existentialism Is a Humanism,* 49.

52. See Baring, "Humanist Pretensions," 592–95; Flynn, *Sartre and Marxist Existentialism,* 33–48. The political goals of the talk are evident from the examples Sartre uses to illustrate his argument, such as whether to join a communist or Catholic trade union (24) or whether to vote for the MRP or the PCF (47).

53. See the sources listed in note 3. Even Baring, in *Converts to the Real,* suggests that the role of Catholics in the development of French phenomenology largely came to an end after 1945.

54. See especially Baring, *Converts to the Real;* Jonathan Judaken, "Sisyphus' Progeny"; Samuel Moyn, *Origins of the Other: Levinas between Revelation and Ethics* (Ithaca, NY: Cornell University Press, 2005).

55. Baring, "Humanist Pretensions," 595–98.

56. Gabriel Marcel, *Philosophy of Existentialism,* trans. Manya Harari (New York: Citadel, 1956), 100.

57. Baring, *Converts to the Real,* 153.

58. Quoted in Baring, "Humanist Pretensions," 597.

59. The text is available in *La Phénoménologie: Journées d'études de la Société thomiste* (Juvisy: Cerf, 1932). Emmanuel Levinas and Gabriel Marcel were also invited: see Chenu to Maritain, 8 July 1932, CEJRM, Chenu-Maritain Correspondence. See also Christian Dupont, *Phenomenology in French Philosophy:*

Early Encounters (New York: Springer, 2014), 279–94; Baring, *Converts to the Real*, 8.

60. Yves de Montcheuil, "Une philosophie du devoir," *Nouvelle revue théologique* 59 (June 1932): 481–523; Gaston Fessard, "Une Phénomenologie de l'existence: La philosophie de M. Le Senne," *Recherches de science religieuse* 25 (April 1935): 131.

61. Gabriel Marcel to Gaston Fessard, 1 August 1934, *Gabriel Marcel–Gaston Fessard*, 69. On Marcel's break with Maritain, see *Gabriel Marcel–Gaston Fessard*, 74–82.

62. See Fessard's review of *Existentialisme chrétien*, an edited volume devoted to Gabriel Marcel, in *Études* 255 (October 1947): 122–24.

63. Gaston Fessard, "L'existentialisme et ses problèmes," (undated), AFCJ, Fonds Fessard, 4/23.

64. Fessard, *France, prends garde de perdre ta liberté* (Paris: Éditions du Témoignage Chrétien, 1946), 137.

65. Fessard, *France, prends garde*, 137, 138.

66. Fessard, *France, prends garde*, 165.

67. Daniélou, "Les catholiques face au marxisme et à l'existentialisme," *Travaux et documents du CCIF* (May 1946), AFCJ, Fonds Jean Daniélou, 47/2, p. 62; Daniélou, *Dialogues avec les marxistes, les existentialistes, les protestants, les juifs, l'hindouisme* (Paris: Le Portulan, 1948),100. For an earlier instance of Kierkegaard's Catholic reception in France, see Yves Congar, "Actualité de Kierkegaard," *La Vie intellectuelle* 32, no. 1 (1934): 9–34.

68. Daniélou, *Dialogues*, 103. Emphasis added.

69. Daniélou, *Dialogues*, 103.

70. See Baring, *Converts to the Real*, chap. 10.

71. The politico-theological significance of incarnation and transcendence would be central to the theory of secularization developed by Marcel Gauchet in *The Disenchantment of the World: A Political History of Religion*, trans. Oscar Burge (Princeton, NJ: Princeton University Press, 1997).

72. Maurice Merleau-Ponty, "Foi et bonne foi," *Les Temps modernes* 5 (February 1946): 777.

73. Jean Daniélou, "Transcendance et Incarnation," *Dieu vivant* 6 (1946): 95.

74. Daniélou, "Transcendance et Incarnation," 95.

75. Daniélou, "Transcendance et Incarnation," 95, 93, 95.

76. Daniélou, "Transcendance et Incarnation," 93.

77. Daniélou, "Transcendance et Incarnation," 92.

78. See Baring, *Converts to the Real*.

79. Jacques Maritain, *Court traité de l'existence et de l'existant* (Paris: Hartmann, 1964 [1947]), 9.

80. Étienne Gilson, *L'être et l'essence* (1948), quoted in Judaken, "Sisyphus's Progeny," 96 (emphasis added); Étienne Gilson, "Le thomisme et les philosophies existentielles," *La Vie intellectuelle* 13 (June 1945): 145.

81. Maritain, *Court traité*, 9; Gilson, "Le thomisme et les philosophies existentielles," 149.

82. Maritain, *Court traité*, 15.

83. Fessard's review of Joseph de Tonquédec's *Une philosophie existentielle: L'existence d'après Jaspers* exemplifies his objections to the Thomist approach. Fessard criticizes Tonquédec for simply "measuring the philosophy he attacks [Jaspers'] against his own traditional Thomism, as one compares a copy to the model" (*Études* 247 [November 1945]: 268–70).

84. Baring, *Converts to the Real,* chap. 3.

85. Martin Heidegger, "Letter on Humanism," in *Basic Writings,* ed. David Farrell Krell (New York: Harper, 2008), 253. See George Kovacs, *The Question of God in Heidegger's Phenomenology* (Evanston, IL: Northwestern University Press, 1990), 252; Baring, "Humanist Pretentions," 607.

86. See the discussion in Dominique Janicaud, *Heidegger en France,* vol. 1 (Paris: Albin Michel, 2001), 140–43.

87. This article was mistakenly attributed to Hugo Rahner, Karl's brother: "Introduction au concept de philosophie existentiale chez Heidegger," *Recherches de science religieuse* 30 (1940): 152–71. Rahner's Heideggerian Thomism was one of the most important developments in twentieth-century Catholic theology and indicates that by no means all Thomists were hostile to Heidegger's thought, as the cases of Max Müller and Edith Stein likewise attest. On Heidegger's influence on German Catholic theology, see Judith Wolfe, *Heidegger and Theology* (London: Bloomsbury, 2014), 128–31, 140–42, 149–54; Thomas Sheehan, *Karl Rahner: The Philosophical Foundations* (Athens: Ohio University Press, 1987), chap. 8.

88. On Fessard's role in the translation, see Roger Munier's letters to Fessard, AFCJ, Fonds Fessard, 33; Janicaud, *Heidegger en France,* 145.

89. See Robert Scherer's report on the visit, 20 September 1947, AFCJ, Fonds Henri Bouillard, 3/40bis.

90. See Bouillard's account of the visit, AFCJ, Fonds Bouillard, 3/40bis. On "anthropological" versus "ontological" readings of Heidegger, see Kleinberg, *Generation Existential,* esp. 17–18.

91. Scherer report, AFCJ, Fonds Bouillard, 3/40bis.

92. See Samuel Moyn, *Christian Human Rights* (Philadelphia: University of Pennsylvania Press, 2015); Marco Duranti, *The Conservative Human Rights Revolution: European Identity, Transnational Politics, and the Origins of the European Convention* (New York: Oxford University Press, 2017); Linde Lindkvist, *Religious Freedom and the Universal Declaration of Human Rights* (Cambridge: Cambridge University Press, 2017), esp. 32–60; Sarah Shortall and Daniel Steinmetz-Jenkins, eds., *Christianity and Human Rights Reconsidered* (Cambridge: Cambridge University Press, 2020).

93. Fessard presentation notes.

94. Gaston Fessard, "Réflexions en conclusion des classes sur Hegel et Heidegger," 29 May 1943, AFCJ, Fonds Fessard, 29/G, p. 3.

95. Gaston Fessard, "Théologie et histoire: À propos du temps de la conversion d'Israël," *Dieu vivant* 8 (1947): 50.

96. Fessard, "Théologie et histoire," 53. Emphasis in original

97. Fessard, "Réflexions en conclusion des classes sur Hegel et Heidegger," 5.

98. Jean Daniélou, *Dialogues,* 64.

99. On the genesis of this antihumanism, especially considered in relation to the postwar "humanism" moment, see Geroulanos, *An Atheism That Is Not Humanist.*

100. "Discussion sur le péché," *Dieu vivant* 4 (1945): 83–133. The entire discussion is reproduced in Georges Bataille, *Discussion sur le péché,* ed. Michel Surya (Paris: Lignes, 2010).

101. "Discussion sur le péché," 93.

102. "Discussion sur le péché," 93.

103. "Discussion sur le péché," 93–94.

104. "Discussion sur le péché," 95.

105. Henri de Lubac, "La recherche d'un Homme Nouveau," reprinted in *Affrontements mystiques* (Paris: Éditions du Témoignage Chrétien, 1950), 46.

106. De Lubac, "La recherche d'un Homme Nouveau," 45 (de Lubac is here quoting Ferdinand Alquié); Jean-Paul Sartre, *Being and Nothingness,* trans. H. E. Barnes (New York: Washington Square Press, 1992), 174.

107. De Lubac, "La recherche d'un Homme Nouveau," 47, 89. Despite these affinities with existentialism, de Lubac always refused the label for himself. See *Mémoire sur l'occasion de mes écrits,* 73.

108. Henri de Lubac, *Surnaturel: Études historiques* (Paris: Lethielleux, 2010 [1946]), 107. David Grummett makes this comparison to the "state of nature" in "De Lubac, Grace, and the Pure Nature Debate," 131.

109. Henri de Lubac, "Remarques sur l'histoire du mot 'surnaturel,'" *Nouvelle revue théologique* 61 (1934): 364; see also De Lubac, *Surnaturel,* 153.

110. De Lubac, *Surnaturel,* 488–89. Emphasis in original.

111. De Lubac here adopts the concept of "deification" (*theosis*), which is central to Orthodox theology. See Adam G. Cooper, *Naturally Human, Supernaturally God: Deification in Pre-Conciliar Catholicism* (Minneapolis, MN: Fortress Press, 2014), 151–68.

112. De Lubac, *Surnaturel,* 487, 493.

113. The report was published as *Human Rights: Comments and Interpretations,* ed. UNESCO (London: Wingate, 1949). It seems to have ultimately had little effect on the drafting of the UDHR, however. See Mark Goodale, ed. *Letters to the Contrary: A Curated History of the UNESCO Human Rights Survey* (Stanford, CA: University of Stanford Press, 2018), 25.

114. Maritain, "Introduction," in *Human Rights: Comments and Interpretations,* 9.

115. Maritain, *Man and the State* (Washington D.C.: Catholic University of America Press, 1998 [1951]), 110–11.

116. Maritain, *Man and the State,* 96–97.

117. Maritain, *Man and the State,* 159, 110. Emphasis in original.

118. John Milbank makes a similar argument in *The Suspended Middle,* 20. For an example of the critique of *Surnaturel* for denying the gratuity of grace, see Charles Boyer, "Nature pur et surnaturel dans le 'Surnaturel' du Père de Lubac," *Gregorianum* 28 (1947): 379–95.

119. De Lubac, *Surnaturel,* 107.

120. De Lubac, *Surnaturel,* 107–8, 494.

121. Wendy Brown, "'The Most We Can Hope For . . .': Human Rights and the Politics of Fatalism," *South Atlantic Quarterly* 103, no. 2/3 (2004): 451–63; Talal Asad, *Formations of the Secular: Christianity, Islam, Modernity* (Stanford, CA: Stanford University Press, 2003), 127–58.

122. Many Catholics, including at the Vatican, were in fact deeply suspicious of the UDHR. See Duranti, *Conservative Human Rights Revolution*, 299.

123. They include, most notably, John Milbank and William Cavanaugh. See, for instance, the critique of human rights discourse in William Cavanaugh, *Torture and Eucharist: Theology, Politics, and the Body of Christ* (Oxford: Blackwell, 1998).

124. Jacques Maritain, "On the Philosophy of Human Rights," in *Human Rights: Comments and Interpretations,* 77; Benedict XVI, "Address to the General Assembly of the United Nations" (April 18, 2008).

125. See, for instance, the caveats in *Gaudium et Spes* (December 7, 1965), §41.

126. De Lubac, "La recherche d'un Homme Nouveau," 75.

127. See Anthony O'Mahoney, "Catholic Theological Perspectives on Islam at the Second Vatican Council," *New Blackfriars* 88 (July 2007): 385–98; Jerrold Seigel, *Between Cultures: Europe and Its Others in Five Exemplary Lives* (Philadelphia: University of Pennsylvania Press, 2016), 115–51.

128. On Moré's "conversion," see Étienne Fouilloux, "Une vision eschatologique du christianisme: *Dieu vivant* (1945–1955)," *Revue d'histoire de l'Église de France* 57 (1971): 51.

129. On the composition of these meetings, see Madeleine Davy to Jean Daniélou, 7 November 1941, AFCJ, Fonds Jean Daniélou, 49/B. They appear to have involved about thirty men and seven or eight women.

130. The structure is explained in the journal's "organizing statement," which was signed by Massignon, Moré, Daniélou, and Flamand (the publisher), AFCJ, Fonds Daniélou, 49/B.

131. Fouilloux, "Une vision eschatologique," 49.

132. "Liminaire," *Dieu vivant* 1 (1945): 9.

133. "Liminaire," 5.

134. "Liminaire," 5.

135. Jean Daniélou, "Transcendance de Dieu," *Dieu vivant* 12 (1951): 21.

136. "Liminaire," 9.

137. "Liminaire," 6.

138. "Liminaire," *Dieu vivant* 2 (1945): 10, 8.

139. "Liminaire," *Dieu vivant* 1 (1945): 9.

140. Walter Benjamin, "On the Concept of History," in *Selected Writings,* vol. 4 (Cambridge, MA: Belknap/Harvard University Press, 2003), 395.

141. "Liminaire," *Dieu vivant* 1 (1945): 10. Emphasis in original.

142. "Liminaire," *Dieu vivant* 2 (1945): 10.

143. Marcel Moré to Jean Daniélou, 3 September 1951, AFCJ, Fonds Daniélou, 2/3.

144. This is according to Étienne Fouilloux' calculation in "Une vision eschatologique," 66. See, for instance, Hans Urs von Balthasar, "Kierkegaard et Nietzsche," *Dieu vivant* 1 (1945): 53–80.

145. Karl Jaspers, "L'homme se produit lui-même," *Dieu vivant* 9 (1947): 77–102; Karl Barth, "Le problème de la religion en théologie," *Dieu vivant* 9 (1947): 47–74; Erik Peterson, "Existentialisme et théologie protestante," *Dieu vivant* 10 (1948): 45–48; Martin Buber, "Le message hassidique," *Dieu vivant* 2 (1945): 13–33; "Autour de la philosophie de l'existence," *Dieu vivant* 6 (1946): 121–26; Gabriel Marcel, "Autour de Heidegger," *Dieu vivant* 2 (1945): 89–102.

146. "Liminaire," *Dieu vivant* 1 (1945): 10. See also Enrico Castelli, "L'univers existentiel de l'histoire," *Dieu vivant* 15 (1950): 51–62.

147. Fessard, "Théologie et histoire," 40.

148. "Liminaire," *Dieu vivant* 10 (1948): 12.

149. "Liminaire," *Dieu vivant* 1 (1945): 10.

150. Fessard, "Théologie et histoire," 40.

151. Henri-Marie Féret, *L'Apocalypse de Saint Jean* (Paris: Corréa, 1943). He published a version of this as "Apocalypse, histoire et eschatologie chrétienne," *Dieu vivant* 2 (1945): 117–34. For an excellent overview of the broader debate on the theology of history, see Joseph S. Flipper, *Between Apocalypse and Eschaton: History and Eternity in Henri de Lubac* (Minneapolis, MN: Fortress Press, 2015), 57–88.

152. Féret, *L'Apocalypse de Saint Jean*, 328.

153. Joseph Huby, "Autour de l'apocalypse," *Dieu vivant* 5 (1946): 128–29.

154. Fessard made this argument much more explicitly in later works such as *De l'actualité historique*, vol. 2 (Paris: Desclée de Brouwer, 1960), 257–303.

155. Fessard, "Théologie et histoire," 58. Emphasis in original.

156. Fessard introduced this new dialectic in "Le mystère de la société: Recherches sur le sens de l'histoire," *Recherches de science religieuse* 35 (1948): 5–54, 161–225.

157. On gender complementarity and republicanism, see Judith Surkis, *Sexing the Citizen: Morality and Masculinity in France, 1870–1920* (Ithaca, NY: Cornell University Press, 2006); Camille Robcis, *The Law of Kinship: Anthropology, Psychoanalysis, and the Family in France* (Ithaca, NY: Cornell University Press, 2013).

158. Here we see the beginnings of Fessard's engagement with the structuralist anthropology of Claude Lévi-Strauss, which would develop more fully in the 1960s. Like Lévi-Strauss, Fessard invoked the universality of the incest taboo as the nexus between nature and culture, or in Fessard's formulation, between the family and the social unit.

159. Fessard, "Théologie et histoire," 57.

160. Fessard, "Théologie et histoire," 62.

161. See Féret-Fessard correspondence, APDF, Fonds Féret (V-810), 03/3.

162. Jean Daniélou, *Essai sur le mystère de l'histoire* (Paris: Cerf, 2011 [1955]), 30.

163. Daniélou, *Essai sur le mystère de l'histoire*, 30, 31.

164. See, for instance, "Le martyr et l'église," *Dieu vivant* 5 (1946): 17–31; "Le traitement de la rage par les Elkésaites d'après Hippolyte," *Recherches de science religieuse* 34 (1947): 232–38; "Existentialisme et théologie protestante," *Dieu vivant* 10 (1948): 45–48; Le problème du nationalisme dans le christianisme des premiers siècles," *Dieu vivant* 22 (1952): 87–97; "L'église," *Dieu vivant* 25 (1953): 99–112.

165. Erik Peterson, *Der Monotheismus als politisches Problem: Ein Beitrag zur Geschichte der politischen Theologie im Imperium Romanum* (Leipzig: Hegner, 1935). On the dispute between Peterson and Schmitt, see György Geréby, "Political Theology Versus Theological Politics: Erik Peterson and Carl Schmitt," *New German Critique* 35, no. 3 (2008): 7–33.

166. De Lubac was, in fact, critical of *Dieu vivant* for not stressing the social dimension of eschatology enough. See Marcel Moré to Henri de Lubac, 5 June 1946, CAEHL, 73917.

167. Henri de Lubac, *Paradoxes* (Paris: Éditions du Livre Français, 1946), 103.

168. De Lubac, *Paradoxes*, 115.

169. See Benjamin, "On the Concept of History."

170. Walter Benjamin, *The Arcades Project,* trans. Howard Eiland and Kevin McLaughlin (Cambridge, MA: Belknap / Harvard University Press, 1999), 462. On the theologico-political dimension of Benjamin's critique of historicism, see Stéphane Mosès, "The Theological-Political Model of History in the Thought of Walter Benjamin," *History and Memory* 1, no. 2 (1989): 5–33.

171. This term comes from Michel Foucault, who used it to describe his approach in *Discipline and Punish: The Birth of the Prison,* trans. Alan Sheridan (New York: Vintage, 1975), 30–31. It has been taken up more recently by historians and is the animating principle behind the journal *History of the Present.*

172. On the relationship between de Lubac and de Certeau, see François Dosse, *Michel de Certeau: Le marcheur blessé* (Paris: La Découverte, 2002), 47–58; Brenna Moore, "How to Awaken the Dead: Michel de Certeau, Henri de Lubac, and the Instabilities of the Past and the Present," *Spiritus* 12 (2012): 172–79. For examples of de Certeau's influence on the "linguistic turn," see Joan Scott, "The Evidence of Experience," *Critical Inquiry* 17, no. 4 (Summer 1991): 773–97; Judith Surkis, "When Was the Linguistic Turn? A Genealogy," *American Historical Review* 117, no. 3 (June 2012): 700–722, esp. 717.

173. "Liminaire," *Dieu vivant* 1 (1945): 10.

174. On the political power of such "untimely" reflections, which disrupt the presumption of a linear chronology, see Wendy Brown, "Untimeliness and Punctuality: Critical Theory in Dark Times," in *Edgework: Critical Essays on Knowledge and Politics* (Princeton, NJ: Princeton University Press, 2005), 1–16; Gary Wilder, *Freedom Time: Negritude, Decolonization, and the Future of the World* (Durham, NC: Duke University Press, 2015).

175. Henri Bouillard, *Conversion et grâce chez saint Thomas d'Aquin* (Paris: Aubier, 1944). On the controversy elicited by the book, see Étienne Fouilloux, "Henri Bouillard et Saint Thomas d'Aquin (1941–1951)," *Recherches de science religieuse* 97 (2009): 173–83.

7. The Death and Resurrection of the *Nouvelle Théologie*

1. This description comes from the Dominican Réginald Garrigou-Lagrange. See Étienne Fouilloux, *Une Église en quête de liberté: La pensée catholique française entre modernisme et Vatican II (1914–1962)* (Paris: Desclée de Brouwer, 1998), 283.

2. The literature on *ressourcement* is vast, but see especially: Jon Kirwan, *An Avant-garde Theological Generation: The* Nouvelle Théologie *and the French Crisis of Modernity* (Oxford: Oxford University Press, 2018); Gabriel Flynn and Paul D. Murray, eds., *Ressourcement: A Movement for Renewal in Twentieth-Century Catholic Theology* (Oxford: Oxford University Press, 2012); Jürgen Mettepenningen, *Nouvelle Théologie—New Theology: Inheritor of Modernism, Prescursor of Vatican II* (London: T&T Clark, 2010); Hans Boersma, *Nouvelle Théologie and Sacramental Ontology: A Return to Mystery* (Oxford: Oxford University Press, 2009).

3. The first installment was Bouillard's *Conversion et grâce chez saint Thomas d'Aquin* (1944), which, along with de Lubac's *Surnaturel,* would become a primary target for critics of the *nouvelle théologie.*

4. On the liturgical movement, see Keith F. Pecklers, "*Ressourcement* and the Renewal of Catholic Liturgy: On Celebrating the New Rite," in Flynn and Murray, eds., *Ressourcement,* 318–32; John Fenwick and Bryan Spinks, *Worship in Transition: The Twentieth Century Liturgical Movement* (New York: Continuum, 2005). On the revival of biblical studies, see Benedict Viviano, "The Renewal of Biblical Studies in France 1934–1954 as an Element in Theological *Ressourcement,*" in Flynn and Murray, eds., *Ressourcement,* 305–17.

5. Labourdette, Nicolas, and Bruckberger, eds., *Dialogue théologique. Pièces du débat entre "La Revue thomiste" d'une part et les R.R. P.P. de Lubac, Daniélou, Bouillard, Fessard, von Balthasar, S.J., d'autre part* (Saint-Maximin: Les Arcades, 1947), 96.

6. Jean Daniélou, "Les orientations présentes de la pensée religieuse," *Études* 249 (April 1946): 7.

7. Daniélou, "Les orientations présentes de la pensée religieuse," 14.

8. Daniélou, "Les orientations présentes de la pensée religieuse," 11.

9. Jean Daniélou to Henri de Lubac, 2 June 1947, CAEHL, 74086. Emphasis added.

10. Henri de Lubac to Gaston Fessard, 6 January 1946, AFCJ, Fonds Gaston Fessard, 73/3. On the Fourvière Affair, see Fouilloux, *Une Église en quête de liberté,* 279–94; Étienne Fouilloux, "Dialogue Théologique? (1946–1948)," in *Saint Thomas au XXe siècle,* ed. Serge-Thomas Bonino, 153–95 (Paris: Éditions Saint-Paul, 1994).

11. The article was labeled as such by fellow Dominicans, Louis-Bertrand Gillon and Paul Philippe (Fouilloux, *Une Église en quête de liberté,* 283).

12. The first use of the term appears in Pietro Parente, "Nuove tendenze teologiche," *L'Osservatore Romano,* February 9–10, 1942, 1.

13. Réginald Garrigou-Lagrange, "La nouvelle théologie où va-t-elle?" *Angelicum* 23 (1946): 144. Although it was attached to the late-1946 issue of *Angelicum,* the article was made public in February 1947.

14. Garrigou-Lagrange, "La nouvelle théologie où va-t-elle?," 143.

15. Michael Kerlin, "Reginald Garrigou-Lagrange: Defending the Faith from *Pascendi dominici gregis* to *Humani generis,*" *U.S. Catholic Historian* 25 (Winter 2007): 111.

16. Pius XII, *Humani Generis* (August 12, 1950), §14–15.

17. The encyclical did not mention anyone by name, but the Father General of the Jesuit order made clear who the primary targets were (de Lubac, Montcheuil, and Teilhard de Chardin) in his official explanation of *Humani Generis,* which was circulated to all French Jesuits. See Jean-Baptiste Janssens, "De executione Encyclicae 'Humani Generis,'" 11 February 1951, AFCJ, Fonds Henri Bouillard, 3/45.

18. See Henri de Lubac to Fr. Girardon, 17 July 1947, CAEHL, 74101. Here, de Lubac in fact claims that the text was disseminated by Montcheuil's critics in order to discredit him.

19. Garrigou-Lagrange, "La nouvelle théologie où va-t-elle?," 134.

20. Jacques Maritain to Charles Journet, 11 February 1947, in *Journet-Maritain Correspondance,* vol. 3 (Fribourg, Switzerland: Éditions Universitaires Fribourg Suisse, 1996), 525.

21. Charles Journet to Jacques Maritain, 25 May 1945, in *Journet-Maritain Correspondance,* 320.

22. Marie-Michel Labourdette, "Fermes propos," *Revue thomiste* 47 (1947): 16; Garrigou-Lagrange, "La nouvelle théologie où va-t-elle?," 136.

23. Gaston Fessard to Henri de Lubac, 7 November 1946, AFCJ, Fonds Fessard, 73/3; Gaston Fessard to Henri de Lubac, 4 January 1948, AFCJ, Fonds Fessard, 73/3.

24. Marie-Dominique Chenu to Bruno de Solages, 19 August 1946, CAEHL, 73929–73931.

25. Yves Congar, "Bulletin d'écclésiologie," *Revue des sciences philosophiques et théologiques* 31 (1947): 86.

26. Congar, "Bulletin d'écclésiologie," 87.

27. Congar, "Bulletin d'écclésiologie," 88.

28. Henri-Marie Féret, "L'impossible dialogue," 18–19 January 1950, APDF, Fonds Henri-Marie Féret (V-810), 303/3. See also the Fessard–de Lubac correspondence from February 1950, AFCJ, Fonds Fessard, 73/3. Féret even suggested that his own quarrel with Fessard in the pages of *Dieu vivant* might have been motivated by the Jesuit's anger at the Dominicans over Labourdette's critique in the *Revue thomiste.* See Henri-Marie Féret to Gaston Fessard, 24 April 1947, APDF, Fonds Féret, 303/3.

29. Henri de Lubac to Yves Congar, 27 February 1947, CAEHL, 74017. See also See Henri de Lubac to Gaston Fessard, February 1947, AFCJ, Fonds Fessard, 73/3.

30. Jean Lacroix to René d'Ouince, 17 March 1949, AFCJ, Fonds Fessard, 5/28.

31. See de Lubac's resignation letter, 26 February 1950, CAEHL, 74372.

32. Henri de Lubac, *Mémoire sur l'occasion de mes écrits* (Namur, Belgium: Culture et Vérité, 1989), 71–73.

33. Several letters in de Lubac's archive refer to "pressure" from outside the order at "the highest levels." See, for instance, Bernard de Gorostarzu to Henri de Lubac, 27 July 1948, CAEHL, 74189.

34. See the ACA's "Communiqué relatif à 'Jeunesse de l'Église," 14–16 October 1953, reprinted in Thierry Keck, *Jeunesse de l'Église, 1936–1955. Aux sources de la crise progressiste en France* (Paris: Karthala, 2004), 415.

35. Oscar Arnal, *Priests in Working-Class Blue: The History of the Worker-Priests (1945–1954)* (New York: Paulist, 1986), 154.

36. François Leprieur, *Quand Rome condamne: Dominicains et prêtres-ouvriers* (Paris: Cerf, 1989), 73.

37. See Congar's account in *Journal d'un théologien: 1946–1956* (Paris: Cerf, 2001), 232–72, and Féret's in APDF, Fonds Féret (V-810), 203.

38. Marie-Dominique Chenu, *Un théologien en liberté: Jacques Duquesne interroge le Père Chenu* (Paris: Le Centurion, 1975), 156–57.

39. Both quoted in Chenaux, *L'Église catholique et le communisme en Europe (1917–1989)* (Paris: Cerf, 2009), 195.

40. Quoted in Nora Beloff, "France and the Vatican," *The Observer*, February 28, 1954, APDF, Fonds Yves Congar (V-832), 400; Yves Congar to Rosaire Gagnebet, 4 December 1946, quoted in Fouilloux, *Une Église en quête de liberté*, 257.

41. Fouilloux, *Une Église en quête de liberté*, 260n45.

42. The crisis reached its apex in 1956, when *Civiltà Cattolica* published a vituperative review of *Integral Humanism*: Antonio Messineo, "L'umanenismo integrale," *Civilità Cattolica*, August 25, 1956, 449–63.

43. See Leprieur, *Quand Rome condamne*; Fouilloux, *Une église en quête de liberté*, 296–98.

44. On the sanctions against *Vraie et fausse réforme*, see Yves Congar, *Journal d'un théologien*, 181–222. On *Humani Generis*, see APDF, Fonds Congar (V-832), 400/9.

45. "Les Dominicains frappés par la nouvelle Inquisition," *L'Observateur d'aujourd'hui*, February 11, 1954, APDF, Fonds Yves Congar (V-832), 400/14, p. 5.

46. Jürgen Mettepenningen describes this as the "phase of the internationalization of the 'nouvelle théologie.'" See Mettepenningen, *Nouvelle Théologie—New Theology*, chap. 3.

47. See Mettepenningen, *Nouvelle Théologie—New Theology*, 117–25.

48. See Joseph Ratzinger, *Milestones: Memoirs, 1927–1977* (San Francisco: Ignatius, 1998), 97–98. Ratzinger also wrote the preface to the English translation of de Lubac's *Catholicism*.

49. On Alioune Diop, see Elizabeth Foster, *African and Catholic: Decolonization and the Transformation of the Church* (Cambridge, MA: Harvard University Press, 2019), 58–94. On Senghor, see Gary Wilder, *Freedom Time: Negritude, Decolonization, and the Future of the World* (Durham, NC: Duke University Press, 2015).

50. This argument is laid out in Léopold Sédar Senghor, *Pierre Teilhard de Chardin et la politique africaine* (Paris: Seuil, 1962). On Senghor's debt to Teilhard, see Wilder, *Freedom Time*, 225–36.

51. Pierre Teilhard de Chardin, *Le phénomène humain* (Paris: Seuil, 1955), 263. Emphasis in original.

52. Léopold Sédar Senghor, "La Négritude, comme culture des peuples noirs, ne saurait être dépassé," quoted in Wilder, *Freedom Time,* 51–52; Senghor, *Teilhard de Chardin et la politique africaine,* 33.

53. See Wilder, *Freedom Time,* esp. 133–43, 218–25; Frederick Cooper, *Citizenship between Empire and Nation: Remaking France and French Africa, 1945–1960* (Princeton, NJ: Princeton University Press, 2014), esp. 251–76, 290–301, 328–34.

54. On the role of international opinion in the Algerian War, see Matthew Connelly, *A Diplomatic Revolution: Algeria's Fight for Independence and the Origins of the Post–Cold War Era* (Oxford: Oxford University Press, 2002). On the role of Christians in the conflict, see Darcie Fontaine, *Decolonizing Christianity: Religion and the End of Empire in France and Algeria* (Cambridge: Cambridge University Press, 2016); André Nozière, *Algérie: Les chrétiens dans la guerre* (Paris: Cana, 2001).

55. Foster, *African Catholic,* 152–92.

56. De Lubac, *Mémoire sur l'occasion de mes écrits,* 117.

57. Quoted in Brian E. Daley, "Knowing God in History and in the Church: *Dei Verbum* and 'Nouvelle Théologie,'" in Flynn and Murray, eds., *Ressourcement,* 344.

58. De Lubac wrote five book-length defenses of Teilhard in the 1960s and 1970s, in addition to editing two volumes of his correspondence.

59. See especially Gerald O'Collins, "*Ressourcement* and Vatican II," in Flynn and Murray, eds., *Ressourcement,* 372–91; Daley, "Knowing God in History," 344–51; John O'Malley, *What Happened at Vatican II* (Cambridge, MA: Belknap/Harvard University Press, 2008), 63, 88–89, 147–48.

60. See O'Collins, "*Ressourcement* and Vatican II," 379–85.

61. Quoted in Joseph A. Komonchak, "*Humani Generis* and *Nouvelle Théologie,*" in Flynn and Murray, eds., *Ressourcement,* 155.

62. See Henri de Lubac, *Carnets du concile,* vol. 1 (Paris: Cerf, 2007), 77–78.

63. Quoted in Jared Wicks "Vatican II on Revelation—From behind the Scenes," *Theological Studies* 71, no. 3 (2010): 643.

64. On these alternative texts, see Wicks, "Vatican II on Revelation"; O'Collins, "*Ressourcement* and Vatican II," 379–81, 385–86.

65. Quoted in O'Malley, *What Happened at Vatican II,* 144.

66. Quoted in O'Malley, *What Happened at Vatican II,* 155–56.

67. Robert Rouquette, "Bilan du concile," *Études* 316 (January 1963): 104.

68. See Chenu, *Un théologien en liberté,* 173–89.

69. See Yves Congar, *Mon journal du concile,* vol. 2 (Paris: Cerf, 2002), 419, 421, 429–30; Rudolf Voderholzer, *Meet Henri de Lubac: His Life and Work,* trans. Michael J. Miller (San Francisco: Ignatius, 2008), 85.

70. *Gaudium et Spes* (December 7, 1965), §21.

71. On the content and significance of this draft, see Wicks, "Vatican II on Revelation," 647–49; O'Collins, "*Ressourcement* and Vatican II," 381–82.

72. In addition to the contributions already mentioned, Congar also played a role in drafting *Dei Verbum* (§21 and parts of chapter 2), *Gaudium et Spes* (§4),

Dignitatis Humanae (esp. the preface), *Presbyterorum Ordinis* (preface, §2–9, §12–14, and conclusion). For the full list, see Yves Congar, *Mon journal du concile,* 2:511. See also Étienne Fouilloux, "Comment devient-on expert à Vatican II? Le cas du Père Yves Congar," in *Le deuxième concile du Vatican (1959–1965),* 307–31 (Rome: École Française de Rome, 1989).

73. On the genesis of *Lumen Gentium,* see Giuseppe Ruggieri, "Beyond an Ecclesiology of Polemics: The Debate on the Church," in *History of Vatican II,* vol. 2, ed. Giuseppe Alberigo and Joseph A. Komonchak, 281–357 (Maryknoll, NY: Orbis, 1995–2006).

74. *Lumen Gentium* (21 November 1964), §8. Emphasis added.

75. Congar, *Mon journal du concile,* 511.

76. *Ad Gentes* (December 7, 1965), §9.

77. O'Malley, *What Happened at Vatican II,* 120.

78. See Gabriel Flynn, *Yves Congar's Vision of the Church in a World of Unbelief* (Aldershot, UK: Ashgate, 2004), 100–107; Jared Wicks, "Yves Congar's Doctrinal Service of the People of God," *Gregorianum* 84, no. 3 (2003): 499–550; Paul Murray, "Expanding Catholicity through Ecumenicity in the Work of Yves Congar: *Ressourcement,* Receptive Ecumenism, and Catholic Reform," in Flynn and Murrary, eds., *Ressourcement,* 457–81.

79. The debt to de Lubac is evident from a footnote to the second draft of the document, which paraphrased his 1953 book, *Méditation sur l'Église,* almost verbatim. See Paul McPartlan, "*Ressourcement,* Vatican II, and Eucharistic Ecclesiology," in Flynn and Murray, eds., *Ressourcement,* 392–93. John O'Malley argues that both "the form and substance" of *Lumen Gentium* were deeply indebted to de Lubac (*What Happened at Vatican II,* 163, 119).

80. Chenu, *Un théologien en liberté,* 182–83. See Stephen Schloesser, "Against Forgetting: Memory, History, Vatican II," *Theological Studies* 67, no. 2 (2006): 305–10, 315–19.

81. Giovanni Miccoli, "Two Sensitive Issues: Religious Freedom and the Jews," in Alberigo and Komonchak, eds., *History of Vatican II,* 4:95–193.

82. *Nostra* Aetate (October 28, 1965), §4. On the genesis of the document, see John Connelly, *From Enemy to Brother: The Revolution in Catholic Teaching on the Jews, 1933–1965* (Cambridge, MA: Harvard University Press, 2012), chap. 8.

83. Connelly, *From Enemy to Brother,* 265–66.

84. Gilbert Rosenthal, quoted in Connelly, *From Enemy to Brother,* 267.

85. Giuliana Chamedes, *A Twentieth-Century Crusade: The Vatican's Battle to Remake Christian Europe* (Cambridge, MA: Cambridge University Press, 2019), 239, 291–93; Michael Phayer, *The Catholic Church and the Holocaust, 1930–1965* (Bloomington: Indiana University Press, 2000), 159–83. On the controversy over these issues in postwar Germany, see Mark Ruff, *The Battle for the Catholic Past in Germany, 1946–1980* (Cambridge: Cambridge University Press, 2017).

86. Gregory XVI, *Mirari Vos* (August 15, 1832), §14, reprinted in Claudia Carlen, *Papal Encyclicals, 1740–1878,* vol. 1 (Raleigh, NC: McGrath, 1981), 235–41. See Schloesser, "Against Forgetting," 297–301.

87. On the Cold War context, see Gerald P. Fogerty, "Vatican II and the Cold War," in *Vatican II Behind the Iron Curtain,* ed. Piotr Kosicki, 27–49 (Washington, D.C.: Catholic University of America Press, 2017); Schloesser, "Against Forgetting," 281–82, 301.

88. See John Courtney Murray, "This Matter of Religious Freedom," *America* 112 (January 9, 1965): 40–43; John T. Noonan, *A Church That Can and Cannot Change: The Development of Catholic Moral Teaching* (Notre Dame, IN: University of Notre Dame Press, 2005), 145–58.

89. *Optatam Totius* (October 28, 1965), §13, §16. This principle is also reaffirmed in *Presbyterorum Ordinis* (December 7, 1965), §19.

90. See, for instance, *Presbyterorum Ordinis,* §19; *Optatam Totius,* §16; *Dei Verbum* (November 18, 1965), §23.

91. O'Malley, *What Happened at Vatican II,* 43–52, 76.

92. *Perfectae Caritatis* (October 28, 1965), §2.

93. O'Malley, *What Happened at Vatican II,* 301–3.

94. O'Malley, *What Happened at Vatican II,* 301.

95. See O'Malley, *What Happened at Vatican II,* 36–43, and John O'Malley, "Reform, Historical Consciousness, and Vatican II's Aggiornamento," *Theological Studies* 32, no. 4 (1971): 573–601.

96. André Duval, "Le message au monde," in *Vatican II commence . . . Approches Francophones,* ed. Étienne Fouilloux, 105–18 (Leuven: Bibliotheek van de Faculteit der Godgeleerdheid, 1993).

97. Chenu, *Un théologien en liberté,* 178.

98. "Message to Humanity," in *The Documents of Vatican II,* ed. Walter M. Abbott (New York: Corpus, 1966), 6.

99. "Message to Humanity," 5.

100. Edward Schillebeeckx, "Church and World," reprinted in *World and Church* (London: Sheed and Ward, 1971), 97–114. De Lubac published a strongly worded critique of this position in *Petite catéchèse sur nature et grace* (Paris: Fayard, 1980), Appendix B.

101. Chenu, *Un théologien en liberté,* 180. Emphasis added in last instance.

102. Marie-Dominique Chenu, "A Council for All Peoples," in *Vatican II Revisited by Those Who Were There,* ed. Alberic Stacpoole (Minneapolis, MN: Winston Press, 1986), 22.

103. De Lubac, *Carnets du concile,* 2:453.

104. Excerpted in de Lubac, *Mémoire sur l'occasion de mes écrits,* 343.

105. De Lubac, *Mémoire sur l'occasion de mes écrits,* 343.

106. This line comes from the concerns de Lubac communicated to the chair of the French working-group for Schema 13 in September 1964. It is quoted in Jared Wicks, "Further Light on Vatican Council II," *Catholic Historical Review* 95, no. 3 (2009): 558. For the letter, see de Lubac, *Carnets du concile,* 2:138–42.

107. See de Lubac, *Carnets du concile,* 2:221–22; Wicks, "Further Light on Vatican Council II," 559.

108. Excerpted in de Lubac, *Mémoire sur l'occasion de mes écrtits,* 342.

109. This distinction between Thomists and Augustinians is drawn by O'Malley in *What Happened at Vatican II*, 234–35.

110. Chenu, *Un théologien en liberté*, 192, 193.

111. See Henri de Lubac, *Autres paradoxes* (Namur, Belgium: Culture et Vérité, 1994), 47–50; *Entretien autour de Vatican II: Souvenirs et réflexions* (Paris: Cerf, 1985), 21–23.

112. See de Lubac, *Entretien autour de Vatican II*, 71–3. For an example of this critique, see Michel Foucault, *The History of Sexuality*, vol. 1 (New York, Pantheon: 1978).

113. See, for instance, Jean Daniélou, *Why the Church?* (Chicago: Franciscan Herald Press, 1975).

114. De Lubac, *Mémoire sur l'occasion de mes écrits*, 346. See also de Lubac, *Carnets du concile*, 2:395–96; Kirwan, *Avant-garde Theological Generation*, 267–68.

115. De Lubac, *Autres paradoxes*, 60–61.

116. De Lubac, *Mémoire sur l'occasion de mes écrits*, 149. On the parallels between the two, see also de Lubac, *Carnets du concile*, 2:398; Christopher Walsh, "De Lubac's Critique of the Postconciliar Church," *Communio* 19, no. 3 (Fall 1992): 407–8, 424.

117. De Lubac frequently appealed to a "true" *aggiornamento* against what he perceived to be misunderstandings of this principle. See the letters reproduced in *Mémoire sur l'occasion de mes écrits*, 343, 346, as well as his comments on a speech by Schillebeeckx at the council in *Carnets du concile*, 2:327.

118. Quoted in Walsh, "De Lubac's Critique of the Postconciliar Church," 422–23. Emphasis in original.

119. Quoted in Walsh, "De Lubac's Critique of the Postconciliar Church," 423.

120. Jorge Mario Bergoglio and Abraham Skorka, *On Heaven and Earth: Pope Francis on Faith, Family, and the Church in the Twenty-First Century* (New York: Random House, 2013), 45.

121. On Pope Francis's debt to de Lubac, see Carl E. Olson, "Pope Francis and Henri de Lubac, SJ," *Catholic World Report*, March 28, 2013: https://www.catholicworldreport.com/2013/03/28/pope-francis-and-henri-de-lubac-sj/. Massimo Borghesi stresses the influence of both de Lubac and Fessard in *The Mind of Pope Francis: Jorge Mario Bergoglio's Intellectual Journey* (Collegeville, MN: Liturgical Press Academic, 2017), 6–14, 75–85.

Epilogue

1. José Casanova, *Public Religions in the Modern World* (Chicago: University of Chicago Press, 1994), esp. 211–34.

2. See, for instance, Jürgen Habermas, "Notes on a Post-Secular Society," *New Perspectives Quarterly* 25, no. 4 (2008): 17–19. The literature on postsecularism is vast, but an excellent introduction is Hent de Vries and Lawrence

Sullivan, eds., *Political Theologies: Public Religions in a Post-Secular World* (New York: Fordham University Press, 2006).

3. For an introduction to liberation theology, see Lilian Calles Barger, *The World Come of Age: An Intellectual History of Liberation Theology* (Oxford: Oxford University Press, 2018); Christopher Rowland, ed., *The Cambridge Companion to Liberation Theology* (Cambridge: Cambridge University Press, 2006). On the history of the Church since Vatican II more broadly, see Ian Linden, *Global Catholicism: Diversity and Change since Vatican II* (New York: Columbia University Press, 2009).

4. On the intellectual links between Brazil and France in particular, see Michaël Löwy and Jesús García-Ruiz, "Les sources françaises du christianisme de la libération au Brésil," *Archives de sciences sociales des religions* 97 (January–March 1997): 9–32. On the institutional as well as intellectual links between Europe and Latin America more broadly, see Olivier Chatelan, "Les circulations intra-ecclésiales Europe-Amérique latine au XXe siècle: Un repérage dans l'historiographie francophone récente," *Chrétiens et sociétés* 24 (2017): 133–45.

5. On the influence of Jacques Maritain in Latin America, see Olivier Compagnon, *Jacques Maritain et l'Amérique du Sud: Le modèle malgré lui* (Villeneuve-d'Ascq, France: Presses Universitaires du Septentrion, 2003); Alceu Amoroso Lima, "The Influence of Maritain in Latin America," *New Scholasticism* 46 (1972): 70–85.

6. Ivan Petrella, "The Intellectual Roots of Liberation Theology," in *The Cambridge History of Religions in Latin America*, ed. Virginia Garrard, Paul Freston, and Stephen C. Dove (Cambridge: Cambridge University Press, 2016), 362.

7. Gustavo Gutiérrez, *A Theology of Liberation: History, Politics, and Salvation*, trans. Sister Caridad Inda and John Eagleson (Maryknoll, NY: Orbis, 1973), 35–41.

8. Gutiérrez, *A Theology of Liberation*, 40.

9. Gutiérrez, *A Theology of Liberation*, 40–41.

10. Gutiérrez, *A Theology of Liberation*, 45–46.

11. Central to Metz's political theology is the concept of the "eschatological proviso." See Johann Baptist Metz, "The Church's Social Function in the Light of a 'Political Theology,'" in *Love's Strategy: The Political Theology of Johann Baptist Metz,* ed. John K. Downey, 26–38 (Harrisburg, PA: Trinity Press, 1999).

12. On this point, see Barger, *The World Come of Age*, chap. 7.

13. Gutiérrez, *A Theology of Liberation*, 42.

14. Juan Luis Segundo, *The Liberation of Theology,* trans. John Drury (Maryknoll, NY: Orbis, 1976), 74.

15. See Andre Gunder Frank, *Capitalism and Underdevelopment in Latin America: Historical Studies of Chile and Brazil* (New York: Monthly Review Press, 1967).

16. For an introduction to radical orthodoxy, see John Milbank, Catherine Pickstock, and Graham Ward, eds., *Radical Orthodoxy: A New Theology* (London: Routledge, 1999); John Milbank and Simon Oliver, eds., *The Radical*

Orthodoxy Reader (London: Routledge, 2009). For an engagement with de Lubac specifically, see John Milbank, *The Suspended Middle: Henri de Lubac and the Debate Concerning the Supernatural* (Grand Rapids, MI: Eerdmans, 2005).

17. William T. Cavanaugh, "The Church in the Streets: Eucharist and Politics," *Modern Theology* 30, no. 2 (April 2014): 398–400. Cavanaugh lays out this soteriology of the modern state in *Theopolitical Imagination* (London: T&T Clark, 2002), chap. 1.

18. Daniel M. Bell, "State and Civil Society," in *The Blackwell Companion to Political Theology*, ed. Peter Scott and William Cavanaugh (Oxford: Blackwell, 2004), 423.

19. Cavanaugh critiques this model at length in *Torture and Eucharist: Theology, Politics, and the Body of Christ* (Oxford: Blackwell, 1998), chap. 4.

20. See especially John Milbank, *Theology and Social Theory: Beyond Secular Reason* (Oxford: Blackwell, 1990).

21. Marie-Dominique Chenu, "'Civique' ou 'politique'?," *Informations catholiques internationales* (June 15, 1958), reprinted in Chenu, *La parole de Dieu*, vol. 2, *L'Évangile dans le temps* (Paris: Cerf, 1964), 612.

22. Gutiérrez, *Theology of Liberation*, 30.

23. See Dominique Janicaud, Jean-François Courtine, Jean-Louis Chrétien, Michel Henry, and Jean-Luc Marion, *Phenomenology and the "Theological Turn": The French Debate*, trans. Bernard Prusack (New York: Fordham University Press, 2000); Hent de Vries, *Philosophy and the Turn to Religion* (Baltimore, MD: Johns Hopkins University Press, 1999).

24. Giorgio Agamben, *The Time That Remains: A Commentary on the Letter to the Romans* (Stanford, CA: Stanford University Press, 2005); Alain Badiou, *Saint Paul: The Foundations of Universalism* (Stanford, CA: Stanford University Press, 2003); John Milbank, Slavoj Žižek, and Creston Davis, *Paul's New Moment: Continental Philosophy and the Future of Christian Theology* (Grand Rapids, MI: Brazos, 2010); Peter Frick, *Paul in the Grip of the Philosophers: The Apostle and Contemporary Continental Philosophy* (Minneapolis, MN: Fortress Press, 2013).

25. See Bruce Holsinger, *The Premodern Condition: Medievalism and the Making of Theory* (Chicago: University of Chicago Press, 2005); Amy Hollywood, *Sensible Ecstasy: Mysticism, Sexual Difference, and the Demands of History* (Chicago: University of Chicago Press, 2001). This may also explain the interest that many theologians have shown in post-structuralist theory. See, for instance, Graham Ward, *Theology and Contemporary Critical Theory* (New York: St. Martin's Press, 2000).

26. See, for instance, Martin Hägglund, *This Life: Secular Faith and Spiritual Freedom* (New York: Pantheon, 2019); Dominique Janicaud's essay in *Phenomenology and the "Theological Turn,"* 16–193.

27. See especially Jürgen Habermas, *An Awareness of What Is Missing: Faith and Reason in a Post-Secular Age*, trans. Ciaran Cronin (Malden, MA: Polity, 2010); Peter E. Gordon, "Critical Theory between the Sacred and the Profane," *Constellations* 23, no. 4 (2016): 466–81.

28. Kantorowicz acknowledges his debt to de Lubac at the beginning of his all-important fifth chapter: "in the following pages I have merely ransacked the wealth of his material . . . and the wealth of his ideas" (Kantorowicz, *The King's Two Bodies: A Study in Mediaeval Political Theology* [Princeton, NJ: Princeton University Press, 1997], 194n4). See Jennifer Rust, "Political Theologies of the *Corpus Mysticum*: Schmitt, Kantorowicz, and de Lubac," in *Political Theology and Early Modernity,* ed. Graham Hamill and Julia Reinhard Lupton (Chicago: University of Chicago Press, 2012), 147–76.

29. The key text that introduced Kantorowicz to French readers was Marcel Gauchet, "Des deux corps du roi au pouvoir sans corps. Christianisme et politique," *Le débat* 14 (July–August 1981): 133–57, and *Le débat* 15 (September–October 1981): 147–68. On Kantorowicz's influence on Gauchet and Lefort, see Warren Breckman, "Democracy Between Disenchantment and Political Theology," *New German Critique* 94 (Winter 2005): 72–105.

30. Marcel Gauchet, *The Disenchantment of the World: A Political History of Religion,* trans. Oscar Burge (Princeton, NJ: Princeton University Press, 1997), 4. Emphasis in original.

31. Charles Taylor, *Les avenues de la foi: Entretiens avec Jacques Guilbault autour de cinq livres qui rendent libres* (Montreal, Canada: Novalis, 2015), 153–77.

32. Charles Taylor, *A Secular Age* (Cambridge, MA: Belknap/Harvard University Press, 2007), 847–48n39.

33. See Daniel A. Rober, "Grace and the Secular: Reading Charles Taylor through Henri de Lubac," *Philosophy & Theology* 30, no. 1 (2018): esp. 184–90.

34. See especially Talal Asad, *Formations of the Secular: Christianity, Islam, Modernity* (Stanford, CA: Stanford University Press, 2003); Joan Scott, *Sex and Secularism* (Princeton, NJ: Princeton University Press, 2017).

35. Talal Asad, "Trying to Understand French Secularism," in *Political Theologies: Public Religions in a Post-Secular World,* ed. Hent de Vries and Lawrence Sullivan, 494–526 (New York: Fordham University Press, 2006); Mayanthi Fernando, *The Republic Unsettled: Muslim French and the Contradictions of Secularism* (Durham, NC: Duke University Press, 2014); Joan Scott, *The Politics of the Veil* (Princeton, NJ: Princeton University Press, 2007).

36. Saba Mahmood, *Religious Difference in a Secular Age: A Minority Report* (Princeton, NJ: Princeton University Press, 2016); Wendy Brown, *Regulating Aversion: Toleration in the Age of Identity and Empire* (Princeton, NJ: Princeton University Press, 2008); Wendy Brown, "'The Most We Can Hope For . . .': Human Rights and the Politics of Fatalism," *South Atlantic Quarterly* 103, nos. 2–3 (2004): 451–63; Elizabeth Shakman Hurd, *Beyond Religious Freedom: A New Global Politics of Religion* (Princeton, NJ: Princeton University Press, 2015).

37. See, for instance, Gil Anidjar, "Secularism," *Critical Inquiry* 33, no. 1 (Autumn 2006): 52–77.

38. Asad, *Formations of the Secular,* 35, 92, 178–79. See the many references to Asad in William Cavanaugh, *The Myth of Religious Violence: Secular Ideology and the Roots of Modern Conflict* (Oxford: Oxford University Press, 2009).

39. Udi Greenberg and Daniel Steinmetz-Jenkins, "The Cross and the Gavel," *Dissent*, Spring 2018, https://www.dissentmagazine.org/article/cross-gavel -secularism-religious-liberty-asad-milbank; Udi Greenberg, "Radical Orthodoxy and the Rebirth of Christian Opposition to Human Rights," in *Christianity and Human Rights Reconsidered*, ed. Sarah Shortall and Daniel Steinmetz-Jenkins, 103–18 (Cambridge: Cambridge University Press, 2020).

40. Carl Schmitt, *Political Theology: Four Chapters on the Concept of Sovereignty*, trans. George Schwab (Chicago: University of Chicago Press, 2005).

41. Jürgen Habermas makes a similar argument in his latest magnum opus, *Auch eine Geschichte der Philosophie* (Berlin: Suhrkamp Verlag, 2019).

ACKNOWLEDGMENTS

This book is about a set of ideas, but it is also, and perhaps especially, about the relationships and institutions that make ideas possible. This was as true for the priests and intellectuals whom I study as it is for my own work. Just as a friendship formed in exile or the mentorship of a teacher shaped the intellectual vision of these priests, so too has this book been profoundly shaped by my relationships to family, friends, and mentors, and by the institutions that have supported me.

I could not have written this book without the help of archivists and librarians who have been extraordinarily generous with the materials in their possession and helped guide my research. I am particularly grateful to Father Bonfils and the staff who continue his good work at the Archives françaises de la Compagnie de Jésus, Marie-Gabrielle Lemaire at the Centre d'Archives et d'Études Cardinal Henri de Lubac, Father Potin at the Archives de la Province dominicaine de France, René Mougel at the Cercle d'Études Jacques et Raïssa Maritain, and the staff at the Bibliothèque nationale de France. Travel to these archives and libraries was made possible by generous funding from the Social Science Research Council, the Social Sciences and Humanities Research Council of Canada, the Graduate School of Arts and Sciences at Harvard University, the Minda de Gunzburg Center for European Studies at Harvard University, and the Dan David Foundation. A Mellon/ACLS Fellowship allowed me to write up the manuscript that became this book and gave me enormously valuable preparation for the academic job market. I was able to devote a blissful two years of undisturbed study to transforming the manuscript into a book thanks to a Sanderson Junior Research Fellowship at University College, Oxford. Funding from the Institute for Scholarship in the Liberal Arts, the Nanovic Institute for European Studies, and the History Department at Notre Dame made it possible for me to organize an extremely fruitful manuscript workshop. Finally, the Institute for Scholarship in the Liberal Arts at Notre Dame provided a generous publication subvention for the book and funding to hire an indexer. I am deeply grateful to these organizations for their financial and logistical support.

In the ten years since I first began this project, many colleagues have read portions of the manuscript, and their insights, queries, and critiques have enriched the book in countless ways. I am particularly grateful to those colleagues who so generously gave of their time to read a full draft of the manuscript: John

Connelly, Kathleen Sprows Cummings, Carolyn Dean, Udi Greenberg, Brad Gregory, Tom Kselman, John McGreevy, Samuel Moyn, Joshua Specht, and the three anonymous readers at Harvard University Press. The book is immeasurably stronger for their detailed advice and critical prodding. I would also like to thank those who read portions of the manuscript, including Teresa Bejan, Annabel Brett, Emile Chabal, James Chappel, Mayanthi Fernando, Rob Priest, Joshua Ralston, Camille Robcis, Daniel Steinmetz-Jenkins, and the participants in the Cambridge Political Thought Seminar, the Center for History and Economics Workshop, and the Center for European Studies Graduate Workshop at Harvard University. I am also grateful for the many conversations over the years with my fellow travelers in the history of European Catholicism, whose work has so greatly enriched my own, including Edward Baring, Giuliana Chamedes, James Chappel, Elizabeth Foster, Udi Greenberg, Piotr Kosicki, Brenna Moore, Danny Steinmetz-Jenkins, and Albert Wu. Finally, I would like to express my gratitude to Lindsay Waters and Harvard University Press for believing in the project, and to Emily Silk for shepherding it through to publication. Joy Deng, Emeralde Jensen-Roberts, Melissa Rodman, and Stephanie Vyce guided me through the publication process, and Catherine Osborne helped me make much-needed cuts to the manuscript. I am grateful as well to the copy editor and Deborah Grahame-Smith at Westchester Publishing Services for helping me to polish the prose. Every effort has been made to identify copyright holders and obtain their permission for the use of copyrighted material. Notification of any additions or corrections that should be incorporated in future reprints or editions of this book would be greatly appreciated.

I have had the extraordinary good fortune, first as a student and then as a faculty member, to benefit from the wisdom and support of an exceptional group of mentors. I am especially grateful to Harold Mah, who made me want to become an intellectual historian and encouraged me to apply to graduate programs in the United States, as well as to Herb Basser and David Parker. At Harvard, I was lucky to work with professors who modeled both an extraordinary intellectual rigor and a passionate commitment to their students. I am particularly grateful to Ann Blair, Francis Schüssler Fiorenza, and David Armitage, who molded me into the teacher and scholar I am today. At Oxford, I benefited tremendously from the guidance of Martin Conway, Robert Gildea, Ruth Harris, Catherine Holmes, and Ben Jackson, among others. I am also deeply grateful to the mentors I have accrued beyond my home institutions—especially Jonathan Sheehan, who has watched this project progress from a vague idea into a fully formed book, as well as Stefanos Geroulanos and Steve Schloesser. But there are two people to whom I am particularly indebted. Judith Surkis's ability to unearth insights that are only implicit in my work and fashion them into something far more brilliant never ceases to amaze me. Peter Gordon took me on as an orphaned graduate student and has been an unfailing advocate ever since. He is the model of a rigorous scholar, engaged intellectual, and generous mentor, and I only hope I can be half as good an advisor to my own grad students one day.

There are few better places to work as a historian of Catholic thought than the University of Notre Dame. Since moving to South Bend, I have been ceaselessly amazed by my colleagues' generosity, rigor, and commitment to their students. I am particularly grateful to the many colleagues who read and commented on portions of the manuscript, including Pete Cajka, Darren Dochuk, Alex Martin, Linda Przybyszewksi, Sonja Stojanovic, Tom Tweed, Emily Wang, and members of the Colloquium on Religion and History and the Nanovic Institute Cultural Transformations in Modern Europe Reading Group. I would also like to thank John Deak, Patrick Griffin, Margaret Meserve, Bob Sullivan, and Tom Tweed for their mentorship, and Jon Coleman and Elisabeth Köll for their support as department chairs. The companionship of Katlyn Carter, Korey Garibaldi, Randy Goldstein, Katie Jarvis, Jake Lundberg, Rebecca McKenna, Brandon Menke, Nikhil Menon, Paul and Abi Ocobock, Emily Remus, and Francisco Robles have made South Bend feel like home.

Writing a book can be a lonely process, but friends from Boston to Australia and Oxford to South Bend have provided me with ceaseless emotional support over the years. Becky Chang, Ross Mulcare, Ben Siegel, Jeremy Zallen, and especially Philippa Hetherington made graduate school some of the best years of my life. I am also deeply grateful for the friendship and comradery of Greg Afinogenov, Jakub Benes, Eva Bitran, Rowan Dorin, Josh Ehrlich, Katrina Forrester, Kate Greasley, Carla Heelan, Brendan Karch, Joseph Lacey, Philipp Lehmann, Kristen Loveland, Aline-Florence Manent, Jamie Martin, Yael Merkin, Luigi Prada, Mircea Raianu, Tehila Sasson, Kasia Szymanska, Heidi and Michael Tworek, Anand Vaidya, and especially Christine Platt and Gaby Adams. My parents have been a constant source of moral and financial support over the years, never questioning the wisdom of a career in European intellectual history and always encouraging me to excel at whatever I turn my hand to. This book is dedicated to them and to my maternal grandmother, whose humor and intelligence I have missed every day since her death in 2010. Calling herself "square, green, and puritanical," she was at once the most selfless and the most formidable woman I have ever known.

But there is no one who deserves greater thanks than my best friend, intellectual partner, and husband, Josh. He has read every inch of this manuscript, talked me down in moments of panic, and patiently endured my long work hours, pathological indecisiveness, and perfectionist tendencies with truly saintly patience. Having endured a long-distance commute between Indiana and Australia, I am so grateful that we can finally make our life together in South Bend with our well-fed cat, Basil. I could not have written this book without him.

INDEX